ANALYZING PHYSICAL EDUCATION AND SPORT INSTRUCTION

Second Edition

Paul W. Darst, PhD
Arizona State University

Dorothy B. Zakrajsek, PhD
University of Idaho

Victor H. Mancini, EdD
Ithaca College

Editors

Human Kinetics Books
Champaign, Illinois

Library of Congress Cataloging-in-Publication Data

Analyzing physical education and sport instruction / edited by Paul W.
 Darst, Dorothy B. Zakrajsek, Victor H. Mancini.
   p.   cm.
   Rev. ed. of: Systematic observation instrumentation for physical
 education. c1983.
   Bibliography: p.
   ISBN 0-87322-216-4
   1. Physical education and training—Teacher training.
 2. Observation (Educational method)   3. Interaction analysis in
 education.   I. Darst, Paul W.   II. Zakrajsek, Dorothy B.
 III. Mancini, Victor H.   Systematic observation instrumentation for
 physical education.   IV. Title.
 GV363.S95   1989
 613.7'07—dc19   88-30628
                                                                        CIP

ISBN: 0-87322-216-4

Developmental Editor: Jan Progen, EdD
Managing Editor: Valerie Hall
Production Director: Ernie Noa
Copyeditor: Claire Mount
Proofreader: Laurie McGee
Assistant Editors: Julia Anderson, Holly Gilly, and Phaedra Hise
Typesetter: Sandra Meier
Text Design: Keith Blomberg
Text Layout: Denise Mueller and Tara Welsch
Cover Design: Jack Davis
Printed By: Braun-Brumfield

Printed in the United States of America

10 9 8 7 6 5 4 3 2 1

Human Kinetics Books
A Division of Human Kinetics Publishers, Inc.
Box 5076, Champaign, IL 61825-5076
1-800-DIAL-HKP
1-800-334-3665 (in Illinois)

This book is dedicated to our colleagues who contributed their systems to this book and to the first edition. Without their interest in improving teaching and their willingness to share their efforts with the profession, this book would not be possible.

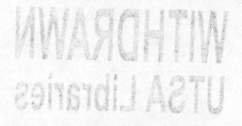

Contents

Preface

The purpose of this book is to provide a catalog of observer systems that can be used to analyze interactive and environmental events that occur in physical education and athletic settings. These systems maximize opportunities for collecting data from many perspectives using different techniques for data sources to explain or modify instructional phenomena.

This latest edition of the text represents the collective works of many sport pedagogists who are currently using these systems in physical education, athletics, adult fitness, and youth sports. The systems are an outgrowth of educational advances in research, theory, and technology and were, for the most part, prompted by the need to study instructional effectiveness in movement environments. This catalog will enable teachers, coaches, administrators, student teachers, researchers, graduate and undergraduate students, and other teachers of movement to select an observer system compatible with their particular needs.

The text helps the reader to understand systematic observation as a tool for studying teaching, coaching, and learning; to develop skills in systematic observation techniques; and to collect data on behaviors occurring in physical education and sport. The user has the option of selecting the system or part of the system that best answers the question at hand; no one system can answer all questions that the user may be asking to study teaching or coaching. Systems in this text focus on specific instructional behaviors such as feedback, time management, student engagement, verbal and nonverbal interaction, pedagogical moves, questioning skills, and so on.

The main body of this text differs from the first edition, *Systematic Observation Instrumentation for Physical Education*, by (a) eliminating many of the earlier interaction systems that were modifications of Flanders' Interaction Analysis System, (b) updating the sections with several new systems, (c) adding an introductory section on systematic observation including computer applications, (d) adding a new section on qualitative methods, and (e) including a summary table of systems in the Appendix.

The scope of this second edition has been broadened to include qualitative methods in Part V. These methods rely on a different set of observation and analytical skills. We hope that this inclusion encourages more opportunities to combine qualitative and quantitative applications for studying the instructional process.

Part I, Introduction to Systematic Observation, should strengthen the user's ability to understand (a) the historical development of systematic observation as a teaching and research tool; (b) data collection methods and training procedures; (c) interobserver agreement and testing; and (d) the use of computer technology with data collection, storage, and analysis. This part should be especially helpful to students and teachers who have not had previous experience with systematic observation. The how-to of recording, training, and establishing interobserver agreement will greatly benefit those who are learning these techniques for the first time.

The summary table in the Appendix briefly describes the capability and data collection factors associated with each system. This information should help the user to quickly identify and compare the merits of each system and to select an appropriate system for possible use.

The following five parts comprise this second edition: I. Introduction to Systematic Observation; II. Verbal and Nonverbal Interaction Analysis; III. Teacher/Student Climate Analysis; IV. Coach/Athlete Climate Analysis; and V. Ethnography: Qualitative Analysis.

Each part is prefaced with a brief description of the systems. In general, the chapters in each part are sequenced in order of complexity, beginning with those instruments that are easier to code and analyze. Each chapter contains a general description of the system, categories, recording procedures, and how to summarize and interpret the data. Recording sheets and research references are included where applicable.

Although some of the systems are more simplistic in terms of their operational demands, this does not diminish their importance. The results of a national survey indicated which systems in the first edition had the highest usage. Based on those results and the need to include some less complicated systems for beginners, we carefully selected the carryover systems.

The intended users of this book include all who engage directly or indirectly in teaching and coaching, whether they are preservice teachers, in-service teachers, supervisors of preservice or in-service teachers, graduate students, adult and continuing education instructors, or researchers. We believe that the systems in this text represent the very best that are available for studying variables in teaching and coaching climates. It is our hope that all who use this book will gain deeper insights into the process dynamics of teaching (coaching) and learning and will apply that knowledge toward upgrading the quality of that experience. We encourage the users to adapt these systems, use a part of a system, or develop a new system to accomplish their objectives. Because research is an ongoing process, continued development and modification of observer systems will probably result in future revisions of this book.

We ask our pedagogical colleagues and all those who aspire to join our ranks to use systematic observation as a tool for improving teaching and coaching in physical education and sport.

Paul W. Darst

Dorothy B. Zakrajsek

Victor H. Mancini

Contributing Authors

William G. Anderson
Department of Movement Sciences and Education
Teachers College-Columbia University
New York, NY 10027

Will Brown
Physical Education Department
Saint Michael's School
Stuart, FL 34996

Damon Burton
Division of Health, Physical Education, Recreation and Dance
University of Idaho
Moscow, ID 83843

B. Robert Carlson
Physical Education Department
San Diego State University
San Diego, CA 92182

John T.F. Cheffers
School of Education
Boston University
Boston, MA 02215

Tchang-Bok Chung
South Korean Armed Forces
Republic of Korea

Paul W. Darst
Department of Health and Physical Education
Arizona State University
Tempe, AZ 85203

Patt Dodds
Department of Physical Education
University of Massachusetts
Amherst, MA 01003

M. Patricia Giebink
Physical Education Department
San Diego State University
San Diego, CA 92182

Grace Goc Karp
Physical Education, Sport & Leisure Studies Department
Washington State University
Pullman, WA 99164-1410

Michael Goldberger
Department of Physical Education
Temple University
Philadelphia, PA 19122

Pat Griffin
Department of Physical Education
University of Massachusetts
Amherst, MA 01003

Andrew H. Hawkins
School of Physical Education
West Virginia University
Morgantown, WV 26506-6116

Theodore W.H. Johnson
952 Cypress Avenue
El Segundo, CA 90245

Alan C. Lacy
Physical Education Department
Texas Christian University
Fort Worth, TX 76129

Edward V. Langsdorf
Department of Health, Physical Education and Athletics
Linfield College
McMinnville, OR 97128

Bennett J. Lombardo
Health, Physical Education, Recreation and Dance Department
Rhode Island College
Providence, RI 02908

Victor H. Mancini
Department of Health and Physical Education
Ithaca College
Ithaca, NY 14850

Thomas J. Martinek
Department of Physical Education
University of North Carolina at Greensboro
Greensboro, NC 27412

Ron McBride
Department of Health and Physical Education
Texas A & M University
College Station, TX 77043

Thomas L. McKenzie
Physical Education Department
San Diego State University
San Diego, CA 92182

Michael Metzler
Department of Health and Physical Education
Virginia Tech
Blacksburg, VA 24061

Bruce L. Morgenegg
Department of Physical Education and Dance
University of Tennessee
Knoxville, TN 37996-2700

Deborah M. O'Brien
Department of Health and Physical Education
Ithaca College
Ithaca, NY 14850

Melissa Parker
Department of Health, Physical Education and Recreation
University of North Dakota
Grand Forks, ND 58202

Jerome Quarterman
Department of Health, Physical Education and Recreation
Kentucky State University
Frankfort, KY 40601

Kelly D. Rankin
Vancouver Public School District #37
Vancouver, WA 98662

Frank Rife
Department of Physical Education
University of Massachusetts
Amherst, MA 01003

Judith E. Rink
Department of Physical Education
University of South Carolina
Columbia, SC 29208

Brent S. Rushall
Physical Education Department
San Diego State University
San Diego, CA 92182

Daryl Siedentop
School of Health, Physical Education and Recreation
The Ohio State University
Columbus, OH 43210-1221

Gary D. Sinclair
Department of Physical Education
University of British Columbia
Vancouver, Canada

Michael J. Stewart
School of Health, Physical Education and Recreation
University of Nebraska
Omaha, NE 68182-0216

Deborah Tannehill
School of Health, Physical Education and Recreation
The Ohio State University
Columbus, OH 43210-1221

Thomas J. Templin
Physical Education, Health and Recreational Studies Department
Purdue University
West Lafayette, IN 47907

Hans van der Mars
Department of Health and Physical Education
Arizona State University
Tempe, AZ 85203

Peter H. Werner
Department of Physical Education
University of South Carolina
Columbia, SC 29208

Robert L. Wiegand
School of Physical Education
West Virginia University
Morgantown, WV 26506-6116

Deborah A. Wuest
School of Health, Physical Education and Recreation
Ithaca College
Ithaca, NY 14850

Dorothy B. Zakrajsek
International Trade & Development
University of Idaho
Moscow, ID 83843

PART I

INTRODUCTION TO SYSTEMATIC OBSERVATION

The first part of this second edition includes four new chapters. The purpose of their inclusion is to provide new users with a basic introduction to the fundamental characteristics and procedures of systematic observation. In chapter 1 systematic observation is defined and contrasted with some of the more traditional methods of observing and recording events in physical education and sport settings. Furthermore, the primary functions and limitations of systematic observation are discussed in the realms of both supervision of teaching and research on teaching. Finally, an overview is provided of the basic steps involved in doing sound systematic observation. Included is a short section on the question of whether to use videotape/audiotape equipment as part of the process of collecting data on teaching or coaching behaviors.

Chapter 2 provides an overview of the four fundamental recording tactics used in systematic observation: event recording, duration recording, interval recording, and time sampling. Each of these four tactics is reviewed in terms of its basic mechanics and limitations. Furthermore, guidelines are provided for novices on how to start using these various recording tactics. This is based on the assumption that use of a 10-category interval recording system is harder to master than one with only 2 or 3 categories. It is also assumed that a sound understanding of the basic tactics will help users in (a) selecting the most appropriate observation system for whatever question is asked and (b) learning the more complex systems with greater ease.

The systems presented in this book are by no means the only systems that can or should be used when studying teachers/coaches and their students/athletes. Depending on what specific aspect of the teaching-learning environment is to be studied, it is possible that none of the systems included in this edition is appropriate. Should that happen, chapter 2 provides basic guidelines for developing a new observation system that would better suit the needs of the user.

In chapter 3 the user is introduced to the various procedures available for determining the degree to which observers are reliable in their observations. Furthermore, a section is included covering various situations that can cause observers to be less reliable and less accurate. Suggestions for minimizing these possibilities are also provided. The final section in this chapter deals with the steps involved in training other people to use systematic observation tools.

Chapter 4 provides an overview of recent developments in computer technology for the purpose of analyzing teacher and student behavior in physical education and sport settings. Following an explanation of the limitations of manual coding procedures, the reader is introduced to some of the critical features that users of computerized recording programs need to be aware of when selecting both hardware and software. In addition, procedures for both training observers and establishing their reliability are different as a result of using electronic data recording devices.

Chapter 1

Systematic Observation: An Introduction

Hans van der Mars

"One hundred rumors are not comparable to one look."
Old Chinese proverb

This chapter provides a short introduction of systematic observation, including its definition, purpose, limitations, and overall process. Darst, Mancini, and Zakrajsek (1983) stated that "systematic observation allows a trained person following stated guidelines and procedures to observe, record, and analyze interactions with the assurance that others viewing the same sequence of events would agree with his [or her] recorded data" (p. 6). As the definition indicates, systematic observation involves both observing and recording. Both differ in their respective purposes. Johnston and Pennypacker (1980) noted that "the goal of observation is to arrange conditions so that man or machine will react sensitively to the defined dimensions of the subject's behavior" (p. 146). The recording act aims to produce an accurate and permanent account of the observation for future examination. Both acts can be performed by humans and/or machines, such as audiorecorders and videorecorders. The reader is alerted to the fact that in the next few chapters the terms *observation* and *recording* are used interchangeably. They represent both unless indicated otherwise.

Systematic, or direct, observation has enjoyed considerable popularity in such areas as anthropology, social psychology, clinical psychology, and cross-cultural psychology. Thus it is by no means a new, revolutionary phenomenon. However, not until the early 1960s did systematic observation become an important investigative procedure in the study of classroom teaching; and it was not until 13 years later that, in the *Second Handbook of Research on Teaching* (Travers, 1973), a whole chapter was devoted to the use of systematic direct observation in the study of teaching. In their closing paragraphs, Rosenshine and Furst (1973) voiced uncertainty over whether systematic observation would ever be able to tease out those variables that discriminate more effective from less effective teachers:

It is possible that the patterns of effective teaching for different ends are so idiosyncratic that they will never be isolated; it is possible that studying teaching in natural settings is unproductive because the settings are not functional for the desired outcomes; it is possible that descriptive systems and research within the descriptive-correlational-experimental loop will be unproductive; it is also possible that linear and nonlinear curriculum approaches and the monitoring of these approaches will be unproductive. At the moment there has not been enough research to make any firm statement about any of these concerns. (p. 175)

Since then, some important variables have been found to contribute to student achievement in classrooms. Furthermore, as Locke (1982) has noted, research on teaching has started to develop a technical common language of its own over the last 20 years. It is safe to say that systematic observation, even with its limitations, has indeed played a major role in generating at least some of the answers regarding good teaching and has contributed to the development of that language of teaching.

The emergence of systematic observation in the realm of teaching is closely related to the advances made in teaching research methodologies. The search for personality traits and effective teaching methods proved fruitless from the 1930s until the mid-1950s, largely because nobody bothered to actually go into regular classrooms and see what was going on. (For a brief historic overview of these phases and their limitations, the reader is directed to Medley, 1979, and Rosenshine, 1979.) It was not until the late 1950s that researchers actually went into classrooms to see what teachers did and said. This constituted a major shift in focus, because, as Medley (1979) noted, "It is what a teacher *does* rather than what the teacher *is* that matters" (p. 13). People like Ned Flanders, Harold Mitzel, Donald Medley, and Nathaniel Gage are but a few of the driving forces in these early efforts. Based on the research paradigm explained by Dunkin and Biddle (1974), numerous process-product studies were conducted in which teacher behaviors were correlated with student achievement. From 1960 until 1970 enough classroom research findings became available for Rosenshine (1971) to publish the now-famous report in which eight teacher behavior variables were found to consistently correlate with student achievement. The eight variables were teacher clarity, variability, enthusiasm, task-oriented or businesslike behavior, teacher indirectness, student opportunity to learn criterion materials, use of structuring comments, and criticism. Since then research efforts that use direct observation have shifted their focus from looking primarily at teachers to including a close systematic analysis of students' behavior.

Here, too, systematic observation played a major role. This shift in attention to students contributed, in part, to the rise of such concepts as time-on-task, student engagement, and academic learning time (ALT). In retrospect, systematic observation has provided some fruitful perspectives of looking at teaching. Each time researchers found new variables to be important, they opened up other avenues for further, more complex analyses of the teaching-learning environment.

With the increased use of systematic observation tactics in the study of teaching, its critics viewed its limitations important enough to suggest alternative investigative techniques. This resulted in the emergence of qualitative, naturalistic, or ethnographic research techniques. Part V in this textbook is devoted to an overview of its major assumptions and characteristics.

The use of systematic observation in the study of physical education and sport settings has a slightly shorter but also productive history. The development of physical education teaching research methodologies and variables lagged behind that in classroom research. This lag could be construed as a shortcoming; however, it could also be regarded as an advantage, in that it allowed physical education teaching researchers to learn from possible mistakes made by others before them.

Systematic observation has played a major role in the emergence of teaching/coaching behavior research as a bona fide area of empirical study in our profession. Although the descriptive findings may not have lived up to our expectations, the answer(s) to the question of what typically goes on in school physical education classes could never have been given with the same confidence in 1970 as they can today. The initial efforts through research programs at Teachers College and Ohio State University were followed by programs at the University of Massachusetts, Boston University, and Ithaca College. In addition, more and more efforts are being made not only to make systematic observation a part of empirical research, but also to use it in the preparation of novice teachers (e.g., Anderson, 1980; Hawkins, Wiegand, & Bahneman, 1983; Mancini, Wuest, & van der Mars, 1985; Siedentop, 1981).

TRADITIONAL METHODS OF DATA COLLECTION

Systematic observation continues to compete with other more traditional methods of collecting information on what teachers/coaches and their students/athletes do, including eyeballing, anecdotal recording, developing rating scales, and using checklists. Each of these techniques has played (and in some cases continues to play) a major part of the evaluation process of teachers, both in preservice teacher preparation programs and in school districts.

Eyeballing

Eyeballing refers to the situation in which an outsider (usually an administrator) enters the teaching setting and looks at the ongoing activities *without making any formal written record* of what is seen. Based on the memory of what was seen, the administrator may provide feedback to the observed teacher. Eyeballing is used in not only official visits to classrooms for evaluation purposes, but also other settings to monitor how teachers conduct themselves in all aspects of their jobs. Whatever the observer picks up in passing may be used as part of a final evaluation of a teacher.

Anecdotal Recording

Anecdotal recording is very similar to eyeballing, with the only difference being that the observer now writes down some of the things that he or she sees and hears. Other labels for this strategy are *narrative recording* and *informal analysis*.

Rating Scales and Checklists

Both *rating scales* and *checklists* are quite popular in the process of (beginning) teachers' performance evaluations. In using rating scales, the observer is asked to give his or her opinion on various aspects of the teaching-learning environment. When checklists are used the observer merely marks whether certain things were said or were attended to by the teacher, again based on his or opinion. For example, a question might read, "Did the teacher use questions?" The observer would need to place a check mark in the "Yes" box, even if the teacher only asked one question. For the question, "Did the instructor attend to safety issues?", the observer gives his or her opinion about whether the environment was arranged in a safe manner and places a check mark in the appropriate box.

Limitations of Traditional Data Collection Methods

The limitations of the traditional techniques lie in their lack of objectivity, reliability, and specificity. First, the resulting data are primarily reflections of the observer's opinions about certain events that were seen. Johnston and Pennypacker (1980) and Siedentop (1983) noted that human beings are notorious for being poor observers. Opinions are based on the observer's personal biases and history of experiences. Thus there is a strong tendency on the part of the observer to report on aspects that he or she thinks are important. As a result, he or she might rate the performance of the instructor as low on, for example, a particular organizational arrangement, not because it did not work as well as it could have, but because the observer simply did not like that approach to organization in itself. Consequently, the resulting record reflects what he or she wanted to see, rather than what actually happened. Thus rating scales lack objectivity.

Second, although rating scales look scientific, there is no way to determine (a) exactly why one person scored a 3 and another person, viewing the same events, scored a 4; and (b) what the exact difference is between 3 and 4 and whether that difference is equal to the one between 4 and 5. This problem becomes more profound as the scale widens from a 2-point scale to maybe a 5- or 7-point scale.

Furthermore, asking two or three independent observers to evaluate a teacher using anecdotal recording most often produces three different narrative records. This, too, is most likely the result of each observer's personal bias in looking for some aspects and not for others. Taken one step further, if one of those three observers were to look at that same class again, he or she would most likely produce a different anecdotal record the second time around. The data collected through anecdotal recording most often lack reliability. It should be noted here that rating scales are not inappropriate in and of themselves, as long as they are used only to obtain a measure of opinion. However, their use as measuring instruments in the process of evaluating teaching (and coaching) performance is highly suspect.

A third problem with the traditional observation methods is their lack of specificity. The information provided through rating scales and/or anecdotal recording cannot provide a specific data base on which recommendations for improvement can be made. Furthermore, subsequent improvement cannot be verified. Rating scales and checklists are simply too crude in showing that an improvement was actually made and measuring its extent. The point of identifying these limitations is to stress that the traditional methods are inherently unreliable ways of collecting data within the context of analyzing and evaluating teaching performance, primarily because there are no strict rules and procedures to follow.

PRIMARY FUNCTIONS AND LIMITATIONS OF SYSTEMATIC OBSERVATION

Systematic observation (also called descriptive-analytic) is not reliable by definition just because it does have specific coding rules and procedures.

As will be shown in chapter 3, there are many sources that influence the observer's ability to observe reliably even with systematic observation tools. However, the use of those strict rules and procedures makes it possible to exert greater control over these sources.

Systematic observation tools play a major role in two different but related arenas: research and supervision. Within these arenas are various ways in which those functions are fulfilled. As part of research projects, systematic observation provides information on both independent and dependent variables. For example, much of the research aimed at changing teaching behaviors of both preservice and in-service teachers used feedback as part of the intervention, and this feedback was typically based on data collected through systematic observation. Verification of behavior changes as a result of these interventions was also established through such data collection procedures.

The second arena into which systematic observation has made its entry is the supervision process. As Locke (1979) noted, supervision can serve a variety of purposes. It plays a role in (a) administrative decisions in public schools regarding the retention of teachers; (b) staff development programs in public schools aimed at improving teachers' instructional effectiveness; (c) a cooperative effort among teachers to guide new, inexperienced student teachers during their internships; and (d) the university supervisor's contributions in that same setting. It should be understood that the specific use of systematic observation and the information it provides differs depending on the supervisory setting in which it is used.

Systematic observation does have some crucial limitations. First and foremost, it concentrates only on observable events and behaviors; that is, only those events that can be detected visually and/or audibly are measured. As will become clear in a later section on the process of systematic observation, this requires great care in first developing proper definitions of the behaviors to be studied. A frequently held misconception about this limitation is that, in light of its focus on only observable events, systematic observation cannot give any information about such aspects as attitudes, emotions, and feelings of teachers/coaches and students/athletes or such constructs as class/team climate. This is not correct. If we assume that attitudes and feelings are somehow going to be reflected in observable behaviors, such behaviors can be categorized and defined. For example, attitude of an athlete toward practice might be reflected in his or her on-time behavior, the amount of time he or she spends taking extra practice, and so on. Although these and other behaviors may not say much about that person's general attitude, they function as indicators of his or her attitude toward practice.

Second, users need to be aware of the fact that, when used appropriately and reliably, systematic observation produces only *descriptive* information that is relatively objective. This is an important limitation. What the user of this descriptive information does with the information can become evaluative in nature depending on how it is interpreted. This fine line between description and evaluation was highlighted by Anderson (1980) when explaining some of the limitations of *informal analysis* (i.e., anecdotal recording). Users of informal analysis have a tendency to make evaluative or judgmental notes and thus superimpose their own beliefs and biases on what they see happening. The use of specific coding rules and procedures in systematic observation forces the observer to first describe the events as accurately as possible and then, based on that descriptive base, make some suggestions for improvement where necessary or reinforce the existing level of performance. The data themselves do not make a judgment about how well or poorly the teacher performed, rather they provide the information for judgments to be made later.

A third limitation is that descriptive data in and of themselves cannot give prescriptions as to what a practitioner could (or should) change. Hawkins, Wiegand, and Landin (1985) recently reported that there is some evidence that data-based feedback to teachers frequently consists largely of reporting to teachers what happened (much like Knowledge of Results [KR]). They indicated that

> although this is perhaps justifiable in the modification of relatively discrete teacher behaviors (e.g., number of feedback statements, first name use, etc.), the exclusive use of KR is more difficult to accept in the modification of more complex criterion process variables. (p. 241)

Hawkins and his colleagues at West Virginia University have begun to study the content of the feedback teacher educators provide to teacher trainees and its relationship to the data collected on teacher and student behavior. These efforts should produce a better understanding of how objective, descriptive data need to be treated in the supervisory process of (new) teachers. The assumption that (preservice) teachers will know exactly what changes to make in their instruction based on only descriptive (i.e., KR) data may thus be a false one.

Fourth, findings obtained through systematic observation are always contextual. In other words, the message they may provide about teaching performance needs to be considered in light of the situation in which they were observed. In teacher preparation programs, for example, it is probably dangerous to make maximum levels of student motor engagement the ultimate and only objective that a supervisor has for a student teacher who is just starting his or her practicum experience. Another example would be to expect the same level of effectiveness from an itinerant teacher who has to travel to three different schools every day as one would for a teacher who is employed in a single school building. The demands placed on the traveling teacher (e.g., having to transport equipment to each school each time) are different from those for the nontraveler. A third example would be to expect the same level of impact from a teacher who has to teach his or her classes in the regular classrooms as one would from the teacher who has his or her own facility complete with ample equipment. In such situations there is a need for establishing differential standards of instructional effectiveness. Systematic observation clearly does not take place in a vacuum.

THE PROCESS OF SYSTEMATIC OBSERVATION

In a way the definition provided earlier does not do justice to systematic observation as a process. It involves more than merely going into a gymnasium with an observation system and collecting data on some selected behaviors and events. The acts of observing and recording behaviors are preceded by a number of steps that need to be taken to ensure that the data to be collected will be reliable, accurate, and valuable. The process of systematic observation involves the following critical steps:

1. Deciding what to observe
2. Developing definitions for the behaviors to be observed
3. Selecting the most appropriate observation tactic(s) and determining if there is an existing observation system that fits the need of the observer
4. Establishing observer reliability
5. Making the observation
6. Summarizing and interpreting the collected data

Deciding What to Observe

Observation of teaching/coaching events is a prominent activity in both research and supervision functions. When part of a research project, observers base their observation focus on the research questions asked. This could be a descriptive, correlational, and/or experimental question. In the supervisory function observation is used to determine performance levels of a great number of instructional skills of teachers and the type/level of involvement of students. In addition, as part of their professional preparation, preservice teachers often are given observation tasks when visiting public schools. The crucial thing here is that there is a specific focus or goal. Observation either for the sake of observation or without any particular goal is a fruitless activity.

In a staff development program where the aim is to improve instructional skills, decisions on what to observe should be made on a collaborative basis between the teacher and the program leader. It is fairly well established that if the latter is the only person deciding where improvements are needed (and thus what to focus the observations on), then the program's success is in jeopardy (Locke, 1984). Teachers who do not have input in the process of staff development are less likely to have any vested interest in making and sustaining change, be it at the program or the instructional level. Anderson (1982) reiterated that "innovations imposed by outsiders tend to disappear when the outsiders leave" (p. 17).

In proposing a model for evaluation of instruction, Siedentop (1983) suggested that one could classify teacher and student behavior into three main groups. The first group of variables is *discrete teaching behaviors*, which include a multitude of individual behaviors exhibited by an instructor that can be coded for frequency of occurrence and appropriateness. Examples of discrete teaching behaviors are cues; feedback on skill performance; feedback on overall conduct; use of questions, praise, and criticism; and so on.

The second group of variables is made up of *analytic units*. An analytic unit (Dunkin & Biddle, 1974) refers to a relatively stable sequence of separate teacher behaviors (possibly combined with some student behaviors). Examples of these units would be a sequence of teacher questions and students' verbal responses during a discussion in some type of guided discovery or problem-solving activity; a sequence in which a coach observes an athlete's trial, provides a correction, monitors the athlete's next response, and praises the athlete for improving his or her performance; and a sequence of events in which a teacher seeks attention from a group of students.

The third group is *criterion process variables*, which provide on-site evidence of student learning (Siedentop, 1983). Two frequently suggested variables are Academic Learning Time-Physical Education (ALT-PE) and Opportunity to Respond (OTR). Both provide detailed information on the type and amount of actual motor involvement on the part of students and/or athletes.

As the numerous systems in this textbook show, there are many different kinds of behaviors, events, and episodes that can be measured and analyzed. It is important to remember that regardless of what aspect of the teaching-learning environment is observed, it should always be tied into some type of goal.

Developing Definitions

As indicated earlier, it is very important to have specific definitions of the behaviors to be observed. Well-developed definitions make the observer's job of discriminating whether an event constitutes an instance of the target behavior much easier. Disagreement between observers can be minimized when definitions are clear, complete, and objective (Hawkins & Dobes, 1977). Typically, the target behavior is first described in more general terms. Once that rough outline is in place the final definition is developed. This definition focuses on either of two aspects of the behavior, namely its topography or its function (Barlow & Hersen, 1984).

When the topography (i.e., the form) of the behavior is emphasized, the definition describes the movements that make up the behavior. However, if function is emphasized, then the definition needs to focus on the outcome or consequence of the behavior. For example, if data were needed on the ability of players to serve overhand in volleyball, it could be described in terms of its physical form. The definition would then most likely include descriptions of foot position from the baseline, point of contact, follow-through, and so on. A definition of the same behavior in terms of its function would most likely include such indicators as "ball will pass over the net and land inbounds in the back third of the opponents' court." Barlow and Hersen (1984) emphasized that regardless of which type is used, the definitions should be meaningful and replicable. Furthermore they noted some characteristics of good definitions:

> They avoid references to intent, internal states, and other private events. . . . Complete definitions include the following components (Hawkins, 1982): a descriptive name; a general description, as in a dictionary; an elaboration that describes the critical parts of the behavior; typical examples of the behavior; and questionable-borderline or difficult examples of both occurrences and nonoccurrences of the behavior. (pp. 111-112)

For additional information on developing sound behavior definitions see chapter 6 in Johnston and Pennypacker (1980).

Selecting the Most Appropriate Observation System

Each behavior or event has two specific dimensional characteristics. The first one is *repeatability* (Johnston & Pennypacker, 1980), which refers to the fact that a behavior can occur over and over again; that is, there is a frequency to each behavior. Certain behaviors typically occur a lot, whereas others may occur only a few times over a long period of time. In other words, there is a pattern to their frequency.

A second inherent feature of each behavior is that it takes time to complete. There is *duration* to each behavior. Certain events last only very short times, whereas others last longer. Both duration and repeatability are critical in the analysis of teaching and coaching environments. Once the definition of the behavior has been developed, one needs to decide whether the behavior is best characterized by its frequency of occurrence or typical duration. In chapter 2 more attention is given to the two main dimensions and the influence of those dimensions on the selection of observation tactics.

Establishing Observer Reliability

Once a person decides which system to use, he or she needs to develop a sufficient level of reliability. Reliability is a critical feature of the process because it is a prerequisite for collecting accurate data. Reliability is most often measured by the degree to which two persons using the same definitions and coding procedures and viewing the same activities agree on their codings. Observer reliability is established through sound training of the observers. Some of the major issues and procedures of reliability and training observers, along with some of the possible threats to observer reliability, are the main focus of chapter 3.

Making the Actual Observations

There are some important considerations observers need to be aware of once they are ready to go into a setting where the observation is going to be held. Primarily, one needs to be concerned with the definite possibility of subject reactivity, particularly if it is the first time that teachers or coaches are observed: Their behavior may change simply because of the presence of observers. The same applies to students in physical education classes. However, after a few sessions their behavior tends to return to its regular pattern. There are a few things that observers can do to minimize their influence on those first few visits. It is a good strategy to suggest to the teacher or coach that he or she explain to his or her students or athletes the presence of the observer(s) *in general terms*, without specifying the exact purpose. In addition, the observer should arrive in the setting early enough so that he or she can start as soon as the first students/athletes enter. This way, the routine of what teachers and students do is less likely to be disrupted. The observer should try to be as inconspicuous as possible, both in dress and behavior. Furthermore, it is best to avoid interaction of any kind with students. If they seek contact it is suggested to be general but courteous. Too much of a "don't bother me" attitude might produce reactive behavior on the part of students or athletes. Also, if a student is the target of observation, the observer needs to ensure that he or she disguises the attention through varying his or her glances.

With regard to the use of audio or video equipment, if cue tapes and earphones are used, try to keep the equipment out of sight as much as possible. Video equipment should be positioned in the same location on each visit. Battery-operated equipment should be checked prior to the visit. Tabletop or lap computers are also making their entry as data collection machines (e.g., Carlson & McKenzie, 1984; Cicciarella & Martinek, 1982). With rapid developments in technology, computers continue to become more compact, less obtrusive, and thus very useful. (For an introduction to the use of computer technology in systematic observation, see chapter 4.)

Summarizing and Interpreting the Data

If data are collected for supervisory purposes they need to be summarized in such a way as to provide feedback to the instructor. If they are collected for research purposes they need to be converted into values appropriate for further (statistical) analyses. Chapter 2 provides guidelines for summarizing data. In addition, each observation system included in this textbook has guidelines for collapsing the data for that particular system.

TO VIDEOTAPE OR NOT TO VIDEOTAPE

Observations can be made live while in the setting, or one can first develop a *permanent record*, such as a videotape, and make the observation from the tape. Initially, there is greater chance of subject reactivity to video equipment than live observation, because of the former's size. One could try to habituate students and teachers to the presence of such equipment by setting it up for four to five sessions and recording them, but not including these tapes in subsequent data analysis.

Another disadvantage of using video equipment is the possibility of equipment failure, which would result in the loss of at least part of a session. Chances of this occurring can be minimized by making sure that camera operators are trained properly in the use of the equipment and equipment is checked prior to each visit.

There are also some important advantages to videotaping the classes or practices. In studying different dimensions of classroom management, Kounin (1970) noted the value of using videotapes for data collection:

> We decided to use videotapes. The combination of a lens and videotape recorder meets the criteria of a good observer and recorder. The lens has no biases, theories, preconceptions, needs, or interests. It takes in all that is occurring in its field and makes no distinction between what is boring or interesting, major or minor, important or

unimportant, outstanding or ordinary, good or bad. And the videotape records it all without forgetting, exaggerating, theorizing, judging, interpreting, or eliminating. (p. 62)

This unbiased record can then be reviewed over and over again, which
is an important feature in case there are some uncertainties about whether
or how a behavior should be coded. An important criterion for a camera
operator is to ensure that the video record be complete and thus valid.
Part of this completeness criterion is the inclusion of teachers' or coaches'
verbal behavior. In live observations the observer is most often forced
to follow teachers and coaches around to make sure he or she can hear
their voices clearly and accurately—this would be quite intrusive. Wireless microphones alleviate this problem. They are of sufficient quality to
provide good records of verbal behavior, and their cost need not be overly
high.

Another value of videotaping the sessions is that it allows the user to
go back later and use the tape for different types of analyses. As will be
shown in chapter 3, an additional advantage of videotaping sessions is
that it guards against certain threats to observer reliability.

In making videotape records of lessons or practice sessions, the observer
should use equipment that has a built-in stopwatch generator. This stopwatch can be superimposed on the screen while recording. Its value lies
in the ease of both capturing the temporal dimensions of behavior and
checking reliability. Some of the recently marketed video (or cam-)
recorders have this as a standard feature.

GLOSSARY

Analytic unit: A group of teacher (and student) behaviors that occurs in
a relatively stable sequence.

Anecdotal recording (Informal analysis): Writing down general comments
without using set rules or procedures.

Criterion process variable: Variables (student or athlete behavior oriented)
that provide indication of learning.

Description: Nonjudgmental overview of events, behaviors, and episodes
as they occur.

Discrete teaching behavior: Behavior exhibited by an instructor that has
a clearly distinguishable beginning and end.

Evaluation: Judgment of events, behaviors, and episodes as they occur.

Eyeballing: Observation of teaching events for the purpose of evaluation by which the observer is depending only on what he or she sees.
No written notations are made for future use.

Permanent record: Record of behavior that can be viewed over and over again (e.g., audiotape and videotape).

Rating scale: Instrument designed to determine the opinion of the user with regard to a list of statements using a scaled continuum (e.g., from strongly agree to strongly disagree).

Repeatability: Dimension of behavior indicating that it can occur again and again.

REFERENCES

Anderson, W.G. (1980). *Analysis of teaching physical education*. St. Louis: C.V. Mosby.

Anderson, W.G. (1982). Working with inservice teachers: Suggestions for teacher educators. *Journal of Teaching in Physical Education*, 1(3), 15-22.

Barlow, D.H., & Hersen, M. (1984). *Single case experimental designs: Strategies for studying behavior change* (2nd ed.). Elmsford, NY: Pergamon Press.

Carlson, B.R., & McKenzie, T.L. (1984). Computer technology for recording, storing, and analyzing temporal data in physical activity settings. *Journal of Teaching in Physical Education*, 4(1), 24-29.

Cicciarella, C.F., & Martinek, T.J. (1982). A microcomputer program for real time collection and immediate analysis of observational data. *Journal of Teaching in Physical Education*, 2(1), 56-62.

Darst, P.W., Mancini, V.H., & Zakrajsek, D.B. (1983). *Systematic observation instrumentation for physical education*. Champaign, IL: Leisure Press.

Dunkin, M.J., & Biddle, B.J. (1974). *The study of teaching*. New York: Holt, Rinehart and Winston.

Hawkins, A., Wiegand, R.L., & Bahneman, C. (1983). Data-based evaluation of a physical education professional preparation program. In T.J. Templin & J.K. Olson (Eds.), *Teaching in physical education, Big Ten Body of Knowledge Symposium Series* (Vol. 14, pp. 131-141). Champaign, IL: Human Kinetics.

Hawkins, A., Wiegand, R.L., & Landin, D.K. (1985). Cataloguing the collective wisdom of teacher educators. *Journal of Teaching in Physical Education*, 4(4), 241-255.

Hawkins, R.P. (1982). Developing a behavior code. In D.P. Hartmann (Ed.), *Using observers to study behavior: New directions for methodology of social and behavioral science* (pp. 21-35). San Francisco, CA: Jossey-Bass.

Hawkins, R.P., & Dobes, R.W. (1977). Behavioral definitions in applied behavior analysis: Explicit or implicit. In B.C. Etzel, J.M. LeBlanc, & D.M. Baer (Eds.), *New directions in behavioral research: Theory, methods, and applications* (pp. 274-296). Hillsdale, NJ: Lawrence Erlbaum.

Johnston, J.M., & Pennypacker, H.S. (1980). *Strategies and tactics of human behavioral research*. Hillsdale, NJ: Lawrence Erlbaum.

Kounin, J.S. (1970). *Discipline and group management in classrooms*. Huntington, NY: Krieger Publishing.

Locke, L.F. (1979). Supervision, schools and student teaching: Why things stay the same. In G. Scott (Ed.), *The academy papers* (No. 13, pp. 65-74). Washington, DC: The American Academy of Physical Education.

Locke, L.F. (1982). Research on teaching physical activity: A modest celebration. In M.L. Howell & J.E. Saunders (Eds.), *Proceedings of the VII Commonwealth and International Conference on Sport, Physical Education, Recreation and Dance* (pp. 189-198). Brisbane, Australia: University of Queensland Press.

Locke, L.F. (1984). Research on teaching teachers: Where are we now? *Journal of Teaching in Physical Education*, Monograph 2.

Mancini, V.H., Wuest, D.A., & van der Mars, H. (1985). Use of instruction and supervision in systematic observation in undergraduate professional preparation. *Journal of Teaching in Physical Education*, 5(1), 22-33.

Medley, D.M. (1979). The effectiveness of teachers. In P.L. Peterson & H.J. Walberg (Eds.), *Research on teaching: Concepts, findings, and implications* (pp. 11-27). Berkeley, CA: McCutchan.

Rosenshine, B.V. (1971). *Teaching behaviors and student achievement*. Windsor, Berkshire, England: National Foundation for Educational Research in England and Wales.

Rosenshine, B.V. (1979). Content, time, and direct instruction. In P.L. Peterson & H.J. Walberg (Eds.), *Research on teaching: Concepts, findings, and implications* (pp. 28-56). Berkeley, CA: McCutchan.

Rosenshine, B.V., & Furst, N. (1972). The use of direct observation to study teaching. In R.M.W. Travers (Ed.), *Second handbook of research on teaching* (pp. 122-183). Chicago: Rand McNally.

Siedentop, D. (1981). The Ohio State University supervision research program summary report. *Journal of Teaching in Physical Education* (Introductory Issue), 30-38.

Siedentop, D. (1983). *Developing teaching skills in physical education* (2nd ed.). Palo Alto, CA: Mayfield.

Travers, R.M.W. (Ed.) (1973). *Second handbook of research on teaching*. Chicago: Rand McNally.

Chapter 2

Basic Recording Tactics

Hans van der Mars

This chapter provides an overview of the recording tactics fundamental to all the quantitative systems presented in this textbook. Each of these systems has its roots in one (or a combination) of four recording tactics: event recording, duration recording, interval recording, and momentary time sampling. A thorough understanding of the characteristics, mechanics, and limitations, combined with actual mastery of these tactics, is important in at least two ways. First, once these two criteria have been met the more complex systems presented in this text should be learned with greater ease. Second, users of systematic observation will be in a better position to choose the appropriate observation system for their needs.

As mentioned in chapter 1, systematic observation involves both observing and recording. Johnston and Pennypacker (1980) noted that "the goal of observation is to arrange conditions so that man or machine will react sensitively to the defined dimensions of the subject's behavior" (p. 146). In contrast, the act of recording provides a permanent and accurate record of the observations for future examination.

Following is a detailed description of each of the four recording tactics. Reference is made to their critical characteristics, the unit of measurement, how to report such data, and advantages and drawbacks to each tactic. Numerous examples are provided. In addition, there is a section on how to get started with each individual tactic. This particular section should lead to a basic mastery of each tactic.

EVENT RECORDING

One of the core properties of observable events or episodes is that they can occur over and over again. *Event recording* is the appropriate tactic for collecting data on this particular aspect of events and/or behaviors. Event recording provides the user with data on the *frequency* of occurrence of a discrete event. It tallies the number of times that this event took place (Cooper, 1974). Events that can be measured through event recording include the number of times that a student has the opportunity to shoot the puck in a floor hockey drill, the number of times that a student talks while the teacher is presenting verbal instructions, the frequency of nonverbal praise by a teacher, the frequency of verbal desists used by a teacher to stop certain student behavior, the frequency of arriving to practice late by an athlete, and the number of times that a coach verbally praises his or her starting athletes versus the number of praises for nonstarters.

The word *discrete* is critical in this context. The observer must be able to discriminate a definite beginning and end to the event. For example, in the case of the student shooting the puck, the beginning of this event will be the initiation of the backswing and the conclusion of this event would be the end of his or her follow-through. The beginning and end of a verbal statement are, of course, characterized by the first and last word of that statement. Event recording thus provides a *numerical* account of the occurrence of events.

Reporting Event Recording Data

If the length of the observation period is constant across sessions, *frequency* is the appropriate unit of measurement in reporting event recording data. If the length of observation varies from one session to the next, then the *rate* of response is more appropriate. The rate of behavior is calculated by dividing the recorded total frequency by the length of observation. The length of observation is typically measured in minutes; hence, the resulting number would be the rate per minute (RPM). Figure 2.1A shows how the apparent increase in the frequency of a coach's verbal specific skill feedback during Observation Sessions 5, 7, 10, and 12 was, in effect, the result of variability in the length of actual observation times. Clearly, RPM is the more appropriate unit of measurement (Figure 2.1B). In addition, it allows for comparisons to be made across a series of observations.

Although not used as often as frequency and rate, ratio and percentage are two additional means of reporting frequency data. *Ratios* are used to indicate the relationship of one behavior pattern to that of another. For example, if a teacher is characterized generally as being "positive," "neutral," or "negative" in interacting with students during class, calculation of a ratio could substantiate this. If a teacher makes 36 positive and 12 nagging or criticizing statements, the ratio would be a positive 3:1. If the teacher maintained that ratio across a large number of classes, then the description of being a positive teacher would be an accurate one. Tharp and Gallimore (1976) found that former UCLA basketball coach John Wooden had a praise-to-scold ratio of virtually 1:1. A similar ratio was found in a study on the verbal behavior patterns of former collegiate football coach Frank Kush (Langsdorf, 1979).

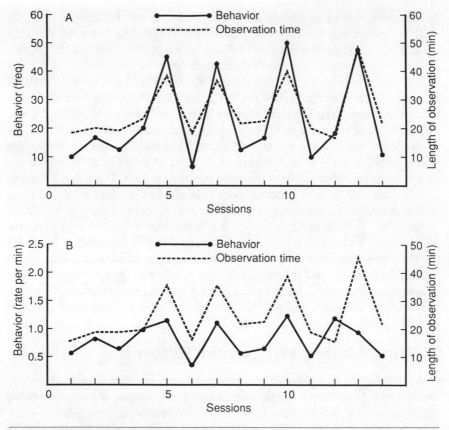

Figure 2.1 Relationship of (A) frequency and (B) rate per minute of behavior to length of observation.

At times frequency data are also expressed in *percentages*. Event recording data expressed in this fashion have their analog, for example, in athletes' game performance statistics. If a basketball player makes 23 of 42 field goal attempts, he or she is shooting 54.7%. Similarly, if a teacher is observed to study which students he or she interacts with most frequently, one could calculate the percentage of total interactions with boys as opposed to girls, high-skilled students as opposed to low-skilled students, and so forth. Another example would be to study the percentage of all positive skill feedback by a coach that carried specific information. It should be emphasized that regardless of how event recording data are reported, their fundamental unit of measurement is always frequency.

With well-defined category definitions, event recording is quite easy to use. There are two situations in which event recording should not be used. Both situations influence the reliability and/or validity of the data. First, if the behavior can occur at extremely high rates, event recording is inappropriate. The observer would probably not be able to keep up with the rapidity of the behavior and still be reliable. For example, it would be difficult to count the number of times that a player dribbled the basketball during practice and maintain a high level of reliability.

Second, a behavior or event can last for extended amounts of time. If that is the case, event recording again would not be the correct choice of observation tactic. In the example of the dribbling basketball player, recording that she only dribbled once throughout the whole practice session would not provide a complete picture of what transpired. She might have dribbled for 4 straight minutes as part of specific dribbling drills, but it would be impossible to tell from numerical data. Thus event recording in this case would produce data that do not give an accurate (i.e., valid) reflection of what actually happened. Another example would be to monitor off-task behavior (e.g., inattentiveness) on the part of a student during instructional episodes. At the end of the observation the coder might have recorded only three tallies for three observed instances of inattentiveness. What these data do not convey is that each instance of inattentiveness might have lasted for extended periods of time. Again, this would seriously jeopardize the validity of such data.

Getting Started With Event Recording

A basic level of competence must be achieved in using event recording before going on to one of the formalized observation systems provided in this textbook. Most of the observation systems comprise a large number of categories. Figure 2.2 provides a blank, all-purpose coding sheet that can be used for recording up to four event data simultaneously. Coding forms typically contain the following components: (a) demographic data, (b) space for recording the behavioral data, (c) space for data summary, (d) space for general comments (usually in the form of keywords, and (e) space for the behavior category definitions (if possible).

Accurately recording all demographic data (i.e., the information on the top portion of the coding form) should not be underestimated. Sloppy record keeping of data results in costly problems, whether it is for staff development or research purposes. Time is wasted if one has to go back and trace the origin of the observation.

The observer needs to get to know the space in which the actual data are recorded very well. Observers need to learn to find their way around this part of the coding form, particularly as the complexity of the system increases. Clearly labeled headings that are placed in the same location across each observation for all categories makes this easier. Although this may seem less important, it is again one of the many factors that influences observer reliability.

Teacher:_____ Date:_____ School: _____

Activity: _____ Time started: _____ Time ended: _____

Length of observation:_____ Observer:_____

Definitions:

1 _____

2 _____

3 _____

4 _____

1	2	3	4

Totals: _____   _____   _____   _____

Data summary:

Behaviors	Total frequency	Rate per minute
1		
2		
3		
4		

Comments: _____

Figure 2.2 All-purpose coding form for use with event recording of up to four behaviors.

As shown in the demographic data portion of Figure 2.2, an entry needs to be made on how long the observation period lasted. This allows the user to convert the frequencies (as shown by the tallies) to rates. The most common rate measure used is rate per minute (RPM). One needs to remember that the length of observation varies not only because the observer might arrive late or have to depart early, but also because of the purpose of the observation. For example, if the focus is solely on certain events that would occur only during transitional (i.e., organizational) episodes, then the observer would need to keep track of the total duration of such episodes. Consequently, the length of actual observation would be shorter and the resulting RPMs would reflect a more accurate depiction of what occurred during the observed episodes. Another example would be the observation of a teacher's use of skill feedback. This behavior is typically exhibited during episodes where students are involved in some kind of motor activity. Calculating an RPM for skill feedback provided by dividing the total frequency of the target behavior by the total class time would give a less than accurate picture of what happened during that class. Dividing the same frequency total by the amount of time students spent in an activity would result in a more accurate indicator.

A small space for writing down general comments and keywords is useful for keeping track of specific events that might be important to note in relation to the target behaviors. It provides the opportunity to enrich the numerical data. This is particularly true in situations where the collected data are used for providing feedback to the observed teacher or coach; being able to record some keywords can help in explaining the data and thus make the feedback more meaningful for the recipient.

As indicated in chapter 1, it is of critical importance to develop sound behavioral definitions of the events to be observed. It is a good strategy to keep the definitions in view while doing the actual observations, particularly in the early stages of learning to observe systematically. The list of definitions thus functions as a quick reference guide for cases in which the observer is undecided. If space allows, the observer should write the category definition(s) right above the area where the actual tallies are recorded. Figure 2.3 is a completed coding form of an observation of four behaviors.

For the novice observer the first few observations should focus on only two behaviors or events. As he or she progresses the complexity can then be increased by adding one, two, or three more categories. Progress should always be measured by establishing sufficient levels of observer reliability. Determining the reliability of observers is the focus of chapter 3.

DURATION RECORDING

A second pivotal dimension of behaviors, events, or episodes is that they can last for extended periods of time. If this dimension is the major focus, *duration recording* is the appropriate tactic. This tactic is used, for example, to collect data on the time spent by students in motor activity, the time spent by a baseball coach to explain the technical aspects of sliding into bases, time used up by a teacher to take attendance, the time that a teacher spends in one particular location of the gymnasium, the time that athletes spend waiting for instructions or for their turn during a drill, and so on.

Teacher: Longlin Date: 3/9 School: Desert H.S.
Activity: Track Time started: 9:05 Time ended: 9:40
Length of observation: 35 Observer: Cusimano

Definitions:
1 Providing exact commendatory information on performance. (motor)
2 Words supporting students' motor response.
3 Providing commendatory statements on behavior, other than motor.
4 Teacher comment to terminate a behavior.

1 Pos. Skill Fb. (specific)	2 Pos. Skill Fb. (General)	3 Behavior Praise	4 Desists
‡‡‡ ‡‡‡ ‡‡‡ I	‡‡‡ ‡‡‡ ‡‡‡ ‡‡‡ ‡‡‡ ‡‡‡ ‡‡‡ ‡‡‡ ‡‡‡ ‡‡‡ ‡‡‡ III	‡‡‡ II	‡‡‡ ‡‡‡ ‡‡‡ ‡‡‡ III

Totals: 16 58 7 23

Data summary:

Behaviors	Total frequency	Rate per minute
1 Pos. Skill Fb. (S)	16	.45
2 Pos. Skill Fb. (G)	58	1.65
3 Praise	7	.20
4 Desists	23	.65

Comments:
* You seem more specific toward male students.
* Let's work on behavior praise! (crucial this time of year)
* Be firm when you desist!!

Figure 2.3 Sample of completed event recording coding form.

As indicated in the previous section, certain behaviors occur at such high rates that event recording is not the appropriate tactic. If this is the case, such as in the dribbling example, then duration recording is the appropriate observation tactic. Duration recording thus provides a *temporal* account of the observed events. When using duration recording, the observer focuses on the whole group of students, a subgroup of students, one individual student, or the teacher.

Alberto and Troutman (1986) and Cooper, Heron, and Heward (1987) differentiated another type of recording procedure that also focuses on temporal dimensions of events: *latency recording*. Latency recording measures the time that elapses between a stimulus or cue and the beginning of the response. The only difference between latency recording and duration recording lies in their respective foci. Conceptually, duration recording starts where latency recording ends. Duration recording measures the time elapsed from the start of a behavior or event until its end. Measuring the amount of time between a teacher's signal for attention and the students' exhibiting that attentive behavior is one example of latency recording. Another example would be measuring the amount of time elapsed from the teacher's "Go" signal until the last student in the group is ready to start an activity. Johnston and Pennypacker (1980) proposed another type of latency, namely, that of time elapsed in between two instances of the same behavior, or Interresponse Time (IRT). Examples of situations or events in physical education and sport settings where latency recording is useful would be the time elapsed between one free throw attempt to the next, one archer's shot attempt to the next, one shot on goal to the next in hockey or soccer, one vault attempt over the horse to the next, and so forth.

Reporting Duration Recording Data

The standard units of measurement for such data are *minutes* and *seconds*. As was the case in event recording, if the length of the observation period is a constant (e.g., 40 minutes) across all observations of one teacher or coach, then the data are reported in the original unit of measurement. However, if it varies in length from one session to the next, then the original data need to be converted to *percentage* of observed time. Percentage of observed time is calculated by using the following equation:

$$\frac{\text{Episode total (seconds)}}{\text{Total time of observation (seconds)}} \times 100$$

The denominator (total amount of observed time) could be the whole class or practice session, or only specific portions of it. If it encompassed the complete class, the label of the denominator would be "percent of class time." However, if the total observation were aimed at only the motor activity portion of the class, the label would read "percent of activity time." The latter would be used if one were interested in determining the degree to which players were actually engaged in motor skill activities during episodes that were designated specifically for motor skill practice.

If the numerator and/or the denominator exceed 60 seconds, those values need to be converted to seconds (see Table 2.1). For example, if the observation lasted 33 minutes and 38 seconds, and during that time the student was off-task 7 minutes and 12 seconds, both values are converted to total seconds first before the division is calculated. Hence, 452 seconds is divided by 2,038 seconds, and the resulting value is multiplied by 100. The off-task behavior is 22.1% of the observed time.

Table 2.1 Time Calculation for Observed Behaviors

Episodes	Minutes:seconds	Total seconds	Percent
Waiting	12:38	758	37.1
Off-task	7:12	452	22.1
Motor engaged	13:48	828	40.6

Needed Hardware

A variety of mechanisms are available to measure the temporal dimensions of behaviors and events. The advent of computer programs for the purpose of collecting observational data has enabled observers to mark the beginning and end of occurrences of behaviors by simply punching the appropriate key on the keyboard. The internal clock in the computer (along with the computer program) keeps a record of how time is spent as viewed by the observer.

The most frequently used mechanism is the manually controlled stopwatch. A digital stopwatch is best for use in duration recording observations, because it is easier to use than the regular second hand wristwatch or wall clock. In addition, the ease with which one can read the elapsed time on the digital stopwatch adds to the collection of accurate records of events. A wall clock or a watch with a second hand is harder to read in terms of speed, causing the observer to miss new changes in the environment that need to be detected and recorded while he or she is reading the clock. The observer's act of viewing the beginning (or end) of an episode or behavior, followed by looking at the clock, finding the correct spot on the coding form, and making the actual recording on the form must take as little time as possible so that the observation can continue.

Getting Started With Duration Recording

The most basic level of duration recording is the observation of a single behavior, event, or episode. Cooper et al. (1987) discriminated between two basic procedures of using duration recording. Both are particularly useful when observing a single behavior or event. The *total duration* procedure provides an accumulative total of the amount of time over which a certain behavior or event occurred. In using this procedure, the observer starts a stopwatch when the event starts and stops it when the event ceases. Without resetting the stopwatch to zero, the observer starts it up again as soon as the behavior occurs for a second time and stops it again when the behavior stops, and so on. Thus the total amount of time slowly accumulates as the observation session progresses.

A second procedure for duration recording is *duration per occurrence*. This is also a useful strategy if only one behavior or event is observed. In using duration per occurrence, the observer starts the stopwatch when the behavior begins and stops it when the behavior ends. After stopping the stopwatch, the observer records on paper the amount of time that elapsed for that specific occurrence of the behavior. After that, the stopwatch is reset to zero and started up once the behavior starts again.

Although not that different from each other, total duration and duration per occurrence provide two alternatives for capturing the temporal dimensions of a behavior or event; the latter also provides a frequency count of the behavior. Latency recording is most often done using duration per occurrence. The decision of which to use depends on the specific type of information that is needed.

Figure 2.4 is an all-purpose duration recording coding form that is used to record temporal data from one to four behaviors or events simultaneously. The time bar is broken down into 30 minutes, and each individual minute is again broken into 10-second segments. The act of using a coding form like this could be described as follows: Once the observer sees (one of) the behavior(s) begin he or she checks the stopwatch to read off the elapsed time (e.g., 3 minutes and 24 seconds). Immediately afterward, the location of that point in time is located on the time bar. The observer places a vertical slash through the time bar between the hash marks that indicate the 3-minute-20-second and the 3-minute-30-second marks. Then, right above the slash, the observer writes "24" to show that the behavior started at exactly that time. Following that, observation of the behavior resumes so that its end can be captured.

In some cases it is appropriate to round off the recorded slashes to the nearest hash mark. For example, if the time elapsed were 3 minutes and 24 seconds, this would be rounded off to the 20-second hash mark. If it were 3 minutes and 28 seconds, it would be rounded off to the 30-second hash mark. This strategy should not become a habit, particularly if the

Teacher: _____ Date: _____ School: _____

Activity: _____ Time started: _____ Time ended: _____

Length of observation: _____ Observer: _____

Definitions:

1 _____

2 _____

3 _____

4 _____

Total time in   1. _____ (min/sec)   Percent of time in   1. _____ %

2. _____ (min/sec)   2. _____ %

3. _____ (min/sec)   3. _____ %

4. _____ (min/sec)   4. _____ %

Comments: _____

_____

_____

Figure 2.4 All-purpose coding form for use with duration recording of up to four behaviors.

collected data are used for research purposes. Rounding off is useful only when an observer is trying to get an initial, general overview of the basic pattern of the behavior(s).

Figure 2.5 is a completed coding form with data collected on four basic time-based variables. The observer should not increase the number of categories until he or she has reached sufficient levels of reliability.

INTERVAL RECORDING

Interval recording allows the observer to measure the occurrence or non-occurrence of behavior within specific intervals. The total observation

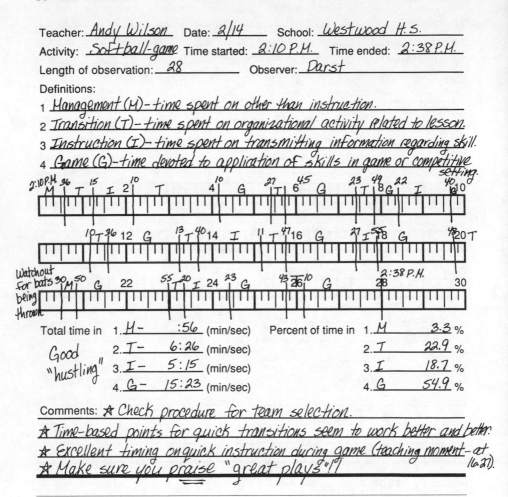

Teacher: _Andy Wilson_   Date: _2/14_   School: _Westwood H.S._
Activity: _Softball-game_   Time started: _2:10 P.M._   Time ended: _2:38 P.M._
Length of observation: _28_   Observer: _Darst_
Definitions:

1 _Management (M) - time spent on other than instruction._
2 _Transition (T) - time spent on organizational activity related to lesson._
3 _Instruction (I) - time spent on transmitting information regarding skill._
4 _Game (G) - time devoted to application of skills in game or competitive setting._

Total time in   1. _M - :56_ (min/sec)   Percent of time in   1. _M   3.3_ %
Good   2. _T - 6:26_ (min/sec)   2. _T   22.9_ %
"hustling"   3. _I - 5:15_ (min/sec)   3. _I   18.7_ %
                4. _G - 15:23_ (min/sec)   4. _G   54.9_ %

Comments: ☆ _Check procedure for team selection._
☆ _Time-based points for quick transitions seem to work better and better._
☆ _Excellent timing on quick instruction during game (teaching moment - at 16:27)._
☆ _Make sure you praise "great plays"!!_

Figure 2.5 Sample of completed duration recording coding form.

period is divided into short intervals of equal length. The range of interval length is normally from 6 to 30 seconds. The choice of interval length depends on two major factors. First, the observer's level of experience in accurately observing and recording behaviors is of influence. As the observer becomes more skilled in detecting the occurrences of events, the interval length can be shortened. Second, the complexity of the observation system also governs the minimum length of the interval. On the one hand, if the observer is focusing on only a single behavior, and thus is concerned with a *dichotomous* decision, then the interval length can remain quite short. On the other hand, if the observation system includes multiple categories, thus forcing the observer to make a decision from a greater number of choices, then the interval length needs to be increased.

Siedentop (1983) noted that there is a danger in lengthening the interval too much, in that a greater number of behaviors or events can occur during that time, thus making the observer's decision harder.

How to Report Interval Recording Data

The unit of measurement for interval recording is frequency of intervals. However, in virtually all cases its derivative, *percentage of intervals* in which the behavior(s) occurred, is used for reporting such data. Percentage of intervals is calculated by dividing the total number of intervals in which the behavior occurred by the total number of intervals observed, multiplied by 100.

Needed Hardware

Some hardware is required to be successful in interval recording. The observer needs to know when each interval has ended. For that reason the standard equipment is an audiocassette recorder with an earphone. Cues signaling the ends of intervals are prerecorded on audiocassettes, thus keeping the observer from having to divert his or her attention to a stopwatch and possibly lessening the accuracy of the data. Typically, the observer hears the following sequence of cues: "Start in 10 seconds. . . . Observe. . . . Record. . . . Record. . . . Record," and so on. The "observe" cue in that sequence constitutes the start of the first interval. Upon the "record" cue, the observer needs to record on the coding form whether the event or behavior occurred during the interval by putting down a check mark (✓) in the appropriate box. If a choice needs to be made from multiple categories, then a representative symbol is placed in the appropriate box. For example, commonly used symbols would be "T" for transition, "P" for practice, and "Of" for off-task.

When the intervals are somewhat longer (i.e., 10 seconds or more) it is sometimes helpful to include additional cues that serve as points of reference for the observer within the interval. For example, if the interval length is 15 seconds, the cue tape would sound as follows: "Start in 10 seconds. . . . Observe. . . . Five. . . . Ten. . . . Record. . . . Five. . . . Ten. . . . Record," and so on.

In developing the cue tape, one should try to make sure that the clock provides a consistent account of time and, furthermore, that the tape recorder runs on outlet power. This ensures that the cues are recorded consistently and accurately. Battery-operated tape recorders are less ideal and should only be used if fully charged batteries are available. Less than adequate power adds to the variability in the data.

Recording Format Procedures

When using interval recording, the observer needs to make decisions regarding both *recording criteria* and *cuing format*. The observer has a choice of two different interval recording procedures. Probably the most widely used is *partial-interval recording*. With this procedure the observer is concerned with the occurrence or nonoccurrence of the behavior, regardless of how many times or when it might have occurred within the interval. Thus, as soon as the behavior occurs for the first time, the observer records its occurrence. Figure 2.6 is a graphic depiction of this procedure. A situation in which the activity is throwing at a target and students are working by themselves with an interval length of 6 seconds results in intervals that may well have more than one trial each. The behavior is coded regardless of how many trials occur or when the first trial is detected by the observer during one interval.

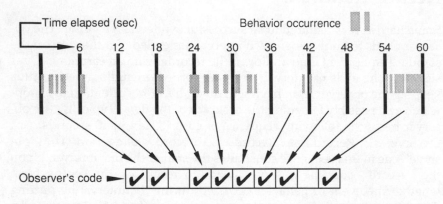

Figure 2.6 Graphic depiction of coding procedure using partial-interval recording.

A second procedure is *whole-interval recording*. In using this strategy, the observer codes the behavior as having occurred only if it lasted for the entire interval. The behavior is not coded if it lasted for only part of the interval. For example, if the observation focused on motor engagement by students or athletes and the activities consisted of continuous, ongoing motor activities such as rope jumping, swimming, running, dribbling a ball, and so forth, they would have to be engaged in those activities for the entire interval to be considered motor engaged (see Figure 2.7).

In using whole-interval recording with multiple categories, observers need to follow *ground rules* that aid in deciding which coding symbol to enter in the case where two (or even three) different behaviors occur with-

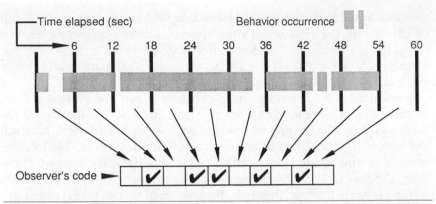

Figure 2.7 Graphic depiction of coding procedure using whole-interval recording.

in one interval. In such cases the ground rule typically has been to code the most predominant behavior observed during the interval. From a contextual perspective, for example, transitional episodes would be coded only if they took up at least 50% of the interval. Figure 2.8 shows how the onset and/or completion of a transition within the interval governs whether that interval is coded as a transition. Other ground rules are applied, of course, depending on the purpose of the investigation.

The observer needs to decide which of the two recording criteria (partial- vs. whole-interval) will produce the closest estimates of both the temporal and the numerical dimensions of the behaviors to be measured. The choice should be made based on the following factors: (a) the average duration of the behavior, (b) the average frequency per time unit of the behavior, and (c) the length of the interval. It is possible to switch from

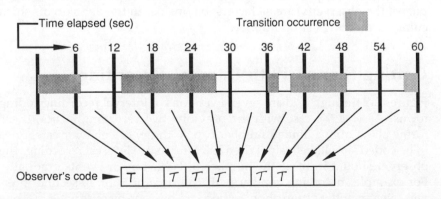

Figure 2.8 Graphic depiction of onset and end of a behavior within the interval and its influence on whether the behavior is coded.

whole-interval to partial-interval recording within one lesson as a result of changes in the type of activities. Some further suggestions on this decision for experimental research efforts are provided in a later section. Communication on these decisions is important, particularly when establishing interobserver agreement (IOA).

In addition to the aforementioned considerations, observers also need to choose from two different kinds of cuing formats. The first one is the format explained in the previous section on "Needed Hardware" in which the observer hears a cue to record every 6 or 10 seconds. Technically, there is no time allotted for recording on paper what was observed. However, the first second of each interval is needed to record what was seen in the previous interval. Springer, Brown, and Duncan (1981) called this the *10/0 format*, where 10 seconds are allotted for observation and 0 seconds for recording.

The second cuing format alternates the observer's tasks of observing and recording. Tawney and Gast (1984) called this *noncontinuous observation control*. For example, the observe interval could be 10 seconds and the record interval could be 5 seconds in length (i.e., a 10/5 format). This format is recommended when the observation system is more complex (i.e., has multiple categories). As the observer becomes more experienced at using a particular system, the length of the record interval can be shortened.

The advantages and disadvantages of both cuing formats as they relate to the validity of resulting data need to be weighed carefully. An observe/record (6/6) format is obviously a reflection of only 50% of the actual observation session. As a rule of thumb, the longer the record interval, the greater the chance of the data being less valid. However, this format does allow a larger number of behaviors to be observed simultaneously. The properties of the behavior to be studied (its frequency and/or duration), the purpose of the analysis, and the level of experience on the part of the observer(s) are all factors to consider in the decision of which cuing format is most appropriate.

Getting Started With Interval Recording

Figures 2.9 through 2.13 are several versions of interval recording coding forms. As was the case with the previous two recording tactics, these forms allow only a limited number (up to three) of behavior categories to be coded simultaneously. When learning to use interval recording, the observer should increase the number of behaviors or events gradually. For example, becoming familiar with the pace of 5- or 10-second intervals over an entire observation session can be done by observing just one behavior, such as student/athlete motor engagement. That can be followed up by adding one or two behaviors as the observer gains experience.

Teacher: _____ Date: _____ School: _____

Activity: _____ Time started: _____ Time ended: _____

Number of total intervals: _____

```
              5           10          15          20          25
  ┌─┬─┬─┬─┬─┬─┬─┬─┬─┬─┬─┬─┬─┬─┬─┬─┬─┬─┬─┬─┬─┬─┬─┬─┬─┐
  └─┴─┴─┴─┴─┴─┴─┴─┴─┴─┴─┴─┴─┴─┴─┴─┴─┴─┴─┴─┴─┴─┴─┴─┴─┘

              30          35          40          45          50
  ┌─┬─┬─┬─┬─┬─┬─┬─┬─┬─┬─┬─┬─┬─┬─┬─┬─┬─┬─┬─┬─┬─┬─┬─┬─┐
  └─┴─┴─┴─┴─┴─┴─┴─┴─┴─┴─┴─┴─┴─┴─┴─┴─┴─┴─┴─┴─┴─┴─┴─┴─┘

              55          60          65          70          75
  ┌─┬─┬─┬─┬─┬─┬─┬─┬─┬─┬─┬─┬─┬─┬─┬─┬─┬─┬─┬─┬─┬─┬─┬─┬─┐
  └─┴─┴─┴─┴─┴─┴─┴─┴─┴─┴─┴─┴─┴─┴─┴─┴─┴─┴─┴─┴─┴─┴─┴─┴─┘

              80          85          90          95          100
  ┌─┬─┬─┬─┬─┬─┬─┬─┬─┬─┬─┬─┬─┬─┬─┬─┬─┬─┬─┬─┬─┬─┬─┬─┬─┐
  └─┴─┴─┴─┴─┴─┴─┴─┴─┴─┴─┴─┴─┴─┴─┴─┴─┴─┴─┴─┴─┴─┴─┴─┴─┘
```

Definitions:

1 _____

2 _____

3 _____

Data summary:

	Total # of intervals	Percentage of intervals
1		
2		
3		

Post-observation comments: _____

_____

_____

Figure 2.9 All-purpose coding form for use with interval recording of up to three behaviors.

Figure 2.9 is an all-purpose coding form that is used for either the record-only cuing format (e.g., 10/0) or the observe/record cuing format (e.g., 10/8). Figure 2.10 is a coding form using the record-only cuing format with an interval length of 10 seconds (10/0). The interval bar is broken down into minutes, as indicated by the black triangles in every sixth interval. In Figure 2.11 the same cuing format (record only) is used, but now the interval length is only 6 seconds (6/0). Figure 2.12 is a coding form for use with an observe/record cuing format of 10/5, and Figure 2.13

Teacher: _____ Date: _____ School: _____

Activity: _____ Time started: _____ Time ended: _____

Number of total intervals: _____

(interval #) 5   10   15   20   25

(min)   1   2   3   4

30   35   40   45   50

5   6   7   8

55   60   65   70   75

9   10   11   12

80   85   90   95   100

13   14   15   16

Definitions:

1 _____

2 _____

3 _____

Data summary:

	Total # of intervals	Percentage of intervals
1		
2		
3		

Post-observation comments: _____

_____

_____

Figure 2.10 Interval recording coding form for use with a record-only format and a 10-second interval.

Teacher: _____   Date: _____   School: _____

Activity: _____   Time started: _____   Time ended: _____

Number of total intervals: _____

(interval #)   5   10   15   20   25

(min)   1   2

30   35   40   45   50

3   4   5

55   60   65   70   75

6   7

80   85   90   95   100

8   9   10

Definitions:

1 _____

2 _____

3 _____

Data summary:

	Total # of intervals	Percentage of intervals
1		
2		
3		

Post-observation comments:

_____

_____

_____

Figure 2.11 Interval recording coding form for use with a record-only format and a 6-second interval.

Teacher:————————   Date:—————   School: ——————————

Activity: ———————————   Time started: ——————————   Time ended: ——————

Number of total intervals: ———————————

(interval #)   5   10   15   20   25

(min)   1   2   3   4   5   6

30   35   40   45   50

7   8   9   10   11   12

55   60   65   70   75

13   14   15   16   17   18

80   85   90   95   100

19   20   21   22   23   24   25

Definitions:

1 ——

2 ——

3 ——

Data summary:

	Total # of intervals	Percentage of intervals
1		
2		
3		

Post-observation comments: ————————————————————————

——

——

——

Figure 2.12   Interval recording coding form for use with an observe/record (10/5 seconds) cuing format.

Teacher: _____ Date: _____ School: _____

Activity: _____ Time started: _____ Time ended: _____

Number of total intervals: _____

(interval #) 5   10   15   20   25

(min)   1   2   3   4

30   35   40   45   50

5   6   7   8

55   60   65   70   75

9   10   11   12

80   85   90   95   100

13   14   15   16

Definitions:

1 _____

2 _____

3 _____

Data summary:

         Total # of intervals   Percentage of intervals

1 _____

2 _____

3 _____

Post-observation comments: _____

_____

_____

Figure 2.13 Interval recording coding form for use with an observe/record (6/6 seconds) cuing format.

Teacher: _Stevens_   Date: _2/28_   School: _Challenger E.S._
Activity: _Jump rope/Jog_ Time started: _10:05_   Time ended: _10:19_
Number of total intervals: _88_

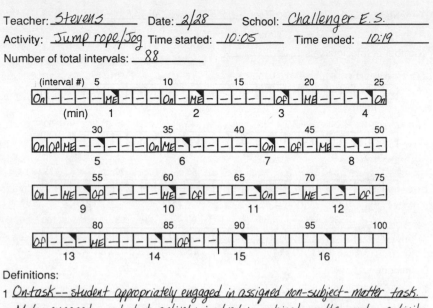

Definitions:

1 _On-task -- student appropriately engaged in assigned non-subject-matter task._
2 _Motor engaged -- student actively involved in subject matter motor activity._
3 _OFF-task -- student engaged in activity other than one he should be_
                                                    engaged in.

Data summary:

	Total # of intervals	Percentage of intervals
1 On-task	17	17/88 × 100 = 19.3
2 Motor engaged	48	48/88 × 100 = 54.5
3 OFF-task	23	23/88 × 100 = 26.1

Post-observation comments: ☆ _As the lesson progressed, the time spent_
waiting allowed OFF-task behavior to increase. ☆ Excellent use of signal
for starting and stopping activities. ☆ Great nonverbal!! ☆ Careful
with spreading students too far.

Figure 2.14 Sample of a completed interval recording coding form.

allows coding with a 6/6 cuing format. Notice that a different cue tape
needs to be developed for each cuing format. Figure 2.14 is a completed
interval recording coding sheet and summary.

MOMENTARY TIME SAMPLING

Momentary time sampling is similar to interval recording in that the observation session is also divided into time intervals. However, the critical

difference lies in the time when the actual act of observation takes place. Figure 2.15 displays the difference between the two tactics graphically. In interval recording the act of observation starts at the beginning of the interval and continues throughout the entire interval, whereas in momentary time sampling the observation act occurs at the end of each interval. After the observation is made the observer marks whether or not the behavior(s) occurred on the coding form.

Most often the length of the interval (i.e., the time in between the actual observation) is longer than that used for interval recording, ranging anywhere from 1 to 10 minutes. The length of the interval depends on the combination of the duration of the total observation session and the number of samples needed. Usually the time intervals are of equal length; however, one can also use variable time intervals. This guards against situations in which the pace of the activities matches the instances where the observation takes place in such a way that the validity of the data is threatened severely. For example, a session in which athletes/students

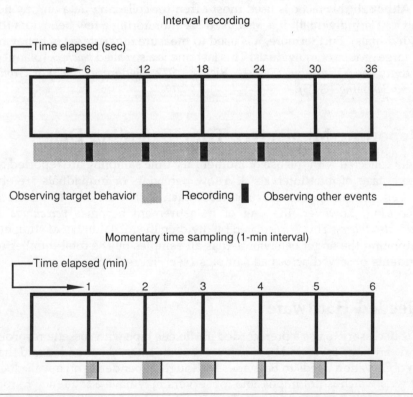

Figure 2.15 Difference between interval recording and momentary time sampling in terms of the sequence and duration of the observation and recording act.

are working on various skills at different work stations usually includes rotating groups from one station to the next. If the time spent at each work station is constant (e.g., 2 minutes) and similar to the length of the time intervals for the observer, it is quite possible that the end of the time interval falls during the rotation. If the observer were measuring the level of motor engagement of students/athletes, the resulting data would indicate a much lower (possibly zero) percentage than what actually happened. Test and Heward (1984) described how a variable schedule of momentary time samples can be developed:

> A random numbers table was used to generate numbers between 1 and 1800, representing the total number of seconds in a 30-minute session. The random numbers were selected and placed on a number line, with the criterion that no two numbers could be less than 10 seconds apart, until 30 observation points had been marked. The list of numbers was then used as a guide for making the variable interval time sampling cuing tape. (p. 181)

Although this tactic is used most often for collecting data on one behavior (or individual), it is also used for monitoring a few behaviors (or individuals). Furthermore, it is used to measure the patterns of behavior of large groups of individuals. This last one is also called *placheck* (planned activity check) *recording* (Doke & Risley, 1972; Siedentop, 1983) or *Group Time Sampling* (GTS).

Reporting Momentary Time Sampling Data

Data collected with the use of momentary time sampling are reported as percentage of total intervals. If a few behaviors or individuals are observed, percentages are calculated for each individual one. In placheck recording, however, the unit of measurement becomes *percentage of students/athletes*. This is calculated by dividing the total number of students exhibiting the target behavior across all samples by the total number of students observed across all samples (see Figure 2.16).

Needed Hardware

It is necessary to use a prerecorded audio cue tape with cassette recorder and earphone to remind the observer that the interval has ended and that an observation needs to be made. Although dependence on a wall clock or wristwatch is not impossible, observers may have a tendency to forget to monitor the clock, particularly if the intervals are somewhat longer (i.e., 2 minutes or more) and attention is focused on other events in the setting.

Behavior observed: Athletes's waiting behavior
Number of samples: 10
Number of athletes present: 12

Sample	# of players waiting
1	1 of 12
2	0 of 12
3	6 of 12
4	8 of 12
5	2 of 12
6	4 of 12
7	6 of 12
8	6 of 12
9	1 of 12
10	2 of 12

Total 36

Equation:

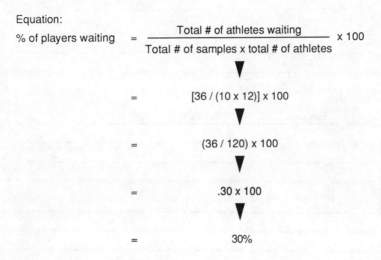

$$\% \text{ of players waiting} = \frac{\text{Total \# of athletes waiting}}{\text{Total \# of samples x total \# of athletes}} \times 100$$

$$= [36 / (10 \times 12)] \times 100$$

$$= (36 / 120) \times 100$$

$$= .30 \times 100$$

$$= 30\%$$

Figure 2.16 Calculation of percentage of students/players from Group Time Sampling data.

Getting Started With Momentary Time Sampling

Momentary time sampling should first be used by itself with a focus on one specific behavior. To practice using this tactic, the observer should use a 1-minute interval. Later, as this tactic is used in combination with other observation tactics, the interval length will increase. Figure 2.17 can be used for this purpose.

As coding experience increases, observations of multiple behaviors or events or of one behavior across a number of individuals can be made.

Teacher: _____   Date: _____   School: _____

Activity: _____   Time started: _____   Time ended: _____

Number of total samples: _____

```
            5 (min)      10         15         20         25
  □□□□□□□□□□□□□□□□□□□□□□□□□□

            30         35         40         45         50
  □□□□□□□□□□□□□□□□□□□□□□□□□□

            55         60         65         70         75
  □□□□□□□□□□□□□□□□□□□□□□□□□□

            80         85         90         95         100
  □□□□□□□□□□□□□□□□□□□□□□□□□□
```

Definitions:

1 _____

2 _____

3 _____

Data summary:

	Total # of samples	Percentage of samples
1		
2		
3		

Comments: _____

_____

_____

Figure 2.17 All-purpose coding form for use with momentary time sampling of up to three behaviors.

Figure 2.18 is a sample coding form for use with three individual students or athletes. The interval length here is 1 minute. When monitoring the behavior patterns of more than one individual, the observer should observe and record in sequence. In other words, upon cue, the observer quickly locates the first player (or student), detects the behavior, and makes the recording. This is followed by the same sequence for the second and third players. Figure 2.19 is a completed coding form.

Teacher:_____   Date:_____   School:_____

Activity: _____   Time started: _____   Time ended: _____

Length of observation: _____   Observer:_____

Student name:
Behaviors   5 (min)   10   15   20 Totals

Student name:
Behaviors   5 (min)   10   15   20 Totals

Student name:
Behaviors   5 (min)   10   15   20 Totals

Student name:	Student name:	Student name:
_____	_____	_____
Behavior percentages	Behavior percentages	Behavior percentages
1. ____ / 20 x 100 = ____	1. ____ / 20 x 100 = ____	1. ____ / 20 x 100 = ____
2. ____ / 20 x 100 = ____	2. ____ / 20 x 100 = ____	2. ____ / 20 x 100 = ____
3. ____ / 20 x 100 = ____	3. ____ / 20 x 100 = ____	3. ____ / 20 x 100 = ____
4. ____ / 20 x 100 = ____	4. ____ / 20 x 100 = ____	4. ____ / 20 x 100 = ____

Figure 2.18 Coding form for use with momentary time sampling across four behaviors for three different students.

MEASUREMENT LIMITATIONS OF TIME-BASED RECORDING TACTICS

One of the advantages of interval recording is that it provides an *estimate* of both the frequency and the duration of behaviors. This is one of the reasons interval recording has become a widely used observation tactic.

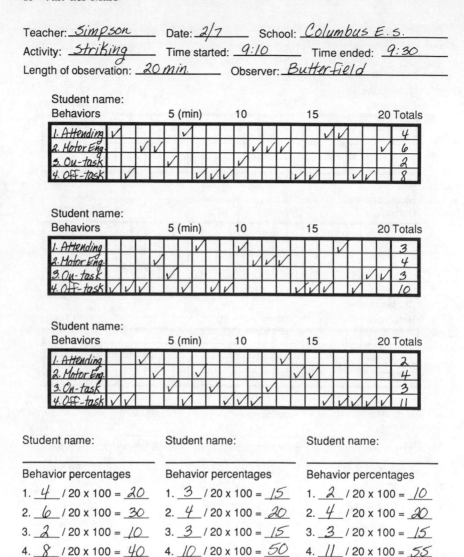

Teacher: *Simpson*   Date: *2/7*   School: *Columbus E.S.*
Activity: *Striking*   Time started: *9:10*   Time ended: *9:30*
Length of observation: *20 min.*   Observer: *Butterfield*

Student name:

Behaviors			5 (min)		10		15		20	Totals
1. Attending	✓		✓				✓	✓		4
2. Motor Eng.		✓	✓		✓	✓	✓		✓	6
3. On-task			✓		✓					2
4. Off-task	✓		✓	✓	✓		✓	✓	✓	✓	8

Student name:

Behaviors			5 (min)		10		15		20	Totals
1. Attending			✓		✓		✓			3
2. Motor Eng.		✓			✓	✓	✓			4
3. On-task		✓						✓	✓	3
4. Off-task	✓	✓	✓		✓	✓	✓	✓	✓	✓	✓	10

Student name:

Behaviors			5 (min)		10		15		20	Totals
1. Attending		✓				✓				2
2. Motor Eng.		✓		✓		✓	✓			4
3. On-task		✓		✓		✓				3
4. Off-task	✓	✓	✓	✓	✓		✓	✓	✓	✓	✓	11

Student name: Student name: Student name:
_____   _____   _____

Behavior percentages   Behavior percentages   Behavior percentages
1. *4* / 20 x 100 = *20*   1. *3* / 20 x 100 = *15*   1. *2* / 20 x 100 = *10*
2. *6* / 20 x 100 = *30*   2. *4* / 20 x 100 = *20*   2. *4* / 20 x 100 = *20*
3. *2* / 20 x 100 = *10*   3. *3* / 20 x 100 = *15*   3. *3* / 20 x 100 = *15*
4. *8* / 20 x 100 = *40*   4. *10* / 20 x 100 = *50*   4. *11* / 20 x 100 = *55*

Figure 2.19 Sample of completed momentary time sampling coding form for three students.

However, unlike event and duration recording, which provide exact measures on those dimensions of any observable event, interval recording and time sampling can only estimate both properties. Springer, Brown, and Duncan (1981) argued that discontinuous, time-based recording tactics such as interval recording and time sampling may produce highly distorted records of behavior, because the recording of the behavior is governed by the passage of time rather than by its natural presence or absence. There is a considerable body of research on this issue. For example, in a comparison of whole-interval, partial-interval, and momentary time sampling recording, Powell, Martindale, and Kulp (1975) reported that whole-interval data repeatedly underestimated the true dimensions of behavior, partial-interval data consistently overestimated the true dimensions, and both occurred when time sampling intervals were longer than 2 minutes. More recently, Test and Heward (1984) found that overestimation and underestimation occurred even with time sampling intervals of only 1 minute and suggested that when momentary time sampling is used as the primary observation tactic some form of calibration should be used to ensure accuracy of data. This calibration would be done using either event recording or duration recording as a backup measure, depending on the dimension of interest.

The accuracy of frequency estimates (i.e., total number of intervals) is influenced by the length of the interval and typical duration of each instance of the behavior. If both match, then the estimate is more likely to be close to the actual frequency of the behavior. If the interval length is long and the typical duration of the behavior is very short, it produces an underestimated frequency count.

Overestimation occurs when the duration of a single instance of the behavior consistently covers a number of consecutive intervals. Barlow and Hersen (1984) indicated that "the interval method will only provide a good estimate of duration when observation intervals are very short in comparison with the mean duration of the target behavior" (p. 118). (See Springer, Brown, & Duncan, 1981, for a more detailed discussion on this issue.)

Cooper et al. (1987) provided useful guidelines for making decisions on which recording procedure to use in experimental research:

> It is recommended that (1) whole-interval recording be used when the goal is to produce a behavior increase since whole-interval may generate an underestimate of the true parameter, (2) partial-interval recording be used when the goal is to produce a decrease in the behavior since this technique may generate an overestimate of the true parameter, and (3) momentary time sampling be used with time intervals of less than 2 minutes. (p. 84)

Momentary time sampling provides two major advantages over interval recording. First, momentary time can be used by teachers/coaches *while* instructing. Depending on how frequent the cues occur, instructional activities can continue normally in between them. Second, it is possible for an outside observer to use the time in between the observations to monitor other events and episodes. From that perspective this tactic can be combined easily with duration recording.

CHOOSING AN OBSERVATION SYSTEM

As indicated in chapter 1, any use of systematic observation tools should be done with a specific purpose, be it for research on or evaluation of instructional episodes. Once a decision has been made on what behaviors or episodes to monitor, they need to be defined in observable terms, keeping in mind their numerical and temporal characteristics. Once these properties have been established, a decision can be made on which recording tactic will produce the most records of events. Given that decision, a system can be selected by using the summary table of systems in the Appendix. Figure 2.20 provides a general reference guide to use in deciding which recording tactic to utilize. Furthermore, it lists the chapter numbers of the systems that correspond with the recording tactics.

DEVELOPING A NEW OBSERVATION SYSTEM

Although the formal observation systems presented in this text allow a great number of behaviors, events, and episodes to be measured and analyzed, users of systematic observation tools may find themselves faced with a possibility that none of the available systems provides appropriate data for the analysis of a specific situation. As research on teaching and coaching in physical activity settings develops, new dimensions and variables will be uncovered, making a more fine-grained study possible and necessary. Siedentop (1983) provided some useful guidelines for developing one's own observation system. First, one needs to develop a sound, behavioral definition of the phenomenon to be studied. Second, an appropriate observation tactic needs to be selected that captures the occurrence of the phenomenon most accurately. And third, a coding form needs to be developed. It is hoped that the information provided so far in this textbook will aid the user in developing new, valid, and practical observation instruments.

GLOSSARY

Cuing format: Type of cuing sequence used in interval recording.

Dichotomous decision: Decision based on a one-choice situation (i.e., either yes or no).

Discrete behavior: Behavior that has a clearly definable beginning and end, and is short in duration.

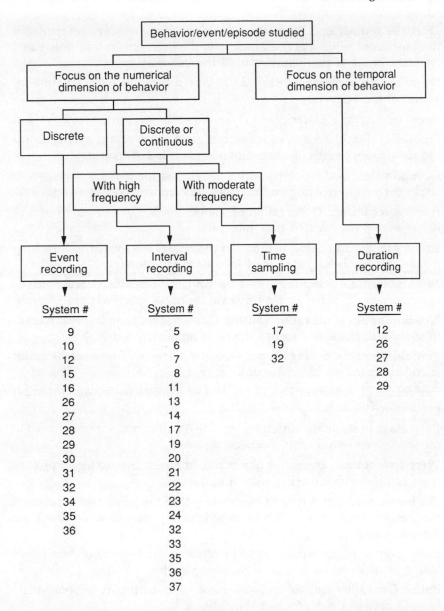

Figure 2.20 Decision chart for selecting appropriate observation systems. *Note.* Adapted from APPLIED BEHAVIOR ANALYSIS FOR TEACHERS, SECOND EDITION by P.A. Alberto and A.C. Troutman (p. 126). Copyright © 1986 by Merrill Publishing Company, Columbus, OH. Reprinted by permission.

Duration recording: Observation tactic used to measure the temporal dimensions of behaviors (i.e., how long the behavior lasted); measured from the onset of the behavior until the behavior ends.

Duration per occurrence: Record of elapsed time for each separate instance of the behavior.

Event recording: Frequency or tally count of the occurrence of behavior.

Frequency: Standard unit of measurement used to report event recording data when length of observation session is constant.

Ground rules: Coding conventions developed for making decisions in situations where existing coding rules lack information or specificity.

Interval recording: Observation of the occurrence or nonoccurrence of behavior *during* specified time intervals.

Latency recording: Same as duration recording, but measures how long it takes for the behavior to start following its stimulus.

Momentary time sampling: Observation tactic for which occurrence or nonoccurrence of behavior is recorded at the *end* of specified time intervals.

Noncontinuous observation control: Cuing sequence in interval recording where observe and record intervals are alternated.

Partial-interval recording: Type of interval recording for which behavior is coded regardless of its duration or frequency during the interval.

Percentage of behavior: Derivative unit of measurement used to report proportions of data.

Percentage of students/athletes: Derivative unit of measurement used to report data collected with placheck recording.

Percentage of time: Derivative unit of measurement used to report proportions of time with duration recording data.

Placheck recording: A type of momentary time sampling that focuses on the performance of a group of individuals (also called Group Time Sampling, GTS).

Rate: Unit of measurement used to report event recording data when length of observation across sessions is variable.

Ratio: Derivative unit of measurement used to report proportionate balance between two sets of behaviors.

Total duration: Accumulative record of the time elapsed between the beginning and the end of a behavior.

Whole-interval recording: Type of interval recording in which behavior is coded only if it lasts throughout the entire interval.

REFERENCES

Alberto, P.A., & Troutman, A.C. (1986). *Applied behavior analysis for teachers* (2nd ed.). Columbus, OH: Merrill.

Barlow, D.H., & Hersen, M. (1984). *Single case experimental designs: Strategies for studying behavior change* (2nd ed.). New York: Pergamon.

Cooper, J.O. (1974). *Measurement and analysis of behavioral techniques.* Columbus, OH: Merrill.

Cooper, J.O., Heron, T.E., & Heward, W.L. (1987). *Applied behavior analysis.* Columbus, OH: Merrill.

Doke, L.A., & Risley, T.R. (1972). The organization of day care environments: Required vs. optional activities. *Journal of Applied Behavior Analysis*, **5**, 405-420.

Johnston, J.M., & Pennypacker, H.S. (1980). *Strategies and tactics of human behavioral research.* Hillsdale, NJ: Lawrence Erlbaum.

Langsdorf, E.V. (1979). *A systematic observation of football coaching behavior in a major university environment.* Unpublished doctoral dissertation, Arizona State University, Tempe.

Powell, J., Martindale, A., & Kulp, S. (1975). An evaluation of time-sample measures of behavior. *Journal of Applied Behavior Analysis*, **8**(4), 463-469.

Siedentop, D. (1983). *Developing teaching skills in physical education* (2nd ed.). Palo Alto, CA: Mayfield.

Springer, B., Brown, T., & Duncan, P.K. (1981). Current measurement in applied behavior analysis. *The Behavior Analyst*, **4**(1), 19-31.

Tawney, J., & Gast, D. (1984). *Single subject research in special education.* Columbus, OH: Merrill.

Test, D.W., & Heward, W.L. (1984). Accuracy of momentary time sampling: A comparison of fixed- and variable-interval observation schedules. In W.L. Heward, T.E. Heron, D.S. Hill, & J. Trap-Porter (Eds.), *Focus on behavior analysis in education* (pp. 177-194). Columbus, OH: Merrill.

Tharp, R.G., & Gallimore, R. (1976). What a coach can teach a teacher. *Psychology Today*, **9**(8), 75-78.

Chapter 3

Observer Reliability: Issues and Procedures

Hans van der Mars

This chapter provides an overview of the concept of reliability in systematic observation. Furthermore, guidelines are provided for the various ways in which observer agreement is measured and reported. Also included is a section on factors that influence the observer's ability to observe and record reliably and accurately. The last part of this chapter presents guidelines to follow when training others to use a systematic observation system.

VALIDITY AND RELIABILITY OF OBSERVATION: DEFINITIONS

The goal of any observation made of the teaching-learning environment is for the resulting data to be an accurate reflection of what really happened. This should hold true whether the observation is made as part of a research project or part of an evaluation of an experienced teacher, a coach, or a teaching/coaching intern. As indicated in chapter 1, human beings are unfortunately not well qualified to perform the acts of observation and recording. Our history of experiences, biases, and beliefs influences dramatically our ability to report accurately what we saw (Johnston & Pennypacker, 1980; Siedentop, 1983). Therefore, it is critical that users of systematic observation tools take measures to ensure that (a) the observation instrument they select to use provides a valid reflection of events and (b) they can use that instrument reliably.

In the context of systematic observation, *validity*, also called *accuracy*, refers to the extent to which an instrument measures what it is supposed to measure. Kazdin (1977) defined it as "the extent to which observations scored by an observer match those of a predetermined standard for the same data" (p. 141). The goal is for the measurements to approximate as closely as possible the true value of events as they occur in the environment (Johnston & Pennypacker, 1980).

Reliability refers to "the capacity of the instrument to yield the same measurement value when brought into repeated contact with the same state of nature" (Johnston & Pennypacker, 1980, p. 191). This definition stresses the importance of consistency. In the situation where teachers or coaches are observed by others, those who make the observations would thus be the instrument. From the consistency perspective, if the same observer using the same behavior definitions and coding procedures views a videotape of the same class, he or she should produce the same data to be considered reliable. Reliability has also been labeled *consistency, stability,* and *observer agreement.*

In most research projects involving systematic observation, *percent of observer agreement* is used as an indicator of observer reliability. Consequently, many have come to regard the two as being the same. However, using the classical definition of consistency over time, Johnson and Bolstad (1973) noted that "it is quite possible to have perfect observer agreement or accuracy on a given behavioral score with absolutely no reliability or consistency of measurement in the traditional sense" (p. 10). (For a detailed discussion on the need for this distinction between observer agreement and reliability, see Johnson and Bolstad, 1973.)

Observer agreement indicates the degree to which observers who viewed certain events agree in their recording of them. Agreement not only has been equated with reliability, but has also come to represent the accuracy of data. Kazdin (1977) noted that

> although accuracy and agreement are related, they need not go together. For example, an observer may observe accurately (relative to pre-established standard) but show low interobserver agreement (with another observer whose observations are quite inaccurate), or observe inaccurately (in relation to the standard) but show high interobserver agreement (with another observer who is inaccurate in an identical fashion). (p. 142)

There are two types of observer agreement procedures. *Interobserver agreement* refers to a situation in which the observation records of one observer are compared to those of a second person. *Intraobserver agreement* refers to the situation in which one observer makes an observation of events on one day and then comes back at a later point in time to observe the same events. In this situation the term *agreement* is closest in meaning to the term *reliability.*

When using interobserver agreement procedures in live coding situations, both observers should locate themselves far enough apart from each other so that neither can detect visually or orally what the other is recording. This is referred to as *independence.* In that same situation it is critical that both observers start and end their observations at the exact same time, otherwise their agreement levels will be lower. Two observers can ensure a simultaneous start by using stopwatches. A target for a starting point is decided upon (e.g., 3 minutes), and then both start their stopwatches at the same time. This gives them 3 minutes to get situated for the observation. As the stopwatch reaches the 3-minute mark both persons commence their observations. Another way to ensure a simultaneous start is to use the official starting point of a class period, which is usually announced over the school's public address (PA) system. If no such signal is given, both observers should synchronize their watches with the school's clock. Although it is possible to use a specific teaching or coaching behavior as a cue to start the observation, there is a good chance that on any given day the teacher or coach will not exhibit that cue, causing possible confusion on when to start the observation.

If a permanent record (i.e., a videotape or audiotape) is available of the class or practice session, interobserver agreement can be completed with both observers viewing the record either simultaneously or on separate occasions. If the latter option is used, care must be taken to ensure that both observers start at the same point on the permanent record.

Independence can be achieved in interval recording or momentary time sampling through the use of a Y-adapter, which allows two persons to listen in to the cues played on a single cassette recorder. This ensures that both observers hear the "observe" and/or "record" cues exactly at the same time. The configuration of this hardware is shown in Figure 3.1. To connect the earphones to the Y-adapter two shielded monaural adapters are needed (see Figure 3.2). The earphones should have at least 6-foot cords.

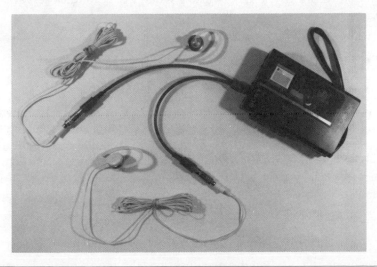

Figure 3.1 Configuration of hardware needed to establish independence when using interval recording.

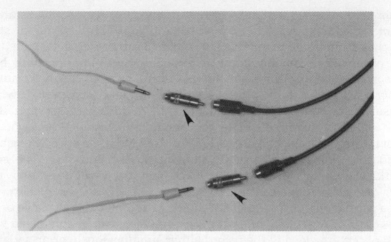

Figure 3.2   Adapters needed to connect earphones with Y-adapter.

To complete the intraobserver agreement the observer needs to have a permanent record of events available, such as an audiotaped or a videotaped record. A live observation cannot be repeated. The time span between the two observation sessions should be at least 1 week, and preferably longer. The longer this time period, the less likely the observer will be able to remember and thus predict his or her codings from the first observation session. Independence with the intraobserver agreement procedure can be achieved by not allowing the observer access to the observation record of the first session when the second observation is made.

CALCULATING PERCENTAGES OF AGREEMENT

Equation 3.1 is used to calculate the percentage of agreement between two observers (or two separate observations of a single observer). In this equation an agreement would be an aspect of the total observation for which both saw or heard the same behavior and recorded it as such. As will become clear later on, if both observers code the absence of behavior this is also considered an agreement.

$$\frac{\text{Agreements}}{\text{Agreements + disagreements}} \times 100 \tag{3.1}$$

Disagreement occurs when the two observers differ on a particular aspect of the observation. Differences in observation records can take on two forms. First, the difference could be one of *omission*, where one observer detects and records the behavior and the other does not detect or record anything. For example, during an interval recording session one of the two observers simply did not see that the target student completed a trial at the throwing station, whereas the other observer did. The causes for not seeing the behavior, of course, could be manifold. Second, a disagreement occurs when both observers code an episode as having occurred, but one records it as being one type of episode (e.g., transition), whereas the other records it as being another (e.g., management).

This basic equation is used with event recording, duration recording, interval recording, and Group Time Sampling (or momentary time sampling), but the resulting percentages take on a different meaning for each. The following sections provide an overview of the basic calculations for each of the observation tactics with the use of some examples.

Agreement Calculations for Numerical Data

The basic equation (3.1) shown earlier applies to event data, in that it is stated as follows: smaller total frequency divided by the larger total frequency, multiplied by 100. For example, let us assume that two individuals observed a volleyball practice session and measured the number of responses (i.e., trials) made by one player on the following four skills: sets, bumps, spikes, and blocks. Following the practice session, both observers tally all observations for each of the four skills monitored. Observer A had the following totals: 86 sets, 57 bumps, 18 spikes, and 21 blocks. Observer B recorded these skill totals: 83, 56, 18, and 22, respectively. Table 3.1 shows the resulting agreement percentages. The range of 95.4% to 100% is very high. Notice, however, that these percentages indicate only the level of agreement on how many trials each observer detected and recorded. As Baer (1977) noted,

the fact that one observer saw four occurrences and the other saw five, yielding a supposed percentage of agreement of 80%, has very

Table 3.1 Event Recording Agreement Percentages of Observers A and B Across Four Skills

Skill	Frequency A	B	Percent agreement
Sets	86	83	96.4
Bumps	57	56	98.2
Spikes	18	18	100.0
Blocks	21	22	95.4

little usefulness: no one knows whether the first observer's four were seen at the same times as any of the second observer's five. Thus their seeing the same behaviors in the same way at the same times could easily be nil. (p. 118)

Thus, in our volleyball example, the 100% agreement does not say anything about whether both observers saw the target athlete's fifth spike (or any of the other eighteen for that matter) also at the same point in time. Figure 3.3 shows graphically how some of the spikes were in fact reported at different times during the observed practice session. In a later section on calculation of agreement percentages with interval recording data, a backup strategy is provided to deal with this problem.

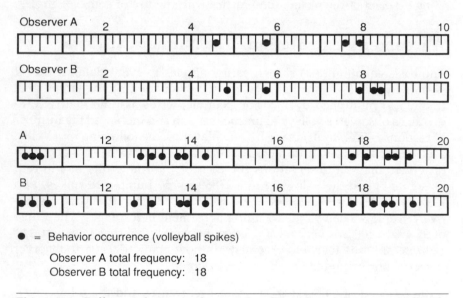

● = Behavior occurrence (volleyball spikes)

Observer A total frequency: 18
Observer B total frequency: 18

Figure 3.3 Difference between observers' coding when spikes occurred with equal frequencies.

Agreement Calculation for Temporal Data

The procedure for obtaining agreement scores for duration recording data is virtually the same as for event data, with the exception of one extra step. Before the totals of both observers are entered into the equation ''smaller divided by the larger, multiplied by 100,'' minutes are converted into seconds. Thus, in the example shown in Table 3.2, the amount of time recorded by Observer A is converted from 6 minutes and 38 seconds to 398 seconds. Observer B's time is converted from 6 minutes and 54 seconds to 414 seconds. Both values are then entered into the same equation as the one used for frequency data. Thus, in Table 3.2 the agreement percentage is 96.1%.

Table 3.2 Duration Recording Agreement Percentage of Observers A and B on Transition Time

Observer	Minutes:seconds	Total seconds	Percent agreement
A	6:38	398	96.1
B	6:54	414	

As was the case with the agreement percentage for event recording data, this 96.1% only indicates the level of agreement on how much total time both observers detected and recorded a transition time. There might still be considerable disagreement on exactly when they saw the transitional activities start and end (see Figure 3.4 for an example). Notice that the total amount of time in "Instruction" is the same for both observers, but that there are disagreements on when some of the episodes started and ended.

Agreement Calculation for Interval and Time Sampling Data

As indicated by Barlow and Hersen (1984), one of the reasons that interval recording has enjoyed widespread popularity is that it allows for easy

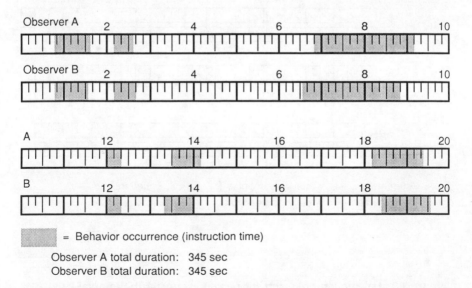

= Behavior occurrence (instruction time)

Observer A total duration: 345 sec
Observer B total duration: 345 sec

Figure 3.4 Difference between two observers' coding when episode started and ended with total duration being equal.

detection of sources of disagreement among observers. The following procedures also alleviate, in part, the problem explained in Figures 3.3 and 3.4 and discussed in the previous two sections. Interval data from two observers can be screened for levels of (dis)agreement in a variety of ways, including the interval-by-interval (I-I), total-interval (T-I), scored-interval (S-I)), and unscored-interval (U-I) methods.

Interval-by-Interval (I-I) Method

In this method each interval is used in the comparison of the two sets of data. An agreement is counted for each interval in which both observers coded the behavior as having occurred or in which they both coded its absence (i.e., the intervals left blank) during the interval. A disagreement is counted for each interval in which one observer did code the occurrence and the other did not. These totals of agreements and disagreements can be placed in the basic equation (3.1). In Figure 3.5 the agreement percentage would be 83%. It should be noted that this procedure is the same regardless of whether one is measuring just one behavior, as in this example, or a series of behaviors simultaneously (see Figure 3.6).

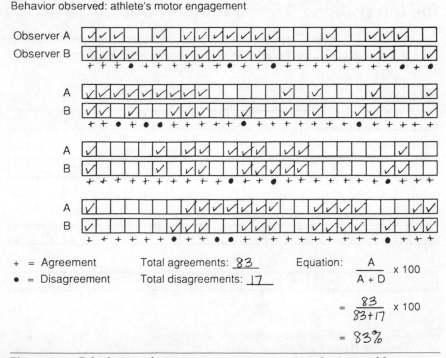

Figure 3.5 Calculation of agreement percentage using the interval-by-interval method between two observers on a single behavior.

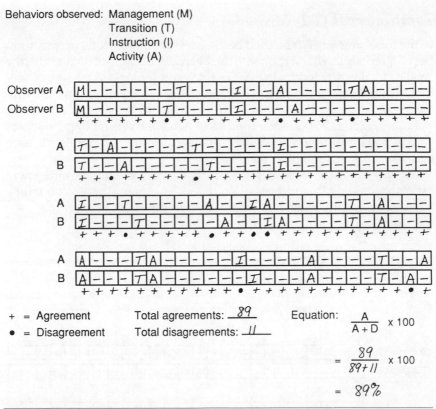

Figure 3.6 Calculation of agreement percentage using the interval-by-interval method between two observers on four behaviors.

Until Hawkins and Dotson (1975) pointed out its limitations, which tend to cause spuriously high agreement scores, I-I was the predominant method used for calculating and reporting observer agreement in research projects that used direct observation. They argued that estimating observer reliability should not be seen as providing only a reflection of data accuracy. Reliability estimates also reflect an indication of behavior definition adequacy and observer competence and can increase (or decrease) the believability of any experimental effect.

The limitation of the I-I method is that high I-I agreement percentages cannot account for possible errors in observation caused by inadequate definitions of target behaviors and/or incompetent observers, particularly when the rate of behavior is either very high or very low. In one of their tests, Hawkins and Dotson (1975) showed how agreement between a fictitious sleeping observer (i.e., a blank coding form) and an alert observer ranged anywhere from 77% to 100%. The following three methods are alternatives to the I-I method.

Total-Interval (T-I) Method

In the total-interval (T-I) method both observers merely total up the number of intervals in which they saw the behavior occur. Subsequently, the smaller total is divided by the larger total and multiplied by 100. Notice that, as opposed to the I-I method, in using this method, one only includes those intervals in which the behavior or event did occur. For example, Figure 3.7 shows the codings of two observers on four behaviors of one athlete during a basketball practice, along with totals for each behavior and agreement percentages.

The disadvantage of the T-I method is that it accounts for agreement estimates on only the number of occurrences. Again, there is no telling whether or not the behaviors were coded in the same interval (e.g., see the discrepancies in coding off-task behavior in Figure 3.7).

Behaviors observed: On-task (On)
Motor engaged (Me)
Waiting (W)
Off-task (Of)

Frequency Totals and Percentage Agreement of Observers A and B

Behavior	A	B	< / >	Percent
On-task	23	27	23 / 27	85.1
Motor engaged	25	27	25 / 27	92.5
Waiting	42	36	36 / 42	85.7
Off-task	10	10	10 / 10	100.0

Figure 3.7 Calculation of agreement percentage using the total-interval method between two observers on four behaviors.

Scored-Interval (S-I) Method

The scored-interval (S-I) method is probably the most widely used for reporting observer agreement percentages in physical education teaching research. Although it has some limitations, the S-I method, when combined with the unscored-interval (U-I) method, is the most rigorous way of estimating observer reliability. To calculate the percentage of agreement between two observers with the use of S-I, we concern ourselves only with those intervals in which *either both observers coded the same behavior or only one of the two observers coded the behavior.* Thus, in Figure 3.8, if we wanted to determine the agreement between two observers on coding Waiting (W) behavior we would include only the intervals displayed in Figure 3.9. Agreements are signified by + right below the codings of Observer B, and disagreements are denoted by •. The totals of both agreements (+) and disagreements (•) are entered into the basic equation. The

Behaviors observed: On-task (On)
Motor engaged (Me)
Waiting (W)
Off-task (Of)

	5	10	15	20	25
Observer A	On – W – – – On – – Of – W – – –	Me – W – – Me – W – –
Observer B	On – – W – – On – – – W – – – – Me – W – – Me – W –

	30	35	40	45	50
A	Me – W Of – – W – – Me – – W Me – – – – – – Of – – W On –
B	Me – – W – Of W – Me – – – W Me – – – – – Of – – W – On

	55	60	65	70	75
A	On – – – W – Of – Me – – W – Me – – Of – W – – On – Of
B	On – – – W – – Of Me – – W – Me – – – W – – – – On Of On

	80	85	90	95	100
A	Of – – W – – – Me – W – – – – Of – – – Me – Of – – W –
B	Of – – – W – – – Me – W – – – Of – – – Me – Of – – – W

Total Frequencies of Observers A and B

Behavior	A	B
Motor engaged	25	28
On-task	13	14
Off-task	24	18
Waiting	38	40

Figure 3.8 Sample codings of two observers using interval recording.

64   van der Mars

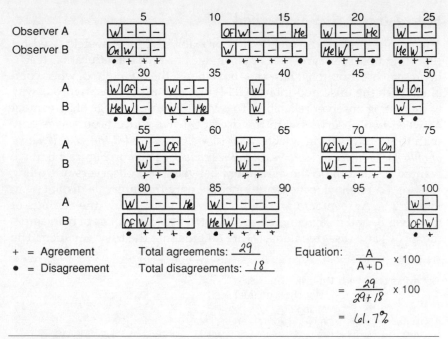

+ = Agreement   Total agreements: _29_   Equation: $\dfrac{A}{A+D} \times 100$

● = Disagreement   Total disagreements: _18_

$$= \dfrac{29}{29+18} \times 100$$

$$= 61.7\%$$

Figure 3.9 Intervals used in completing the scored-interval method of calculating interobserver agreement. *Note.* Scored intervals are those for which either both or one of the observers recorded the occurrence of a behavior.

resulting percentage thus reflects the degree to which both observers saw the athlete's waiting behavior occur at the same time.

If we had used the T-I method, the percentage of agreement would have been substantially higher because both observers had approximately the same number of intervals in which they coded waiting behavior. The S-I method, however, also accounts for whether both observers saw the behavior occur at the same time.

To measure multiple behaviors, this procedure is applied to each of those behaviors separately. Consequently, intervals for which disagreements were found in coding waiting behavior (e.g., intervals 3, 11, 16, 18, 21, 23, 28, and 29 in Figure 3.9) also become disagreements in the calculation of agreement for the remaining behaviors.

As noted, S-I does have limitations. Hawkins and Dotson (1975) indicated that (a) in light of the rigor of this test, new standards would need to be developed on acceptable levels of agreement; (b) when the behavior frequency is very low, S-I percentages become very vulnerable (e.g., if less than 10 intervals are coded, even one disagreement alters the S-I agreement percentage dramatically); and (c) when the behavior has a very high frequency, S-I percentages take on the characteristics of I-I percentages. It was argued that these three constraints could be alleviated by using the U-I method introduced in the next subsection. Despite these limitations, S-I is considered the most rigorous method of estimating observer agreement for interval data.

Unscored-Interval (U-I) Method

The unscored interval (U-I) method is exactly the same as the S-I method, except that the intervals used for this calculation are different. Using the same codings (Figure 3.8), we now look at only those intervals in which either *both observers agreed that the behavior did not occur (agreements) or one of the two did record its occurrence (disagreements)*. Those intervals are shown in Figure 3.10. Agreements (+) and disagreements (•) are marked and their totals are then entered into the basic equation. To measure more than one behavior, this agreement percentage must be calculated for each individual category. When U-I is used as the only measure of agreement,

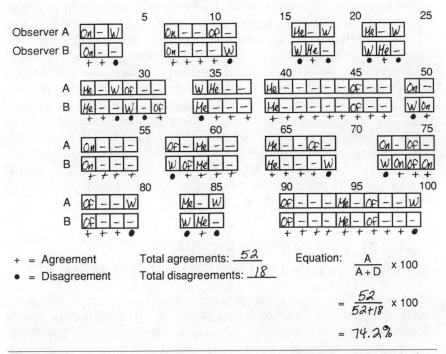

Figure 3.10 Intervals used in completing the unscored-interval method of calculating interobserver agreement. *Note.* Unscored intervals are those for which either both or one of the observers recorded the behavior as not occurring.

it has the same limitations as those reported for S-I. However, the combined use of S-I and U-I should solve these problems (Hawkins & Dotson, 1975).

Using S-I and U-I
With Numerical and Temporal Data

Dunbar and O'Sullivan (1986) were the first to publish research data in the physical education and sport teaching research literature that used S-I and U-I as backup measures to strengthen the agreement percentages on numerical data. As noted earlier, the agreement percentage of numerical data indicates an agreement on only the frequency of occurrence, and not on whether they were detected and coded at the same time. The same problem also exists with temporal data in terms of the starting and ending time of behavior. Use of S-I and U-I as a backup provides a means of verifying that observers agreed on not only how many times they saw or heard the behavior, but also *when* they did.

This backup measure can only be used if there is a videotape or audiotape record available of the behavior(s) studied. The procedure for using S-I and U-I methods with numerical and temporal data is as follows: After completing the regular IOA (interobserver agreement) on the numerical data, develop an audio cue tape with an interval length that matches the average duration of the target behavior. If this average is fairly low, such as with verbal behaviors, the interval length should probably be no more than 5 seconds. Make sure that both observers start the observation at the same time, coding the occurrence of behaviors by intervals. After completing the second coding session, apply S-I and U-I methods to these interval data. The resulting agreement percentages provide an added dimension to the original agreement score. This backup procedure can also be used for temporal data.

CORRELATION COEFFICIENTS
AS ESTIMATES OF OBSERVER RELIABILITY

Some of the observation systems, most notably the interaction analysis systems presented in Part II of this textbook, rely on correlational methods to estimate observer reliability. Johnson and Bolstad (1973) noted that "studies using correlation methods have generally been those in which one cannot be sure that the same behaviors are being jointly observed at the same time" (p. 14). Typically, raw data collected with interaction analysis systems are entered into matrix cell loadings and converted into percent and ratio values. Using Cheffers' Adaptation of Flanders' Interaction Analysis System (CAFIAS; Cheffers, Mancini, & Martinek, 1980) as an example in light of its frequent use, one can use any of three nonparametric statistical procedures (Martinek, Nolen, & Cheffers, 1980). They recommended using Scott's coefficient of reliability, Kendall's W coefficient of concordance, or the Spearman rho correlation. A brief overview of each procedure follows.

Scott's Pi Coefficient of Reliability

Scott's coefficient of reliability is found using Equation 3.2, where Po is the proportion of interobserver agreement and Pe is the proportion of agreement that is expected by chance. Pe can be determined by squaring the percent of tallies in each category and summing these over all the categories.

$$pi = \frac{Po - Pe}{100 - Pe} \tag{3.2}$$

To complete the calculation of Scott's coefficient of reliability, we fill in a table (Table 3.3) according to the following steps:

Table 3.3 Sample Data for Calculation of Scott's Coefficient of Reliability

Category	Frequency A	Frequency B	Percent A	Percent B	% difference	$(\overline{X}\%)^2$
2	13	12	2.56	2.29	0.27	0.059
12	4	4	0.79	0.76	0.03	0.006
3	8	6	1.58	1.14	0.44	0.018
13	2	2	0.39	0.38	0.01	0.001
4	7	5	1.38	0.95	0.43	0.013
14	6	3	1.18	0.57	0.61	0.007
5	130	141	25.69	26.95	1.26	6.930
15	118	121	23.32	23.13	0.19	5.390
6	83	80	16.40	15.29	1.11	2.509
16	24	30	4.74	5.73	0.99	0.275
7	5	5	0.98	0.95	0.03	0.009
17	1	1	0.19	0.19	0.00	0.003
8	12	13	2.37	2.48	0.11	0.059
18	74	76	14.62	14.53	0.09	2.120
8\	4	6	0.79	1.14	0.35	0.009
18\	3	5	0.59	0.95	0.36	0.006
9	0	1	0.00	0.19	0.19	0.000
19	0	1	0.00	0.19	0.19	0.000
10	12	11	2.37	2.10	0.27	0.049
20	0	0	0.00	0.00	0.00	0.000
Totals	506	523	99.94	99.91	6.93	17.450

1. Sum the number of tallies in each of the 20 categories for each observer (Columns 2 and 3).
2. Divide each category total by the grand total and multiply by 100 to convert to percent figures (Columns 4 and 5).
3. Determine the percent of disagreement between observers by subtracting the percent figures corresponding to each category, and then total the differences (Column 6).
4. Divide the total amount of tallies for each category by the sum total of all 20 categories for both observers. To determine the percent of disagreement expected by chance (Pe), the square of the average amount of tallies in each category is multiplied by 100 and the sum of these overall categories is calculated (Column 7).
5. To determine Po, subtract the total percent disagreement (Column 5) from 100. (Martinek et al., 1980, pp. 78-79).

The pi value is then calculated as follows:

$$\text{pi} = \frac{(100 - 6.93) - 17.45}{100 - 17.45} = \frac{75.62}{82.55} = .916$$

Spearman Rho Correlation

The Spearman rho correlation is used when the agreement of observers is measured on the ranking of the top 10 matrix cell loadings (see Cheffers et al., 1980, for determining matrix cell loadings). Table 3.4 is an example with the rankings for two observers, along with the difference (d) and the squared difference (d^2) in rankings.

Rho is calculated using Equation 3.3:

$$\text{rho} = 1 - \frac{6\sum d^2}{n(n^2 - 1)} = 1 - \frac{6 \times 9.50}{10(10^2 - 1)}$$

$$= 1 - \frac{57}{990} = 1 - .057 = .943$$

(3.3)

Kendall's *W* Coefficient of Concordance

Martinek at al. (1980) recommended Kendall's coefficient for determining levels of reliability of more than two observers at the same time. As was the case with Spearman's rho, agreement is measured based on the top 10 matrix cell loadings.

Table 3.5 is the top 10 cell rankings of the primary observer (A) along with the rankings of the four remaining observers and the difference

Table 3.4 Sample Data Rankings for Calculation of Spearman's Rho for Observers A and B

Top 10 cell loadings	Ranking A	B	d	d²
10 - 8	1	1	0	0
8 - 10	2	2	0	0
8 - 2	3	3	0	0
6 - 8	4	4	0	0
2 - 8	5	5.5	0.5	0.25
9 - 3	6	5.5	0.5	0.25
8 - 3	7	7.5	0.5	0.25
5 - 6	8.5[a]	9	0.5	0.25
5 - 8	8.5[a]	10	1.5	2.25
5 - 5	10	7.5	2.5	6.25
Total				9.50

[a]In case of tied ranks the two ranks are averaged (e.g., 8 + 9/2 = 8.5).

Table 3.5 Sample Data Ranking of Five Coders for Calculating Kendall's W Coefficient of Concordance

Cell	Observer A	B	C	D	E	d²
6 - 6	1	1	1	1	1	$(5 - E)^2 = 506.25$
18 - 18	2	2	3	2	3	$(12 - E)^2 = 240.25$
2 - 18	3	3	2	3	4	$(15 - E)^2 = 156.25$
15 - 14	4	7	4	4	2	$(21 - E)^2 = 42.25$
8 - 12	5	4	7	5	6	$(27 - E)^2 = .25$
12 - 15	6	5	6	6	5	$(28 - E)^2 = .25$
4 - 20	7	9	5	8	8	$(37 - E)^2 = 90.25$
5 - 5	8	10	9	7	7	$(41 - E)^2 = 182.25$
18 - 3	9	8	10	9	9	$(45 - E)^2 = 306.25$
2 - 3	10	6	8	10	10	$(44 - E)^2 = 272.25$
						Total d² = 1,796.5

between observed and expected totals in the ranking procedure and its total (d^2). Expected totals (E) are derived from Equation 3.4:

$$E = \frac{kn(n + 1)}{2n} = \frac{5 \times 10(11)}{20} = \frac{50 \times 11}{20} = \frac{550}{20} = 27.5 \quad (3.4)$$

where k is the number of observers and n is the number of cells.

The value of d^2 is determined as follows: Add the observers' rankings for each cell (e.g., the total for the "2-18" cell is 15). Subtract E (27.5) from this value and square the difference. Do this for each of the 10 cells and then sum these squared values. In the example, d^2 is 1,796.5. Once the value of d^2 has been determined, W is calculated in Equation 3.5:

$$W = \frac{12\sum d^2}{k^2(n^3 - n)} = \frac{12 \times 1,796.5}{5^2(10^3 - 10)} = \frac{21,558}{25(1,000 - 10)}$$

$$= \frac{21,558}{25 \times 990} = \frac{21,558}{24,750} = .871$$

(3.5)

Its level of significance is determined by using a table of critical values for W (e.g., Siegel, 1956).

WHICH METHOD OF AGREEMENT ESTIMATES TO CHOOSE?

The procedures outlined earlier for numerical and temporal data are fairly standard, keeping in mind that the percent-agreement value is related to the frequency of behavior. If the frequency is high, the percent agreement will be high. Using the S-I method as a backup measure should add confidence to this.

In the case of interval and momentary time sampling data, the answer of which method to use is not straightforward. It is fairly clear, however, that there isn't one particular calculation method that can be used in every situation. According to Birkimer and Brown (1979), Hartmann (1977), Hawkins and Dotson (1975), and Johnson and Bolstad (1973), the frequency of occurrence is a critical factor in selecting the most appropriate method. As indicated, extremely high and low frequencies of behavior overestimate or underestimate observer agreement scores. In interval recording systems with a large number of behavior categories there could be considerable differences in frequencies among the categories. Metzler (1983) suggested using more than one method if this occurs. The S-I method is recommended in light of its rigor, but the user should consider using other methods when the situation calls for it. (e.g., in cases of very high or low frequencies).

ARE THERE MINIMUM LEVELS OF AGREEMENT PERCENTAGES?

Although there is no fully accepted minimum standard for direct observation data, 80%-85% levels of agreement are deemed sufficiently high (Hartmann, 1977; Johnson & Bolstad, 1973), particularly when using complex observation systems. The level should reach 90% or higher when measuring only one or a few behaviors.

Metzler (1983) suggested flexible levels of agreement for variable frequencies of intervals across behaviors:

When the number of scored intervals of the target category is five or less, acceptable S-I agreement is 60 percent. When the number of scored intervals of the target category is six to ten, acceptable S-I agreement is 70 percent. When the number of scored intervals of the target category is 11 or more, acceptable S-I agreement is 80 percent. (pp. 189-190)

When using correlational methods for estimating observer agreement, researchers should screen coefficients for statistical significance. Gelfland and Hartmann (1975) recommended that correlation coefficients for reliability that take into account chance agreements should be higher than .60.

REPORTING OBSERVER AGREEMENT VALUES

Presenting estimates of observer agreement in research reports is done in a variety of ways. The one criterion that fits across all situations is that authors must be as specific as possible about the number of observers used, the number of reliability checks made, the amount of time in between observations (if intraobserver agreement procedures were used), the methods for conducting (double) blind reliability checks, and so forth.

With regard to assessing the reliability values, Siedentop, Tousignant, and Parker (1982) provided the following rule: "Reliability should be assessed for the variables that are included in the data presentation. That is, if data are to be shown by category, then reliability by category should be established" (p. 34). That recommendation basically holds true for the actual reporting of reliability estimates. Reporting only the averages of multiple agreement scores should be avoided at all costs. Mean scores simply do not allow the reader to make a judgment about the accuracy of the reported data and, in the case of experimental research, the believability of the experimental effect. Reporting a range of reliability scores is more acceptable with large numbers of variables (i.e., categories), as long as the range remains narrow and the variables with the extreme values are named.

SOURCES OF OBSERVER ERROR

The goal of making systematic observations in physical education and sport settings is to produce reliable and accurate records of what happened, regardless of whether they are to be used for research, staff evaluation, self-analysis, or instructor training. During this rather involved process a myriad of pitfalls needs to be avoided. Factors such as behavior definition, research design, and problems of measurements all influence how accurate and complete the coding records will be. If these problems are ignored, the data will not provide a true picture, and, consequently, the evidence to support the statement, ''Your coaching skills have really improved,'' might as well have been collected through eyeballing or rating scales.

Another factor that influences data accuracy is the observers themselves. The following five sections outline some of the major obstacles that relate directly to the observer. Where possible, some recommendations are made to minimize or eliminate these influences. The five major influences on observers are observer drift, complexity of the observation system, expectancies (or bias), reactivity, and cheating.

Observer Drift

Observer drift pertains to an observer's tendency to change coding rules and interpret category definitions differently. It is also called *instrument decay* (Johnson & Bolstad, 1973). Observer drift is a gradual process that has many causes, such as going for a long period without using a system, mixing definitions from one system with those of another, and observing individual instances of behavior that do not neatly fit into any one category and making accommodations for that. Weick (1968) reported that satiation and boredom also cause drift tendencies. Barlow and Hersen (1984) recommended the following procedures for identifying observer drift. First, continue the observer training. Just because you have established a sufficient level of reliability at the completion of observer training does not mean that you will never lose it (it is not the same as learning how to ride a bicycle). Second, periodically code prescored videotapes and check your agreement with the standard. And finally, periodically rotate the person with whom you compare your codings. Staying together with one colleague for too long might actually cause both parties to drift together without realizing it, thus remaining in agreement but no longer being accurate (Kazdin, 1977). Cooper, Heron, and Heward (1987) noted that drift decreases when videotapes are used, because observer agreement can then be measured in random order.

Complexity of the Observation System

The difficulty in making correct coding decisions increases as the number of categories and students/athletes who need to be observed simultaneously increases. The observer may have a hard time keeping up with the fast pace of change in behavior patterns. Adding shorter time intervals to interval recording also tends to increase the pressure on the observer, regardless of whether it is in the record-only or observe/record cuing format. Kazdin (1977) noted that although no specific guidelines exist for ensuring proper coding decisions, that in light of the complexities,

the influence of complexity within an observational system on interobserver agreement can be controlled by assessing agreement across all phases of an investigation and across all subjects, or at least a large sample of subjects, to ensure that agreement is not confounded with complexity. (p. 146)

Depending on the type of investigation and observation system used, one can reduce complexity by reducing the number of categories that are coded simultaneously, or increasing the length of the intervals slightly. The former is easier to implement if permanent records are available, because the observer can review the session over and over again. Although this may be more time-consuming, the accuracy of the data is less likely to be influenced by system complexity.

Observer Expectancies/Biases

Evidence suggests that if observers are told that certain changes in behavior patterns of teachers/coaches and students/athletes might occur as a result of some type of intervention, coupled with feedback about their behavior patterns, they are more likely to produce a *bias* in the data that reflect a change, even if the behavior did not really change. Although expectancies in and of themselves do not seem to influence observers' recording behaviors, if combined with feedback or information about target subjects' characteristics and/or prejudices of the investigator, they can produce seriously distorted data (O'Leary, Kent, & Kanowitz, 1975).

Kazdin (1977) and Cooper et al. (1987) recommended that observer bias can be minimized by (a) videotaping the sessions and coding these permanent records in random order, (b) frequently inserting new observers, and (c) keeping observers naive as to the purpose(s) of the investigation.

Observer Reactivity

Knowing that someone else is also doing an observation for the purpose of checking your reliability is called *observer reactivity*. This factor is probably harder to control than any of the others (Johnson & Bolstad, 1973). Evidence suggests that when observers know they are being tested, agreement percentages tend to be higher (Kent, Kanowitz, O'Leary, & Cheiken, 1977).

Reactivity can be minimized by keeping the assessment of reliability as inobtrusive as possible, notifying observers that all sessions may be screened, and videotaping each session so that there never needs to be contact between the observer and his or her assessor for reliability check purposes.

Observer Cheating

Barlow and Hersen (1984) noted that cheating does not occur very often. Cheating occurs by way of data fabrication, alteration of data, and incorrect calculation of agreement scores or derivatives from the raw data. Cheating opportunities can be minimized by (a) collecting the coding sheets immediately after an observation session is completed; (b) using pens rather than pencils; (c) letting persons other than the observers do the calculation of agreement percentages; and (d) conducting unannounced, random reliability checks (Barlow & Hersen, 1984).

OBSERVER TRAINING

One aspect that facilitates observer reliability is proper training in the use of an observation system. Sound training in systematic observation is an involved, time-consuming process. If done correctly, however, it saves numerous hours of frustration later when one finds that observers' data do not reach minimum levels of reliability. This section provides an overview of the major phases of learning how to use a systematic observation system. Depending on the purpose of the investigation and the complexity of the observation system itself, some of the steps may be less time-consuming than others. Barlow and Hersen (1984) stressed that instructors "utilize appropriate instructional principles, such as successive approximations and ample positive reinforcement in teaching their observer trainees appropriate observation, recording and interpersonal skills" (p. 123).

Phase 1: Orientation to the System

In this first phase the new user is introduced to the basic purpose of the observation system, including a description of the types of events or behaviors that can be studied. Barlow and Hersen (1984) noted that this first introduction should stress the need for *tunnel vision*, which is adhering strictly to definitions and procedures of the particular system, and not being influenced by personal beliefs, history, and previous personal experiences. Each of these might lead to different interpretations of behavior categories.

Phase 2: Learning the Categories

During Phase 2 the definitions of all categories need to be learned verbatim! Users need to be able to discriminate among the basic categories with 100% accuracy. At the same time, when necessary, the correct category symbols need to be memorized with equal accuracy. In the introduction of the categories it is good to show as many videotaped examples of them as possible, making sure that each category cannot be confused with other closely related categories. Successful completion of this phase should be based on passing a written or oral test.

Phase 3: Using the Coding Form Correctly

Once users learn categories by heart, it is critical for them to learn how to use the coding form. It takes practice to successfully place the coding symbols in the appropriate areas of more complex forms. Here, too, accuracy ought be established before the next phase is started.

Phase 4: Initial Coding Practice

In Phase 4 the users need to be overtrained (Barlow & Hersen, 1984). Novices get their first opportunity to practice coding by using part of the observation tool while viewing a videotape of a physical education lesson or practice session. Use of appropriate videotapes is critical at this stage; no single tape fits each observation tool. For example, if the observation system focuses on the analysis of verbal teacher behavior, the videotape should meet at least the following criteria. First, it should provide a clear record in terms of sound quality. The trainee's progress should not be inhibited by poor sound quality.

Second, the videotape should keep the teacher in view at all time. This facilitates making definite coding decisions. For example, in the Student Teacher Observing Peers (STOP) system (see chapter 11), the user needs to be able to see whether the interactions were directed at one individual, a small group, or the whole class. If the camera recorded only students, such decisions would be very hard to make and, consequently, unnecessarily lengthen the process of learning this system. Similarly, if the system is to capture the students'/athletes' opportunities to respond, the videotape should provide a *complete* record of their movements throughout the practice session.

Third, the initial videotapes should provide simple sequences of behavior; that is, they should not force the new users to make too many coding decisions in short amounts of time. However, the videotape should include a reasonable amount of behaviors for the user to react to. If the system aims to collect data on how time is being spent during classes or practices, the early videotapes ought not to have too rapid a pace of changes. For example, learning the Academic Learning Time-Physical Education (ALT-PE) system (see chapter 17) would be slowed if the first videotape depicted a coach who, during a practice session, constantly changed from technique to strategy to rules back to strategy and so on. In the early stage this videotape would be too complex to code, causing frustration on the part of the learner and the instructor.

As the user gains more successful experience, the videotapes can gradually become complex, reflecting variable patterns of events and behaviors. As the above-mentioned criteria show, those who introduce observation systems should be very careful in their selection of instructional videotape segments. Although editing videotape segments is a time-consuming process, high-quality videotaped examples facilitate the learning process.

Furthermore, it is critical to introduce new videotapes as the training process continues. Repeated use of the same videotapes causes new users to be able to predict the behavioral patterns, hence producing questionable scores when reliability is checked. As the learner goes through this phase, the length of individual observation sessions can be increased to approximate normal lengths.

Another critical aspect of this phase is for the instructor and learner to discuss each instance of behavior that needs to be detected and coded. Frequent discussion of unclear instances of the behavior (or coding rules and procedures) helps avoid many mistakes. The user should be encouraged to write down critical information and develop a *decision log*. This log contains *ground rules* that the user refers to during observation sessions. Ground rules, or coding conventions, are coding rules employed specifically for certain situations that may occur. For example, if off-task behavior is the focus of a study using interval recording, a ground rule might be that off-task behavior takes precedence over any other behavior, regardless of how long (or short) it might be during the interval.

Phase 5: Live Observation Practice

Many of the considerations in Phase 4 also apply to Phase 5. Live observation practices are held in locations where some type of motor skill instruction is going on. Ideal settings are regular physical education classes in elementary or secondary schools; activity classes at colleges, universities, or local YMCAs; and youth sport practices. Observation sites should be chosen with care in terms of the complexity of behavior patterns to be coded.

When training involves learning an interval recording system, particular attention should be given to the gradual increase in complexity. One of two methods is best for the early stages. The first is for the interval lengths to be somewhat longer, so that the observer has more time to make correct decisions, particularly with multiple category systems. As the learner gains experience, the intervals can be shortened. The second method is to keep the interval length at the official length and start with fewer categories. As the user becomes more proficient (i.e., more reliable) more categories can be added.

GLOSSARY

Accuracy: Degree to which data coincide with how events actually occurred (or a set of predetermined standards); has been used as an analog for the term *validity*.

Bias: Error in measurement as a result of expectancies and prejudices; also called *observer expectancy*.

Consistency: Degree to which an instrument produces the same data values when brought in contact with the same situation over and over again; analog for the term *reliability*.

Decision log: Written notes collected by observer that provide guidelines for coding decisions under specific circumstances.

Ground rules: Specific coding rules that are used to make decisions in special situations.

Independence: Observers are located far enough apart so that neither can detect what the other is recording. Minimum distance should be at least 10 ft.

Instrument decay: Degree to which the original category definitions and coding rules are altered by user over time; also called *observer drift*.

Interobserver agreement: Degree to which two persons viewing the same activity with the same coding rules and procedures at the same time agree on what they see/hear.

Intraobserver agreement: Degree to which one person records the same data on two separate occasions using the same coding rules and procedures while viewing the same events.

Observer cheating: Fabrication and/or alteration of data by the observer.

Observer drift: Degree to which accuracy of data decreases as a result of changes in interpretations of category definitions or other coding procedures.

Observer expectancy: Degree to which observers who expect certain behaviors (changes) to occur are more likely to find them, even though the behaviors did not really occur (or change).

Observer reactivity: Degree to which an observer's accuracy of observation is influenced by the awareness of being checked for reliability.

Omission: Observer fails to detect and record the occurrence of an instance of behavior.

Percent of observer agreement: Indicator used to report level of agreement between two observers.

Stability: Degree to which observation of the same record of events is consistent over time; has been used as an analog for *reliability* and *consistency*.

Validity: Degree to which the instrument measures what it is supposed to measure; that is, the degree to which the recorded data are an accurate reflection of what actually occurred.

REFERENCES

Baer, D.M. (1977). Reviewer's comment: Just because it is reliable doesn't mean that you can use it. *Journal of Applied Behavior Analysis*, **10**(1), 117-119.

Barlow, D.H., & Hersen, M. (1984). *Single case experimental designs: Strategies for studying behavior change* (2nd ed.). Elmsford, NY: Pergamon.

Birkimer, J.C., & Brown, J.H. (1979). A graphical judgmental aid which summarizes obtained and chance reliability data and helps assess the believability of experimental effects. *Journal of Applied Behavior Analysis*, **12**(4), 523-533.

Cheffers, J.T.F., Mancini, V.H., & Martinek, T.J. (1980). *Interaction analysis: An application to nonverbal activity* (2nd ed.). Minneapolis, MN: Association for Productive Teaching.

Cooper, J.O., Heron, T.E., & Heward, W.L. (1987). *Applied behavior analysis*. Columbus, OH: Merrill.

Dunbar, R.R., & O'Sullivan, M.M. (1986). Effects of intervention on differential treatment of boys and girls in elementary physical education lessons. *Journal of Teaching in Physical Education*, **5**(3) 166-175.

Gelfland, D.M., & Hartmann, D.P. (1975). *Child behavior and therapy*. Elmsford, NY: Pergamon.

Hartmann, D.P. (1977). Considerations in the choice of interobserver reliability estimates. *Journal of Applied Behavior Analysis*, **10**(1), 103-116.

Hawkins, R.P., & Dotson, V.A. (1975). Reliability scores that delude: An Alice in Wonderland trip through the misleading characteristics of inter-observer agreement scores in interval recording. In E. Ramp & E. Semb (Eds.), *Behavior analysis: Areas of research and application* (pp. 359-376). Englewood Cliffs, NJ: Prentice-Hall.

Johnson, S.M., & Bolstad, O.D. (1973). Methodological issues in naturalistic observation: Some problems and solutions for field research. In L.A. Hamerlynck, L.C. Handy, & E.J. Mash (Eds.), *Behavior change: Methodology, concepts, and practice* (pp. 7-67). Champaign, IL: Research Press.

Johnston, J.M., & Pennypacker, H.S. (1980). *Strategies and tactics of human behavioral research*. Hillsdale, NJ: Lawrence Erlbaum.

Kazdin, A.E. (1977). Artifact, bias, and complexity of assessment: The ABCs of reliability. *Journal of Applied Behavior Analysis*, **10**(1), 141-150.

Kent, R.N., Kanowitz, J., O'Leary, K.D., & Cheiken, M. (1977). Observer reliability as a function of circumstances of assessment. *Journal of Applied Behavior Analysis*, **10**(2), 317-324.

Martinek, T.J., Nolen, W.F., & Cheffers, J.T.F. (1980). Reliability measurement. In J.T.F. Cheffers, V.H. Mancini, & T.J. Martinek, *Interaction analysis: An application to nonverbal activity* (2nd ed., pp. 77-102). Minneapolis, MN: Association for Productive Teaching.

Metzler, M. (1983). An interval recording system for measuring academic learning time. In P.W. Darst, V.H. Mancini, & D.B. Zakrajsek (Eds.), *Systematic observation instrumentation for physical education* (pp. 181-195). Champaign, IL: Leisure Press.

O'Leary, K.D., Kent, R.N., & Kanowitz, J. (1975). Shaping data collection congruent with experimental hypotheses. *Journal of Applied Behavior Analysis*, **8**(1), 43-51.

Siedentop, D. (1983). *Developing teaching skills in physical education* (2nd ed.). Palo Alto, CA: Mayfield.

Siedentop, D., Tousignant, M., & Parker, M. (1982). *Academic learning time-physical education* (rev. ed.). Columbus, OH: The Ohio State University, School of Health, Physical Education, and Recreation.

Siegel, S. (1956). *Nonparametric statistics for the behavioral sciences*. NY: McGraw-Hill.

Weick, K.E. (1968). Systematic observational methods. In G. Lindzey & E. Aronson (Eds.), *The handbook of social psychology* (Vol. 2, 2nd ed., pp. 357-451). Menlo Park, CA: Addison-Wesley.

Chapter 4

Systematic Observation and Computer Technology

Thomas L. McKenzie
B. Robert Carlson

Direct observation in natural physical education and sport settings is heading into a new era, in which electronic data collection will merge with older measurement techniques to enhance the efficiency of observing, storing, analyzing, and transporting data. The rapid development of microcomputing technology has produced portable computers that are practical, state-of-the-art tools for on-site supervision of teachers and research involving systematic observation.

In direct observation, researchers typically employ one or more of the standard observation methods: frequency, duration, or time sampling using interval, momentary time sampling, or placheck recording. Frequency recording, which involves counting the number of occurrences of an event, is the most commonly used method. Duration recording is used when the observer is interested in the length of the occurrence of a particular event. Frequency and duration recording are the preferred methods of data collection because they provide the most accurate data. However, with the inefficiencies of standard paper-and-pencil data recording techniques, these methods are not effective for studying a large number of variables that occur simultaneously or with long time periods normally encountered in physical education classes. For these applications, time sampling techniques such as interval recording have become widely accepted and frequently used. The most widely used time sampling system is the Academic Learning Time-Physical Education (ALT-PE) system (Siedentop, Tousignant & Parker, 1982). It uses interval recording during which the subject is observed for a time interval (e.g., 6 seconds) and the data are recorded for the next time interval (e.g., 6 seconds). A detailed description of this system is found in chapter 17. Other time-sampling methods include momentary time sampling and placheck recording (see chapter 2).

PROBLEMS WITH
STANDARD DATA COLLECTION PROCEDURES

Although all of the previously mentioned data collection methods are valuable and have a place in sport pedagogy research, most observers, when using the methods, limit their effectiveness by not taking advantage of recent progress in electronic technology. For example, in studies using duration recording, an observer can operate only one or two stopwatches and thus is restricted to obtaining data on only one or two variables. Because most researchers are interested in both the frequency and the duration of many variables that typically occur simultaneously, they are forced to adopt time-sampling techniques. These techniques, which sample behaviors, are inferior to event and duration methods because they provide only an estimation of the frequency or the duration of an event. Traditional observational methods using paper-and-pencil technology are also limited because data cannot be recorded in real time, thereby negating the potential for studying sequence effects.

The historical method of manually recording the data requires that observers spend a great deal of time focusing on the recording sheet to enter data into the correct spaces. This shift in focus from the subject to the recording sheet causes observers to miss valuable data. Additionally, once data have been entered on recording sheets, they must be manually scored and transferred to summary sheets. This lengthy process makes it impossible for results of data collection to be available in time to take immediate action, is prone to calculation and copying errors, and requires researchers to spend considerable time performing menial tasks. Manual recording also limits the extent of the data analysis by limiting the number of variables and/or subjects that can be observed simultaneously and reducing the on-task observation time. It is important to note that qualitative researchers also lose valuable observation and analysis time by continuing to use traditional pencil-and-paper techniques.

COMPUTERIZATION
OF OBSERVATION SYSTEMS

The need to efficiently collect and analyze more complex data led several exercise and sport pedagogy researchers to computerized observation systems. Electronic behavioral processors such as the Apple II (Cicciarella & Martinek, 1982), Datamyte (Hawkins, Wiegand, & Bahneman, 1983), TICOR-DAC (Wurzer, 1983), the SSR-7 (Gray, 1983), and the Radio Shack TRS 80 Model 100 (Carlson & McKenzie, 1984; McKenzie & Carlson, 1984) have been used to study behaviors in physical activity settings. Unfortunately, most of these systems have one or more of the following deficiencies: they are expensive, lack portability, have limited long-term storage, provide no immediate analysis of the data, and/or have limited storage capacity.

A review of the sport pedagogy literature indicates that, although several researchers use computers for analysis, only a few use this technology to record and store data. Of the few that do, Cicciarella and Martinek (1982) described a microcomputer program suitable for real-time data recording and immediate analysis. Although their program is a tremendous asset to pedagogical researchers, it is limited to observations made in a single, stationary setting or from videotape recordings. Because their program requires a computer, disk drive, television monitor, and printer, it is neither sufficiently portable nor unobtrusive enough for data collection in most physical activity settings. Additionally, the cost of this equipment (approx $2,000) is beyond the budget of most pedagogical researchers. Recently, the computer industry has produced several small battery-operated portable computers, referred to as briefcase-size. For exercise and sport pedagogy researchers, these computers appear to be more functional than stationary systems and may be purchased at almost one-third the cost.

The selection of a computer system, which includes both the hardware and software, should be based on factors related to acquiring, storing, and analyzing the data of interest. Once the computer characteristics have been established, a search for a computer system that meets the needs of the specific researcher should be undertaken.

HARDWARE REQUIREMENTS

Frequently cited hardware requirements have been compiled into a list of nine characteristics that may be used as criteria for evaluating different pieces of equipment. According to the criteria, a primary characteristic is a computer that can operate in both field and laboratory settings. Because research studies call for data acquisition from the far reaches of a playing field, the bleachers of a gymnasium, or the solitude of a laboratory, the equipment has to be portable. Ideally, a portable computer should be no larger than a clipboard with a weight of no more than 4 to 5 pounds. In addition, the computer should be either AC or battery-operated, with an internal power source that protects against loss of data when the external power fails or is removed.

A second characteristic is the ability to communicate with external storage devices for the downloading of data files. Communication capability is fundamental to having long-term data storage, making subsequent analyses of the data via merging of data files, and accessing sophisticated statistical analysis packages. The ability to communicate via a modem with another computer is preferable to using a cassette recorder due to the greater speed and accuracy of transmission. A third factor to be considered is the cost. Given that the equipment is usually purchased without outside funding, total price is directly related to the ability of the school or individual to purchase the equipment. The fourth hardware characteristic is a full keyboard with a normal typewriter key arrangement. This characteristic reduces recording errors and increases the speed of data entry.

The inclusion of an internal clock on the criteria list enables the timing of events or intervals, which is an essential component of duration and time-sampling methods. An internal clock provides for the programming of intervals, thereby reducing the need for external timing devices such as time generators or programmed cassette recorders. A sixth hardware characteristic is a screen for prompting the observer and showing the data being recorded. Although the size priority of the computer reduces the likelihood of a full-size screen, the purchaser's goal should be to secure as large a screen as possible. The seventh factor to consider is the quality of the computer industry's support for the hardware selected. This includes the availability of repair services, consultation personnel, and software packages. The eighth factor is the ability to correct errors when entering data in the field. The ninth hardware characteristic is the capability for word processing. The ability to enter and modify words/ sentences efficiently is a tool crucial to the performance of qualitative research and to writing/modifying software programs.

HARDWARE SELECTION

Three categories of portable computers meet the criteria presented: hand-held computers, suitcase computers, and briefcase computers. Hand-held computers are the least expensive, but their keyboards are too small and at present they do not offer adequate programming capability and storage capacity for the anticipated research designs. The size and weight (approx 26 lb) of the suitcase computers are significant deficiencies, as well as their total dependency on AC power. In contrast, the briefcase computers more closely meet the requirements described in the previous section. These computers are becoming more powerful and less expensive each year. To illustrate the ease of use and power of a briefcase computer that is currently available, two useful public domain software programs that are available free of cost are briefly described.

COMPUTER PROGRAM DEVELOPMENT

An interval recording and data analysis program written in TRS BASIC and suitable for the TRS Model 100 and 200 has been described by McKenzie and Carlson (1984). It is ALT-PE compatible and provides for the coding of three factors (levels) and three subjects simultaneously. The three factors are setting (ALT-PE context), student (ALT-PE learner), and teacher. When using this program, the observer monitors for a 6-second interval and then depresses coded keys during the next 6 seconds. The observer is cued to observe both visually by messages on the computer screen and aurally by a beeping sound. At the end of the observation interval, the computer beeps again and cues the observer to record data by subject and observation number. The observation cues "setting," "student," and "teacher," appear sequentially on the screen. A digital clock on the screen also indicates the amount of elapsed time during each interval.

After the program is terminated, the data are analyzed immediately or are stored to await further data collection and/or later analysis. Data entry errors are corrected before analysis. The data analysis program computes and displays the frequency and percentage of occurrence for each code that is used to describe any of the three factors for each subject. The data are written to separate files for each subject. The files may be stored in the computer or transferred via the internal modem. This sample program goes beyond the usual demands of the ALT-PE system. It provides for coding three variables and three subjects over a longer period of time than described in the ALT-PE revised coding manual (Siedentop et al., 1982). It allows for the simultaneous coding of a third level, teacher behavior (TEACHER). With the coding of teacher behavior, the researcher adds information to the data base that is potentially useful in examining the complexities of instructional settings.

DURATION PROGRAM

Carlson and McKenzie (1984) also describe a duration software program for the TRS Models 100 and 200 that enables observers to do on-site duration recording in real time and permits immediate data analysis. To collect data, a coded keyboard letter is depressed at the beginning of the behavior and again at the end of the behavior. After the data entry portion of the program is terminated, the data are then analyzed immediately, or stored to await further data collection and/or later analysis. Five behaviors can be recorded simultaneously, and up to 25 different behavior categories can be recorded and analyzed during any one observation period. From the observer's point of view, these behaviors could be of one subject or of several different subjects in the same setting.

Errors in coding are often made during data collection. Because the program automatically stores data in a separate data file, errors cannot be corrected immediately. However, if an error is made, the observer can note the exact time of the error on the digital clock in the upper right corner of the screen and correct the behavior through the computer's text editing function after completion of the observations but prior to data analysis. The data for a single observation are stored on a single line with the behavior code being followed by a space and the real time in hours, minutes, and seconds. This format permits easy visual inspection by the observer after data collection. Thus, once the data have been entered at the keyboard, it is not necessary to handle the data again, because all computations and communication can be done electronically.

This BASIC software program is relatively simple in design but sufficiently powerful in function to provide the measures demanded by pedagogical researchers. Once observations have ended and any errors are corrected, the program presents the following data for each occurrence of any measured behavior: behavior name, beginning time, ending time, length of behavior, and percent of total time. The program also summarizes the data for the different behavior categories: (a) total time of observation, (b) total time for the behavior category, (c) frequency of occurrence, (d) average length of each occurrence, and (e) percent of total time during which that behavior category was observed. If additional data are added to the file at a later time, all results are recalculated. The results are written to an output file to be retained for later detailed analysis. All data and output reports are written to separate ASCII files up to a maximum of three data files and three output files. The ASCII format permits easy transfer of the data via a modem to a remote computer or directly to a cassette recorder or printer. Should the researcher desire to merge files, the merger would normally be done after the transfer of files to the remote computer facilities. In the remote computer, data can then be analyzed using more complex data analysis software packages (e.g., SPSS, BMDP).

PROGRAM ADAPTABILITY

Although software programs are designed to collect data according to a particular model (e.g., modified ALT-PE protocol), the computer equipment can be programmed for many different protocols. For example, with the previously described interval program, slight modifications can accommodate the data collection for one subject over an extended period of time before commencing data collection for a second subject. Collecting for two factors rather than three also necessitates only slight programming changes. With the internal clock, intervals either between or within behavioral occurrences can be varied. Although the screen size is a limiting factor for displaying information, the data are presented visually to enhance communication when using the machine for feedback. In a laboratory setting, the data are presented through larger screens. With this flexibility, it seems that the range of applications for the study of teacher and learner behaviors is limited only by one's imagination and ability to communicate with a programmer!

RELIABILITY OF OBSERVATIONS

Using electronic data collection devices requires researchers to rethink procedures for maximizing the reliability of data. During training, observers must become familiar with more complex instruments and tasks. In addition to all of the traditional tasks, they must learn how to initiate programs, enter data, correct errors, run the analysis program, dump files to external devices, and solve any problems if the previous tasks fail. These tasks are more difficult to learn than starting a tape recorder or filling out a data sheet and thus require a longer training period. A second procedure involves simultaneous observations by independent observers. For live recording, two identical electronic devices are necessary, and observers must be careful to initiate the observation programs at the same moment. If coding is done from videotapes or audiotapes, then only one electronic device is necessary to do either intraobserver or interobserver agreement calculations. The recorded data must be initiated at the exact spot on the tape for multiple playbacks. Because the speed of video playback machines slows slightly with weakened batteries, it is better to use AC power.

For standard frequency, duration, and interval measures, the common interobserver agreement calculations remain suitable (i.e., agreements divided by agreements plus disagreements multiplied by 100; sometimes adjusted for kappa values). However, increased use of portable electronic data collection devices in sport pedagogy research is likely to increase the use of continuous measures in real time. Data collection using real-time measures requires a modification of the traditional methods for calculating interobserver agreement scores. For example, one should determine not only if two independent observers record the same event but also whether the observers record the event to both start and end at the same moment (e.g., within 1/100th of a second). BASIC language programs for calculating interobserver agreement for data yielded by continuous data collection on multiple behaviors have already been devised (MacLean, Tapp, & Johnson, 1985) and are likely to be more readily available in the future.

FINAL COMMENTS

The advantages of using a portable briefcase computer in sport pedagogy research are numerous. With its capacity for recording, storing, analyzing, and transmitting data, the briefcase computer serves as a time-saving device that allows more data to be recorded over extended time periods. Consequently, more complex questions concerning learner and instructor behavior can be addressed with minimal increase in the time demanded of the researcher. Errors due to human handling of the data, which may occur when recording, transcribing, or making calculations, are virtually eliminated. It should be noted, however, that human error when entering data remains a possibility and needs to be controlled through observer training. Meanwhile, the hardware of the briefcase computer described in this chapter is sufficiently flexible that the machine is not likely to be the limiting factor for most research efforts. In all likelihood, the limiting factors will be (a) the complexity of the research hypotheses and (b) access to computer programs that are designed to accommodate the complexities of the gymnasium and playing field.

When using the portable computer as a research tool, one can gather observational data more easily and more accurately than through traditional procedures. The hardware and software systems that record, store, analyze, and transmit relevant data, although providing immediate output in the physical activity setting, vary in cost and capability. However, some systems are relatively inexpensive (approx $500), fully portable, and useful for researching a variety of sport pedagogy questions involving student/athlete and teacher/coach behavior. The portable computers described here also are potentially useful in preservice and in-service teacher training.

REFERENCES

Carlson, B.R., & McKenzie, T.L. (1984). Computer technology for recording, storing, and analyzing temporal data in physical activity settings. *Journal of Teaching in Physical Education*, **4**(1), 24-29.

Cicciarella, C.F., & Martinek, T.J. (1982). A microcomputer program for real time collection and immediate analysis of observational data. *Journal of Teaching in Physical Education*, **2**(1), 56-62.

Gray, J.A. (1983). The dance teacher: A computerized behavioral profile. *Journal of Physical Education, Recreation and Dance*, **54**(9), 34-35.

Hawkins, A., Wiegand, R., & Bahneman, C. (1983). The conceptual nature of ALT-PE and its use in an undergraduate teacher preparation program [Monograph 1]. *Journal of Teaching in Physical Education*, 11-16.

MacLean, W.E., Tapp, J.T., Sr., & Johnson, W.L. (1985). Alternate methods and software for calculating interobserver agreement for continuous observation data. *Journal of Psychopathology and Behavioral Assessment*, 7(1), 65-73.

McKenzie, T.L., & Carlson, B. R. (1984). Computer technology for exercise and sport pedagogy: Recording, storing, and analyzing interval data. *Journal of Teaching in Physical Education*, 3(3), 17-27.

Siedentop, D., Tousignant, M., & Parker, M. (1982). *Academic learning time–physical education: Coding manual, 1982 revision*. Columbus: Ohio State University, School of Health, Physical Education, and Recreation.

Wurzer, D.J. (1983). Correlation between academic learning time-physical education and student achievement in cardiopulmonary resuscitation. In R. Telama (Ed.), *Research in School Physical Education* (pp. 197-202). Jyvaskyla, Finland: Foundation for Promotion of Physical Culture and Health.

■ *PART II*

VERBAL AND NONVERBAL INTERACTION ANALYSIS

Flanders' Interaction Analysis System (FIAS) served as the standard model for studying classroom verbal behaviors throughout the sixties and most of the seventies. It still enjoys widespread usage, although today the observer has the luxury of selecting from many instruments. During this time period when FIAS was the primary observation tool, multiple adaptations of FIAS followed that increased behavior analysis, refined them, and provided better analysis within subject matter specializations.

To increase the usefulness of FIAS in physical education, several adaptations were made available. Most of these were included in the first edition, *Systematic Observation Instrumentation for Physical Education*.

We have excluded most of the adaptations from this text because of the sophistication of teacher/coach behavior research and the need to include many of the newer systems. Rankin's and Goldberger's adaptations were retained to provide a transitional link between FIAS and CAFIAS. Additionally, they are broader in data interpretation and are frequently used in preservice preparation.

Because Flanders' system was the precursor for developing observation tools, we have included it for historical and operational reference. The system is also easily learned, allowing for transfer of observation skills to more complex instruments. FIAS focuses totally on verbal interactions between teacher and students and provides a measure of direct and indirect teacher influence in the classroom. Plotting of the data allows for studying sequences and patterns of verbal discourse.

The Rankin Interaction Analysis System (RIAS) was designed to measure verbal and nonverbal interaction occurring during the teaching experience of student teachers in elementary physical education classes. Parts of Rankin's system came directly from Flanders, whereas others were more original. The system consists of five verbal and five nonverbal categories. The information generated through RIAS suggests that teaching behaviors are influenced by student behavior as well as educational instruction.

In 1970 Goldberger used an adaptation of FIAS as part of a cognitive and affective training program on in-class behavior of physical education student teachers. This adaptation focused on the theoretical teaching styles of Mosston (1966). The Behavior Analysis Tool (BAT) is a further modification of his original attempt to answer specific questions about the teaching process. BAT provides verbal and nonverbal teacher behavior, learner behavior, and interaction between teacher and learners during the impact phase of instruction in 25 different categories.

Cheffers' Adaptation of Flanders' Interaction Analysis System (CAFIAS), described by Cheffers and Mancini, is one of the most popular and widely used interaction analysis systems in physical education and sport. CAFIAS was designed to provide information about teachers' and students' verbal and nonverbal behaviors and interactions in physical activity settings, both in physical education classes and in the athletic environment. In addition to describing behaviors, this instrument permits the identification of patterns of interactions, class structure, and varieties of teaching agencies.

The CAFIAS Supervisory Feedback Instrument (CSFI), designed by Wuest and Mancini, allows supervisors to provide systematic feedback to preservice and in-service teachers immediately following the conclusion of the instructional episode. The CSFI's categories are similar to those employed in CAFIAS; however, a modification of the CAFIAS coding procedures permits observers to offer teachers information concerning the type and frequency of behaviors exhibited, without using the computer for data analysis. The procedures employed with this instrument also make it easy for beginning observers to use it for a variety of purposes.

The purpose of Mancini and Wuest's Self-Assessment Feedback Instrument (SAFI) is to provide teachers and coaches with a means to easily evaluate their own behaviors, specifically the manner in which they give feedback during instruction. This self-assessment instrument allows teachers and coaches to analyze both the type and the frequency of feedback they provide to their students and athletes. The information generated from the SAFI can be used by a teacher or a coach to determine areas of improvement, set personal goals, and monitor progress toward attainment of these goals.

The Dyadic Adaptation of CAFIAS, designed by Martinek and Mancini, provides teachers with descriptive information about their interactions with a specific student or a small group of students (i.e., fewer than five students). DAC permits teachers to compare their interactions with students possessing certain characteristics, such as high or low skill ability. The system allows for analyses of teacher expectancy effects in physical activity settings.

REFERENCE

Mosston, M. (1966). *Teaching physical education*. Columbus, OH: Charles E. Merrill.

Chapter 5

Interaction Analysis: A System for Coding Direct and Indirect Teaching Behaviors

Paul W. Darst
Dorothy B. Zakrajsek
Victor H. Mancini

Systematic observation as a quantitative tool for categorizing teaching behavior is, for the most part, an outgrowth of Flanders' work in the 1960s. The Flanders' Interaction Analysis System (FIAS) (Flanders, 1965) was the forerunner for several adaptations of early physical education observation systems (Darst, Mancini, & Zakrajsek, 1983). Because the next six chapters describe systems derived from FIAS, it is necessary not only to review FIAS for its historical significance but to ground the reader in the purpose, limitations, categories, and procedures for using this system or the adaptations based on it.

Flanders' system is designed for observing, recording, and analyzing verbal behavior only. The assumption is that the verbal behavior of the teacher is an adequate sample of the teacher's total behavior. The display of verbal behaviors is organized such that the sequence of behaviors can be studied.

CATEGORY DESCRIPTIONS

All teacher-student interactions are divided into 10 categories that are mutually exclusive yet together include all verbal interaction that occurs. Interactions are categorized in one of three major sections: teacher talk, student talk, and silence or confusion. Teacher talk is subdivided into two headings: indirect teacher influence and direct teacher influence. Categories within these subdivisions provide information about the climate for more or less student participation.

Teacher Talk—Indirect Influence

This environment increases student participation and maximizes the freedom of student response and action.

Accepts Feelings (1)

The teacher accepts and clarifies the feeling tone of the students in a non-threatening manner. Feelings may be positive or negative. Predicting or recalling feelings is included. *Examples:* "I know that this skill will be difficult for many of you." "Not all of you will be successful on the first few attempts."

Praises or Encourages (2)

The teacher praises or encourages student action or behavior. He or she makes jokes that release tension but not at the expense of another individual. Category also includes nodding head or saying "mm-hm" or "go on."

Accepts or Uses Ideas of Students (3)

The teacher clarifies, builds, or develops ideas suggested by student. As the teacher moves from the idea to the teacher's own thoughts, the observer should shift to Category 5.

Asks Questions (4)

The teacher asks questions about content or procedure with the intent that a student answer. This does not include rhetorical questions.

Teacher Talk—Direct Influence

This environment increases the active control of the teacher and restricts the freedom of student response.

Lectures (5)

The teacher gives facts or opinions about content or procedures, expresses own ideas, and asks rhetorical questions.

Gives Directions (6)

The teacher gives directions, commands, or orders with which the student is expected to comply.

Criticizes or Justifies Authority (7)

The teacher makes statements intended to change student behavior from nonacceptable to acceptable, bawls someone out, or states why he or she is behaving in such a way. This category involves extreme self-reference.

Student Talk

This environment provides a check on the freedom of student action.

Student Talk—Responds (8)

Students talk in response to teacher. The teacher initiates the contact and solicits student response.

Student Talk—Initiates (9)

Students initiate talk. If a teacher calls on a student only to indicate who may talk next, the observer must decide if student wants to talk. If so, then observer uses this category.

Silence or Confusion

Category used when the observer cannot determine who is talking or when no one is talking.

Silence or Confusion (10)

Pauses, short periods of silence, and periods of confusion in which communication cannot be understood by the observer.

RECORDING PROCEDURES

The observer's location in the classroom should cause the least amount of distraction to the teacher and students. Before recording, the observer should spend about 5 to 10 minutes becoming oriented and getting a feeling for the total situation; then the recording begins. Every 3 seconds the observer records the category number of the verbal behavior that has just been observed. The numbers are recorded sequentially in a column. Several long columns of numbers are recorded during a normal observational period (15 to 20 minutes), because approximately 20 numbers are recorded per minute. The observer should maintain accuracy and a steady tempo. Marginal notes can be written to explain unusual happenings.

In addition, a change in the activity being observed should be noted because interaction may vary. The observer should draw a line under the recorded numbers, make a marginal note of the new activity, and begin categorizing again when interaction resumes.

Due to the complexity of the system in terms of categorization, ground rules have been established. These rules of observation have been found helpful in developing consistency. Selected ground rules that appear common to a variety of teaching situations are identified here. A complete set of ground rules is available in Amidon and Flanders (1971).

1. When not certain in which of two or more categories a statement belongs, choose the category that is numerically farthest from Category 5. This is true except when one of the two categories in doubt is Category 10, which is never chosen if there is an alternative category under consideration.

2. If the primary tone of the teacher's behavior has been consistently direct or indirect, do not shift into the opposite classification unless a clear indication of shift is given. The trained person observing a particular action is in the best position to judge whether the teacher is restricting or expanding the freedom of action of class members.

3. Do not be overly concerned with your own biases or with the teacher's intent. Rather, you must ask, "What does this behavior mean to the students as far as restriction or expansion of their freedom is concerned?"

4. If more than one category occurs during the 3-second interval, then record all categories used in that interval. In other words, record each change in category. If no change occurs within 3 seconds, repeat the category number.

SUMMARIZING AND INTERPRETING THE DATA

The observer maintains the sequences of interaction by recording the category numbers in columns. These tallies are entered into a 10-row by 10-column table called a *matrix*. Before making entries in the matrix, the observer places a "10" at the beginning and end of the sequence; it is assumed that each episode begins and ends with silence. The numbers are marked off in pairs as shown here. Note that each pair of numbers overlaps with the previous pair, and each number, except the first and last, is used twice. Otherwise, two tallies would be lost.

```
   10                          1
    5                          1
    5                          4
    5                          9
    6                          9
    6                          9
   10                          2
    7                          3
    7                          3
    6                         10
    6
```

Tabulations are then made in the matrix. The cell in which a pair is recorded is determined by using the first number in the pair to indicate the row and the second number to indicate the column. Thus the first pair (10-5) is entered in Row 10, Column 5. A tally for the second pair (5-5) is shown in the cell formed by Row 5, Column 5. The completed matrix for this interaction sequence is revealed in Figure 5.1. This procedure permits the total of each column to equal the total of the corresponding row. The tabulations in the matrix can be checked for accuracy by noting that there should be one less tally in the matrix than there are numbers in the original sequence $(N - 1)$. In this example, with 21 numbers in the sequence, the total number of tallies in the matrix is 20. After the number of tallies is determined for each column, a corresponding percentage of tallies is computed.

After the interaction analysis matrix is tabulated, the observer or teacher can describe and interpret the interaction in several ways. The simplest analysis is to compute the percentage of tallies in each category (columns). This is shown in Figure 5.1 by dividing each of the column totals by the total number of tallies in the matrix. A complete description of teacher and student interaction can be developed by examining various areas of the matrix. In doing so, recognize that only the individual teacher can make the final decisions about what behavior is good or bad, desirable or undesirable. The special areas of the matrix are identified and briefly defined in the following subsections.

Teacher Influence

The percentage of teacher influence represents that proportion of total interaction during which the teacher is engaged in verbal behavior. The total number of tallies in Columns 1 through 7 is divided by the total number of tallies in the matrix. In the previous example, teacher influence was 70% (15 ÷ 20).

	1	2	3	4	5	6	7	8	9	10	
1	I			I							
2			I								
3			I							I	
4									I		
5					II	I					
6	I					II				I	
7						I	I				
8											
9		I							II		
10					I		I				Matrix total
Total	2	1	2	1	3	4	2	0	3	2	20
%	10	5	10	5	15	20	10	0	15	10	

Figure 5.1 Sample interaction analysis matrix.

Student Influence

The percentage of student influence represents that proportion of total interaction during which the student is engaged in verbal behavior. The total number of tallies in Columns 8 and 9 is divided by the total number of tallies in the matrix. In the previous example, student influence was 15% (3 ÷ 20).

I/D Ratio

To determine whether the teacher is predominantly indirect or direct, the total number of tallies in Columns 1, 2, 3, and 4 is divided by the total number of tallies in Columns 5, 6, and 7 plus the total in Columns 1, 2, 3, and 4. This results in the ratio of indirect to direct teacher influence (I/D ratio). An I/D ratio of .67 means that there were two indirect behaviors for every one direct behavior. In Figure 5.1, less than half of the teacher's influence was indirect (I/D ratio = .40).

Revised I/D Ratio

To find out the kind of emphasis given to motivation and control, the number of tallies in Columns 1, 2, and 3 is divided by the total number of tallies in Columns 6 and 7 plus the total in Columns 1, 2, and 3. These categories are more concerned with motivation and control and less concerned with presentation of content. By eliminating the effects of Categories 4 and 5, the observer reveals information about whether the teacher approaches motivation and control directly or indirectly. In Figure 5.1, slightly less than half of the teacher's approach to motivation and control was indirect (revised I/D ratio = .45).

Content Cross

In Figure 5.2, tallies that indicated the content cross are shown by Area A. This area represents teacher behavior consisting primarily of teacher questions; lecture; and presentation of opinions, ideas, and information. A heavy concentration of tallies in this area indicates an emphasis on content. From Figure 5.1, six of the tallies were represented by the content cross (30%).

Categories		1	2	3	4	5	6	7	8	9	10
Accepts feelings	1										
Praises/encourages	2		B								
Uses students' ideas	3										
Asks questions	4					A					
Presents/lectures	5										
Gives directions	6							C			
Criticizes	7										
Student response	8			E				F		D	
Student initiation	9										
Silence/confusion	10										

Figure 5.2 Areas of matrix analysis.

Extended Indirect Influence

High frequency in the cells that comprise the intersection of Columns 1, 2, and 3 and Rows 1, 2, and 3 indicates the use of extended indirect influence. This area of the matrix, Area B in Figure 5.2, represents the emphasis the teacher gives to accepting and expanding upon student feelings, reinforcing student behavior, and using student ideas. From Figure 5.1, only three of the tallies were found in this area (15%).

Extended Direct Influence

High frequency in the cells that comprise the intersection of Columns 6 and 7 and Rows 6 and 7 indicates the use of extended direct influence. This area of the matrix, Area C in Figure 5.2, represents the teacher's emphasis on giving lengthy directions and criticism and using authority. The behavior pattern, 6-6, 6-7, 7-6, 7-7, means the teacher gives a direction that is not followed and criticism ensues. This may reveal discipline problems or student rejection of teacher influence. From Figure 5.1, four of the tallies were found in this area (20%).

Sustained Student Influence

Area D in Figure 5.2 represents student influence, which is prolonged verbal behavior by one student and sustained verbal behavior by several students. Sustained student influence is indicated by a high frequency in the matrix cells located at the intersection of Columns 8 and 9 and Rows 8 and 9. From Figure 5.1, only two of the tallies were found in this area (10%).

Teacher Response to Students

An important aspect of interaction is the way the teacher responds to student comment. In Figure 5.2, Area E represents indirect response to students; Area F reveals direct response. A comparison of the relative number of tallies in these two areas indicates the pattern of behavior used by the teacher in response to students. The number of tallies in these areas from Figure 5.1 was 1 and 0 for indirect response and direct response, respectively.

Interpretation of matrices should be made on the basis that interaction data reveal current, rather than the best or most desired, practices. Other aspects of the matrix providing interpretation of teacher-student interaction are as follows (Amidon & Flanders, 1971):

- Direct and indirect teachers seem to use the same number of behaviors fitting into Category 2.

- There appears to be very little difference in the use of Categories 4 and 5 between direct and indirect teachers.
- Direct and indirect teachers differ in their use of Categories 6 and 7. The direct teacher gives more directions and spends more time in criticism and self-justification. The indirect teacher rarely uses the 6-7 and 7-6 cells.
- Rows 4 and 8 and Columns 4 and 8 indicate the question-and-answer pattern. A heavy 4-8 cell indicates that the teacher asks many direct questions that limit the range of student response. A heavy 8-4 cell, with few tallies in other Row 8 cells, means the teacher is following the student's answer with another question.
- A high number of tallies in the 4-8, 8-2, 8-3, 2-4, and 3-4 cells indicates a modified question-and-answer pattern. The teacher asks a question and then encourages or accepts student ideas before asking another question.
- Frequent use of the 4-10 cells reflects periods of silence following teacher questions. Heavily loaded 10-8 or 10-9 cells could mean the teacher asks thought-provoking questions and allows time for students to think. Heavy loadings in the 4-5 and 4-6 cells means the teacher is directing students to answer or extending Category 5 after questioning.
- Frequent use of the 5-7 cell suggests the teacher is attempting to maintain order and control while presenting information either verbally or nonverbally.
- Considerable use of the 5-5 cell with little use of other Row 5 cells means the teacher uses concentrated periods of lecture/presentation/demonstration with few teacher questions or student contributions.

Matrix analysis is designed to help the teacher gain a systematic and thorough understanding of the important cells and areas of the matrix. Accurate descriptions and meaningful interpretations depend on the teacher's specific teaching objectives. The interaction indexes provide an objective basis for interpretation of classroom interaction in terms of the teacher's objectives. For example, teacher objectives could focus on the following aspects:

- Amount of time spent in teacher verbal behavior
- Degree to which an indirect or direct teaching pattern is used
- Kind of response to student verbal behavior
- Amount of time spent in presenting/lecturing
- Amount of time spent in extending student ideas
- Use of accepting and encouraging behaviors
- Effectiveness in the use of praise
- Effectiveness in the use of criticism
- Degree of student behavior

For the purpose of synthesis, a complete interaction analysis matrix is presented in Figure 5.3. Note that the cells reflect percentages rather than actual tallies; this makes it easier to tabulate teacher-student interaction data (Amidon & Flanders, 1971). The basic indexes that are revealed at the bottom of Figure 5.3 may be interpreted as follows:

- The teacher's influence (59%) approximates that of the average teacher, who engages in verbal behavior about two-thirds of the time.

	1	2	3	4	5	6	7	8	9	10	
1	0.28	0.07		0.28	0.14	0.07					
2		1.62	1.19	1.62	0.84	1.12		0.21	0.14	0.56	
3		0.77	3.51	5.55	2.32	0.56		0.14	0.28	0.14	
4		0.14	0.14	1.54	0.14	0.28		11.17	2.25	0.56	
5	0.14	0.28	0.14	3.86	6.54	1.19	0.07	0.17	0.56	0.49	
6	0.07	0.21		0.42	0.77	2.18	0.14	2.25		1.34	
7				0.07	0.28	0.21	0.21				
8	0.28	3.65	5.41	2.32	1.05	0.98	0.21	8.43	0.35	0.28	
9		0.35	2.81	0.28	0.77				7.31	0.42	
10	0.07	0.21	0.07	0.28	0.84	0.77	0.14	0.63	1.05	2.03	Matrix total
Total											
%	0.84	7.31	13.28	16.23	13.42	7.38	0.77	22.98	11.94	5.83	

Matrix subsections		Percent
Teacher influence	=	59.23
Student influence	=	34.92
I/D ratio	=	0.636
Revised I/D ratio	=	0.724
Content cross	=	46.18
Extended indirect influence	=	7.44
Extended direct influence	=	2.74
Sustained student influence	=	16.09
Indirect response to students	=	15.10
Direct response to students	=	3.01

Figure 5.3 Sample percentage matrix for interpretation.

- Student influence (35%) is slightly more than average: About one-third of all student influence is student-initiated behavior (Column 8).
- Over half of the teacher's influence is indirect as indicated by the I/D ratio (.636). As high as 70% of teachers employ predominantly direct patterns. This ratio is supported by a fairly high percentage of extended indirect influence (7.44%).
- Nearly half (46%) of teacher behavior emphasizes content as revealed by the number of tallies comprising the intersection of Rows 4 and 5 and Columns 4 and 5.
- Four of the steady state cells contain over 3% of the matrix total, that is, cells 3-3, 5-5, 8-8, and 9-9. The student behavior cells (8-8 and 9-9) account for almost all of sustained student influence.
- Five of the transition cells contain over 3% of the matrix total (cells 3-4, 4-8, 5-4, 8-2, and 8-3). These high-frequency cells indicate question-answer patterns followed by praise or teacher acceptance that is relatively long in duration. The nature of the teacher's response to students is clearly indirect (15%) as opposed to direct (3%).

Data from this instrument help teachers understand their classroom verbal behavior and their interactions with their students. With this information teachers make conscious decisions about whether they wish to modify their behavior; if they do, they better understand the reasons underlying their decision.

ACKNOWLEDGMENT

The authors would like to credit Vincent Melograno for his help in providing a major portion of this chapter.

REFERENCES

Amidon, E.J., & Flanders, N.A. (1971). *The role of the teacher in the classroom*. Minneapolis, MN: Association for Productive Teaching.

Darst, P.W., Mancini, V.H., & Zakrajsek, D.B. (1983). *Systematic observation instrumentation for physical education*. Champaign, IL: Leisure Press.

Flanders, N.A. (1965). Teacher influence, pupil attitudes, and achievement (Cooperative Research Monograph No. 12). Washington, DC: U.S. Office of Education.

Chapter 6

The Rankin Interaction Analysis System (RIAS)

Kelly D. Rankin

The purpose of any interaction analysis system is to give precise and objective feedback to the individuals being observed in a teaching environment. As researchers began using systems to collect verbal information in the classrooms, the area of nonverbal interaction came to be looked at as an essential part of the communication game.

The gymnasium is a classroom, and various authors began adopting interaction instruments to investigate both verbal and nonverbal interaction occurring in physical education. The purpose of the Rankin Interaction Analysis System (RIAS) is to look at both verbal and nonverbal behaviors in the area of elementary physical education. Its objective is to provide a practical method for the teacher and supervisor to more easily evaluate verbal and nonverbal behaviors of their student teachers in elementary physical education. RIAS can also be used in secondary physical education.

The reliability of the RIAS for $r_s = .93$. The Cheffers' Adaptation of Flanders' Interaction Analysis System (CAFIAS) was used to establish validity because this measure included both verbal and nonverbal behaviors. Pearson's product moment correlation technique was used to determine the validity of the RIAS. For three expert observers the correlation coefficients were $r = .72$, $r = .65$, and $r = .62$.

CATEGORY DESCRIPTIONS

Teacher Talk (1)

The teacher gives directions, commands, or orders with which a student is expected to comply; this category also includes lecturing, giving facts or opinions, expressing ideas, and answering questions directed by students.

Teacher Rejection (2)

Teacher makes statements intended to change or control student behavior and gives negative or sarcastic response to student action.

Student Talk (3)

Students talk among themselves without teacher direction and without following the teacher's comments.

Student Feedback (4)

Students talk when teacher asks questions or elicits comments.

Teacher Praise (5)

Teacher accepts and reinforces student action.

Student Smiling (6)

Student reacts to comments or instructions from teacher or classmates with laughing, giggling, joking, and giving facial signs of approval.

Student Motion (7)

Student moves body or parts of the body as in exercises or other activities.

Student Frowning (8)

Student shows negative feelings toward criticism or comments from the teacher. Student shows disapproval of the activity or of classmates through facial expressions and body gestures.

Teacher Gestures (9)

Teacher smiles, shakes head affirmatively, pats student on the back, winks, places hand on student's shoulder or head, claps, raises eyebrows, maintains eye contact, or uses body to emphasize idea. Teacher frowns, stares, taps foot, negatively shakes head, or looks away from the deviant and ignores student behavior.

Nonresponse or Confusion (10)

Students stand or sit listening to teacher or student talk; class creates considerable noise and disrupts the planned activity.

RECORDING PROCEDURES

Once the teacher has learned the 10 categories, he or she may begin observing the student teacher and recording the numbers as they occur in the lesson. An inference is made every 3 seconds, or whenever the behavior changes about which category of behavior was witnessed. By observing and recording behavioral events every 3 seconds, the supervisor can collect accurate, objective information.

SUMMARIZING AND INTERPRETING THE DATA

When the observer finishes the recordings after a 20- to 30-minute lesson, the numbers are then paired in the following manner.

$$
\begin{array}{ll}
& 1 \\
& \quad \Big]\text{1st pair} \\
\text{2nd pair} & 4 \\
& 9 \\
& \quad \Big]\text{3rd pair} \\
\text{4th pair} & 2 \\
& 9 \\
& \quad \Big]\text{5th pair} \\
& 1 \\
& 5 \\
& 3 \\
& 1 \\
& 1 \\
& 9
\end{array}
$$

These data are then placed on a 10-by-10 matrix (Figure 6.1). Pair 1-4 is shown by a tabulation in the cell formed by Row 1 and Column 4. The second pair, 4-9, is shown in the cell formed by Row 4 and Column 9. Once the tallies are entered in the 10-by-10 matrix, the interaction patterns in the classroom can be interpreted by studying the matrix. The 10 categories are then totaled, the percentages are figured, and comparisons between verbal and nonverbal behavior for teacher and students are made.

Working with the total percentages, the observer-recorder adds Columns 1, 2, and 5 for teacher verbalization and Column 9 for how much the teacher interacted nonverbally. Figures in Columns 2 and 3 show how much student talk was going on. Nonverbal student interaction is determined by adding Columns 6, 7, and 8. Column 10 hows how much time was wasted with confusion and nonresponse. A high percentage in Columns 1, 2, and 5 may indicate that the student teacher is talking too much during the lesson and that the atmosphere is negative.

	1	2	3	4	5	6	7	8	9	10	
1	I			I	I				I		
2									I		
3	I										
4									I		
5			I								
6											
7											
8											
9	I	I									
10											Matrix total
Total	3	1	1	1	1	0	0	0	3	0	10
%	30	10	10	10	10	0	0	0	30	0	

Figure 6.1 Rankin Interaction Analysis Matrix.

Once the data have been recorded in the matrix, the observer begins to see clusters of tallies. These clusters with the percentage results are used to show the student teacher the types of interaction that occurred in the lesson.

RIAS is used in discriminating between patterns of teaching and studying the teaching behaviors of student teachers in elementary physical education, preservice and in-service training of teachers, and in-service training clinics.

RELATED REFERENCES

Rankin, K.D. (1975). *Verbal and non-verbal interaction analysis of student teachers with students in elementary physical education*. Unpublished doctoral dissertation, University of Kansas, Lawrence.

Rankin, K.D. (1978). An objective approach to student teacher evaluation. *The Physical Educator*, **35**(1), 43-46.

Twa, H. (1979). *A comparison of male and female physical education teachers' verbal and non-verbal interaction at the elementary level*. Unpublished doctoral dissertation, University of Oregon, Eugene.

Chapter 7

The Behavior Analysis Tool (BAT)

Michael Goldberger

The Behavior Analysis Tool (BAT) is a modification of Flanders' Interaction Analysis System. I and several graduate students at Temple University developed BAT in 1977 to study fidelity between teaching behavior and several theoretical teaching styles (Mosston, 1972). The purpose of BAT is to objectively record verbal and nonverbal teacher behavior, learner behavior, and the interaction between teacher and learners during the impact phase of instruction. A trained observer closely watches the instructional process and systematically notes the behavior just witnessed.

RECORDING PROCEDURES

An inference is made every 5 seconds, or whenever the behavior changes, about which category of behavior occurred. The observer makes a literal inference of the observed behavior; that is, the data should reflect the actual behavior and not necessarily the intent. Data are recorded in numbered columns for later analysis.

It should be noted that no distinction is made here between verbal and nonverbal behavior. A teacher presenting information to the students is recorded as Category 4 whether the information is a verbal description or a nonverbal demonstration. Similarly, a predictable response from the student is recorded as an 11 whether the response is verbal or nonverbal (Table 7.1). A nonverbal nuance, however, like a faint smile, should not be recorded unless it is clearly seen as a behavior by the recipient of the communication.

For convenience, BAT categories are arranged in terms of teacher initiation, student response, and teacher reinforcement. This arrangement reflects the usual flow of classroom interaction, although not the only or

Table 7.1   Category Descriptions for the Behavior Analysis Tool (BAT)

Teacher initiation behavior

Direct

1. *Teacher commands:* Teacher directs student to do something and compliance is commanded.
2. *Teacher directs:* Teacher directs student to do something but compliance is not commanded.
3. *Teacher suggests:* Teacher makes specific suggestions but compliance is left to student.
4. *Teacher lectures:* Teacher presents information but compliance is not suggested. Use the following subscripts: (a) presents orally, (b) uses printed materials, (c) uses A/V aids, and (d) uses demonstration.
5. *Teacher offers opinions:* Teacher offers personal ideas or goes off on a tangent.
6. *Teacher asks convergent questions:* Use the following subscripts: (a) rhetorical questions, (b) singular (one-answer) questions, and (c) narrow (few answers possible) questions.

Indirect

7. *Teacher asks divergent questions:* Teacher presents a problem that has many possible solutions.
8. *Teacher asks opinions:* Teacher requests student to present ideas or personal opinions.

Student response behavior

On-target response

9. *Student works on task:* Student is thinking or preparing to respond to the task.
10. *Student initiates contact with other:* Sanctioned on-task contacts with the teacher, other students, or materials.
11. *Student produces predictable response:* Student responds to direct teacher initiation.
12. *Student produces divergent response:* Student responds to indirect teacher initiation and expresses ideas, opinions, or feelings.

Off-target response

13. *Student produces off-target response:* Student tries to do the task but does it incorrectly.
14. *Student is off-task:* Student is not engaged in the task, unsanctioned, but not causing a disturbance.
15. *Student exhibits deviant behavior:* The teacher must respond to the student's unsanctioned, disruptive behavior.

Teacher reinforcement behavior

Positive reinforcement

16. *Teacher empathizes:* Teacher accepts student's feelings and tries to understand.

17. *Teacher offers enthusiastic positive reinforcement:* Teacher clearly reinforces student response or behavior and is unusually energetic in feeling tone.
18. *Teacher offers positive value statements:* Teacher statements are intended to positively reinforce student behavior.

Neutral reinforcement

19. *Teacher encouragement:* Teacher makes statements that reinforce the continuance of task or problem engagement (including praise).
20. *Teacher accepts student behavior:* Teacher accepts, uses, and builds upon student ideas or responses.
21. *Teacher provides corrective feedback:* Teacher makes specific suggestions for correct performance.

Negative reinforcement

22. *Teacher offers negative value statements:* Teacher uses language intended to discourage student behavior.
23. *Teacher critical:* Teacher uses harsh reprimands to move a student from off-task to on-task behavior.
24. *Teacher justifies own authority:* Teacher uses punishment or humiliation to justify his or her own authority in the setting.
25. *Confusion:* Neither teacher nor student behavior can be coded.

---

necessarily the best flow. For example, a student might initiate the interaction, coded as 10, and this might be intended on the part of the teacher and very appropriate.

Instructional episodes usually have a climate associated with them that affects the interaction between teacher and students. Before recording data, the observer should become aware of this climate and operate within the contextual parameters of that milieu while recording information. If during the orientation period the observer becomes aware of behaviors that are not accurately represented by the existing 25 categories, he or she may add categories to the system by clearly describing the observed behavior on the back of the rating form and identifying it with a new category number (i.e., 26 or above).

SUMMARIZING AND INTERPRETING THE DATA

When the observer completes the recordings, the numbers are then paired in the following manner and entered into a matrix.

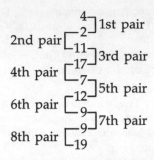

Data are summarized on a 25-by-25 matrix (or larger if additional categories are included) following procedures suggested by Amidon and Flanders (1967). Column percentages are determined and a variety of ratios computed to answer specific research questions. For example, the following ratios have been used to assess the affective climate during instruction:

Pattern/Description	Ratio
Empathetic/positive teacher behavior ratio	$\dfrac{16 + 17 + 18 + 19 + 20}{\text{Teacher reinforcement}} \times 100$
Punitive/negative teacher behavior ratio	$\dfrac{22 + 23 + 24}{\text{Teacher reinforcement}} \times 100$
Businesslike transaction	$\dfrac{2 + 4 + 9 + 11 + 18 + 22}{\text{Entire matrix}} = 100$

These computer-generated ratios and over 50 like them have added to the richness of data analysis. Ratios have also been developed for each of the eight theoretical styles of teaching described by Mosston (1972).

BAT has been used in facilitating teacher education, helping teachers objectively analyze videotaped sessions, and conducting several areas of research. Modified versions of BAT have been used to study the effects of different educational programs on teacher behavior and to examine the effects of alternative teaching styles on selected learner outcomes.

REFERENCES

Amidon, E.J., & Flanders, N.A. (1967). Interaction analysis as a feedback system. In E.J. Amidon & J.B. Hough (Eds.), *Interaction analysis: Theory, research, and application* (pp. 25-26). Reading, MA: Addison-Wesley.

Mosston, M. (1972). *Teaching from command to discovery*. Belmont, CA: Wadsworth.

RELATED REFERENCE

Goldberger, M.S. (1974). Studying your teaching behavior. *Journal of Health, Physical Education, and Recreation, 45*(4), 33-36.

Chapter 8

Cheffers' Adaptation of the Flanders' Interaction Analysis System (CAFIAS)

John T.F. Cheffers
Victor H. Mancini

The Cheffers' Adaptation of the Flanders' Interaction Analysis System (CAFIAS) was developed primarily for use in physical activity settings. The system uses numbered categories to objectively code verbal and non-verbal behaviors between teacher and student, identifies specific teaching agencies and class structure, and elaborates on student response behavior. Because CAFIAS was designed to record not only the actual events that take place within a classroom but also the sequence of these interactions, it has proven to be a valuable observation tool in research and in teacher education programs.

CAFIAS is not a new system, but an adaptation for specific application in predominantly movement-oriented settings. CAFIAS makes two changes in the Flanders' Interaction Analysis System (FIAS). It provides a device for the coding of nonverbal behavior through a double category system so any behavior can be categorized as verbal, nonverbal, or both. In addition, it provides for diversification of the agency responsible for performing the teaching function.

The classroom teacher is only one of the agents responsible for teaching. Peers and structures within the local environment are critical factors often overlooked in the general assessment of teaching. Based on the philosophy that when learning occurs teaching has taken place, CAFIAS, through postscripting, permits the classification of the teaching agency as the teacher, other students, or the local environment. For coding, the *s* is placed beside the appropriate tally each time the students assume the teaching responsibilities. An *e* is placed beside each tally when the environment is the teaching agency.

The current system of assigning many students to a single teacher has proved economical, but it has been seriously questioned by those interested in providing opportunities to learn at differing rates by involving the learners more as participants than as recipients in the learning process.

CAFIAS permits the coding of the class as whole (W), where the entire class is functioning as one unit; part (P), where the class is broken down into small groups or the students are working individually; or no teacher influence (I), where the teacher is not present. This is accomplished by placing a W, a P, or an I beside each tally when the structure of the class changes. This makes it possible to have a time-line analysis of the class structure for comparative purposes. A series of postscripts and subscripts, supported by a minimum of ground rules, make up the operating procedures. For example, in CAFIAS, Flanders' Category 1, acceptance of strong student feelings by the teacher, is coded as a 3/1. Category 1 is removed from the matrix, so these behaviors are simply recorded separately at the bottom of the matrix.

Cheffers (1972) measured the performance of CAFIAS compared to FIAS using the blind-live interpretation technique on four selected physical education classes. In this method of establishing validity, the accuracy of assessments made by observers who have seen a videotape of a class is compared to a similar number of impartial observers who have not witnessed the lesson but have seen and interpreted a matrix of the class. Pearson's product moment correlations between the blind and live interpretations established a ratio of .80. This was converted to a t ratio of 3.5, which was significant at the .05 confidence level.

Cheffers (1972) determined the reliability of CAFIAS through submitting cell rankings to Kendall's coefficient of concordance. Two comparisons were made. One compared the total matrices and established a W ranging from .60 to .81. The second compared the 10 main cells and found a W ranging from .44 to .87. Both comparisons were found to be reliable at or beyond the .05 level of significance.

CATEGORY DESCRIPTIONS

CAFIAS divides behaviors into two major categories: teacher behaviors and student behaviors. A third major category encompasses behaviors such as silence and confusion. CAFIAS permits observers to describe both verbal and nonverbal behaviors. The definitions of the CAFIAS categories, expressed as relevant behaviors, and the corresponding CAFIAS code, noted in parentheses, are presented below:

Teacher Behaviors

Praises or Encourages

Verbal (2).   Teacher praises, commends, jokes, and encourages.

Nonverbal (12).   Teacher smiles, nods energetically with smile, winks, laughs, applauds by clapping hands or patting student on shoulder or head, shakes student's hand, embraces joyfully, and laughs to encourage.

Accepts or Uses Ideas of Students

Verbal (3).   Teacher accepts, clarifies, uses, and develops suggestions and feelings of the student.

Nonverbal (13).   Teacher nods without smiling, tilts head or sighs empathetically, shakes hands, embraces sympathetically, and places arm around student's shoulder. Teacher elevates student performance to a par with teacher performance, accepts facilitation from students, takes part in student activities, catches an implement thrown by student, takes part in a game with students, or supports student during activity or spots in gymnastics.

Asks Questions

Verbal (4).   Teacher asks questions requiring student answers.

Nonverbal (14).   Teacher wrinkles brow, opens mouth, turns head with quizzical look. He or she raises hands in air to invite an answer, stares awaiting answer, scratches head, or cups hand to ear and stands still awaiting answer.

Gives Information

Verbal (5).   Teacher gives facts or opinions, expresses ideas, or asks rhetorical questions.

Nonverbal (15).   Teacher whispers words audibly, sings, or whistles. He or she gesticulates, draws, writes, demonstrates activities, or points to board.

Gives Directions

Verbal (6).   Teacher gives directions or orders that will result in immediate observable student response.

Nonverbal (16).   Teacher points with head, beckons with head, yells commands, points finger, blows whistle, or pushes a student in a given direction.

Criticizes or Justifies Authority

Verbal (7).   Teacher provides a negative value assessment; he or she criticizes, expresses anger or distrust, or uses sarcasm or extreme self-reference.

Nonverbal (17).   Teacher grimaces, growls, frowns, drops head, throws head back in derisive laughter, rolls eyes, spits, or shakes head. He or she hits, pushes away, pinches, grapples with student, pushes hands at student, bangs table or wall, damages equipment, or throws things down.

Student Behaviors

Student Predictable Response

Verbal (8).   Student response entirely predictable, such as obedience to orders and responses not requiring thinking beyond the comprehension phase of knowledge.

Nonverbal (18).   Poker-face response; student nods or shakes head or gives small grunts or a quick smile. Student moves mechanically to questions or directions, responds to any action with minimal nervous activity, is robotlike, follows rote practice drills, waits in line, or raises hand in response to teacher direction.

Student Interpretive Behavior

Verbal (8\).   Predictable student response that requires some measure of evaluation, synthesis, and interpretation from the student. The initial behavior is in response to teacher initiation, that is, student interpretation from teacher in discussed activity, or student questioning that relates strictly to topic under discussion.

Nonverbal (18\).   Student shows look of thinking, or pensive, formal expressions. He or she interprets movements, tries to show some arrangement that requires interpretive thinking, works on gymnastic routine, takes a test, or interprets task cards or game play. Student puts hand in air to give answer to teacher's question.

Student Initiative Behavior

Verbal (9).   Student-initiated talk that is unpredictable. This talk could be either positive or negative.

Nonverbal (19).   Student makes interrupting sounds, gasps, sighs; puts hands in air to ask unsolicited question of teacher; or gets up and walks around without provocation. Student begins creative movement education, makes up own games or movements, shows initiative in supportive movement, or introduces new movements into games not predictable in the rules of the games.

Other Behaviors

Confusion or Silence

Verbal (10). Periods of confusion in which communication cannot be understood by the observer. Student-to-student verbal interaction that cannot be understood or that happens during activity.

Nonverbal (20). Pauses or short periods of silence; students noiselessly awaiting teacher just prior to teacher entry; student-to-student nonverbal interaction, such as when students are participating with other students silently in a drill or game play.

RECORDING PROCEDURES

Observers record numerical symbols of the appropriate behavior in order of occurrence. This is sometimes referred to as spontaneous event recording. A time limitation of 3 seconds is placed on extended behaviors, but the recorder codes all behaviors that are observable. CAFIAS permits the coding of teaching behavior either in live educational settings or from a videotaped lesson. A completed recording sheet is shown in Figure 8.1.

SUMMARIZING AND INTERPRETING THE DATA

Each tally recorded by the coder is transferred to a 20-by-20 matrix. The data are presented in the frequency counts of each CAFIAS category, as well as percentages and ratios of each CAFIAS parameter and the patterns of interaction between teacher and students and among students. The data may be calculated manually or with a computer. Figure 8.2 is a completed CAFIAS matrix. The data collected from the coding of CAFIAS are entered into the computer for analysis. The computer compiles the raw data into frequency counts, ratios, and percentages for all the parameters of CAFIAS. The data are presented in three major components.

The Use of Each CAFIAS Category

This will tell us the number of each CAFIAS category usage and the percentage of the specific category usage in the lesson observed.

Teacher _Jones_ _____ Observer _Smith_ _____
Class _Badminton_ _____ Date _4/25_ _____
School _Central_ _____ Time: _10 a.m._ _____

1. 20W	21. 5	41. 8	61. 18	81. 18
2. 5	22. (5)	42. 2	62. 18	82. 18
3. 5	23. (5)	43. 4	63. 18	83. 18
4. 5	24. (5)	44. 8	64. 18	84. 18
5. 5	25. 5	45. 2	65. 18	85. 6
6. 5	26. 5	46. 4	66. 18	86. 18
7. 5	27. 5	47. 8	67. 18	87. 5
8. 5	28. 4	48. 2	68. 18	88. 5
9. 5	29. 8	49. 6	69. 18	89. 5
10. 5	30. 2	50. 18	70. 18	90. 5
11. 5	31. 4	51. 18	71. 18	91. 5
12. 5	32. 8	52. 18	72. 18	92. 5
13. 5	33. 2	53. 18	73. 18	93. 5
14. 5	34. 4	54. 18	74. 18	94. 5
15. 5	35. 8	55. 18	75. 18	95. 5
16. 5	36. 2	56. 18	76. 18	96. 5
17. 5	37. 4	57. 18	77. 18	97. 5
18. 5	38. 8	58. 18	78. 18	98. 5
19. 5	39. 2	59. 18	79. 18	99. 5
20. 5	40. 4	60. 18	80. 18	100. 20

Figure 8.1 Completed Cheffers' Adaptation of the Flanders' Interaction Analysis System (CAFIAS) recording sheet.

Patterns of Interaction
Between Teacher and Students and Among Students

The top 10 cell frequencies for the lesson are studied. The density of tallies in cells determines not only the predominant teacher and student behaviors but also the sequence of those behaviors. The use of a matrix permits the determination of patterns of interaction, which in turn permits succinct and objective descriptions of the patterns of interaction in each class.

Major CAFIAS Parameters in Percentages and Ratios

The following are the major CAFIAS parameters studied for interpretation.

Teacher __Jones__   Grade __Junior High__
Class __Badminton__   Setting __Gymnasium__
No. __Ⓖ, B, Coed__   Time __10 a.m.__

	2	12	3	13	4	14	5	15	6	16	7	17	8	18	8\	18\	9	19	10	20
2	4	2		5			5	3	3	1				6	3	14	1	1		
12	2	2			2		1	1	2	1				2	1	1				
3	1				4	1	5	4	2					1	1	8				1
13					4		2	2						2	1	1				
4						2	1		1				4	4	31	9	1	1		3
14													1		1					
5	1	1			8	11	9	5						8	2	11				
15					8	10	9	2						5	2	4				
6					1	1								26	1	1				
16														7						
7	3																			
17																				
8	1				3															
18	9	5		5	7		9	5	11	5	1			6	4	5				3
8\	6	2	15	2	12		6	5	2	1	1			1	2	5			9	
18\	13		12	3	8		9	3	4		2			1	3	14			9	5
9			2	1																
19			2	1																
10															9	9				
20					2										3	1	6			
Teacher	40	12	31	12	65	2	59	42	33	8	4	0	5	72	62	88	2	2	18	12
Environ.	0	0	0	0	0	0	0	0	0	0	0	0	0	0	0	0	0	0	0	0
Student	0	0	0	0	0	0	0	0	0	0	0	0	0	0	0	0	0	0	0	0
Total	40	12	31	12	65	2	59	42	33	8	4	0	5	72	62	88	2	2	18	12
Percent	7.0	2.1	5.4	2.1	11.4	0.4	10.4	7.4	5.8	1.4	0.7	0.0	0.9	12.7	0.9	15.5	0.4	0.4	3.2	2.1

Figure 8.2 Completed Cheffers' Adaptation of the Flanders' Interaction Analysis System (CAFIAS) matrix.

Teacher Contribution, Verbal (TCV). This involves all teacher verbal behaviors observed during the coding period, including praise, acceptance, questions, lecturing, directions, criticism, and empathy. For numerical calculations, all tallies recorded for Categories 2, 3, 4, 5, 6, and 7 are added together.

Teacher Contribution, Nonverbal (TCNV). This involves all teacher nonverbal behaviors observed during the coding period, including praise, acceptance, questions, lecturing, directions, criticism, and empathy. For numerical calculations, all tallies recorded for Categories 12, 13, 14, 15, 16, and 17 are added together.

Total Teacher Contribution (TTC). This involves all teacher behaviors observed during the coding period, verbal and nonverbal, including praise, acceptance, questions, lecturing, directions, criticism, and empathy. For numerical calculations, all tallies recorded for Categories 2, 12, 3, 13, 4, 14, 5, 15, 6, 16, 7, and 17 are added together.

Student Contribution, Verbal (SCV). This is all student verbal behaviors observed during the coding period, including rote (expected or automatic manner) predictable responses, interpretative or evaluative responses, and student-initiated unexpected or unpredictable behavior. For numerical calculations, all tallies recorded for Categories 8, 8\, and 9 are added together.

Student Contribution, Nonverbal (SCNV). This refers to all student nonverbal behaviors observed during the coding period, including rote predictable responses, interpretative or evaluative responses, and student-initiated unexpected or unpredictable behavior. For numerical calculations, all tallies recorded for Categories 18, 18\, and 19 are added together.

Total Student Contribution (TSC). TSC includes all student behavior, verbal and nonverbal, observed during the coding period, including rote predictable responses, interpretive or evaluative responses, and student-initiated unexpected or unpredictable behavior. For numerical calculations, all tallies recorded for Categories 8, 18, 8\, 18\, 9, and 19 are added together.

Silence (S). This parameter refers to each 3-second period of silence during the observation. For numerical calculations, all tallies recorded in Category 20 are added together.

Confusion (C). This parameter refers to each 3-second period during the observation when there is confusion. For numerical calculations, all tallies recorded in Category 10 are added together.

Total Silence and/or Confusion (TSC). This parameter refers to each 3-second period during the observation when there is silence, confusion, or anything other than student or teacher talk. For numerical calculations, all tallies recorded for Categories 10 and 20 are added together.

Teacher Use of Questioning, Verbal (TQRV). The verbal questions of the teacher are compared to verbal lecturing behaviors. The numerical calculation is as follows:

$$\frac{4}{4+5}$$

Teacher Use of Questioning, Nonverbal (TQRNV).   The nonverbal questions of the teacher are compared to nonverbal lecturing behaviors. The numerical calculation is as follows:

$$\frac{14}{14 + 15}$$

Total Teacher Use of Questioning (TTQR).   The verbal and nonverbal questions of the teacher are compared to verbal and nonverbal lecturing behaviors. The numerical calculation is as follows:

$$\frac{4 + 14}{4 + 14 + 5 + 15}$$

Teacher Use of Acceptance and Praise, Verbal (TAPRV).   The teacher's verbal use of acceptance, praise, encouragement, and empathy is compared to verbal use of direction and criticism. The numerical calculation is as follows:

$$\frac{2 + 3}{2 + 3 + 6 + 7}$$

Teacher Use of Acceptance and Praise, Nonverbal (TAPRNV).   The teacher's nonverbal use of acceptance, praise, encouragement, and empathy is compared to nonverbal use of direction and criticism. The numerical calculation is as follows:

$$\frac{12 + 13}{12 + 13 + 16 + 17}$$

Total Teacher Use of Acceptance and Praise (TTAPR).   The teacher's verbal and nonverbal use of acceptance, praise, encouragement, and empathy is compared to verbal and nonverbal use of direction and criticism. The numerical calculation is as follows:

$$\frac{2 + 12 + 3 + 13}{2 + 12 + 3 + 13 + 6 + 16 + 7 + 17}$$

Student Verbal Narrow Dependence (SVNDR).   The rote, predictable verbal responses are compared to all student verbal behaviors. The numerical calculation is as follows:

$$\frac{8}{8 + 8 + 9}$$

Student Nonverbal Narrow Dependence (SNVNDR).   The rote, predictable nonverbal responses are compared to all student nonverbal behaviors. The numerical calculation is as follows:

$$\frac{18}{18 + 18 + 19}$$

Total Student Narrow Dependence (TSNDR).   All student verbal and non-verbal rote, predictable responses are compared to all student verbal and nonverbal behaviors. The numerical calculation is as follows:

$$\frac{8 + 18}{8 + 18 + 8\backslash + 18\backslash + 9 + 19}$$

Student Verbal Interpretation (SVIR).   The interpretive or evaluative verbal responses are compared to all student verbal behaviors. The numerical calculation is as follows:

$$\frac{8\backslash}{8 + 8\backslash + 9}$$

Student Nonverbal Interpretation (NVIR).   The interpretive or evaluative nonverbal responses are compared to all student nonverbal behaviors. The numerical calculation is as follows:

$$\frac{18\backslash}{18 + 18\backslash + 19}$$

Total Student Interpretation (TSIR).   All student verbal and nonverbal interpretive responses are compared to all student behaviors. The numerical calculation is as follows:

$$\frac{8\backslash + 18\backslash}{8 + 18 + 8\backslash + 18 + 9 + 19}$$

Total Student Verbal Dependent (TSVDR).   The rote, predictable verbal and the interpretive or evaluative verbal responses are compared to all student verbal behaviors. The numerical calculation is as follows:

$$\frac{8 + 8\backslash}{8 + 8\backslash + 9}$$

Total Student Nonverbal Dependent (TSNVDR).   The rote, predictable nonverbal and the interpretive or evaluative nonverbal responses are compared to all student nonverbal behaviors. The numerical calculation is as follows:

$$\frac{18 + 18\backslash}{18 + 18\backslash + 19}$$

Total Student Dependent (TSDR).   All student verbal and nonverbal rote, predictable responses and the interpretive or evaluative responses are compared to all student verbal and nonverbal behaviors. The numerical calculation is as follows:

$$\frac{8 + 18 + 8\backslash + 18\backslash}{8 + 18 + 8\backslash + 18\backslash + 9 + 19}$$

Student Verbal Initiation, Teacher Suggested (SVITSR).   The interpretive or evaluative student verbal responses and the unexpected or unpredictable verbal student behaviors are compared to all student verbal behaviors. The numerical calculation is as follows:

$$\frac{8\!\!\backslash\ + 9}{8 + 8\!\!\backslash\ + 9}$$

Student Nonverbal Initiation, Teacher Suggested (SNVITSR).   The interpretive or evaluative student nonverbal responses and the unexpected or unpredictable nonverbal student behaviors are compared to all student nonverbal behaviors. The numerical calculation is as follows:

$$\frac{18\!\!\backslash\ + 19}{18 + 18\!\!\backslash\ + 19}$$

Total Student Initiation, Teacher Suggested (TSITSR).   All student verbal and nonverbal interpretive or evaluative responses and their unexpected or unpredictable behaviors are compared to all student verbal and nonverbal behaviors. The numerical calculation is as follows:

$$\frac{8\!\!\backslash\ + 18 + 9 + 19}{8 + 18 + 8\!\!\backslash\ + 18\!\!\backslash\ + 9 + 19}$$

Student Verbal Initiation, Student Suggested (SVISSR).   The unexpected or unpredictable self-initiated student verbal behaviors are compared to all student verbal behaviors. The numerical calculation is as follows:

$$\frac{9}{8 + 8\!\!\backslash\ + 9}$$

Student Nonverbal Initiation, Student Suggested (SNVISSR).   The unexpected or unpredictable self-initiated student nonverbal behaviors are compared to all student nonverbal behaviors. The numerical calculation is as follows:

$$\frac{19}{18 + 18\!\!\backslash\ + 19}$$

Total Student Initiation, Student Suggested (TSISSR).   All student verbal and nonverbal unexpected or unpredictable self-initiated student behaviors are compared to all student verbal and nonverbal behaviors. The numerical calculation is as follows:

$$\frac{9 + 19}{8 + 18 + 8\!\!\backslash\ + 18\!\!\backslash\ + 9 + 19}$$

Content Emphasis-Teacher Input (CETI).   This is the amount of class time that the teacher devotes to subject matter. For numerical calculation, all tallies in Categories 4, 14, 5, and 15 rows and columns are added together, with steady state cells counted one time only. This total is divided by the total matrix tally count.

Content Emphasis-Student Input (CESI).   All tallies in 8\ and 18\ rows and columns are summed with the steady state cell counted but once. This total is divided by the total matrix tally count.

Teacher as Teacher (TT).   The amount of class time during which the teacher is the teaching agent.

Other Students as Teacher (ST).   The amount of class time during which one (or more) of the students is the teaching agent.

The Environment as Teacher (ET).   The amount of class time during which the environment (e.g., book, film, piece of equipment, etc.) is the teaching agent.

Verbal Emphasis (VE).   All behaviors during the class that are expressed verbally. For numerical calculations, all tallies in Categories 2, 3, 4, 5, 6, 7, 8, 8\, and 9 are added together.

Nonverbal Emphasis (NV).   All observable behaviors during the class that are not expressed verbally. For numerical calculation, all tallies in Categories 12, 13, 14, 15, 16, 17, 18, 18\, and 19 are added together.

Class Structure as One Unit (W).   The amount of class time during which the class is structured to function as a whole unit.

Class Structure as Groups of Individuals (P).   The amount of class time during which the class is structured so that the students work in groups or as individuals.

Class Structure With No Teacher Influence (I).   The amount of class time during which the teacher has no influence over the class (e.g., teacher is talking with another teacher, answering the phone, correcting work at the table, hanging posters, etc.).

Teacher Empathy to Student Emotions (TE).   The number of times during the class when the teacher was empathetic in response to an emotional pupil behavior. For numerical calculation, all tallies in Categories 1 and 11 are added together. This is a frequency count. Percentage descriptions can be obtained by summing tallies in these various ratios, dividing them by the total matrix tally count, and multiplying by 100.

Percentage descriptions can be obtained by summing the tallies in these variations, having them divided by the total matrix tally count, and multiplying by 100.

CAFIAS provides researchers, teachers, and coaches with information about the occurrence of specific behaviors, interaction patterns, and ratios of various types of behaviors. This information permits the description of moment-to-moment events in the gymnasium and in coaching environments as well as serving as a basis for changing and monitoring teachers' and coaches' behaviors.

REFERENCE

Cheffers, J.T.F. (1972). *The validation of an instrument designed to expand the Flanders' system of interaction analysis to describe nonverbal interaction, different varieties of teacher behavior and pupil response.* Unpublished doctoral dissertation, Temple University, Philadelphia.

RELATED REFERENCES

Agnew, M. (1977). *Comparison of female teaching and coaching behaviors in secondary schools.* Unpublished master's thesis, Ithaca College, Ithaca, NY.

Batchelder, A. (1975). *Process objectives, observed behaviors, and teaching patterns in elementary math, English, and physical education classes.* Unpublished doctoral dissertation, Boston University, MA.

Batchelder, A., & Cheffers, J. (1976, July). *CAFIAS: An interaction analysis instrument for describing student-teacher behaviors in different learning settings.* Paper presented at the International Congress for Physical Activity Sciences, Quebec City, Ontario, Canada.

Batchelder, A., & Keane, F. (1979). BAKE: An analysis of lecture in the college classroom. *The Journal of Classroom Interaction,* **14**(2), 33-34.

Bechtold, W. (1976). *The study of the effect of tutorial relationships between volunteer high school students and moderate retarded peer-aged students participating in individually prescribed physical education programs.* Unpublished doctoral dissertation, Boston University, MA.

Cheffers, J. (1972). *The validation of an instrument designed to expand the Flanders' system of interaction analysis to describe non-verbal interaction, different varieties of teacher behavior and pupil response.* Unpublished doctoral dissertation, Temple University, Philadelphia, PA.

Cheffers, J.T.F., & Mancini, V.H. (1978). Teacher-student interaction. In W.G. Anderson & G.T. Banette (Eds.), *What's going on in gym: Descriptive studies of physical education classes* (pp. 39-50, Monograph No. 1). Newtown, CT: Motor Skills: Theory into Practice.

Devlin, G.L., Mancini, V.H., & Frye, P.A. (1980, April). *Teaching contingency management skills to disruptive elementary students: Its effect on student self-concept and student influence on physical educators' behaviors.* Paper presented at the American Alliance for Health, Physical Education, Recreation and Dance National Convention, Detroit.

Fisher, A.C., Mancini, V.H., Hirsch, R.L., Proulx, T., & Staurowsky, E.J. (1982). Coach-athlete interactions and team climate. *Journal of Sport Psychology*, **4**, 388-404.

Frye, P.A., Furey, J., & Mancini, V.H. (1982, April). *A comparison of interaction behavior patterns in elementary physical education classes differing in attitude toward physical education*. Paper presented at the American Alliance for Health, Physical Education, Recreation and Dance National Convention, Houston, TX.

Griec, J., Mancini, V.H., & Wuest, D.A. (1984, March). *Lasting effects of supervision using interaction analysis on inservice physical educators and their students' Academic Learning Time-Physical Education*. Paper presented at the American Alliance for Health, Physical Education, Recreation and Dance National Convention, Anaheim, CA.

Hayes, J.E. (1978). *The effects of three teaching styles on the acquisition of badminton skills and knowledge*. Unpublished master's thesis, Ithaca College, Ithaca, NY.

Hendrickson, C.E., Mancini, V.H., Morris, H.H., & Fisher, A.C. (1976, April). *Interaction analysis of preservice physical educators' teaching behavior*. Paper presented at the American Alliance for Health, Physical Education, and Recreation Convention, Milwaukee.

Hope, D.M. (1978). *The development and evaluation of recreation programs and their effect upon morale and functioning of elderly nursing home residents*. Unpublished doctoral dissertation, Boston University, MA.

Keane, F.J. (1976). *The relationship of sex, teacher leadership style, and teacher leader behavior in teacher-student interaction*. Unpublished doctoral dissertation, Boston University, MA.

Kenyon, D.L. (1981). *A comparison of coaching behaviors of physical educators and non-physical educators*. Unpublished master's thesis, Ithaca College, Ithaca, NY.

Lydon, M. (1978). *Decision-making in elementary school-age children: Effects of a convergent curriculum model upon motor skill development, self-concept and group interaction*. Unpublished doctoral dissertation, Boston University, MA.

Lombardo, B.J. (1979). *The observation and description of the teaching and behavioral interaction of selected physical education teachers*. Unpublished doctoral dissertation, Boston University, MA.

Mancini, V.H. (1974). *A comparison of two decision-making models in an elementary human movement program based on attitudes and interaction patterns*. Unpublished doctoral dissertation, Boston University, MA.

Mancini, V.H., & Avery, D.E. (1980, April). *Interaction patterns of effective coaches*. Paper presented at the American Alliance for Health, Physical Education, Recreation and Dance National Convention, Detroit.

Mancini, V.H., Cheffers, J.T.F., & Zaichkowsky, L.D. (1975). Decision making in elementary children: Effects on attitudes and interaction patterns. *Research Quarterly*, **46**, 420-426.

Mancini, V.H., Frye, P.A., & Quinn, P.A. (1982). Long term effects of instruction and supervision in interaction analysis on teacher behavior effectiveness and attitudes of inservice physical educators. In M. Piernon & J.T.F. Cheffers (Eds.), *Studying the teaching in physical education* (pp. 179-188). Leige, Belgium: Association Internationale des Ecoles Superieures d'Education Physique (AIESEP).

Mancini, V.H., Getty, H.L., & Morris, H.H. (1979, July). *The effects of instruction and supervision in interaction analysis on the teaching behavior and effectiveness of student teachers*. Paper presented at the International Conference for Health, Physical Education, and Recreation, World Congress Kiel International Conference, Kiel, Germany.

Mancini, V.H., Goss, J., & Frye, P.A. (1982, April). *Relationships of interaction behavior patterns of student teachers and their cooperating teachers*. Paper presented at the American Alliance for Health, Physical Education, Recreation and Dance National Convention, Houston, TX.

Mancini, V.H., Inturrisi, E., & Frye, P.A. (1979, March). *The use of interaction analysis: Its effects on attitudes and teaching behaviors of student teachers*. Paper presented at the American Association for Health, Physical Education, Recreation and Dance Convention, New Orleans.

Mancini, V.H., Rochester, D.A., & Morris, H.H. (1977, March). *The effects of supervision and instruction in the use of interaction analysis on the teaching behavior of preservice teachers*. Paper presented at the American Association for Health, Physical Education, and Recreation Convention, Seattle.

Mancini, V.H., Wuest, D.A., Cheffers, J.T.F., & Rich, S.M. (1983). Promoting student involvement by sharing decisions. *International Journal of Physical Education*, **20**(3), 16-23.

Mancini, V.H., Wuest, D.A., Clark, E.K., & Ridosh, N. (1983). A comparison of the interaction patterns and academic learning time of low- and high-burnout secondary physical educators. In T. Templin & A. Olsen (Eds.), *Teaching in physical education* (pp. 197-208). Champaign, IL: Human Kinetics.

Mancini, V.H., Wuest, D.A., & Craven, J. (1984, April). *A comparison of the teaching behaviors of low- and high-burnout elementary physical education teachers*. Paper presented at the American Alliance for Health, Physical Education, Recreation and Dance National Convention, Cincinnati, OH.

Mancini, V.H., Wuest, D.A., & van der Mars, H. (1985). Use of instruction and supervision in systematic observation during undergraduate professional preparation. *Journal of Teaching in Physical Education*, **4**(5), 22-33.

Mancini, V.H., Wuest, D.A., Vantine, W.K., & Clark, E.K. (1984). Effects of instruction and supervision in interaction analysis on burned-out physical educators' teaching behavior, level of burnout, and their students' academic learning time. *Journal of Teaching in Physical Education, 3*(2), 29-46.

Martinek, T.J., & Johnson, S.B. (1979). Teacher expectations: Effects on dyadic interactions and self-concept in elementary age children. *Research Quarterly, 50*(1), 60-70.

Martinek, T.J., & Mancini, V.H. (1979). CAFIAS: Observing dyadic interaction between teacher and student. *The Journal of Classroom Interaction, 14*(2), 18-23.

Martinek, T., Zaichkowsky, L., & Cheffers, J.T.F. (1977). Decision-making in elementary children: Effects on self-concept and motor skills. *Research Quarterly, 48*, 350-357.

Mawdsley, R.H. (1977). *Comparison of teacher behaviors in regular and adapted movement classes*. Unpublished doctoral dissertation, Boston University, MA.

Reisenweaver, P.J., Mancini, V.H., & Frye, P.A. (1981, April). *Teaching interaction patterns of secondary female physical educators with high-skilled and low-skilled students*. Paper presented at the American Alliance for Health, Physical Education, Recreation and Dance Convention, Boston.

Rich, S.M., Mancini, V.H., Sherrill, C., & Frye, P.A. (1983, November). *Teaching behaviors in physical education classes for the handicapped*. Paper presented at the Third International Symposium of Adapted Activities, New Orleans.

Rich, S.A., Wuest, D.A., & Mancini, V.H. (1988). CAFIAS: A systematic observation tool to improve teaching behaviors of preservice physical education. In C. Sherrill (Ed.), *Foundations of adapted physical education teacher training* (pp. 373-378). Champaign, IL: Human Kinetics.

Rotsko, A. (1979). *A comparison of coaching behaviors of successful and less successful coaches*. Unpublished master's thesis, Ithaca College, Ithaca, NY.

Savitz, J. (1982). *Comparison of interaction behavior patterns of males and females coaching women's basketball teams*. Unpublished master's thesis, Ithaca College, Ithaca, NY.

Sciera, J.R. (1983). *Interaction behavior patterns of college football coaches during various phases of the football season*. Unpublished master's thesis, Ithaca College, Ithaca, NY.

Scriber, K., Mancini, V.H., & Wuest, D.A. (1984, March). *The relationship between perceived teaching behaviors and actual teaching behaviors of school health educators*. Paper presented at the American Alliance for Health, Physical Education, Recreation and Dance National Convention, Anaheim, CA.

Steffen, M.M., Mancini, V.H., & Wuest, D.A. (1983, April). *Effects of instruction and supervision in interaction analysis on teaching behaviors exhibited by elementary school physical educators toward disruptive children*. Paper presented at the American Alliance for Health, Physical Education, Recreation and Dance National Convention, Minneapolis, MN.

Stevens, M.E., Mancini, V.H., & Frye, P.A. (1981, April). *Effects of instruction and supervision in interaction analysis on the teaching behavior of selected physical education teachers*. Paper presented at the American Alliance for Health, Physical Education, Recreation and Dance National Convention, Boston.

Streeter, B., Mancini, V.H., & Frye, P.A. (1981, April). *Interaction behavior patterns of male secondary physical educators with high-skilled and low-skilled students*. Paper presented at the American Alliance for Health, Physical Education, Recreation and Dance National Convention, Boston.

Underwood, T.E. (1979). *A comparison of interaction patterns of high-anxiety and low-anxiety student teachers*. Unpublished master's thesis, Ithaca College, Ithaca, NY.

van der Mars, H., Mancini, V.H., & Frye, P.A. (1981). The effects of interaction analysis training on perceived and observed physical education teaching behavior. *Journal of Teaching in Physical Education* (Introductory Issue), 57-65.

Vogel, R. (1976). *Effects of instruction and supervision in Cheffers' adaptation of Flanders' interaction analysis system on the teaching behavior of student teachers*. Unpublished master's thesis, Ithaca College, Ithaca, NY.

Wood, D. (1978). *Adventure-education through participant observation and interaction analysis*. Unpublished doctoral dissertation, Boston University, MA.

□ *Chapter 9*

CAFIAS Supervisory Feedback Instrument (CSFI)

Deborah A. Wuest
Victor H. Mancini

The CAFIAS Supervisory Feedback Instrument (CSFI) was designed to assist supervisors of in-service and preservice teachers to provide immediate feedback concerning the behaviors exhibited during instruction. The CSFI permits supervisors to provide teachers with feedback concerning the type and frequency of behaviors exhibited immediately following the conclusion of the instructional session, without waiting for the computer analysis of the data. The procedures used with the CSFI are also easier for beginning observers to use for a variety of purposes.

The CSFI is derived from Cheffers' Adaptation of Flanders' Interaction Analysis System (Cheffers, 1983). Several modifications in coding procedures have been made to facilitate its use:

- The number of behavior categories are reduced by combining verbal and nonverbal behaviors and by eliminating the circling of behaviors when both verbal and nonverbal behaviors occur (e.g., 5 + 15, as opposed to writing 5 and then a 15 on the CAFIAS coding sheet).
- New categories were developed to provide for coding various types of student-to-student interaction.
- The observation interval was extended from 3 to 5 seconds. This allows the observer more time to make decisions regarding the type of behavior that occurred.
- A tally is placed in the appropriate box rather than recording the specific CAFIAS category code. This makes the coding process faster.
- The observation sheet is divided into time periods to make it easier for the observer to keep track of the time. Information is then also available about the timing of behaviors, such as the predominant use of information in the early part of the instructional session and the dominance of student interpretive behaviors in the latter part of the session.
- Information regarding the type and frequency of behaviors is hand calculated as opposed to using the computer for analysis.

The CSFI is not without limitations. Information about the sequence of behaviors (i.e., the interaction patterns) is not available because computer analysis or the hand-calculated matrix is not used. Additionally, information about major CAFIAS parameters, such as the ratio of teacher use of acceptance to praise, is not immediately available as it would be with computer analysis. However, the CSFI does meet the objective of providing immediate feedback about teaching behaviors.

CATEGORY DESCRIPTIONS

The CSFI categories are derived from CAFIAS. Unlike CAFIAS, which has specific verbal and nonverbal behavior categories, the CSFI combines both verbal and nonverbal behaviors. The categories for teacher behaviors are the same as those for CAFIAS. The student behaviors are the same as in CAFIAS; however, three categories have been added in an effort to help the observer more easily code the various types of student-to-student interactions that occur in an instructional session. The CSFI categories, with the appropriate codes noted in parentheses, are listed here.

Teacher Behaviors

Praise (2 + 12)

Teacher praises or encourages student behaviors, actions, ideas, and efforts.

Acceptance (3 + 13)

Teacher accepts student behaviors, clarifies or builds upon their ideas, and participates with students during an activity.

Asks Questions (4 + 14)

Teacher asks questions about content or procedures that require students to answer.

Lectures (5 + 15)

Teacher lectures, demonstrates, and relates information to students.

Gives Direction (6 + 16)

Teacher gives directions or commands that result in immediate student response.

Criticizes (7 + 17)

Teacher criticizes student behaviors, expresses anger or sarcasm, and uses statements to change student behavior from nonacceptable to acceptable standards.

Student Behaviors

Student Predictable Response (8 + 18)

Student responses that are predictable. *Example:* Student obeys orders or participates in mechanical practice drills.

Student-to-Student Predictable Interaction (88)

Extended student-to-student interaction in a predictable manner. *Example:* Students work together as part of a skill drill. (In CAFIAS, this would have been coded as 8-10-8.)

Student Interpretive Behavior (8\ + 18\)

Predictable student responses that require some measure of evaluation, synthesis, and interpretation from the student. Student interprets movements, game playing, or working from a task card.

Student-to-Student Interpretive Interaction (89)

Extended student-to-student interaction involving interpretive activities. *Examples:* Game playing or scrimmaging. (In CAFIAS, these would have been coded as 8\-10-8\.)

Student Initiative Behavior (9 + 19)

Student initiates behavior, such as making up own game or movements or contributing his or her own ideas. This behavior arises from the student's own initiation and is not in response to teacher's behavior. This behavior may be positive (e.g., offering a novel solution to a movement problem) or negative (e.g., expressing off-task behavior or creating disciplinary problems) in nature.

Student-to-Student Initiative Behavior (99)

Extended student-to-student initiative behavior. *Examples*: Students work together independently or involve each other in off-task or disruptive behavior that may go on for a period of time. (In CAFIAS, this would have been coded as 9-10-9.)

Other Behaviors

Confusion or Silence (10/20)

Periods of confusion or disorder. *Example:* Students enter the gym as class is starting. Periods of silence. *Example:* Students sit silently and wait for the class to begin.

RECORDING PROCEDURES

Most of the CAFIAS ground rules are observed for the CSFI. However, several changes in the coding procedures have been made to facilitate coding (Figure 9.1). A tally is placed in the appropriate column every 5 seconds or every change in behaviors; if more than one behavior occurs at the same time the dominant behavior is recorded. Both verbal and nonverbal behaviors are included in the same category.

The coding sheet is divided into 1-minute intervals; because the coding sheet only accommodates 15 minutes, several sheets may be necessary. Brief notes can also be recorded regarding the structure of the class and class activities. The CSFI assumes that the teacher is the predominant teaching agent. When a student or the environment is the teaching agent, then an *s* or an *e*, respectively, is entered in the appropriate column in lieu of the tally.

Coding is also easier because verbal and nonverbal behaviors are combined into a single category. Additionally, the use of three categories to record various types of student-to-student interaction speeds up the coding process while reducing confusion for the coder. For example, according to CAFIAS coding conventions, student-to-student interpretive interaction, or game play, would be coded 8\-10-8\, requiring the observer to enter three coding symbols on the coding sheet. With the CSFI only one tally is entered in the appropriate column on the coding sheet; the CSFI codes student-to-student interpretive interaction as 89.

CAFIAS Supervisory Feedback Instrument (CSFI)

Directions: Place a tally mark (•) in the appropriate column of the behaviors observed. Record a tally every 5 seconds or for every change in behaviors.

Name _____ Date _____

Class/practice no._____ Length _____

	Teacher behaviors (2-17)						Student behaviors (8-99)					Other
Time	2+12	3+13	4+14	5+15	6+16	7+17	8+18	88	8\+18\	89	9+19	99	10/20
0-59													
1-1:59													
2-2:59													
3-3:59													
4-4:59													
5-5:59													
6-6:59													
7-7:59													
8-8:59													
9-9:59													
10-10:59													
11-11:59													
12-12:59													
13-13:59													
14-14:59														Total
Total													
Percent														100

Figure 9.1 CAFIAS Supervisory Feedback Instrument (CSFI) recording sheet.

SUMMARIZING AND INTERPRETING THE DATA

Following the conclusion of the observation session, the data are summarized. The tallies entered in each column are totaled and recorded in the space provided. Tally totals from all coding sheets are placed on the last coding sheet used. The total number of tallies recorded for each category are added, and the total tallies recorded for the session are recorded in the appropriate space. Percentages for each category are calculated.

The CSFI yields information about the percentages of behaviors exhibited by the teacher and students. Its greatest strength is that it allows the supervisor to provide the teacher with immediate feedback about his or her teaching behaviors. The CSFI can also be used by student teacher supervisors and in the coaching environment. The CSFI has been used by peers to provide preservice teachers with immediate feedback about their teaching. Its streamlined coding procedures and immediacy of feedback make the CSFI a valuable supervisory instrument.

REFERENCE

Cheffers, J.T.F. (1983). Cheffers' Adaptation of the Flanders' Interaction Analysis System (CAFIAS). In P.W. Darst, V.H. Mancini, & D.B. Zakrajsek (Eds.), *Systematic observation instrumentation for physical education* (pp. 76-95). Champaign, IL: Leisure Press.

Chapter 10

Self-Assessment Feedback Instrument (SAFI)

Victor H. Mancini
Deborah A. Wuest

Self-evaluation instruments based on systematic observation techniques provide teachers and coaches aspiring to improve their effectiveness with a means of quantifying their behaviors relative to their specific concerns. Information generated from such instruments is used to help determine areas of improvement, set personal goals, and monitor one's progress toward their attainment.

One concern relative to the process of self-evaluation is that it can be time-consuming. Most teachers and coaches are already hard-pressed to fulfill their myriad responsibilities. Moreover, teachers and coaches, although recognizing the need for self-evaluation, may believe they lack the time to learn how to use systematic observation instruments. Yet, time spent on self-evaluation may yield large dividends. For example, coaches spend hours analyzing films of athletes' game performances, yet they rarely spend time videotaping themselves and analyzing their own practice behaviors (Mancini & Wuest, 1987). Self-analysis through directed observations can contribute measurably to the improvement of instructional effectiveness (Mancini, Wuest, & van der Mars, 1985).

The Self-Assessment Feedback Instrument (SAFI) was designed as a self-evaluation instrument that can be easily used by teachers and coaches to identify the manner in which they give feedback during instruction. A modification of Cheffers' Adaptation of Flanders' Interaction Analysis System (CAFIAS) (Cheffers, 1983), the SAFI allows teachers and coaches to monitor both the type and the frequency of feedback they provide either during or following physical performance. The SAFI offers teachers and coaches a simple, yet effective, means to become more aware of their behaviors without the time-consuming process of learning the intricacies of CAFIAS and mastering the computer analysis. To use the SAFI, teachers and coaches must only become familiar with the various CAFIAS categories, such as praise, and be able to recognize certain sequences of behavior, such as praise followed by information.

To use the SAFI, the teacher or coach should audiotape or videotape the instructional session. The tape is then reviewed, and the SAFI is used by the teacher or coach to code the behaviors exhibited. The SAFI is also used by other individuals to assist teachers and coaches to become more cognizant of the various behaviors they are exhibiting. However, having teachers or coaches analyze tapes of their own instruction using SAFI is less threatening than allowing other individuals to view their instructional endeavors. Additionally, the process of actually reviewing their instructional endeavors and personally coding may in and of itself contribute to their awareness of their behaviors (Mancini et al., 1985).

CATEGORY DESCRIPTIONS

The SAFI categories are derived from the various CAFIAS behaviors and common sequences of behaviors or interaction patterns. The CAFIAS categories and their descriptions are listed in chapter 8. The focus of the SAFI is limited to feedback provided either during or following physical performance. There are 12 categories, 11 of which are related to CAFIAS and one for which the teacher or coach can record behaviors of interest, such as the use of names. The 11 categories related to CAFIAS encompass both verbal and nonverbal behaviors. These 11 categories, the corresponding CAFIAS code(s), a description of the behaviors, and an illustration of each category are listed here.

Praise (2)

Teacher praises and encourages efforts, actions, and behaviors. *Example:* "Good job!"

Praise/Reinstruct (2-5)

Teacher praises and encourages efforts, actions, and behaviors and then provides information. *Examples:* "Good job!" "A longer step on your follow-through will help you."

Acceptance (3)

Teacher accepts actions, behaviors, and feelings. *Example:* "I understand your concern about your ability to continue to guard the taller forward."

Question (4)

Teacher asks questions requiring answers from participants. *Example:* "If the ball is hit to you, where should you throw it to make the out?"

Instruction During Performance (8-5-8, 8\-5-8\, 9-5-9)

Information given to participants while they are involved in performing activities such as drills, scrimmages, and games or their own initiated behavior. *Example:* "Remember to cut the angle between the ball and the goal."

Directions (6)

Orders or directions specifying a response. *Example:* "Run play Number 5."

Hustle (6H)

Orders or directions employed to encourage participants' efforts or execution of desired responses. *Example:* "Let's go! Let's go! Get moving!"

Criticism (7)

Criticism, anger, or sarcasm directed at participants' efforts, actions, or behaviors. *Example:* "That's terrible! How stupid can you be!" "You're wrong!"

Constructive Criticism (7-2)

Criticism designed to help participants improve their efforts, actions, or behaviors. *Example:* "Close. Much better than last time, but still not quite right."

Criticism/Reinstruct (7-5)

Criticism, anger, or sarcasm followed by information. *Example:* "Are you dumb? How many times do I have to tell you? Step forward with your opposite foot when you throw."

Constructive Criticism/Reinstruct (7-2-5)

Constructive criticism followed by information. *Example:* "That's better than the last dive. Now, if you tighten your tuck, you'll be able to spin faster during the dive. Bring your chin down to your chest and tighten up."

RECORDING PROCEDURES

A tally is placed in the appropriate category each time a feedback statement occurs. For ease of observation, the observation period is divided

Self-Assessment Feedback Instrument (SAFI)

Directions: Classes or practices are divided into 10-minute segments for ease of observation. During each 10-minute segment, place a tally next to the appropriate behavior category each time this behavior occurs. The use of various behaviors may be calculated in terms of percentage of total behaviors or as rate per minute.

Name _____   Date _____

Class/practice no._____   Length _____

Category	0-10	11-20	21-30	31-40	41-50	Total	Percent or Rate
Praise (2)							
Praise/reinstruct (2-5)							
Acceptance (3)							
Questions (4)							
Instruction during performance (8-5, 8-5 or 9-5)							
Gives directions (6)							
Hustle behavior (6H)							
Criticism (7)							
Constructive criticism (7-2)							
Criticism/reinstruct (7-5)							
Constructive criticism/ reinstruct (7-2-5)							
Other behavior of interest							
Total							

Figure 10.1   Self-Assessment Feedback Instrument (SAFI) recording sheet.

into 10-minute segments. A sample recording sheet is shown in Figure 10.1.

SUMMARIZING AND INTERPRETING THE DATA

After completing the observation, the recorder totals the number of tallies in each category. Tally frequencies may be converted to percentages by dividing the tallies totaled for each category by the total number of tallies recorded; alternately, the rate at which various behaviors are exhibited may be determined by dividing the total tallies for each category by the length in minutes of the observation period.

The data provide the teacher and coach with information regarding the type and frequency of feedback employed. The division of the observation time into 10-minute segments helps the professional determine whether more feedback was concentrated at the beginning, middle, or end of the instructional session.

The SAFI is used by teachers and coaches initially to establish their normal patterns of behavior. This may involve using the SAFI for several sessions. Next, the professional determines which behaviors he or she would like to improve and identifies specific target percentages or rates. It is suggested that only one or two behaviors be improved at a time. The SAFI is then used several times to monitor progress toward attainment of the desired behaviors. The SAFI and other self-evaluation instruments are of great assistance to teachers and coaches aspiring to improve their effectiveness and allows them to serve as self-change agents throughout their careers.

REFERENCES

Cheffers, J.T.F. (1983). Cheffers' Adaptation of Flanders' Interaction Analysis System. In P.W. Darst, V.H. Mancini, & D.B. Zakrajsek (Eds.), *Systematic observation instrumentation for physical education* (pp. 76-95). Champaign, IL: Leisure Press.

Mancini, V.H., & Wuest, D.A. (1987). Coaches' interactions and their athletes' ALT-PE: A systematic perspective. In G.T. Barrette, R.S. Feingold, C.R. Rees, & M. Pieron (Eds.), *Sport pedagogy: Myths, models, and methods* (pp. 231-237). Champaign, IL: Human Kinetics.

Mancini, V.H., Wuest, D.A., & van der Mars, H. (1985). Use of instruction and supervision in systematic observation in undergraduate preparation. *Journal of Teaching in Physical Education, 5*(1), 22-33.

Chapter 11

The Dyadic Adaptation of the Cheffers' Adaptation of the Flanders' Interaction Analysis System (DAC)

Thomas J. Martinek
Victor H. Mancini

The Dyadic Adaptation of the Cheffers' Adaptation of the Flanders' Interaction Analysis System (DAC) was developed to further sensitize the teacher to the type of interactions that occur in the classroom (Martinek & Mancini, 1979). Like FIAS, CAFIAS provides a teacher with the knowledge of general interaction between the teacher and his or her students in a particular class (Cheffers, 1983). But what about the interaction between the teacher and a single student? Much of the interactions between a particular student and the teacher go unnoticed in CAFIAS. This dyadic interaction is not distinct in the mind of the observer or on the descriptive records of a researcher.

Obtaining a more thorough description of the interaction between a teacher and a particular student enables both researcher and educator to capture the unique relationship that exists between the two. Further, by studying the interactions of teacher-student dyads, the teacher might become more sensitive to and aware of that person's characteristics, behaviors, and individuality, as well as the manner in which he or she, the teacher, interacts with the student. Thus an important aspect of teacher influence is behavior directed toward individual students rather than to an entire class. DAC provides a method by which interactions between teacher and student are recorded and analyzed.

DAC does not involve coding everything that happens in the classroom or physical activity setting, such as interactions with groups of students or interactions with the class as a whole unit. Rather, the emphasis is on the word *dyadic* (i.e., the interaction between the student and the teacher). DAC is intended to provide preservice and in-service teachers with descriptive data regarding their teaching behavior directed to individual students.

CATEGORY DESCRIPTIONS

DAC uses the same categories as CAFIAS. Both teacher and student verbal and nonverbal behaviors are recorded. Brief descriptions of each behavior category and DAC codes, noted in parentheses, are listed below. More complete information about each category, including descriptions of characteristic verbal and nonverbal behaviors, is provided in chapter 8.

Teacher Behavior

Praise (Verbal, 2; Nonverbal, 12)

Teacher praises or encourages student's behavior or ideas.

Acceptance (Verbal, 3; Nonverbal, 13)

Teacher accepts or clarifies student's behavior, ideas, or feelings.

Asks Questions (Verbal, 4; Nonverbal, 14)

Teacher asks question requiring student's response.

Gives Information (Verbal, 5; Nonverbal, 15)

Teacher lectures, provides information, or demonstrates.

Gives Directions (Verbal, 6; Nonverbal, 16)

Teacher gives directions or orders resulting in an immediate, observable student response.

Criticizes (Verbal, 7; Nonverbal, 17)

Teacher criticizes student's behavior or ideas, or justifies authority as a teacher.

Student Behavior

Student Predictable Response (Verbal, 8; Nonverbal, 18)

Student responds in a predictable manner, obeys orders, or participates in mechanical drills.

Student Interpretive Behavior (Verbal, 8; Nonverbal, 18)

Student exhibits interpretive behavior or participates in scrimmaging or game play.

Student Initiative Behavior (Verbal, 9; Nonverbal, 19)

Student behavior is the result of the student's own initiative; behavior is either positive or negative.

Other Behavior

Confusion (10)

Brief periods of disorder, chaos, or confusion or periods when communication cannot be understood.

Silence (20)

Brief periods of silence.

RECORDING PROCEDURES

All CAFIAS coding procedures and ground rules are basically the same for DAC. However, to facilitate the use of CAFIAS for the purposes of analyzing dyadic interaction, the following coding procedures were added:

1. A procedure for the identification of each student must be established prior to the start of the class to be observed. The system of student identification may vary depending on specific circumstances. It is important, however, that a separate identifying symbol for each student be recorded for various dyadic interactions. The following alternatives for student identification may be used:
   - *Student names:* Observer must know the names of all students or observe the class with someone who does.
   - *Row and seat numbers:* This is appropriate only when students are positioned in stationary seats.
   - *Numbered pinnies:* These are worn on the back and front by each student. For repeated observations, students must always wear the same number.

2. When a teacher directs a behavior to one student (or a small group), the observer codes the interaction that transpires between them. The observer does not code situations when the teacher is directing behaviors toward the entire class or to large groups of students (i.e., more than four). To code small group interaction, the subscripts should accompany the coded tally (e.g., $6_{1,2,3,8}$).

3. When teacher behavior toward the same student or small groups continues for more than 3 seconds, the observer places another tally on the coding sheet and continues this practice at 3-second intervals until the behavior switches categories or is directed toward another student or the interaction stops. Figure 11.1 is a tally sheet used for coding a class with DAC. CAFIAS can be learned with high reliability in a period of approximately 20 hours. DAC requires

Teacher __Jordon__   Observer __Hall__

Class __Badminton__   Date __10/19__

School __Lincoln__   Time __10 a.m.__

1. 20	21. $5_{6,7}$	41. $18_{6,9}$	61. 9_2	81. 18_1
2. 5_1	22. $\textcircled{6}_{6,7}$	42. $2_{6,9}$	62. 7_2	82. 18_1
3. 5_1	23. $18_{6,7}$	43. $52_{6,9}$	63. 2_2	83. 2_5
4. $\textcircled{5}_7$	24. $6_{3,4}$	44. $7_{6,9}$	64. 7_2	84. 3_5
5. $\textcircled{5}_7$	25. $18_{3,4}$	45. $\textcircled{6}_8$	65. 2_2	85. 3_5
6. 6_7	26. $\textcircled{6}_{3,4}$	46. 18_8	66. 6_9	86. $\textcircled{3}_5$
7. 18_7	27. $18_{3,4}$	47. $\textcircled{6}_8$	67. 18_9	87. 6_5
8. 18_7	28. $\textcircled{6}_1$	48. 18_8	68. 7_9	88. 18_5
9. $\textcircled{2}_7$	29. 18_1	49. $\textcircled{6}_8$	69. 2_9	89. 18_5
10. 9_4	30. $\textcircled{6}_1$	50. $18_{3,4}$	70. $\textcircled{6}_1$	90. $\textcircled{6}_{6,7}$
11. 13_4	31. 18_1	51. $\textcircled{6}_{3,4}$	71. 18_1	91. $18_{6,7}$
12. 5_4	32. $\textcircled{6}_1$	52. $6_{3,4}$	72. 18_1	92. 9_8
13. 6_4	33. 18_1	53. $18_{3,4}$	73. $7_{3,4}$	93. 9_8
14. 18_4	34. $\textcircled{6}_2$	54. $2_{3,4}$	74. $2_{3,4}$	94. 9_8
15. 5_9	35. 18_2	55. $\textcircled{6}_1$	75. $7_{3,4}$	95. 5_8
16. 5_9	36. $\textcircled{6}_2$	56. 18_1	76. $2_{3,4}$	96. 5_8
17. 5_9	37. 18_2	57. 18_1	77. $5_{3,4}$	97. 6_3
18. 5_9	38. $\textcircled{6}_9$	58. 9_1	78. $5_{3,4}$	98. 18_3
19. 6_9	39. 18_9	59. 9_1	79. $5_{3,4}$	99. 6_3
20. 18_9	40. $\textcircled{6}_9$	60. 9_1	80. 6_1	100. 20

Figure 11.1 Completed Dyadic Adaptation of the Cheffers' Adaptation of the Flanders' Interaction Analysis System (DAC) tally sheet.

approximately 1 to 2 additional hours of practice to obtain similar reliability measures.

The decision to code live or to use a videotape recorder depends on a number of considerations. Traditionally, the live method has been found to be more effective for obtaining valid data. Such things as voice inflection, clarity of identification symbols worn by students, and various behavioral subtleties are easier for the observer to perceive when coding takes place in the classroom. However, the ability to reevaluate episodes and further clarify coding about questionable behaviors are convincing reasons for the use of videotape. Furthermore, the development of portable tape recorders and the use of wireless microphones provide greater sophistication in obtaining and storing observational data.

SUMMARIZING AND INTERPRETING THE DATA

Following the conclusion of a lesson, the data are transferred to a recording form. A dot is placed in the appropriate cell across from the student's name or identification symbol. Figure 11.2 is a completed recording sheet used for summarizing the observational data taken from Figure 11.1.

After all the data have been transferred to the recording form, they are summarized in the following sequence:

1. Sum and record each cell total. Write over the tally dots.
2. Sum each column. Total and record in the space provided.
3. Sum and record each row.
4. Compute all column and row total percentages and record in the spaces provided.

In analyzing the data presented in Figure 11.2, we can view each student's interaction independently (by row) or all students as a group (by columns). For example, looking at Student 1, we can see that much of the teacher's behavior with that student was in the form of direction-giving. Also, the teacher appeared to generate a significant amount of both predictable and unpredictable student response. Student 1's total amount of class involvement was also highest among the nine students (20%), indicating that more time was spent by the teacher with that particular student. It is also interesting to note that the reverse was found for Student 5, showing differential treatment by the teacher.

The column total and percentages reveal information regarding the group as a whole. For example, verbal and nonverbal direction-giving appears to be the predominant teacher behavior given to the individuals in this group (34%). Also, there is evidence that the students demonstrated

Teacher __Jordan__   Demographic identity __White, middle-class__

Grade __6th__

Categories

Student ID#	1	11	2	12	3	13	4	14	5	15	6	16	7	17	8	18	8	18	9	19	10	20	Total	Percent
1									4	2	7	6				6		4	3				32	20
2			2								2	2	2			2			1				11	7
3			3		3						6	3	2			6							23	15
4			3			1			4		5	3	2			6			1				25	16
5			2						2		3					1							8	5
6			2						3		1	2	1			2							11	7
7				1	1				1		2	1		1		4							11	7
8										2	2	3				3			3				13	8
9			3			1			8		4	2	1			4							23	15
Totals	0	0	15	1	4	2	0	0	22	4	32	22	8	1	0	34	0	4	8	0	0	0	157	
Percent	0	0	10	1	3	1	0	0	14	3	20	14	5	1	0	22	0	3	5	0	0	0	102	

Figure 11.2 Completed Dyadic Adaptation of the Cheffers' Adaptation of the Flanders' Interaction Analysis System recording sheet.

predictable nonverbal behaviors as a result of the types of directions given by the teacher. Although the data may have little significance about this group of nine students, when compared to other groups (e.g., whites/ blacks, males/females, etc.), there may be significant group differences. This, in turn, would have important sociopsychological implications for the teaching-learning process.

The expansion of social scientific inquiry in physical education is a crucial enterprise. To provide researchers and practitioners with effective means for assessing their relationships with their students, the development of reliable and valid measures of observation must continue. The DAC system provides a vehicle by which dyadic inquiry will be expanded, thus ensuring a clearer understanding of teacher-student relationships. DAC has been used in research on preservice and in-service physical educators and their students, as well as on coaches and their athletes.

REFERENCES

Cheffers, J.T.F. (1983). Cheffers' Adaptation of Flanders' Interaction Analysis System. In P.W. Darst, V.H. Mancini, & D.B. Zakrajsek (Eds.), *Systematic observation instrumentation for physical education* (pp. 76-95). Champaign, IL: Leisure Press.

Martinek, T.J., & Mancini, V.H. (1979). CAFIAS: Observing dyadic interaction between teacher and student. *Journal of Classroom Interaction,* 14(2), 18-22.

RELATED REFERENCES

Boyes, J. (1981). *The interaction behavior patterns of college football coaches with their starting and nonstarting athletes*. Unpublished master's thesis, Ithaca College, Ithaca, NY.

Devlin, G.L. (1979). *The effects of teacher contingency management skills to elementary students on the students' self-concept and physical educators' behaviors*. Unpublished master's thesis, Ithaca College, Ithaca, NY.

Devlin, G.L., Mancini, V.H., & Frye, P.A. (1981). Teaching contingency management skills to disruptive elementary students: Its effect on student self-concept and physical educators' behaviors. *Journal of Teaching in Physical Education,* 1(1), 47-58.

Hoffman, A.F. (1981). *The interaction patterns of collegiate lacrosse coaches with high-skilled and low-skilled athletes*. Unpublished master's thesis, Ithaca College, Ithaca, NY.

King, R.B. (1985). *Environmental analysis and interaction patterns of high school baseball coaches and athletes.* Unpublished master's thesis, Ithaca College, Ithaca, NY.

Mancini, V.H., & Wuest, D.A. (1987). Coaches' interactions and their high- and low-skilled athletes' academic learning time: A systematic perspective. In G.S. Barrette, R.S. Feingold, C.R. Rees, & M. Pieron (Eds.), *Sport pedagogy: Myths, models, and methods* (pp. 231-237). Champaign, IL: Human Kinetics.

Mancini, V.H., Wuest, D.A., & Smith, K. (1985, August). *A comparison of teachers' behaviors and students' academic learning time-physical education (ALT-PE) with command style and movement education style of instruction.* Paper presented at the Association Internationale des Ecoles Superieures d'Education Physique (AIESEP), Adelphi University, Garden City, NY.

Martinek, T.J., & Johnson, S.B. (1979). Teacher expectations: Effects of dyadic interactions and self-concept in elementary age children. *Research Quarterly,* **50**(1), 60-70.

Martinek, T.J., & Mancini, V.H. (1979). CAFIAS: Observing dyadic interaction between teacher and student. *Journal of Classroom Interaction,* **14**(2), 18-22.

Metcalfe, T., Mancini, V.H., & Wuest, D.A. (1985, April). *A comparison of the interactions of a male and a female physical educator and their students' ALT-PE.* Paper presented at the American Alliance for Health, Physical Education, Recreation and Dance National Convention, Cincinnati, OH.

Reisenweaver, P.J. (1980). *The teaching interaction patterns of secondary female physical education teachers with high-skilled students and with low-skilled students.* Unpublished master's thesis, Ithaca College, Ithaca, NY.

Rush, D.A., Mancini, V.H., & Wuest, D.A. (1985, April). *A comparison of coach's interactions with high- and low-skilled intercollegiate divers.* Paper presented at the American Alliance for Health, Physical Education, Recreation and Dance National Convention, Cincinnati, OH.

Ryan, M.A. (1983). *Academic learning time and teacher interaction patterns in an elementary physical education unit: Comparisons among high-skilled, average-skilled, and low-skilled students.* Unpublished master's thesis, Ithaca College, Ithaca, NY.

Silvernail, S. (1985). *A comparison of teacher interaction patterns with high-skilled and low-skilled middle school students during an instructional unit.* Unpublished master's thesis, Ithaca College, Ithaca, NY.

Streeter, B.I. (1980). *Interaction behavior patterns of male secondary physical education teachers with high-skilled and low-skilled students.* Unpublished master's thesis, Ithaca College, Ithaca, NY.

Ware, J. (1985). *Interactions of an intercollegiate volleyball coach with female players of different abilities.* Unpublished master's thesis, Ithaca College, Ithaca, NY.

TEACHER/STUDENT CLIMATE ANALYSIS

Part III focuses on instruments that have been used primarily with teachers and students in physical education classes. Several of the instruments have been used with teachers in nonschool settings such as the YMCA. Many different kinds of real-world teacher and student behaviors have been observed and classified with these instruments.

Data Collection for Managerial Efficiency in Physical Education (DACOME-PE), developed by Siedentop and Rife, is used for coding the managerial efficiency of physical education classes. It combines event and duration recording procedures to look at the number of teacher managerial behaviors, the positive and negative teacher reactions to student management, and the percentage of class time spent in management. With DACOME-PE results, teachers gain a clear picture of overall management procedures.

Zakrajsek's Pattern Analysis system looks at how students spend time in a physical education class. It consists of 10 time-coded functions that are grouped according to class management or positive or negative functions. The time values obtained provide an account of how physical education teachers allot class time. Johnson's Flow of Teacher Organizational Patterns (FOTOP) is an initiating system used primarily as a preservice instrument. The purpose of FOTOP is to discern teacher organizational patterns used in conducting physical education classes by coding teaching and nonteaching functions. The data display the frequency and the sequential flow of these organizational behaviors.

Dodds' instrument, Student Teachers Observing Peers (STOP), is designed to be used by teachers that are working together in the same teaching situation. Teachers observe and provide feedback to each other in four major categories of teacher behavior: management, instructional input, skill feedback, and social behavior feedback. A combination of event, duration, and placheck recording procedures is used. This peer approach is effective in helping teachers to obtain objective data for making future decisions about their teaching behaviors.

Brown's instrument, Systematic Observation of Student Opportunities to Respond (SOSOR), is designed to analyze the effects of game modifications on student opportunities to participate. The system focuses on the opportunities to respond, the specific skill responses, and whether the responses were acceptable or unacceptable and successful or unsuccessful. The instrument is based on the assumption that the most educationally efficient modifications provide more opportunities for quality participation.

Academic Learning Time-Physical Education Version II (ALT-PE) discussed by Parker is one of the most popular and widely used observation systems. It was designed to measure the portion of time in a physical education class that a student is involved in motor activity at an appropriate success rate. The instrument is capable of describing not only the type of motor activity (e.g., skill practice, scrimmage, game, or fitness) in which selected students are involved, but also the context (general or subject matter) in which the total class is involved. It uses an interval recording technique with 12-second intervals.

The Teacher's Questionnaire on Students' Activities (TQSA) by Mancini, Wuest, and O'Brien has been used to determine the accuracy of teachers' awareness of their behaviors and their students' behavior. It is a 16-item questionnaire based on the revised ALT-PE. The questionnaire should be used in conjunction with ALT-PE so that teachers can compare their preclass and postclass perceptions with what actually occurred in the class.

The purpose of Teacher Monitoring Analysis System (TMAS), developed by van der Mars, is to provide the user with information on the physical (re)location patterns of teachers or coaches. Relocation behavior patterns have been found to influence student behavior in classroom settings, yet their influence on student behavior in physical education and sport settings remains largely unknown. The system is an interval recording tool that is built around the previously developed ALT-PE Version II. This allows for analyses to be made on the relationship between (re)location patterns of teachers, contextual variables, and learner involvement variables. Subscripts are used to identify the various class structures used by the teacher. This observation system helps provide answers to at least some dimensions of teacher monitoring behavior.

The Microcomputer Data Collection System (MCDCS) by Metzler is another academic learning time instrument that is designed to allow electronic collection, storage, analysis, and retrieval of the data. Although the behavior categories include several new variations, they are basically the same as the original ALT-PE categories. The system uses a modified and more content-specific set of 22 defined categories, coded on four decision levels: pacing, content, learner moves, and difficulty.

Chung's Time-on-Fitness Instrument (TOFI) was developed to describe student time on task in the specific context and for the specific content of *The Y's Way to Physical Fitness* programs. It consists of nine exhaustive and mutually exclusive activity categories in four major divisions. Behaviors are recorded at 5-second intervals during alternate 1-minute class segments. TOFI is one of the few descriptive instruments that has been used in a teaching environment outside of the schools.

The categories of the Direct Instruction Behavior Analysis (DIBA), developed by Zakrajsek and Tannehill, were derived from a cluster of research-based teaching behaviors that are associated with the teaching model, direct instruction. DIBA allows for an examination of these effective teaching behaviors including on-task student behavior. Subscripts provide refinements within the major categories that strengthen the overall analysis of direct instruction.

The Observational Recording Record of Physical Educator's Teaching Behavior (ORRPETB), developed by Stewart, is multidirectional with capabilities for observing instructional climate, interaction possibilities, teacher behavior, and various combinations. It can be used in a lab or field setting to look at 27 teacher behavior categories, 4 student behavior categories, and 5 teacher-student interaction categories.

The Observation Instrument for Content Development in Physical Education (OSCD-PE) by Rink is used to describe the process of content development in physical education activity classes. All teaching behaviors are simultaneously coded into the following three major facets: the source (to whom the behavior is directed), the communication function (soliciting, responding, initiating, or appraisal), and the content function (informing, refining, extending, applying, conduct, or organization).

Rink and Werner's Qualitative Measures of Teacher Performance Scale (QMTPS) was designed to assist researchers in gaining more qualitative insight as to how more effective teachers differ from less effective teachers in affecting student learning. The QMTPS is divided into four major constructs: type of task, task presentation, student response appropriate to task focus, and specific congruent feedback. The construct of task presentation has five major categories: clarity, demonstration, appropriate number of cues, accuracy of cues, and qualitative cues provided. Responses in each category are summed and converted to percentages of the teacher task-student response unit of analysis. Responses in the most desirable column are also summed and averaged for a total QMTPS score.

The West Virginia University Teaching Evaluation System (WVUTES), designed by Hawkins and Wiegand, provides a sound empirical basis on which teacher educators can make reasoned judgments and provide helpful suggestions for the solution of lesson problems encountered by preservice trainees. The core of the system is a set of 11 teacher response class categories and 8 student response class categories. The system is designed for use with an electronic data collection regimen (microcomputer) but is adaptable to interval recording regimens. Especially unique to this system is the feedback taxonomy, which comprises strategies to correct lesson problems that are revealed through data analysis. Teacher educators are thus provided with a means of collecting empirical information about classes that are observed as well as equipped with practical suggestions designed to solve specific data problems.

Morgenegg's descriptive system, Instrument for the Analysis of the Pedagogical Functions of Physical Education Teachers (PEDFUNC), is based on the work of Bellack and represents a study of language behavior. PEDFUNC allows analysis of the teacher's language and its attendant stimulus. Language is coded as structuring, soliciting, responding, or reacting. There are further subclassifications of verbal or nonverbal; substantive or nonsubstantive; positive, negative, or neutral; teacher or student initiated; and individual, group, or whole class directed.

Anderson's system, Physical Education Teachers' Professional Functions, was conceived as a part of the Videotape Data Bank Project that was carried out at Columbia University. It provides a means to accurately describe videotape teaching behaviors across several dimensions. Each videotaped segment is subjected to several codings, one for each dimension. The analysis of all codings provides a classification of teacher behaviors according to the teacher's function, how it is carried out, the manner of communication, to whom it is communicated, and the subject matter. Because all behaviors are time coded, duration is calculated for each function category, and a descriptive analysis is provided of how time was spent across several teacher roles.

Chapter 12

Data Collection for Managerial Efficiency in Physical Education (DACOME-PE)

Daryl Siedentop
Frank Rife

The Data Collection for Managerial Efficiency in Physical Education (DACOME-PE) instrument focuses on the management component of physical education classes. It uses an event and duration recording procedure to measure the number of managerial behaviors practiced by the teachers, the number of positive and negative teacher reactions to student on-and off-task behavior, and the amount of class time spent in a management-related activity. These three components include a *managerial episode* that occurs at different times during a class period. An interobserver agreement of over 90% has been achieved for this observation instrument. DACOME-PE does not attend to teacher or student behavior related to course content or subject matter.

CATEGORY DESCRIPTIONS

Types of Managerial Episodes

This refers to the managerial episodes that differ according to their purpose and the type of activity that immediately follows.

At the Beginning of a Class Activity to Get the Class Organized for Initial Instruction. Example: A signal to begin and the time it takes to call roll or set up equipment.

Class Change Within a Current Activity. Example: A signal and the class time it takes to move from one teaching station to another.

Change Prior to a Different But Familiar Activity. *Example:* A signal and the time it takes to move to a large group so the teacher can review a previous activity that the class will practice.

Change Prior to a New Activity. *Example:* A signal and the time it takes for the class to move to a large group so the teacher can give instructions about a new activity they will practice.

At the End of Class for Additional Managerial and Noninstructional Purposes. *Example:* A signal to meet and collect equipment.

Length of Managerial Episode

This refers to a continuous time segment that begins when a teacher displays the first managerial behavior and ends when all the students have responded appropriately to the teacher's managerial directions. Appropriate student compliance is measured when all the students start such a new, nonmanagerial activity. The new, nonmanagerial activity may be one of the following:

- The teacher begins to explain a game.
- The teacher begins to explain and describe a skill to be learned.
- The teacher gives group or individual feedback for student skill attempt(s).
- The students begin practicing a skill.
- The students begin playing a game.

Initial managerial episodes usually begin when the teacher signals the class to organize (in squads, in the bleachers, etc.). This episode terminates when the teacher begins the instructional part of the day's lesson. Interim managerial episodes occur when the teacher directs the class to change an activity (e.g., move from one station to another) or calls the class together in order to explain something. Interim episodes begin when the teacher gives a managerial cue (e.g., a whistle) and end when all the students begin the new activity (e.g., students begin practicing the new skill or begin a game situation). The terminal managerial episode in a class period comes toward the end of the class, and the episode begins at the end of the final class learning activity when the teacher calls the class together. The managerial episode stops if the teacher begins to tell the class about what they've learned for that day or gives them information about the next class (all considered instructional behavior). If the teacher stops the learning activity (a game or a skill practice) and organizes the students so they can leave the gym, the managerial episode would begin with the managerial cue to end class and would be over when all the students left the gymnasium area.

Managerial Behavior

This is any teacher behavior that includes preparation for an activity or a signal to change from one activity to another. It is important to remember that managerial behaviors fall into the generic category of instructional behavior, as these behaviors precede expected student behavior. Any behavior that is a reaction to and contingent upon student behavior comes under the generic category of teacher reactions or feedback.

Positive Teacher Reactions to Student On-Task Behavior

This is teacher behavior falling into the generic category of feedback, as it is a reaction to and contingent upon student on-task behavior. This includes all verbal (e.g., "Thanks for lining up so quickly!") and nonverbal (e.g., a thumbs-up gesture for lining up quickly) teacher reactions to student behavior that are considered essential for the orderly conduct of class other than student skill attempts.

Negative Teacher Reaction to Student Off-Task Behavior

This is a teacher feedback behavior that includes all verbal (e.g., "Get back in line!") and nonverbal (e.g., a scowl at a student getting out of line) teacher reactions to student misbehavior that are defined by the teacher as interfering with the orderly conduct of class.

RECORDING PROCEDURES

To obtain the data for teacher behavior and the time-related components of teacher managerial efficiency, DACOME-PE uses both an event and a duration recording procedure. The former collects teacher managerial and feedback behavior related to student on- and off-task performance. The latter collects the time of each managerial episode. A tally sheet records the collected data with a conventional stopwatch to record the time component of each managerial episode.

Observers code for an entire class period and should sit at opposite ends of the gym or playing fields yet be close enough to hear the verbal behavior of the teacher and observe any nonverbal teacher behavior. There are no rest intervals in the observing and recording of target behaviors, and observers record data for the entire class period. Observers note the beginning and end of recording to adjust the data and make comparisons of results for class periods of unequal length (Cooper, 1974; Siedentop, 1976).

To avoid possible observer confusion about whether a teacher displayed this or that behavior, or meant this or that, observer(s) should watch the effect of a teacher behavior on a target student's behavior. To strengthen interobserver agreement and avoid observer confusion, observer(s) must note whether a teacher's verbal or nonverbal behavior has a particular effect upon the target student. With regard to a teacher's positive or negative comments, these behaviors should precede a corresponding increase or decrease in a target student's behavior. This ensures the validity of a particular behavior category, which in turn ensures the validity of the observation instrument itself. Allowing observer bias to interfere with the observation and recording of a particular behavior results in low interobserver agreement and possibly negates the data collected during a particular class period.

SUMMARIZING AND INTERPRETING THE DATA

The raw data are tabulated at the end of each class period with calculations made for the total number of the different type of managerial episodes, the total amount of time of the episodes, the total number of teacher managerial responses, the total number of positive teacher reactions to student on-task behavior, and the total number of negative teacher reactions to student off-task behavior.

In addition, calculations must be made for the average number of teacher managerial behaviors and positive and negative teacher reactions to related student behavior, as well as the average time per each managerial episode. A completed recording sheet displaying collected data is shown in Figure 12.1. Each daily sheet is kept and the information accumulated on a permanent master recording sheet until the end of the observation and recording project.

The collected data provide baseline information about the managerial picture of a particular physical education class. Total and average calculations of managerial behavior and time spent in managerial episodes are designed to indicate the amounts of behavior the teacher devotes to managing his or her class and how much time the students spend in a management-related activity. Such teacher management behavior detracts from student learning, as the class time spent in management-related activity competes with the class time available for student learning (Siedentop, Birdwell, & Metzler, 1979).

Student teacher _Student A_____   Date and time _3/10   10:13 A.M._____

Class _5th Grade—coed—gymnastics___   Observer _Observer B_____

Length of class period _10:30-11:00_____

Type of managerial episode (a) begin (b) change within (c) change different (d) change new (e) end	Length of managerial episode	Managerial behaviors	Positive reactions to task behavior	Negative reactions to off-task behavior
a	:33	1		
b	:60	3		2
b	:30	1		
b	:38	1		2
b	:31	1		1
b	:37	2		1
d	:57	2		1
e	:05	1	1	

Total episodes R = 8	Total time 4:51	Total managerial 12	Total + 1	Total − 7
	Mean time 36.5 sec per episode	Mean managerial 1.5/episode	Mean + .12/episode	Mean − .87/episode

Figure 12.1 Completed Data Collection for Managerial Efficiency in Physical Education (DACOME-PE) recording sheet.

REFERENCES

Cooper, J. (1974). *Measurement and analysis of behavioral techniques*. Columbus, OH: Charles E. Merrill.

Siedentop, D. (1976). *Developing teaching skills in physical education*. Boston: Houghton Mifflin.

Siedentop, D., Birdwell, D., & Metzler, M.A. (1979, April). *A process approach to measuring teaching effectiveness in physical education*. Paper presented at the American Association of Health, Physical Education, and Recreation Research Symposium, New Orleans.

Chapter 13

Pattern Analysis

Dorothy B. Zakrajsek

Pattern Analysis describes how instructional time is used in the physical education classroom. The purpose is to obtain accurate time values of events as they occur during the lesson. The system is based on the assumption that the teacher has control over time decisions. In other words, the teacher decides when to start and stop class activities as well as which methods and procedures to use.

The instrument identifies 10 functions that could occur during a physical education lesson. The observer makes a function identification every 5 seconds. A quick processing of tallies at the completion of the class shows how class time was spent and allows for various analyses and interpretations. Interobserver reliability of objectivity correlation coefficients has been established over several years with a range of .94 to .99.

The instrument is nonresponsive to individualized programming where students are working on their own learning package and where learning centers are the major delivery system. However, meaningful information can still be generated with modification.

CATEGORY DESCRIPTIONS

The instrument identifies 10 functions that occur in the physical education classroom and that the observer identifies every 5 seconds. The functions are preparatory, organizational, content presentation (teaching), developmental, recreational, controlling, summation, departure, and nondirected. The last category, evaluation, is optional and would probably have more appeal when describing an entire unit of instruction. Functions 1 and 7 have been delineated for independent examination of events characteristic of that function.

Preparatory (1)

This category includes activities preceding the lesson: changing clothes (1.1), roll call (1.2), and warm-up (1.3). Each is delineated by separate indicators so the subfunction can be partialed out of the total function for independent analysis. The time frame for the changing of clothes can be accurately clocked instead of time coded. It should be noted that time is coded as "preparatory" until an official act by the teacher commences class activities.

Organizational (2)

This category includes getting equipment out; setting up equipment; and grouping for instruction, drills, games, or teams. Direction-giving and direction clarification are subsumed under this category, as is giving class assignments.

Content Presentation (Teaching) (3)

This category includes only the act of teaching or presenting content. Demonstrations that contribute to understanding or learning are coded here, but demonstrations used for motivation would be coded under Category 2. For indirect lessons, cuing would be coded in this category, whereas the response would be coded under Category 4. This category also includes individual and small-group teaching even though the majority of the class is actively engaged in skill acquisition (Category 4). The coder would use "4_3" to indicate that most of the class is in developmental activities while the teacher is engaged in teaching. However, the coder must be certain that the teacher is engaged in teaching and not giving reinforcement or chatting. Interruptive teacher feedback that aims at correcting or helping student response would be coded here.

Developmental (4)

This category includes all practice sessions such as drills and games that follow teaching and have planned objectives. Group or individual demonstrations presented as a culminating activity or presentation would be included here. Subscripts can be used to indicate approximately how many students are motor engaged (e.g., 4_1—less than 25% and 4_2—about 50%). This allows for a more accurate accounting of developmental time in terms of student participation.

Recreational (5)

This category includes only those play functions that do not follow purposeful and planned teaching (supervised play as an end in itself).

Controlling (6)

This category includes disciplinary verbalization and punishment when given to the whole class as a means of controlling deviant behavior. This category includes direction clarification if it is presented in a disciplinary manner. The clue in coding "6" is that the whole class has been interrupted to correct or call attention to deviant behavior.

Summation (7)

This category is subdivided into teaching summation, organizational summation, and motivational summation. If a review of something that was taught is reinforced, it is coded "7.1" (teaching). If reference is made to the next day's procedure, it is coded "7.2" (organizational). If a summation is attitudinal or motivational, it is coded "7.3." This allows for a closer examination of the summation function.

Departure (8)

This category includes the time allotted to dress and shower. If roll call is taken at the end of the period, it is recorded "8.1" here. This time frame need not be coded, but can be accurately clocked.

Nondirected (9)

This category includes times when nothing is happening because of teacher absence or no direction from the teacher. This includes periods when the students are doing whatever they want to while awaiting direction. Nondirected time is only coded after the class has officially begun.

Evaluation (Optional) (10)

This category refers to all formal evaluation such as written or skill testing. Demonstrations subjected to formalized evaluation by students or teacher would apply. (Analysis of skills or performances would be Category 3 if the intent were to correct or reinforce performance.)

RECORDING PROCEDURES

The Pattern Analysis system is functional and can be taught with a consistent rate of reliability achievement. The Pattern Analysis recording sheet

Pattern Analysis

Name _____   School _____

Activity _____   Time: (Beginning) _____ (End) _____Total _____

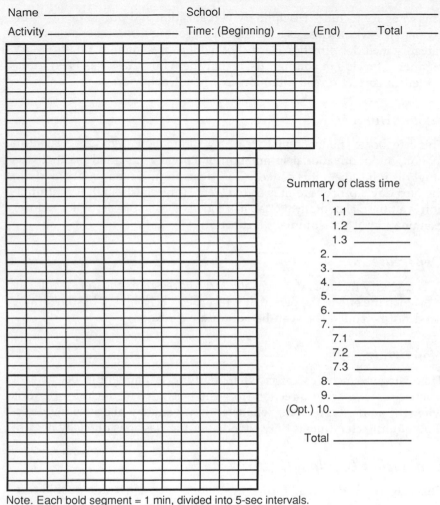

Summary of class time
1. _____
1.1 _____
1.2 _____
1.3 _____
2. _____
3. _____
4. _____
5. _____
6. _____
7. _____
7.1 _____
7.2 _____
7.3 _____
8. _____
9. _____
(Opt.) 10. _____

Total _____

Note. Each bold segment = 1 min, divided into 5-sec intervals.

Figure 13.1 Pattern Analysis recording sheet.

is shown in Figure 13.1. Ground rules for systematic recording are as follows:

- A complete class session must be observed.
- Function coding is recorded in 5-second intervals.
- Clock time may be recorded for the changing of clothes in preparatory and departure categories if accuracy can be obtained.
- If the developmental phase is set for all or the major portion of the class (e.g., a volleyball game or tournament), the time is clock-

recorded and only interruptive functions (e.g., substitutions, changing teams, clarifying rules) are coded. This time is subtracted from the developmental activity and entered into the appropriate category.
- All recording follows a column system.
- All event changes are recorded even if the changes occur between 5-second intervals. Excess tallies can be adjusted by slowing the subsequent recording pace.
- If in doubt about the category, observe what the class is doing. If the class is engaged in practice, stay with Category 4, unless the teacher is interjecting information, which would be a subscript of Development, or 4_3.
- It should be noted that the total time observed for a lesson can be less than the composite of the total time observed in each function. This is due to recording Category 4 when it is recorded simultaneously with a subscript 3.

SUMMARIZING AND INTERPRETING THE DATA

All tallies on the recording sheet are totaled by function and multiplied by five to obtain the total seconds allotted to that function. Next, the total class time observed is converted to seconds. This allows for a quick mathematical percentage computation:

$$\text{Percentage} = \frac{\text{Time observed in function}}{\text{Total observed instructional time}}$$

The observed time for each function is computed and expressed as a percentage of the total observed instructional time. The percentage becomes an objective record describing categorically how time is used. Seconds are reconverted to minutes to provide mean time per function.

After the observer tabulates and studies time used for each function separately, three groupings are suggested for additional assessment:

- Class management: Add percentages in 1, 2, 6, and 8.
- Positive functions: Add percentages in 3, 4, and 7.
- Negative functions: Add percentages in 5 and 9.

(If function 10 is used it is added to positive functions.)

Class management activities are legitimate time-consumers, but should be scrutinized for efficiency. Positive functions are central to the purpose of education and should reveal major consumption of class time. Negative functions are detrimental to the development and advancement of physical education as an educational program and should be minimized, if not eliminated.

The uses of Pattern Analysis are many. As a supervisory tool, it promises objective feedback about conducting the lesson. Integral to the interpretation of feedback in a supervisor-teacher relationship is the active and willing involvement of the teacher. Preservice and in-service training provides additional motives for exploiting the value of the instrument. This potential is acknowledged for the undergraduate student in direct observation and clinical experiences using peer or supervisory personnel. The practitioner is encouraged to participate in self-analysis through videotape replay or peer recording. An outcome for all would be the identification and, if needed, the selection of appropriate organizational strategies.

The system offers a workable method for garnering time-allocation data that heretofore have not been available. The collection of such information could aid the profession in knowing what really happens in the physical education classroom. General uses include courses in undergraduate physical education methods, student teaching seminars, directed-study projects, and graduate courses in pedagogy and supervision.

RELATED REFERENCES

McCombs, J. (1980). *A study to quantify and compare how selected secondary physical education teachers who are head varsity basketball coaches utilize physical education time during and after basketball season*. Unpublished master's thesis, University of Idaho, Moscow.

Pettigrew, F. (1977). *Systematic observation applied to graduate assistants teaching in the basic instruction program*. Unpublished master's thesis, Kent State University, Kent, OH.

Zakrajsek, D.B. (1977). *Patterns of instructional time utilization and related teacher characteristics for seventh grade physical education in selected schools*. Unpublished doctoral dissertation, Kent State University, Kent, OH.

□ *Chapter 14*

Flow of Teacher Organizational Patterns (FOTOP)

Theodore W.H. Johnson

Flow of Teacher Organization Patterns (FOTOP) was developed at the University of New Mexico and has been used primarily as a training tool in teacher preparation activities conducted at State University of New York-Brockport. FOTOP describes the manner in which a teacher uses various organizational patterns necessary to conduct physical education activities. The observer reliability of FOTOP was determined by using the formula described in chapter 3. Both interobserver and intraobserver results were found to be above the 80% level of acceptance. Feedback from FOTOP does not determine teaching effectiveness in terms of how well skills were taught by the teachers or learned by students. The primary focus is on the sequential behavior patterns of the teacher, not the student.

CATEGORY DESCRIPTIONS

The FOTOP categories make it possible for the observer to record the frequency and sequential order in which they are employed. The organizational patterns have been subdivided into two major classes: teaching and nonteaching. Teaching includes all teacher organizational patterns directly related to acquisition of motor skills. The teaching categories are cognitive structuring, mass activity instruction, group instruction, individual instruction, and testing. Nonteaching includes all teacher patterns not directly related to teacher acts. The nonteaching categories include managerial functions, supervision, officiating, participating, and other, which is included to pick up any procedure that cannot be placed in the above categories.

Teaching

Cognitive Structuring (1)

Teacher speaks directly to the entire class; class physical movement is restricted (standing, sitting); includes lecturing, demonstrating, asking questions, and so forth.

Mass Activity Instruction (2)

Entire class actively engages in teacher-directed controlled learning movements; instructional actions are directed toward class as a whole. *Examples:* Drills, controlled game situations.

Small Group Instruction (3)

Any cluster of two or more students but not the entire class engaged in teacher-directed controlled learning movements; the teacher's attention must be focused on the group at the time the observation is recorded. *Example:* Station teaching.

Individual Instruction (4)

Teaching on a one-to-one basis; instructional actions are directed to one individual. This supersedes mass activity instruction and small group instruction and is recorded regardless of the category in which it occurs.

Testing (5)

Any procedure that involves formal evaluation; this is recorded when it is observed regardless of the category in which it occurs. Testing supersedes individual instruction.

Nonteaching

Managerial Functions (6)

This includes all nonteaching operations involving paperwork or the performance of administrative duties. *Examples:* Calling roll, reading bulletins, writing passes, issuing equipment, moving class to instruction area, and giving directions.

Supervisional Functions (7)

This involves no direct instruction on the part of the teacher, but the teacher must be aware of what the class is doing. *Example:* Students play games or practice skills on their own.

Officiating (8)

Operations involving the enforcement of previously learned behaviors and regulations. The teacher performs only in the role of an official.

Participating (Informal Interactions) (9)

Teacher enters into activity or discussion for self-recreational or non-task-directed purposes.

Other (10)

Any teacher organizational pattern or function that cannot be placed in one of the previous nine categories.

RECORDING PROCEDURES

The FOTOP recording sheet lists the categories on the left side separated from each other by parallel lines. Teaching categories are listed on the top half of the sheet and Nonteaching on the bottom half. There are five 2-minute time module columns separated by vertical lines. A person observing a 10-minute segment of class begins recording in the first 2-minute module with Number 1 and at ensuing 15-second intervals records numbers 2-8 in the appropriate category slots. If more than one organizational behavior occurs in the 15-second interval, the observer decides what behavior predominated and records that behavior in the appropriate category. Simultaneous observations of the same teachers were made using 10- and 15-second intervals. Significant differences in recorded behaviors were not noted. Therefore, the 15-second interval was selected to make it easier for the observer.

SUMMARIZING AND INTERPRETING THE DATA

Upon completion of all five 2-minute segments, the total time in each category is summarized in minutes and seconds. For further study, a percentage of the total time observed (10 minutes) can be determined for each category by converting time to seconds and dividing by 600. Upon completion of the observation period, it is possible for the teacher to receive objective feedback regarding time spent in the various categories and the flow pattern employed. Feedback from FOTOP should enable physical education teachers to organize their operational procedures more effectively.

Figure 14.1 is a completed recording sheet for a college volleyball class. The first minute (Numbers 1-4) was spent in managerial functions, in this case taking roll. The next 1 minute and 45 seconds were spent in cognitive structure, in this case reviewing technique. The instructor then moved to mass activity instruction (Numbers 4-8) for a warm-up activity, after which the teams began playing the game and the instructor moved to officiating through the next 3 minutes. The next category was individual instruction (Column 4, Numbers 5 and 6). The Numbers 5 and 6 are circled, indicating that the two 15-second intervals were spent with one

Instructor _Instructor A_   Date _10/14_

Observer _Observer A_   Activity _Volleyball_   Teaching station _Gym 203_

Class beginning time _10:00_   Ending time _10:50_

Coding beginning time _10:00_   Ending time _10:10_

Teaching	2 min 1	2 min 2	2 min 3	2 min 4	2 min 5	Total time min:sec	% of total time
Cognitive structure	5, 6, 7, 8	1, 2, 3				1:45	17.5
Mass activity instruction		4, 5, 6, 7, 8				1:15	12.5
Group instruction							
Individual instruction				(5, 6)	1, 2	1:00	10
Testing							
Nonteaching							
Managerial functions	1, 2, 3, 4					1:00	10
Supervising				7, 8	3, 4	1:00	10
Officiating			1, 2, 3, 4, 5, 6, 7, 8	1, 2, 3, 4		3:00	30
Participating					5, 6, 7, 8	1:00	10
Other							

Instructions: Record by placing Numbers 1-8 in the appropriate category and time module every 15 sec. To find percentage, convert time to seconds and divide by 600.

Comments: (Use back of sheet if necessary)

Figure 14.1 Completed Flow of Teacher Organizational Patterns (FOTOP) recording sheet.

student. The instructor next began supervising (Column 4, Numbers 7 and 8) and then in Column 5 gave individual instruction. This instruction was given to two different students (Numbers 1 and 2). The instructor returned to supervising (Column 5, Numbers 3 and 4). After supervising for 30 seconds, the instructor began participating in the game (Column 5, Numbers 5-8). At the conclusion it was determined that the instructor had spent his time as follows: cognitive structure, 17.5%; mass activity instruction, 12.5%; individual instruction, 10%; managerial functions, 10%; supervising, 10%; officiating, 30%; and participating, 10%. By reviewing the FOTOP, the instructor could decide if the flow pattern and time spent in the various categories were in keeping with his or her expectations.

In addition to observing individual teachers, student teachers, and undergraduate minilessons, FOTOP has been used to compare two teachers (a male and a female) in a team-teaching situation, to observe 3 hr of a high school varsity basketball practice, to compare elementary teaching patterns with secondary patterns, to compare the time spent in teaching categories with nonteaching categories at the secondary level, and to observe teacher behavior while working with emotionally disturbed and educable mentally retarded children.

FOTOP was designed primarily for use by teachers in the field. Students can be trained to use it in a very short time, much like learning to keep statistics and shot charts. With some sophistication it is acceptable as a research instrument. Some categories, such as Managerial Functions, are very general. Therefore, it is suggested that FOTOP be used as an initial observation instrument. As patterns are identified, more specific instruments could be used to observe particular teaching-learning behaviors more closely.

Chapter 15

Student Teachers Observing Peers (STOP)

Patt Dodds

Student Teachers Observing Peers (STOP) is designed for use by student teachers paired in the same setting so they can observe and provide feedback to each other. Four major categories of teacher behavior are recorded using event recording, duration recording, and placheck: instructional input, skill feedback, social behavior feedback, and management. Interobserver agreement (observational reliability) by simultaneous recording in a live setting ranges from .86 to .98. Construct validity of these behavior categories was established from a review of literature on teacher behavior research and applied behavior analysis (behavioral psychology).

Because student behaviors are not recorded (except by a periodic placheck), the data do not show direct relationships between teacher and student actions in the learning environment. In addition, when a time-sampling recording format is not superimposed (Siedentop, 1976), a continuous recording in all categories at the same time may contribute to observer fatigue before the end of the class session. One or more portions of the instrument may be used separately to collect data on teacher behaviors particularly important to a given student teacher.

CATEGORY DESCRIPTIONS

Within each major category, more than one subcategory label is used for each instance of teacher behavior. The coding form has separate boxes for recording event tallies of each possible combination of subcategories.

Instructional Input

Teacher cues (statements or questions) before movement activities are attempted to tell students what to do or how to do it. Instructional input must be directly related to the movement activities and tasks. It may be further labeled as Question or Statement, Open or Closed. *Example*: ''First we will practice moving a large ball with different body parts. Think about control at all times so you can stop the ball within 2 seconds whenever you hear the signal. Which body parts might you use to have the best control?''

Open Instruction.   Questions or statements allowing students a variety or choice of movement responses. *Example:* ''Decide which of the five soccer dribbling tasks you need the most practice on and see if you can improve your time or score from yesterday. Be sure to mark your new scores or times on your activity card.''

Closed Instruction.   Questions or statements specifying the same movement task for all students with no choice or decisions by students. *Example:* ''Everyone keep both hands together on the bat and try to do level swings.''

Skill Feedback

Verbal reactions, after student attempts to perform the next movement skill, intended to provide additional information to improve the next skill attempt. It may be further labeled as positive, corrective, or negative; general or specific.

Positive.   Verbal reactions to correct, well-executed aspects of the movement skill attempt. *Example:* ''Good forehand, John. You really shifted your weight forward at the right time.''

Corrective.   Verbal reactions to incorrect, poorly executed aspects of the movement skill attempt without the additional flavoring of a personal put-down. *Example:* ''Sue, if you took the racket head back a little sooner your swing might not feel so rushed.''

Negative.   Verbal reactions to incorrect, poorly executed aspects of the movement skill attempt with the explicit addition of a personal put-down. *Example:* ''Ted, you're a rotten tennis player for being so good at racquetball! Pay more attention to those next services and get them in the court.''

General.   Verbal reactions conveying positive, corrective, or negative teacher appraisal of movement skill attempts without either exact prescriptions for improving subsequent performance or precise targeting of the specific aspect of performance that triggered the teacher comment. *Example:* ''I can't believe you keep sending those lobs over the fence, Jane.''

Specific.   Verbal reactions conveying positive, corrective, or negative appraisal of movement skill attempts including either precise targeting of the aspect of performance that triggered the comment or exact prescriptions for improving subsequent performance. *Example:* ''Jim, swing your racket upward more. That should help keep your lobs in the court rather than beyond the baseline where they're landing now."

Social Behavior Feedback

Verbal reactions to all student actions other than movement skill attempts for the purpose of providing additional information about those actions. Student actions include, but are not limited to, approved or unapproved physical or verbal interactions with other students, individual attending or not attending to the movement tasks set, or any type of behavior contributing to learning or detracting from it. Social behavior feedback may be further labeled as positive, corrective, or negative; general or specific.

Subcategory Labels. The definitions for positive, corrective, negative, general, and specific subcategories are the same as for the skill feedback category, but teacher reactions are to student actions not directly involving movement skill attempts. *Examples:* (Positive, specific) "Thank you, Group 3, for getting into your soccer positions so quickly—now we have more time for the game." (Corrective, general) "Stop that, Sam, and get back to work." (Positive, general) "Thanks for being so good today, Paul." (Negative, specific) "If I ever see you hit him again, Joe, I'll send you to the principal so fast it'll make your head swim. But I guess I shouldn't expect anything better from a member of the notorious Smith family, anyway."

Management

Teacher actions for organizing students and equipment and for beginning, changing, and terminating activities within the learning environment.

Episode Length. The duration of a teacher's managerial episode. An episode is a continuous set of teacher managerial actions, beginning with the first teacher managerial comment and ending when the teacher begins a different kind of activity, usually when most students are engaged in the new activity.

Episode endings are sometimes difficult to determine. The clearest arbitrary definition is to end the episode when the first student begins the new activity. An alternative is to end when the last student becomes engaged. In the first instance, teacher management time estimates are unrealistically short, whereas in the second, management time estimates are too long. Perhaps the most accurate end for a managerial episode is determined by the teacher's own expectations for student compliance with a request. When a teacher turns attention to other aspects of the learning environment after a managerial request, observers can assume the teacher is satisfied that enough students have responded, and other teaching activities can be pursued. Teachers may do any of the following to terminate a managerial episode: (a) start explaining a movement skill or rules for a game (Instructional Input), (b) give feedback to one or more students about movement performance or social behaviors unrelated to the managerial episode (skill feedback or social behavior feedback), (c) obviously monitor or watch without speaking to one or more students engaged in the new activity, (d) begin an entirely different managerial episode (e.g., change one's mind about how to organize students and start over with a different request), or (e) attend to functions not directly related to the learning situation (e.g., filling out attendance forms, talking with another teacher). *Example:* Teacher asks for groups of four (begin episode: observer's stopwatch starts), repeats the direction to one girl, then hustles all students to get into groups of four. Teacher waits. Teacher gives feedback to the five groups who are ready (end episode: stopwatch stops when this social behavior feedback is given; duration of episode = 4 minutes, 23 seconds).

Number of (Teacher Managerial) Behaviors.   Each separate teacher comment within the managerial episode, including the initial request, additional information, and direct or paraphrased repetitions of the initial request. The number of teacher managerial behaviors indicates to some degree how tuned in students are to that teacher's management strategies. Teachers who have few managerial behaviors and short episodes are getting students to respond quickly, whereas teachers with many behaviors and long episodes organize students very slowly. *Example:* "Get yourselves into groups of four as quickly as possible. Jill, did you hear? Groups of four, not five or six—four! Let's go, kids, everybody in groups of four; we've wasted 3 minutes already" (three managerial behaviors).

Pl(acheck) Appr(opriate).   A quick all-inclusive (3-5 second) glance around the whole class to count the number of students who are engaged in movement performance or directly related behaviors that, in the observer's mind, contribute to a positive learning environment. *Example:* Twenty students wait in line, five are dribbling soccer balls, two are listening to the teacher answer a question, three are hitting each other: Pl Appr = 27 (three are off-task, not contributing to the learning environment).

Pl(acheck) Ac(tive).   A quick glance around the entire class to count those students who are actually moving and practicing the teacher-designated movement tasks. *Example:* Only the five students dribbling soccer balls (from the previous example) would be included here (the other 25 are inactive or involved in other kinds of activity).

Targeting Students

In the three major categories discussed so far, teacher comments may be directed to all students present (class), to a subgroup of two or more students (group), or to a single student (individual). Boxes in the coding form allow for separate tallies for each target possibility.

RECORDING PROCEDURES

Three recording procedures are used to collect the data (Cooper, 1974). Event recording yields all information for the instructional input, skill feedback, and social behavior feedback categories, whereas duration recording and placheck are used to record management data. Observers code for the entire class period or make prior arrangements to observe for any portion of a class. Recording is continuous with no rest periods, and the observers note the exact starting and ending times for each recording session. This allows comparisons to be made across several observations. Observers record behaviors in all four categories whenever those behaviors occur. The recording sheet is shown in Figure 15.1.

Observers must decide which major category each teacher comment fits into and then further label the comment with the appropriate subcategories. For example, a tally is marked in the box for positive specific skill feedback to a group, rather than skill feedback only. For beginners, the STOP subcategories are ignored and recordings done for the four major categories only. Subcategory distinctions are added gradually for one major category at a time as soon as observers can handle them.

Duration recording is used for episode length under management. The observer starts a stopwatch at the beginning of the managerial episode and stops it when the end of the episode is apparent. Times are recorded in seconds on the recording sheet.

Placheck is used for placheck appropriate and placheck active in management. Observers listen via earphones to a prerecorded audiocassette tape with timed intervals. Plachecks are generally done every 2-3 minutes during an observation session, but intervals may be longer or shorter depending on the observers' skill level and the situation. Observers record the number of students engaged in either appropriate or active behaviors. This is usually easier to do by counting the students not doing appropriate or active behaviors (because this number is usually smaller, it takes less time to count).

ST teaching _Patt_   Start time _10:19_

ST observing _Frank_   Stop time _10:54_

Date _9/18_   Total minutes _37 min_

Class/activity   _5th grade/volleyball_

Instructional input (II)						II
	Question		Statement		Totals ▶	
	Open	Closed	Open	Closed		57
Class	5	10	0	25	40	
Group	0	2	0	5	7	
Individual	6	0	0	4	10	
	11	12	0	34	Totals ▼	

Skill feedback (SKFB)							SKFB
	Positive		Corrective		Negative		Totals ▶
	Specific	General	Specific	General	Specific	General	59
Class	2	14	7	2	0	0	25
Group	1	0	8	0	0	0	9
Individual	1	8	15	0	1	0	25
	4	22	30	2	1	0	Totals ▼

Social behavior feedback (SBFB)							SBFB
	Positive		Corrective		Negative		Totals ▶
	Specific	General	Specific	General	Specific	General	14
Class	0	3	0	10	0	0	13
Group	0	0	0	0	0	0	0
Individual	0	0	0	1	0	0	1
	0	3	0	11	0	0	Totals ▼

Management	1	2	3	4	5	6	7	8	Totals
Episode length	53	182	77						$\overline{X}$ = 104 Total = .312 or 5:12
# T. behaviors	2	6	2						$\overline{X}$ = 3.33/Episode
Placheck appr.	27	26	20	10	11	10	28	26	$\overline{X}$ = 19.75
Placheck active	15	15	13	17	15	19	18	13	$\overline{X}$ = 15.50

Figure 15.1 Completed Student Teachers Observing Peers (STOP) recording sheet with grouped data.

SUMMARIZING AND INTERPRETING THE DATA

At the end of each observation session, all data are totaled within each major category and its subcategories (see Figure 15.2). Event recorded and placheck data yield raw numbers, whereas management episode

ST teaching _Patt_____   Start time _10:17_____

ST observing _Frank_____   Stop time _10:54_____

Date _9/18_____   Total minutes _37 min_____

Class/activity _5th grade/volleyball____   Observation # _1_____

Categories	Raw # totals	Percentages	Rates/minute
All sections	130		3.5
Instructional input	57	44 Total behaviors	1.5
Class	40	70	1.1
Group	7	12	0.2
Individual	10	18	0.3
Questions, open	11	19	0.3
Questions, closed	12	21	0.3
Statements, open	0	0	0.0
Statements, closed	34	60	0.9
Skill feedback	59	45 Total behaviors	1.6
Class	25	42	0.7
Group	9	15	0.2
Individual	25	42	0.7
Positive, specific	4	7	0.1
Positive, general	22	37	0.6
Corrective, specific	30	51	0.8
Corrective, general	2	3	0.1
Negative, specific	1	2	0.0
Negative, general	0	0	0.0
Social behavior feedback	14	11 Total behaviors	0.4
Class	13	93	0.4
Group	0	0	0.0
Individual	1	7	0.0
Positive, specific	0	0	0.0
Positive, general	3	21	0.1
Corrective, specific	0	0	0.0
Corrective, general	11	79	0.3
Negative, specific	0	0	0.0
Negative, general	0	0	0.0

Management

Episode length: $\overline{X}$ = 104(1:44)

$$\frac{\text{Total management time}}{\text{Total class time}} = \frac{5:12}{37:00} = 14\% \text{ class time}$$

T Behaviors: $\overline{X}$ = 3.33/episode (Total = 10)

Placheck appropriate: An average of _20_ students were on-task when surveyed.

Placheck active: An average of _15_ students were moving when surveyed.

Figure 15.2 Completed Student Teachers Observing Peers (STOP) data summary sheet.

length is totaled in seconds. Means are calculated for episode length, number of (teacher managerial) behaviors, placheck appropriate, and placheck active.

Rates per minute are calculated for all categories but management by dividing the raw total by the length of the class observation session (beginning and ending times recorded on the recording sheet). Percentages are also calculated for comparing all major categories but management and for all subcategories. To do this, total all events recorded in instructional input, skill feedback, and social behavior feedback, and then divide by the total in the particular category of interest. The same process for calculating percentages can be applied to all subcategories of these three major categories.

Data sheets for each observation session are retained for comparisons across time. Each data category may be extracted from the total recording sheet for separate display (see Figure 15.3) on a line graph. This allows direct comparisons across time of very specific subcategories and can be done as raw totals, rates per minute, or percentages.

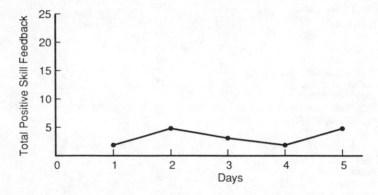

Figure 15.3   Student teaching Week 1: Raw totals for Positive Skill Feedback to Individuals.

Student teachers use STOP data to obtain an objective picture of their own performances in four categories of teaching behavior. They also become aware of those same teacher behaviors by observing their partners, thus being doubly sensitized to a great deal of very specific information about teaching actions. Value judgments about the quality of performance can then be based on such objectively collected data, but they are clearly separate propositions. The STOP instrument provides ongoing, baseline data that may indicate the desirability of applying behavior change strategies for altering certain teaching actions. The effectiveness of those change strategies can then be monitored by continuing to record behavior using the STOP instrument during and after the behavior change intervention occurs.

ACKNOWLEDGMENTS

The author wishes to acknowledge that this observation system is based on behavior categories in dissertations at Ohio State University done by Frank Rife (1973), Carey Hughley (1973), Paul Darst (1974), Keith Hamilton (1974), and Jack Boehm (1974).

REFERENCES

Cooper, J. (1974). *Measurement and analysis of behavioral techniques*. Columbus, OH: Charles E. Merrill.

Siedentop, D. (1976). *Developing teaching skills in physical education*. Boston: Houghton Mifflin.

Chapter 16

Systematic Observation of Student Opportunities to Respond (SOSOR)

Will Brown

Systematic Observation of Student Opportunities to Respond (SOSOR) was developed to determine the effects of game modifications on student opportunities to participate. It was designed to identify opportunities to respond (OTRs) (Hall, Delquadri, & Harris, 1977) and specific skill responses and to qualify the responses as being either acceptable or unacceptable, and either successful or unsuccessful. The assumption was that the most efficient game modification, in terms of student learning, would provide more OTRs and more acceptable/successful responses.

The instrument was used with mean interobserver agreement scores of 80-100% for each unit of analysis: OTRs, responses, acceptable/unacceptable, and successful/unsuccessful. Graduate students learned the system in 8-10 hr of training.

The original instrument was used to analyze videotapes of fifth grade children playing volleyball and soccer game modifications. The skills for each game were chosen and defined in such a way that they formed a facet (Dunkin & Biddle, 1974); that is, all discrete skill responses were codable into one of the selected and defined skills. It is conceivable that SOSOR could be adapted for use with any game modification. The data collection was limited to target students who were assigned to play on courts and fields that were in the camera's range of view.

CATEGORY DESCRIPTIONS

OTR

Players have OTRs when the game puts them in situations in which they *could* emit a discrete skill response.

Skill Response

When the game provides an OTR, the player may choose to emit either a discrete skill response or no response. (The discrete volleyball skills were serving, passing, bumping, digging, spiking, blocking, and dinking. The discrete soccer skills were kicking, trapping, dribbling, throwing, and goalkeeping.)

Acceptable (A)/Unacceptable (UA) Responses

Each discrete skill response has topographical criteria (i.e., form; Merrill, 1971), which are used to determine whether it is acceptable or unacceptable. When the topographical criteria are emitted, the response is acceptable. When they are omitted, the response is unacceptable. In addition, an inappropriate response (i.e., the chosen skill is not the one that should have been emitted) is considered as being unacceptable.

Successful (S)/Unsuccessful (US) Responses

Each discrete skill response has either successful or unsuccessful results. If the intended results occur (e.g., the flow of the game continues), the response is successful. If unintended results occur, the response is unsuccessful.

No Response

When given an OTR, the player must choose not to respond. The player may emit avoidance behavior, escape behavior, or be out of position and be unable to respond.

For the purpose of identifying OTRs, categorizing skill responses, and qualifying the responses, we had to define each discrete skill response and determine topographical and results criteria. An example for the discrete skill of serving in volleyball is shown in Table 16.1.

RECORDING PROCEDURES

The SOSOR provides a chronological picture of the series of OTRs and skill responses for each observed student for the entire length of the game. The recording sheet is shown in Figure 16.1. When an OTR is identified, record the time (a stopwatch may be used or the time can be dubbed onto the videotape) in the "Sequence" column. For each OTR, identify the discrete skill that was emitted and place the code in the "Code" column. If no response was emitted, record "N." If a discrete response was emitted, determine if the topography was acceptable or unacceptable and

Table 16.1 Systematic Observation of Student Opportunities to Respond (SOSOR) Skill Definition and Performance Criteria for the Volleyball Serve

Code   S

Definition
   The ball is propelled over the net by the hand for the purpose of putting the ball in play.

Topography
   For a response to be one of serving, the player must
   1. hold the ball in the nonhitting hand in front of the hitting hand's side of the body (a small toss is acceptable),
   2. swing the hand in an underhand motion and *behind* the back leg *before* swinging it forward, and
   3. step with the opposite foot, or start with the opposite foot forward.

Results
   The *successful* serve travels over the net and initiates the potential for game play. The following is an example:
   1. The ball clears the net and contacts the floor within the boundaries, or is hit by an opponent.
   The *unsuccessful* serve does not initiate game play. The following are examples:
   1. The ball does not clear the net.
   2. The ball hits the ceiling or a wall, or touches the floor outside the boundaries.

if it was an appropriate response and record a tally in the corresponding column. Finally, determine if the response was successful or unsuccessful and record a tally in the corresponding column. If no response was emitted, no tallies are recorded for topography or results.

SUMMARIZING AND INTERPRETING THE DATA

Interobserver agreement (IOA) can be calculated for each unit or combined units of analysis using Equation 3.1.

   Compare the total OTRs (sequence column) recorded by two independent observers. Divide the smaller total by the larger total and multiply by 100.

   Compare, line by line, the responses in the code column. Each line that has matching times and response codes is counted as an agreement. Each line that has matching times and different response codes is counted as a disagreement. Each line in which only one observer recorded a time

Soccer		Volleyball			
Trap—T	Throw—C	Serve—S	Spike—I	Counter start	0268
Kick—K	Goalkeep—G	Pass—P	Block—C	Counter stop	1396
Dribble—D	No response—N	Bump—B	Dink—K	Timer stop	16:41
	Uncodable—X	Dig—D	No response—N	Timer start	1:25
				Total time	15:15

Volleyball/Soccer Class # _1_ of 20   Date of lesson _4/26_ Modification _4_

Observer: _Brown_   Date of observation _2/17_

Subject: _James_   Subject: _Sally_

Response sequence	Skill code	Topography A	UA	Results S	US	Response sequence	Skill code	Topography A	UA	Results S	US
1 1:29	P	1		1		1 1:35	P		1	1	
2 2:13	P		1	1		2 1:46	B		1		1
3 2:25	N					3 1:54	N				
4 2:33	N					4 2:08	N				
5 4:20	P		1	1		5 2:12	P		1	1	
6 6:59	P		1		1	6 2:14	P		1		1
7 8:24	P		1		1	7 2:25	N				
8 8:42	P		1		1	8 3:47	S		1	1	
9 9:23	P		1		1	9 4:02	S		1	1	
10 9:45	P	1		1		10 4:06	P		1	1	
11 12:12	P		1		1	11 5:37	P		1		1
12 14:14	S	1			1	12 5:52	P		1	1	
13 15:01	P		1		1	13 6:43	S		1		1
14						14 8:21	S		1	1	
15						15 9:20	S		1	1	
16						16 9:45	P		1	1	
17						17 10:42	S	1			1
18						18 11:12	P		1		1
19						19 11:58	S		1		1
20						20 14:11	N				
21						21 15:20	P		1	1	
Totals		3	8	4	7	Totals		1	16	10	7

Figure 16.1 Completed Systematic Observation of Student Opportunities to Respond (SOSOR) recording sheet.

is counted as an omission. Omissions are disagreements. No responses (N) are not included in the calculations. IOA scores are calculated by using Equation 3.1 described in chapter 3.

For each skill response, compare the corresponding tallies recorded by two independent observers for acceptable/unacceptable and successful/unsuccessful responses. For each pair of columns, matching tallies are agreements. IOA scores are calculated by using Equation 3.1 shown for responses. Separate IOA scores can be calculated for acceptable/unacceptable and for successful/unsuccessful responses.

The totals for each category are divided by the total game time, minus rests, to provide rates per minute. The rates can be compared to identify any differences between students and/or game modifications. The data can be visually inspected by displaying them on multielement graphs (Ulman & Sulzer-Azaroff, 1973).

ACKNOWLEDGMENTS

The author collaborated with Dr. Susan Lawless and Dr. Melissa Parker, former Ohio State University graduate students, while developing some of the original definitions and skill criteria.

REFERENCES

Dunkin, M.J., & Biddle, B.J. (1974). *The study of teaching*. New York: Holt, Rinehart, & Winston.

Hall, R.V., Delquadri, J., & Harris, J. (1977, May). *Opportunity to respond: A new focus in the field of applied behavior analysis*. Paper presented at the Midwest Association for Applied Behavior Analysis, Chicago.

Merrill, M.D. (1971). Psychomotor and memorization behavior. In M.D. Merrill (Ed.), *Instructional design: Readings* (pp. 196-214). Englewood Cliffs, NJ: Prentice-Hall.

Ulman, J.D., & Sulzer-Azaroff, B. (1973). Multielement baseline design in educational research. In E. Ramp & A. Semb (Eds.), *Behavior analysis: Areas of research and application* (pp. 377-391). Englewood Cliffs, NJ: Prentice-Hall.

Chapter 17

Academic Learning Time-Physical Education (ALT-PE), 1982 Revision

Melissa Parker

The notion that student engagement with the subject matter to be learned is a powerful predictor of achievement is not new (Carroll, 1963; Jackson, 1968). Many descriptors have been applied to the concept, but it was Berliner (1979), in the Beginning Teacher Evaluation Study (BTES), who coined the phrase "academic learning time." In the BTES three measures of instructional time were developed. *Allocated time* referred to the time a teacher allocated for instruction and practice in a particular subject area. *Engaged time* referred to that portion of allocated time that a student was actually involved with the subject matter. *Academic learning time* (ALT) was that portion of engaged time when the student was involved with materials that were appropriate to his or her abilities, resulting in high success and low error rates. Academic Learning Time-Physical Education (ALT-PE) is an application of this notion to the physical education setting.

ALT-PE was originally developed and subsequently refined by Siedentop and graduate students at Ohio State University (Metzler, 1979; Siedentop, Birdwell, & Metzler, 1979; Siedentop, Tousignant, & Parker, 1982). The purpose of the ALT-PE instrument is to measure the portion of time in a physical education lesson that a student is involved in motor activity at an appropriate success rate. The total instrument is capable of describing not only the type of motor activity (e.g., skill practice, scrimmage, game, fitness) in which selected students are involved, but also the context (general or subject matter) in which the total class is involved. The information on motor activity provides the most useful data for physical education.

ALT-PE has several limitations:

- ALT-PE is a time-based concept that commonly uses interval recording techniques. As such, ALT-PE is limited by the nature of interval recording techniques (Siedentop, 1983).

- ALT-PE is not sensitive to differences among motor performances in various physical education activities. A unit of ALT-PE can refer to anything from walking on a balance beam and doing aerobic dance to playing goalie in soccer. Further, even within the game setting, ALT-PE does not delineate what players are doing—whether they are playing the ball or playing off the ball waiting for a play to occur.
- ALT-PE provides a picture of only a small portion of what happens in physical education. As Anderson (1983) states, it provides a "shadow of shadows . . . a meager representation of the richness of realities" (p. 54).
- ALT-PE does not measure the congruence between learner needs and content goal (Rink & Werner, 1985).
- ALT-PE is not sensitive to the goals of a given lesson.
- ALT-PE does not indicate the quality of the practice. Success rate may not be a discriminating enough variable.

CATEGORY DESCRIPTIONS

The ALT-PE interval recording instrument, as currently conceived, is a two-level, hierarchical decision-making system. The first level of the system requires a decision on the context of the setting under observation. The second level involves observations of the individual learner's involvement.

Context Level

The context level describes the context of the setting within which specific individual student behavior is occurring. This level is comprised of two major facets: general content and subject matter content.

General Content

Class time during which students are not intended to be involved in physical education activities.

Transition (T).   Time devoted to managerial and organizational activities related to instruction.

Management (M).   Time devoted to class business that is unrelated to instructional activity.

Break (B).   Time devoted to rest and/or discussion of issues unrelated to subject matter.

Warm-Up (WU). Time devoted to routine execution of physical activities whose purpose is to prepare the individual for engaging in further activity, but not designed to alter the state of the individual on a long-term basis.

Subject Matter Knowledge Content

Class time when the primary focus is intended to be on knowledge related to physical education content.

Technique (TN). Time devoted to transmitting information concerning the physical form (topography) of a motor skill.

Strategy (ST). Time devoted to transmitting information concerning plans of action for performing either individually or as a group.

Rules (R). Time devoted to transmitting information about regulations that govern activity related to the subject matter.

Social Behavior (SB). Time devoted to transmitting information about appropriate and inappropriate ways of behaving within the context of the activity.

Background (BK). Time devoted to transmitting information about a subject matter activity such as its history, traditions, rituals, heroes, heroines, records, importance in later life, or relationship to fitness.

Subject Matter Motor Content

Class time when the primary focus is intended to be on motor involvement in physical education activities.

Skill Practice (P). Time devoted to practice of skills or chains of skills outside the applied context with primary goal of skill development.

Scrimmage/Routine (S). Time devoted to refinement and extension of skills in an applied setting (i.e., in a setting that is like or simulates the setting in which the skill is actually used) and during which there is frequent instruction and feedback for the participants.

Game (G). Time devoted to the application of skills in a game or competitive setting when the participants perform without intervention from the instructor/coach.

Fitness (F). Time devoted to activities whose purpose is to alter the physical state of the individual in terms of strength, cardiovascular endurance, or flexibility.

Learner Involvement Level

The learner involvement level describes how individual learners are involved in the physical education setting described in the context level. The learner involvement level has two facets: not motor engaged and motor engaged.

Not Motor Engaged

Any student involvement other than motor involvement with subject matter-oriented motor activities.

Interim (I).   The student is engaged in a noninstructional aspect of an ongoing activity.

Waiting (W).   The student has completed a task and is waiting for the next instructions or opportunity to respond.

Off-Task (OF).   The student is either not engaged in an activity he or she should be engaged in or is engaged in an activity other than the one he or she should be engaged in.

On-Task (ON).   The student is appropriately engaged in carrying out an assigned non-subject-matter task (e.g., management task, transition task, warm-up task).

Cognitive (C).   The student is appropriately involved in a cognitive task.

Motor Engaged

Motor involvement with subject matter-oriented motor activities related to the goals of the setting. Thus the categories under the heading not motor engaged may include motor activity, but not subject matter-oriented motor activity.

Motor Appropriate (MA).   The student is engaged in a subject matter motor activity in such a way as to produce a high degree of success.

Motor Inappropriate (MI).   The student is engaged in a subject matter-oriented activity, but the activity-task is either too difficult for the individual's capabilities or so easy that practicing it could not contribute to lesson goals.

Supporting (MS).   The student is engaged in subject matter motor activity whose purpose is to assist others in learning or performing the activity.

RECORDING PROCEDURES

ALT-PE was originally conceptualized as an interval recording system, and, though other methods of data collection have since been developed (Metzler, DePaepe, & Reif, 1985; Siedentop, Tousignant, & Parker, 1982), it is referred to here as an interval system. (Those readers who are interested in alternative data collection methods are directed to the original sources for such information.)

Interval recording is an observation technique by which an individual or group is observed for a specific length of time (i.e., interval) and a decision is made as to what behavior category best represents the behavior of the individual or group during that time. Interval recording is a sampling process in that samples of behavior are collected periodically. As with any sampling process, the more samples that are collected and the more evenly those samples are distributed across the total time, the more representative the sample is to what actually transpired during the total length of the observation session.

The length of the observation interval must be consistent and only as long as needed to accurately code the defined behaviors. The typical interval length for the ALT-PE instrument is 12 seconds. The interval recording technique employed by ALT-PE is an observe/record format: the first 6 seconds of the interval are used to observe and the second 6 seconds to record the observation on the coding sheet. To keep observations in the proper order and time, a preprogrammed audiotape is used to provide observe/record cues.

Figure 17.1 depicts the interval recording portion of the coding sheet for the ALT-PE system. Generally, three target students (one high-, one medium-, and one low-skilled) are observed in sequence for an entire class period. If three students are used for observation, the first row of intervals would be assigned to Student 1, the second row to Student 2, the third row to Student 3, the fourth row to Student 1, and so forth. The actual coding moves down columns before moving across rows. The first observe-record interval would focus on Student 1, the second on Student 2, the third on Student 3, the fourth on Student 1, and so on.

The demographic information portion of the ALT-PE recording sheet is shown in Figure 17.2. This portion of the sheet contains spaces to identify the teacher, date, school, activity, observer, allocated time, and other information that is critical to any particular lesson. On the recording portion of the coding sheet (Figure 17.1) the "C" (context) and "LI" (learner involvement) adjacent to rows of intervals correspond to the decision levels of the instrument. The categories are written at the bottom of the coding sheet with an appropriate symbol for each category.

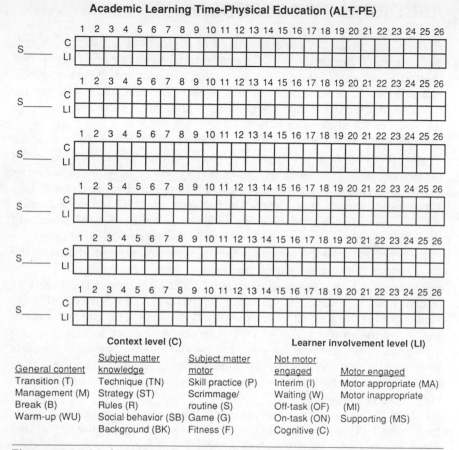

Figure 17.1 Academic Learning Time-Physical Education (ALT-PE) interval recording sheet.

The coding conventions for this two-level decision system are straight-forward. For each observation interval, the context is first noted and then the specific student is observed to ascertain the nature of his or her involvement. If a general content or subject matter knowledge category is chosen at the context level, the second-level decision is from categories in the not motor engaged group. If a subject matter motor category is chosen at the context level, the second-level decision uses the entire learner involvement category system. Any observation sample in which motor appropriate is chosen in the second-level decision becomes one unit of ALT-PE. A completed recording sheet is shown in Figure 17.3; ALT-PE intervals are circled.

After making the appropriate decision in each interval, the observer

Academic Learning Time-Physical
Education (ALT-PE)

Date: _____ Teacher: _____ School: _____

Class/activity: _____ Observer: _____

Start time: _____ Stop time: _____ Duration: _____ Page ___ of ___

This observation is day _____ of _____ days in this unit.

The teacher allocated _____ minutes of activity time for this lesson.

The source of this allocation information was (teacher, lesson plan).

Observer comments on this class:

Data summary

Total time _____ Allocated practice time _____ ALT-PE _____

Context level data: general content _____

    subject matter knowledge _____ subject matter motor _____

Learner involvement data: not motor engaged _____ motor engaged _____

Figure 17.2   Academic Learning Time-Physical Education (ALT-PE) demographic information recording sheet.

writes the appropriate symbol in the appropriate box for each observation interval. If adjacent intervals (across rows) have the same category, this may be represented by a dash (—) rather than repeating the symbol. To review, the ALT-PE system involves a group-focused context decision and an individually focused learner involvement decision for each observation sample. Those observation samples in which a subject matter content motor category is chosen at the context level and motor appropriate is chosen at the learner involvement level are ALT-PE samples. The decision system is summarized below on a step-by-step basis.

Step 1: Context level decision.

What is the context of the class? What is the class doing as a whole?

Choices:	*General Content*	*Knowledge*	*Motor*
	Transition	Technique	Skill practice
	Management	Strategy	Scrimmage
	Break	Rules	Game
	Warm-up	Social behavior	Fitness
		Background	

Academic Learning Time-Physical Education (ALT-PE)

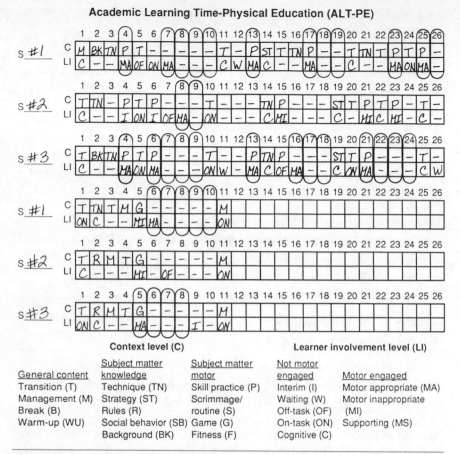

Figure 17.3 Completed Academic Learning Time-Physical Education (ALT-PE) recording sheet.

Step 2: Learner involvement decision.

What is the nature of the individual learner's engagement? What is the individual student doing?

Choices: | *Not Motor Engaged* | *Motor Engaged* |
|---|---|
| Interim | Motor appropriate |
| Waiting | Motor inappropriate |
| Off-task | Supporting |
| On-task | |
| Cognitive | |

The methods used to calculate reliability for the ALT-PE instrument are the Interval-by-Interval (I-I) method and the Scored-Interval (S-I) method.

The Scored-Interval method is preferred. See chapter 3 for a detailed description.

SUMMARIZING AND INTERPRETING THE DATA

ALT-PE data could be summarized in several different ways, but the simplest is to express the category under investigation as a percentage of total intervals. Metzler (1983) suggests that this is a three-step process.

First, the raw data recording sheets are scrutinized for coding errors and exclusions (missed intervals). After the data are cleaned, the number of remaining intervals are counted for each target student.

Second, the data are tabulated. The frequency of occurrence for each behavior category is counted and recorded, then converted to a percentage figure by dividing the frequency by the total number of observed intervals. For example, if ALT-PE figures are needed, then the intervals in which MA was recorded at the learner involvement level would be counted and divided by the total number of observed intervals to arrive at the ALT-PE percentage figure. The total length of the observation period can then be multiplied by this percentage figure to obtain an estimate of total time in ALT-PE.

The third step in the procedure, if desired, is to determine the percentage of occurrences for the facets of the context and learner involvement categories. This is done by summing the frequencies of all the subcategories under the general content, subject matter motor, subject matter knowledge, not motor engaged, and motor engaged facets, and then dividing by the total number of intervals. Data can be summarized for each target student. Further, data can be summed across students in a particular class to allow for a generalization about student time involvement in that class.

The primary objective of the ALT-PE recording system is to measure the amount of time that a student spends in motor activity at an appropriate success rate. These data are expressed as percentage of ALT-PE and as the amount of ALT-PE accrued in minutes. ALT-PE could also be determined for each subject matter motor category by counting the MA codes in each motor category (game, practice, scrimmage) separately.

ALT-PE percentages vary widely from setting to setting and activity to activity; although high and low numbers may not be totally indicative of student achievement, they can provide an indicator of the amount of successful practice in any given physical education environment. Metzler's (1979) original study and one conducted by Godbout, Brunelle, and Tousignant (1983) reported ALT-PE levels ranging from 14 to 22%, yet these ALT-PE data contained categories other than the MA category. When all categories except the MA have been removed from the ALT-PE figure, percentages have ranged from approximately 2 to 30% for public school environments (Parker, 1986; Placek & Randall, 1986; Shute, Dodds, Placek, Rife, & Silverman, 1982). By varying instructional strategies, McKenzie, Clark, and McKenzie (1984) were able to increase ALT-PE in university classes to as high as 97.9%. The average ALT-PE percentage for public school classes appears to be somewhere between 15 and 25%. How high this rate should go is uncertain, as there may well be a plateau effect at some point.

Though ALT-PE data and other motor data are of primary importance to most physical educators, data can be interpreted by combining various variables to obtain a picture of other aspects of the class under observation. For example, how a teacher uses instructional time could be examined by combining the categories of technique, strategy, rules, social behavior, background, and management.

When interpreting ALT-PE data, remember that the major purpose, to indicate the amount of time a student spends in motor activity at an appropriate success rate, must remain paramount. Researchers and readers should be cautioned not to generalize beyond the data or the limits of the system.

ACKNOWLEDGMENTS

Much of the material in this chapter was originally published in and is taken directly from Siedentop, Tousignant, and Parker (1982). Though this chapter was written singularly, credit should be given to the two other authors because much of what is contained here is their work.

REFERENCES

Anderson, W. (1983). Observations from outside the system. In P. Dodds & F. Rife (Eds.), Time to learn in physical education: History, completed research, and potential future for academic learning time in physical education. *Journal of Teaching in Physical Education* (Summer Monograph I), 53-57.

Berliner, D. (1979). Tempus educare. In P. Peterson & H. Walberg (Eds.), *Research on teaching* (pp. 120-135). Berkeley: McCutchan.

Carroll, J. (1963). A model for school learning. *Teachers College Record*, **64**, 723-733.

Godbout, P., Brunelle, J., & Tousignant, M. (1983). Academic learning time in elementary and secondary physical education classes. *Research Quarterly for Exercise and Sport*, **54**(1), 11-19.

Jackson, P. (1968). *Life in classrooms*. New York: Holt, Rinehart & Winston.

McKenzie, T., Clark, E., & McKenzie, R. (1984). Instructional strategies: Influence on teacher and student behavior. *Journal of Teaching in Physical Education*, **3**(2), 20-28.

Metzler, M. (1979). *The measurement of academic learning time in physical education.* (Doctoral dissertation, University Microfilms No. 8008314). Columbus, OH: Ohio State University.

Metzler, M. (1983). An interval recording system for measuring academic learning time in physical education. In P. Darst, V. Mancini, & D. Zakrajsek (Eds.), *Systematic observation instrumentation for physical education* (pp. 181-195). Champaign, IL: Leisure Press.

Metzler, M., DePaepe, J., & Rief, G. (1985). Alternative technologies for measuring academic learning time in physical education. *Journal of Teaching in Physical Education,* 4(4), 271-285.

Parker, M. (1986). *Academic learning time physical education.* Unpublished manual, Department of Physical Education, University of South Carolina, Columbia.

Placek, J., & Randall, L. (1986). Comparison of academic learning time in physical education: Students of specialists and nonspecialists. *Journal of Teaching in Physical Education,* 5(3), 157-165.

Rink, J., & Werner, P. (1985, August). *Student responses as a measure of teacher effectiveness.* Paper presented at the International Association for Physical Education in Higher Education Convention, Garden City, NY.

Shute, S., Dodds, P., Placek, J., Rife, F., & Silverman, S. (1982). Academic learning time in elementary school movement education: A descriptive analytic study. *Journal of Teaching in Physical Education,* 1(2), 3-14.

Siedentop, D. (1983). Academic learning time: Reflections and prospects. In P. Dodds & F. Rife (Eds.), Time to learn in physical education: History, completed research, and potential future for academic learning time in physical education. *Journal of Teaching in Physical Education* (Summer Monograph I), 3-7.

Siedentop, D., Birdwell, D., & Metzler, M. (1979, April). *A process approach to studying teaching effectiveness in physical education.* Paper presented at the national convention of the American Alliance for Health, Physical Education, Recreation and Dance, New Orleans.

Siedentop, D., Tousignant, M., & Parker, M. (1982). *Academic learning time–physical education: 1982 revision coding manual.* Unpublished manual, School of Health, Physical Education and Recreation, The Ohio State University, Columbus, OH.

RELATED REFERENCE

Kim, D. (1986). *A comparison of academic learning time between high rated and low rated secondary physical education teachers in South Korea.* Unpublished doctoral dissertation, University of Idaho, Moscow.

Chapter 18

Teacher's Questionnaire on Students' Activities (TQSA)

Victor H. Mancini
Deborah A. Wuest
Deborah M. O'Brien

The Teacher's Questionnaire on Students' Activities (TQSA) was developed to provide a means to determine the accuracy of teachers' awareness of their behaviors and those of their students. The TQSA is a 16-item questionnaire based on the revised Academic Learning Time-Physical Education instrument (Siedentop, Tousignant, & Parker, 1982).

Several researchers (Good & Brophy, 1973; Martin & Keller, 1976; Withall, 1972) have found that teachers have little awareness of the behaviors they exhibit and those engaged in by their students. According to researchers (Batchelder, 1975; Scriber, Mancini, & Wuest, 1984; van der Mars, Mancini, & Frye, 1981), teachers aspiring to be more effective and to facilitate learning by their students need to become more aware of their own and their students' current behaviors as one of the initial steps in changing their teaching methods. The TQSA offers teachers information about the manner in which they conduct their classes and insight into the behaviors exhibited by their students.

The TQSA requests the teacher to estimate, using percentages, the amount of time spent by students in various activities. The teacher makes this judgment prior to teaching the class and immediately following the completion of the class. The teacher's estimates are referred to as *perceived behaviors*. A trained observer using the revised ALT-PE instrument observes the class live or a videotape of the class. The data generated from the coding yield percentages reflecting the actual participation of students in the class activities. To assess the teacher's awareness of behaviors, the percentages for the perceived behaviors are compared to the percentages for actual behaviors using various statistical techniques. The strength of the relationship between perceived and actual behaviors, or the size of the discrepancy between the percentages, indicates the accuracy of the teacher's awareness.

CATEGORY DESCRIPTIONS

The categories comprising the ALT-PE context level are reflected in Questions 1 through 9 (Figure 18.1). Questions 1 and 2 of the TQSA refer to the General Content subdivision. Question 1 combines the categories of management and transition. Question 2 represents the warm-up category.

The Subject Matter Knowledge subdivision is represented in Questions 3 to 6. Questions 3 and 4 reflect the categories of rules and that of background. The technique category is reflected in Question 5 while the strategy category is encompassed in Question 6.

Questions 7 to 9 refer to the Subject Matter Motor subdivision. The ALT-PE category skill practice is represented in Question 7, while Question 8 combines the categories of scrimmage/routine and game. Question 9 relates to the fitness category.

The categories comprising the ALT-PE learner involvement level are represented in Questions 10 through 16. Questions 10a, 10b, and 11 refer to the Motor Engaged subdivision. Question 10a combines the categories motor appropriate and motor inappropriate, whereas Question 10b specifically refers to motor appropriate behavior of ALT-PE. The motor supporting category is represented by Question 11.

The Not Motor Engaged categories are reflected in Questions 12 through 16. The categories of waiting, cognitive, and off-task are reflected in Questions 12, 13, and 14, respectively. Question 15 reflects the interim category, whereas Question 16 refers to the on-task category.

Teacher's Questionnaire on Students' Activities (TQSA)

Name _____ Class _____ Date _____

For each of the following questions estimate the percentage of class time each of the activities occur (0%, 12%, 30%, etc.). Only give a percentage for the categories you are planning to use or have actually used. The total for the nine questions should equal 100%. These first nine questions refer to the activites of the whole class.

For Questions 1 and 2 the focus is on class time devoted to the general content areas.

	Before class estimate	After class estimate	Actual percentages
1. What percentage of class time was devoted to managerial tasks, such as taking roll call, or to transitions, such as selecting teams, moving from station to station, changing equipment, or moving out to the playing field?	_____	_____	_____
2. What percentage of class time was spent on warm-up activities such as stretching, calisthenics, or routine exercises?	_____	_____	_____

Questions 3-6 refer to class time when the primary focus is on the knowlege of the sport or activity, not movement.

3. What percentage of class time was used for explanation of rules and regulations of the game or activity such as violations, scoring in bowling, or the specific rules in basketball?	_____	_____	_____

(Cont.)

Figure 18.1   Teacher's Questionnaire on Students' Activities (TQSA).

4. What percentage of class time was used for giving information on <u>background</u>, history, rituals, heroes, or the importance of the activity for later years, such as team records or the fitness value? _____ _____ _____

5. What percentage of class time was spent on giving information on the <u>strategy</u> of the game or physical activity such as an explanation of offense and defense or the progressions in a dance or a gymnastic routine? _____ _____ _____

Questions 7-9 refer to the class time students are <u>actively involved or participating</u> in skill practice, scrimmage, a game, or fitness activities.

7. What percentage of class time was spent on <u>control skill practice</u> such as circle drill in passing a volleyball, dribbling around cones, practicing skills on the balance beam, or practicing a step in dance? _____ _____ _____

8. For what percentage of class time were <u>skills applied</u> in a modified game, scrimmage, or the entire game such as a volleyball game, a complete balance beam routine, a relay race, a 100-yard dash, or a complete dance routine? _____ _____ _____

9. What percentage of class time was spent on the development and maintenance of fitness such as doing aerobics, or running a mile? _____ _____ _____

Total should equal 100%   Total _____ _____ _____

For each of the following questions estimate the percentage of class time each of the situations occur. The total for the seven questions should equal 100%. These seven questions refer to the specific type of <u>individual</u> student involvement in the class.

	Before class estimate	After class estimate	Actual percentages
Questions 10 and 11 refer to the percentage of time the student(s) were actively involved or participating in skill practice, scrimmage, or an entire game.			

10a. What percentage of class time was the student actively involved in a skill practice, a scrimmage, or an entire game play? _____ _____ _____

10b. Of the percentage of time in question 10a that the students were actively involved, what percentage of the time were they successful? <u>Example</u>: Students were actively invoved 66% of the time and they were successful 42% of the time. Do not add this percentage to the total percentage. _____ _____ _____

11. What percentage of class time during the physical activity was the student <u>acting as an assistant or in a supporting role</u> such as spotting in gymnastics, feeding the balls to a hitter in tennis, or clapping to keep beat while others are dancing? _____ _____ _____

Questions 12-16 refer to the percentage of time the learners are <u>not</u> involved in a motor activity.

12. What percentage of class time was the student not receiving information but <u>waiting</u> for the next instructions or opportunity to respond, such as waiting in line for the balance beam, waiting as a substitute to play in a game, or waiting for further directions? _____ _____ _____

13. What percentage of class time was the student receiving information by lecture or watching a demonstration such as listening to instructions or having a discussion? _____ _____ _____

Figure 18.1 (Continued)

14.   What percentage of class time was the student off-task, that is, not carrying out an assigned task or engaging in an activity he or she should not, such as fooling around, fighting, disrupting a drill, or talking while the teacher is talking?   _____ _____ _____

15.   What percentage of class time was the student involved in a noninstructional task of an ongoing activity such as retrieving balls, fixing equipment, or changing sides of a court in volleyball?   _____ _____ _____

16.   What percentage of class time was the student carrying out an assigned non-subject-matter task such as doing warm-up activities, moving out to the playing field, or moving into squads?   _____ _____ _____

Total should equal 100%   Total   _____ _____ _____

Figure 18.1   (Continued)

RECORDING PROCEDURES

The teacher completes the TQSA prior to and immediately following the class. The percentage of class time devoted to various activities is estimated and recorded in the appropriate space. For each level of the ALT-PE instrument the percentages must total 100%. Thus the percentage for Questions 1 through 9 must total 100%, and those for Questions 10 through 16 must total 100%. The actual percentages, obtained by coding of the class using ALT-PE, are recorded next to the appropriate question.

SUMMARIZING AND INTERPRETING THE DATA

The TQSA provides a means to assess the accuracy of the teacher's perceptions regarding the students' class activities. It also provides information regarding the teacher's class planning.

To determine the teacher's awareness, the relationship between perceived and actual behaviors is assessed using various statistical analyses. The teacher's postclass estimates are compared to the actual percentages. The postclass estimates are thought to be more accurate, reflecting the various changes that the teacher made during the instructional process to adjust to students' needs and situational factors. When postclass estimates are compared to actual percentages, the stronger the relationship that is expressed or the smaller the difference between the percentages, the more accurate the teacher's perceptions regarding the students' activities. In a similar manner, the relationship or difference between planned activities and the activities in which the students actually participated can be assessed by comparing the teacher's preclass estimates with the actual percentages. The stronger the relationship or the smaller the difference, the more accurate the teacher planning.

The relationship between the teacher's perceptions and the students' actual behaviors may also be determined by visually comparing the percentages recorded for perceived and observed behaviors. The larger the difference between the percentages for perceived and observed behaviors, the less accurate the teacher's perceptions.

It should be noted that the preservice teachers in the studies by O'Brien (1985) and Coulson (1986) found the TQSA helpful in planning for instruction, as it assisted them in describing the specific types of student behaviors desired during instruction. The preservice teachers also reported that completing the postclass estimates was helpful in evaluating their teaching in that it served to guide their thoughts in reviewing their teaching and recalling the specific actions of students in their classes.

REFERENCES

Batchelder, A.S. (1975). *Process objectives and their implementation in elementary math, English, and physical education*. Unpublished doctoral dissertation, Boston University.

Coulson, C. (1986). *The lasting effects of instruction and supervision through academic learning time-physical education on the relationship between perceived and observed students' behaviors in classes taught by inservice physical educators*. Unpublished master's thesis, Ithaca College, Ithaca, NY.

Good, T.L., & Brophy, J.E. (1973). *Looking in classrooms*. New York: Harper & Row.

Martin, R., & Keller, A. (1976). Teacher awareness of dyadic interactions. *Journal of School Psychology*, **14**, 47-55.

O'Brien, D.M. (1985). *The effects of instruction in and supervision through academic learning time-physical education on the relationship between perceived and observed students' behaviors*. Unpublished master's thesis, Ithaca College, Ithaca, NY.

Scriber, K., Mancini, V.H., & Wuest, D.A. (1984, March). *The relationship between perceived teaching behaviors and actual teaching behaviors of school health educators*. Paper presented at the American Alliance of Health, Physical Education, Recreation and Dance National Convention, Anaheim, CA.

Siedentop, D., Tousignant, M., & Parker, M. (1982). *Academic learning time-physical education: 1982 revised, coding manual*. Unpublished manual. School of Health, Physical Education and Recreation. The Ohio State University, Columbus, OH.

van der Mars, H., Mancini, V.H., & Frye, P.A. (1981). Effects of interaction analysis training on perceived and observed teaching behaviors. *Journal of Teaching in Physical Education* (Introductory Issue), 57-65.

Withall, J. (1972). Research in systematic observation in the classroom and its relevance to teachers. *The Journal of Teacher Education, 23,* 330-332.

□ *Chapter 19*

Teacher Monitoring Analysis System (TMAS)

Hans van der Mars

The purpose of the Teacher Monitoring Analysis System (TMAS) is to enable the user to collect information on selected variables related to teacher monitoring behavior, that is, the physical (re)location patterns of teachers and grouping structures of students. This observation tool uses a combination of interval recording and momentary time sampling. It has three levels of categories, and the user has a choice of using one, two, or three levels simultaneously. Subscripts are available to provide additional background data. In addition, the user can preserve the interactive nature of teacher and student behavior through the use of categories of the revised ALT-PE observation system (Siedentop, Tousignant, & Parker, 1982).

As with every descriptive-analytic tool, this instrument does not give its user an all-encompassing description of all the features of a lesson or practice session. For example, the use of TMAS does not provide any indication of how teachers (or coaches) interact verbally with their students (or players). This instrument provides information only on the following dimensions of the teaching-learning environment:

- The context of the class in which the student group as a whole is working.
- The group structures used by the instructor throughout the lesson(s).
- The physical (re)location behavior patterns of the instructor.
- The types of involvement on the part of a randomly selected student, and his or her physical location.

Depending on which of these four dimensions are studied, one can analyze the relationships between the dimensions. For example, one could study the relationship between the group structure selected and the relocation patterns that seem to occur at the time when students are grouped in a particular fashion. Another example would be the relationship between teacher relocation and the types/levels of learner involvement.

TMAS can be used both indoors and outdoors. When it is used outdoors, the observer should make sure that he or she takes responsibility to place large orange cones around the activity area. This should be done well in advance of the start of a class so as not to intrude on the class more than necessary.

CATEGORY DESCRIPTIONS

Context Level

The context level describes the context of the major class activity. The categories are identical in label, code, and definition to those developed by Siedentop, Tousignant, and Parker (1982) for ALT-PE II. The categories included are as follows (see chapter 17 for category descriptions):

- *General content:* transition (T), management (M), break (B), and warm-up (WU).
- *Subject matter knowledge:* technique (TN), strategy (ST), rules (R), social behavior (SB), and background (BK).
- *Subject matter motor:* skill practice (P), scrimmage/routine (S), game (G), and fitness (F).

In addition to the context description this level provides information on the class (or grouping) structure by way of subscripts. The purpose of gathering information on this dimension is that it interacts with both the positioning and the relocating styles of the instructor, particularly during subject matter motor episodes. The following subscripts have been designated for use at this level. They are written in lower case so as not to confuse them with the other symbols of the primary categories.

Whole (w)

Students are located in one concentrated area. *Examples:* Students are lining up for attendance, sitting around a circle, standing along a wall awaiting team selection. Whole also refers to situations in which students are all engaged in the same activity that is led by the teacher or a student. *Example:* The typical stretching and warm-up routine at the beginning of a class period.

Subgroup (s)

Students are divided into groups equal to or greater than three. *Examples:* Stations, teams of five that rotate in, squads.

Partners (p)

Students are divided into groups of two (they need *not* be engaged simultaneously).

Individual (i)

Students work by themselves on a motor task, typically scattered across the activity area.

Disperse (d)

Students spread out in activity area to find space, equipment that is set up, and/or perhaps teammates.

Converge (c)

Students come together as one group at teacher-established location (either implicit or explicit). *Examples:* Students are entering the gymnasium, going to center circle, returning equipment.

Nonstructure (n)

Students are in gymnasium, but not organized in any teacher-directed grouping pattern. *Examples*: Students are entering the gymnasium or waiting for class to start.

Although this information reflects how the group as a whole is organized, any changes in structure (e.g., from i to c or from d to p) should be coded based on what the target student is doing.

Teacher Monitoring Level

The teacher monitoring level of TMAS provides data on both the positioning and the relocating patterns of the instructor throughout the observation period. For this purpose it is necessary to divide the gymnasium floor or field space into designated sectors. To help the observer in discriminating between the sectors, markers (e.g., small orange cones) should be located at the base of the walls at the sector borders. Colored tape or washable (water-based) shoe polish can be used to identify where borderlines of sectors intersect. This helps the observer discriminate the location of either the teacher or the target student more accurately around these areas. The number of sectors used is typically dependent on factors such as reliability of the observer, experience of the observer, and the type of information desired. The standard format is shown in Figure 19.1. It is

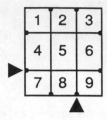

Figure 19.1 Sector map and observer location.

suggested that the observer be located exactly in the extension of one of the borderlines (note the arrows).

The width of the gymnasium space is divided into equal thirds. The four corner sectors (i.e., 1, 3, 7, and 9) should be square shaped. Consequently, Sectors 4, 5, and 6 are rectangular in shape, assuming of course that the activity area is rectangular. If the activity area is virtually square shaped, divide it into nine sectors of equal size. The numbers are the symbols to be used when coding the instructor's positioning and relocating behavior patterns. An additional category is included to indicate that the instructor is not in view. The symbol for this is "0" (i.e., zero).

The following coding ground rules apply to this level:

1. Code only the sector code of the sector in which the instructor is located at the end of the observe interval.
2. Place a "1" in front of the code if the relocation included a change in sectors during the observe interval. For example, if during the observe interval the teacher walked from Sector 6 to Sector 7, code "17."
3. Circle the sector code if the instructor is repositioning within one sector during the observe interval.
4. If the instructor is positioned on a sector border use the code of the sector that he or she is facing and/or attending to.
5. If the instructor is straddling a borderline without facing one specific sector, code the number of the sector from which he or she last came.

Learner Involvement Level

The learner involvement level provides information on the type and degree of involvement on the part of a learner in the class. As was the case for the first level, the categories used to measure this involvement are identical to those used in the ALT-PE system described in chapter 17. The categories include the following:

- *Not motor engaged:* interim (I), waiting (W), off-task (OF), on-task (ON), and cognitive (C).
- *Motor engaged:* motor appropriate (MA), motor inappropriate (MI), and supporting (MS).

In addition, by way of using subscripts, the observer can determine where the student is located on the gymnasium or field space. The subscripts at this level are the same numbers (1-9 and 0) used to code teacher positioning and relocating patterns. When using the subscripts 1-9 at the learner involvement level, the observer doesn't place circles around the code that would indicate the target student's movement within one sector; neither does he or she place a "1" in front of the code to indicate that the target student had changed sectors during the observe interval. Thus, at this coding level of TMAS, one captures two types of information: (a) the type of learner involvement and (b) the location of the target student.

RECORDING PROCEDURES

The user of this multidimensional observation tool has options for recording procedures, depending on the type of information desired. The system presented here is an interval recording system, with a 6-second observe and a 6-second record interval length. To maintain the constant 6-second cadence it is necessary to use a programmed cue tape that provides the cues to either observe or record. This observe-record pattern is the same, regardless of which data option is used. The following three basic data options are available:

1. Basic ALT-PE Version II (Siedentop, Tousignant, & Parker, 1982): In this option the observer uses only the categories in the context and learner involvement levels.
2. Teacher monitoring: In this option the observer uses the categories in the context and teacher monitoring levels. For both Options 1 and 2 he or she should use the coding sheet in Figure 19.2.
3. Interactive: In this option the observer codes categories from the context level for each interval. Furthermore, he or she alternates coding at the teacher monitoring and learner involvement levels. The coding sheet to be used in this option is shown in Figure 19.3.

In the ALT-PE II option, information can be gathered on three students simultaneously. In the interactive option of this system only one student

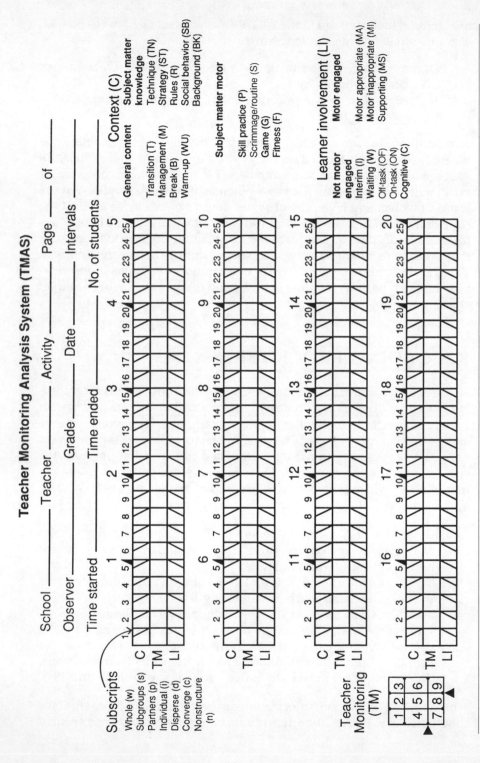

Figure 19.2 Teacher Monitoring Analysis System (TMAS) recording sheet.

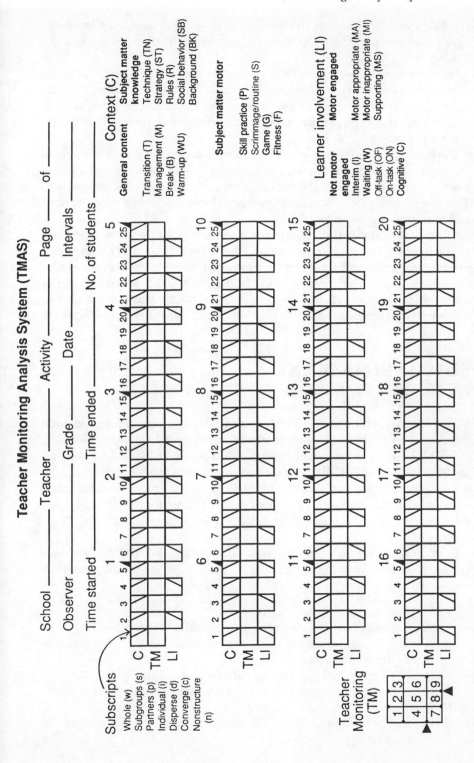

Figure 19.3   Teacher Monitoring Analysis System (TMAS) recording sheet (interactive).

can be observed. Note that the interactive option requires a different cue tape to ensure that the observation is alternated properly between the teacher and the target student.

No subscripts were included in the basic options. The purpose of using subscripts is to provide further detail or background that enriches the data collected through the regular categories. The use of subscripts is dependent on (a) what type of information is desired and/or (b) familiarity with the basic system.

Depending on what type of information is sought, the user can create more recording options than those described. The degree to which one uses a variety of options depends also on his or her level of experience. The user needs to remember to use the appropriate prerecorded programmed cue tape.

Observer reliability is of the utmost importance for the subsequent use of the information that was collected. The reliability of interval and temporary time-sampling data can be estimated using a variety of calculation procedures. The most rigorous and widely used procedure is the scored-interval method, first proposed by Hawkins and Dotson (1975). For a step-by-step explanation of this calculation please refer to chapter 3.

SUMMARIZING AND INTERPRETING THE DATA

Data collected with TMAS can be summarized into percentage of total intervals and percentage of intervals in Category X. An example of the former would be if the teacher were coded as being located in Sector 4 for 10 intervals out of all 150 coded intervals; the percentage would be 6.6 for this category. An example of the latter would be if one were interested in determining levels of student off-task behavior during *only* those intervals in which the group structure was subscripted as ''s'' (i.e., subgroup).

In addition to the basic percentages of intervals, the user can also calculate the following parameters for data collected at the teacher monitoring level:

1. Total number of sector changes.
2. Total number of stays in each individual sector.
3. Average length of stay in each individual sector (i.e., the mean of consecutive intervals).
4. Rate of sector changes per minute (when using Option 2).
5. Rate of sector changes per 2 minutes (when using Option 3).
6. Total number of empty sectors.
7. Percent of total intervals in the peripheral sectors. This would be

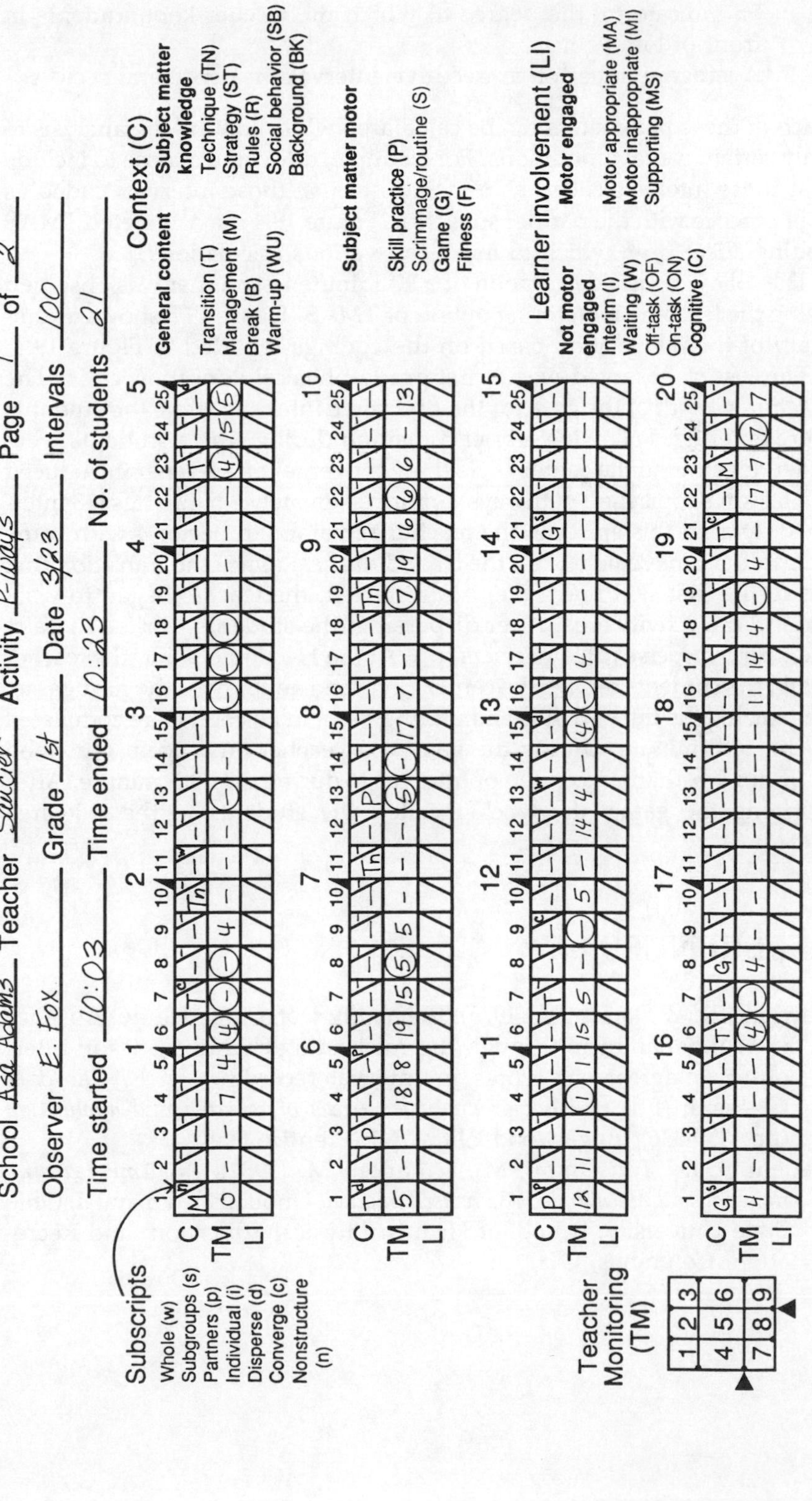

Figure 19.4 Completed Teacher Monitoring Analysis System (TMAS) recording sheet.

     an indicator of the degree to which the teacher kept students in front of him or her.

8. Average number of consecutive intervals in peripheral sectors.

Each of these parameters can be calculated while limiting the analysis to only certain context conditions. For example, one could choose to include just those intervals coded as transition or just those intervals coded as skill practice with the partner subscript. Figure 19.4 is a completed TMAS coding sheet from which to make the various calculations.

The following is a description of a 20-minute lesson that was observed using the teaching monitoring option of TMAS. Figure 19.5 shows a summary of the information based on the codings reported in Figure 19.4.

The lesson observed was a first-grade physical education class. The teacher was out of the gym for the first three intervals while the students were entering. Following a brief transition during which students were called together to the center circle (i.e., converge), the teacher introduced the lesson's topic (i.e., pathways) for approximately 2.5 minutes (13 intervals). During this episode, the teacher remained in Sector 4 with some intermittent movement (i.e., the circled dashes). Once the transition that led to the first skill practice episode started, the teacher began to walk around the activity area. After dispersing, the students worked in pairs (i.e., from disperse [d] to partners [p]). At the 11-minute point, the teacher called the students back to the center circle and announced the next game. Organizing the three squads and placing them in position were completed at the 14th minute. During the game the teacher once again remained in Sector 4 with the exception of Interval 16 during the 18th minute. After stopping the game, the teacher called the students to the exit area (Sector 7).

REFERENCES

Hawkins, R., & Dotson, V. (1975). Reliability scores that delude: An Alice in Wonderland trip through the misleading characteristics in inter-observer agreement scores in interval recording. In E. Ramp & G. Semb (Eds.), *Behavior analysis: Areas of research and application* (pp. 359-376). Englewood Cliffs, NJ: Prentice-Hall.

Siedentop, D., Tousignant, M., & Parker, M. (1982). *Academic learning time-physical education—1982 revised manual*. Unpublished manual. Ohio State University, School of Health, Physical Education, and Recreation, Columbus, OH.

Teacher Monitoring Analysis System (TMAS)

Date: _3/23_ Teacher: _Saucier_ Grade: _1st_ Option: 1 ②　3
School: _Asa Adams_ Observer: _E. Fox_ Activity: _Pathways_

Context

General content	(%)	Subject matter knowledge	(%)
Transition (T)	26	Technique (TN)	17
Management (M)	9	Strategy (ST)	___
Break (B)	___	Rules (R)	___
Warm-up (WU)	___	Social behavior (SB)	___
		Background (BK)	___

Subject matter motor	(%)	Subscripts	(%)
Skill practice (P)	25	Whole (w)	16
Scrimmage (S)	___	Subgroups (s)	25
Game (G)	23	Partners (p)	29
Fitness (F)	___	Individual (i)	___
		Disperse (d)	11
		Converge (c)	13
		Nonstructure (n)	6

Teacher Monitoring

Sector	Intervals (%)	Stay (frequency)	Mean length of stay (intervals)	Within-sector movement (frequency)
1	5	2	2½	1
2	1	1	1	___
3	1	1	1	___
4	53	3	17.6	13
5	19	3	6.3	5
6	4	1	4	1
7	10	3	3.3	2
8	2	1	2	___
9	2	2	1	___
0	3	1	3	___

Sector changes (freq.): _17_
Rate of sector change: _.85_
Average # of consecutive intervals in periphery: _20_

Within-sector movement (%): _22_
Empty sector(s): _0_
Intervals in periphery (%): _81_

Learner involvement

Not motor engaged	(%)	Motor engaged	(%)
Interim (I)	___	Motor appropriate (MA)	___
Waiting (W)	___	Motor inappropriate (MI)	___
Off-task (OF)	___	Motor supporting (MS)	___
On-task (ON)	___		
Cognitive (C)	___		

Figure 19.5 Completed Teacher Monitoring Analysis System (TMAS) data summary sheet.

Chapter 20

The ALT-PE Microcomputer Data Collection System (MCDCS)

Michael Metzler

The Microcomputer Data Collection System (MCDCS) is designed to allow electronic collection, storage, analysis, and retrieval of Academic Learning Time-Physical Education (ALT-PE) interval data. It is intended for use by observers already trained in ALT-PE interval coding systems. Although the MCDCS does include some new variations from existing systems, it relies on those other versions for familiarity with data recording procedures. The system features the dual capability of on-site data entry during instructional episodes or delayed data entry from previously completed observations. Regardless of whether data are entered during or after class, the system provides several conveniences over nonelectronic ALT-PE technologies: (a) it eliminates the need for written records of behavior codes; (b) it can store dozens of observations on a single floppy diskette, which can be copied easily; (c) it performs data analyses by individual students and across students in less than 15 seconds; (d) for on-site coding the system itself can cue the observer, eliminating the need for external cuing devices; and (e) it can combine data across multiple observations of the same class for cumulative analyses.

The current version of the ALT-PE MCDCS is designed for use with any of the Apple II series computers, the II+, IIc, or IIe. It requires 48k of RAM, one disk drive, and a monitor. It can make printouts on the screen or with a printer, so a printer is not necessary for on-site use. The MCDCS program is written in Applesoft BASIC, which can easily be translated into other popular versions of BASIC for use on IBM and IBM-compatible computers. If on-site data collection is desired, the observer must connect the computer to an AC power supply, or use it with a battery pack (available for Apple IIc only).

CATEGORY DESCRIPTIONS

So far, most ALT-PE data have been recorded with either Version I (Siedentop, Birdwell, & Metzler, 1979) or Version II (Siedentop, Tousignant, & Parker, 1982). Although these versions are quite different from one another, they do produce greatly similar data on the frequency of motor appropriate intervals in which students are observed in physical education (Rife, Dodds, & Shute, 1985). The MCDCS uses a modified and more content-specific set of categories than the previous versions, but is still designed to measure the same variable, ALT-PE (Metzler, DePaepe, & Reif, 1985). The MCDCS has 22 defined categories, coded on four decision levels: pacing, content, learner moves, and difficulty (see Figure 20.1).

ALT-PE Microcomputer Data Collection System (MCDCS)

Pacing level
Student
Teacher

Content level

Content—General	Content—PE
Management	Practice unspecified
Wait	Game
Transition	Scrimmage
Rest	Knowledge content
	Wild card A
	Wild card B
	Wild card C
	Nonfocused skill

Learner moves level

Not Engaged	Engaged
Pause	Motor responding
Waiting	Indirect participating
Off-task	Cognitive

Difficulty level
Motor appropriate
Motor inappropriate

Figure 20.1   Microcomputer Data Collection System (MCDCS) categories and decision levels.

Pacing Level

The pacing level denotes who is providing the instructional timing cues during the observed interval, either the student or the teacher.

Student (S)

Student provides the instructional timing cues.

Teacher (T)

Teacher provides the instructional timing cues.

Content Level

The content level divides class time into two main groups, content-general and content-physical education (Content-PE). The MCDCS can code either unspecified practice, or up to three kinds of content-specific practice. This allows for the identification and analysis of intervals spent in the practice of separate skills during class (e.g., volleying, serving, and using forehand for tennis; putting, driving, and playing in sand for golf). The observer enters specified skills under the wild card categories. Each skill is given a label and placed on any printouts of the observation.

Content-General

Noninstructional Time.

Wait (W). Periods of no activity and no movement prior to and between activities.

Transition (T). Periods of change from one activity to another, including lining up or quieting down for the next activity.

Management (M). Time devoted to class business that is unrelated to the instructional activities of the day.

Rest (R). Intentional periods of no activity to rest, drink water, and so forth. Breaks must be initiated by the teacher.

Content-Physical Education

Time devoted directly to learning tasks.

Practice Unspecified (P). Participation in drills and other instructional activities in which the primary goal is individual skill development.

Scrimmage (S). Controlled group practice in which instruction and feedback are frequent. Includes the simulation and/or modification of game playing to focus upon a specific instructional point.

Game (G). Practice under game conditions.

Knowledge (K). Activities that focus on knowledge about skill, fitness, background information, and so forth.

Wild Card A (A). Content-specific practice.

Wild Card B (B). Content-specific practice.

Wild Card C (C). Content-specific practice.

Nonfocused (N). Unrelated motor activity.

Learner Moves Level

The learner moves level denotes the kind of student involvement under content-PE time; it is used only following a content-PE code on the previous level.

Engaged

Engaged Motor Responding (M). Student is performing a skill.

Engaged, Indirect Participation (I). Student is in an activity but not directly involved with the immediate action (includes assisting others in skill practice). *Examples:* Spotting, setting up targets, retrieving balls, and so forth.

Engaged Cognitive (C). Cognitive involvement related to instruction. *Examples:* Listening, questioning, responding verbally, or thinking about the activity.

Not Engaged

Pause (P). Any noninstructional activity that is part of the content-PE activity. *Examples:* Changing sides of the net and taking time outs between points.

Waiting (W). Time during activity when student is waiting for help or waiting to participate again. *Example:* Being a substitute in a game.

Off-Task (O). Student is inappropriately disengaged from the lesson.

Difficulty Level

The difficulty level is used to code the appropriateness of observed motor engagement. An observed motor task is coded as appropriate or inappropriate based on the degree to which it is commensurate with a student's previous experience and current skill level.

Motor Appropriate (A)

Student is engaged in a motor activity that provides a high degree of success.

Motor Inappropriate (N)

Student is engaged in a motor activity that is too difficult or too easy for the student's capabilities.

RECORDING PROCEDURES

The MCDCS can be used in either of two modes, delayed or cued. The delayed mode is intended for those instances when it is not possible to use a computer for data entry. Typical reasons include lack of a direct power supply, obtrusiveness in small areas, or risk of damage to the computer. Data are then coded onto a hand-held recording sheet, similar to those used for Versions I and II (see Figure 20.2). An external cuing device

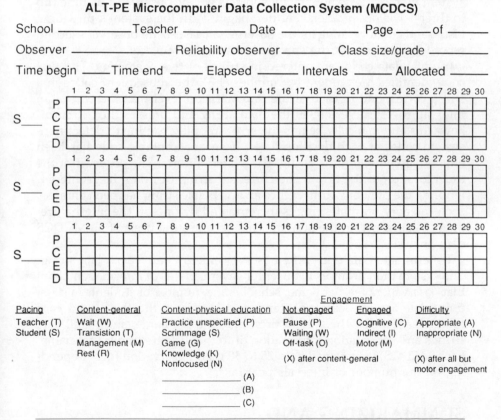

Figure 20.2 Microcomputer Data Collection System (MCDCS) recording sheet.

must be used to alert the observer of the beginning and end of intervals and the correct student sampling sequence. At the completion of the observation, data are then entered into the computer to gain full access to all MCDCS features. The cued mode is designed for on-site data entry during an observation. The observer sets up the computer in the instructional area and makes all entries onto the keyboard, instead of the coding sheet.

The MCDCS is activated automatically when its floppy disk is inserted into the disk drive and the computer is turned on. A main menu appears, showing all program options: (1) begin observation, (2) recall data from storage, (3) run data analysis, (4) get printout, (5) see file list, (6) combine files, and (7) quit ALT program.

The observer enters "1" and the system prompts, "Do you want interval cuing?" If using the delayed mode, the observer rejects this option and data are entered at any rate. If on-site, this option is selected; the system then requests how many subjects will be observed this time (up to three). The observation can then begin, with the system's providing visual and auditory cuing for the observer on a 6-second observe/6-second record rotation across the specified number of subjects.

Interval data codes are entered in strings of five characters. The first code identifies the student by number (1-3); the subsequent codes in a string correspond to each of the four decision levels. At the end of an interval, the observer enters the data string and presses the "Return" key. This automatically begins the error trapping routine to detect non-system codes at each decision level. If an unacceptable code has been entered anywhere in the string, the system informs the observer of the exact location of the error. The corrected string can then be reentered, ignoring the previous string. Once an acceptable string has been entered, each category on that string is incremented by one on the internal frequency count within the system. This becomes the basis of all MCDCS data analyses.

To terminate data entry, the observer enters "end" as a data string. The system then prompts the user for several pieces of information about that observation: teacher name, school name, number of students in class, time, date, grade, lesson content, and labels for the three wild card categories. Finally, the system prompts for a file name, storing all data strings and observation information onto the diskette under that name. Each MCDCS diskette will hold 25 to 30 class observation files, depending on the number of intervals per class.

SUMMARIZING AND INTERPRETING THE DATA

After the file has been named and completed, the MCDCS returns to the main menu. Selecting Option 3 allows the data from the observation to be analyzed in less than 15 seconds. Following that, Option 4 formats the data and files information for screen and/or printed reading (see Figure 20.3). All file information appears on the top four lines. The printout includes frequency of observed intervals for each student and for the

```
***************************************************************
TEACHER: Lesh         SCHOOL: San Rafael HS    GRADE: 11th
#S's: 17              DATE: 6/25               TIME:  2 p.m.
Content Tennis--Forehand Drills
***************************************************************
                    ST 1       ST 2       ST 3        Total
#INTS               70         70         70          210

S-Pace              68/97.1    69/98.5    68/97.1     205/97.6
T-Pace              2/2.8      1/1.4      2/2.8       5/2.3
-----------------------------------------------------------
MANAGE              0/0        0/0        0/0         0/0
WAIT                0/0        0/0        0/0         0/0
TRANS               0/0        0/0        0/0         0/0
REST                0/0        0/0        4/5.7       4/1.9

CONTENT GENERAL     0/0        0/0        4/5.7       4/1.9
-----------------------------------------------------------
PRAC, UN            0/0        0/0        0/0         0/0
GAME                0/0        0/0        0/0         0/0
SCRIM               0/0        0/0        0/0         0/0
KNOW                7/10       1/1.4      7/10        15/7.1
SERVE               0/0        0/0        0/0         0/0
BACK                0/0        0/0        0/0         0/0
FORE                60/85.7    65/92.8    59/84.2     184/87.6
NON FOC             3/4.2      4/5.7      0/0         7/3.3

CONTENT PE          70/100     70/100     66/94.2     206/98
-----------------------------------------------------------
NOT ENG/PAUSE       26/37.1    15/21.4    18/25.7     59/28
WAITING             2/2.8      22/31.4    5/7.1       19/13.8
OFFTASK             0/0        0/0        0/0         0/0

NE (TOT)            28/40      37/52.8    23/32.8     88/41.9
NE (LEV)            28/40      37/52.8    23/34.8     88/42.7
-----------------------------------------------------------
ENG MOT             35/50      32/45.7    36/51.4     103/49
ENG COG             7/10       1/1.4      7/10        15/7.1
ENG IND             0/0        0/0        0/0         0/0

ENG (TOT)           42/60      33/47.1    43/61.4     118/56.1

ENG (LEV)           42/60      33/47.1    43/65.1     118/57.2
-----------------------------------------------------------
ALT (M)             31/44.2    13/18.5    23/32.8     67/31.9

NON ALT             4/5.7      19/27.1    13/18.5     36/17.1

% MOTOR EASY        (88.5)     (40.6)     (63.8)      (65)
***************************************************************
```

Figure 20.3 Microcomputer Data Collection System (MCDCS) printout.

total group, frequencies and percentages for all defined categories by student and across students, and within-level data for the Engaged and Not Engaged categories taken together. The three bottom lines show calculations for ALT-PE, non-ALT-PE and "% Motor Easy." ALT-PE for the MCDCS accrues only for successful motor task engagement; it is not possible to code "appropriate" under cognitive or indirect engagement. The calculation for "% Motor Easy" reflects the success rate for observed motor tasks in the lesson.

If a hard copy printout is requested, the system provides one across 40 columns on a single page. The printout is made on the left side of the page, allowing for handwritten notes on the right half.

The MCDCS can retrieve and combine filed observations for cumulative analyses. If the observer selects Option 6 on the main menu and requests existing files on the diskette, the system reads those files together to form a single data base. Each file takes 2 to 3 minutes to be retrieved. Once combined, the data are analyzed and printed like single files, but reflect the entire set of grouped observations.

The ALT-PE MCDCS has two components, the BASIC program written on a 5 1/4-inch floppy diskette and a system manual. The diskette contains all needed programs and room for 25 to 30 observation files. The system manual provides all necessary descriptions, instructions, and observation assistance for using the MCDCS. The system design requires a working familiarity with ALT-PE observation procedures and assumes the observer is fully trained for reliable data coding. Once familiarized with the MCDCS and trained for ALT-PE coding, an observer should find the combination easy to use and an extremely efficient way to collect ALT-PE data.

REFERENCES

Metzler, M., DePaepe, J., & Reif, G. (1985). Alternative technologies for measuring academic learning time in physical education. *Journal of Teaching in Physical Education, 4*, 271-285.

Rife, F., Dodds, P., & Shute, J. (1985). ALT-PE versions I and II: Evolution of a student-centered observation system in physical education. *Journal of Teaching in Physical Education, 4*, 134-142.

Siedentop, D., Birdwell, D., & Metzler, M. (1979, April). *A process approach to studying teaching in physical education*. Paper presented at the national convention of the American Alliance for Health, Physical Education, Recreation and Dance, New Orleans.

Siedentop, D., Tousignant, M., & Parker, M. (1982). *Academic learning time-physical education: 1982 revision coding manual*. Unpublished manual, School of Health, Physical Education and Recreation, The Ohio State University, Columbus.

Chapter 21

The Time-On-Fitness Instrument (TOFI): Time On-Task in Nonschool Settings

Tchang-Bok Chung

The Time-On-Fitness Instrument (TOFI) is designed to accurately record how the student's time is allocated among the different activities found in YMCA adult physical fitness classes. It is both a context- and a content-specific category system, based on major fitness components. The system is comprehensive enough to provide a continuous account of student behavior—verbal, nonverbal, movement, and nonmovement—in an adult fitness class. It is detailed enough to show the sequence of each occurrence of student behavior. Thus it describes how students spend their time in terms of not only specific task and nontask behaviors, but also when and in what order. In its context and content specificity, it is unique in the literature of descriptive studies of teaching.

The results of the reliability test conducted in March 1985 at a local YMCA indicated that overall interobserver agreement for the system was 96%. For each dimension of the system, agreements were active fitness time, 99%; transitional fitness time, 100%; passive fitness time, 96%; and nonfitness time, 97%. For each category, agreements were strength/stretch, 99%; cardiovascular, 96%; warm-up, 100%; knowledge, 96%; management, 93%; wait, 98%; and other, 100%. There was no interval coded in the rest/relaxation category (but there were five rest/relaxation intervals coded with 100% agreement in the final field test leading to the test of reliability).

As with any other live observation system, the TOFI is limited in scope and must be used in conjunction with *The Y's Way To Physical Fitness* (Golding, Myers, & Sinning, 1982). It is designed to observe student behavior rather than teacher behavior or student-teacher interactions. The system categorizes the cardiovascular, fitness, strength, and flexibility activities derived from *The Y's Way to Physical Fitness* and creates five other categories necessary for descriptive completeness. Within this system, therefore, nine categories describe all observed student behaviors in fitness- and non-fitness-related activities. Behavior is limited by the category definitions.

CATEGORY DESCRIPTIONS

Transitional Fitness Time

Student time spent in a state of motion, which reflects the bidirectional link between inactivity and vigorous activity; based on Y program's suggestion that an exercise session should include warm-up and cool-down periods.

Warm-Up.   Engaging in exercises that prepare the body for the work to come. This phase of exercise is basically geared not to the increase of flexibility but to the actualization of the level of flexibility already attained (e.g., rotation of the neck and extension of the knees). *Example:* Slow walking or jogging at a low level of difficulty is a warm-up for endurance or cardiovascular activity.

Cool-Down.   Engaging in low-intensity exercises that allow the body to gradually recover from high-intensity exercises. This phase of exercise is geared to relaxing the muscles used during vigorous activity and returning heart rates to normal, resting levels.

Active Fitness Time

Student time spent in a state of motion devoted to the fitness activity.

Strength/Stretch.   Engaging in exercises that stretch the muscles, tendons, and ligaments surrounding the joint to increase its range of motion; or that provide moderate resistance to each major muscle group to improve the strength/endurance of these muscles.

Cardiovascular.   Engaging in controlled duration exercises, rhythmical and repetitive in nature, to induce cardiovascular training effects.

Passive Fitness Time

Student time spent physically at rest that is a part of the fitness activity.

Rest/Relaxation.   Engaging in planned or deliberate resting behavior based on the alternating work and rest periods of the interval principle, or engaging in activities that produce relaxation. Rest/relaxation is a period of inactivity, a respite from active fitness time. It is an innovation in the

TOFI system that reflects the recent recognition of the importance of stress management.

Knowledge.   Engaging in communicating or monitoring behavior on the topics related to fitness, the purpose of which is to provide students with the basis for making intelligent decisions about fitness and healthy lifestyles. *Examples:* Receiving instruction, talking, measuring pulse, recognizing heavy breathing, discussing, listening, observing, reading, and writing.

Nonfitness Time

Student time spent in activities not related to fitness.

Management.   Engaging in the managerial activities of the class. *Examples:* Making a transition, changing equipment, taking attendance, and organizing games.

Wait.   Engaging in a holding behavior unrelated to the interval principle until a new or different behavior is required. *Examples:* Waiting one's turn to practice and waiting for the instructor to begin the class.

Other.   Engaging in any behavior not classified in the above categories. *Examples:* Socializing, drinking water, tying shoes, and leaving class.

RECORDING PROCEDURES

The TOFI requires the observer to code behavior as it actually occurs in the classroom. To secure highly reliable data, it is necessary to make sure that the interval is short enough to encode only one behavior and that the coding segments are spread evenly across the class time. Thus the system uses 5-second interval recording during alternate 1-minute segments of the class. In other words, at the end of each 5-second interval, the observer codes the behavior of the target student during that interval. To provide the coder with accurate timing, a prerecorded audiotape (coding audiotape) is used for signaling each 5-second observation interval as well as the 1-minute uncoded periods throughout the class time.

The instrument uses numbers 1 through 12, instead of a check mark, for coding. This ordinal sequencing of behavior in 1-minute segments of observation, having twelve 5-second intervals, proves useful for analysis and reliability tests. The observer codes by placing a numeral while simultaneously assessing the student behavior in the next 5-second interval. The observer/coder continues to code—at a rate of 12 observations per minute—every other minute, coding for 1 minute and relaxing for

1 minute. Each segment of observation always starts with 1 and ends with 12. During the relaxation period, the observer records any comments in the "Segment Notes" column. A typical behavior exhibited by a target student during the field test is illustrated in Figure 21.1.

In the 23rd segment of coding or in the 45th minute of the class, these codes revealed that a student spent the first 10 seconds getting a set of Heavy Hands, 35 seconds waiting for the instructor to start strength exercises, and the last 15 seconds doing strength exercises. The 24th segment indicates that the same target student spent 60 seconds doing strength exercises with Heavy Hands. The 25th segment, which is circled to note that a new target student was selected and observed, indicates that the new student spent 50 seconds doing the same strength exercises, 5 seconds resting, and the last 5 seconds changing position (i.e., getting up from the mat).

As shown in Figure 21.1, using the numerals for coding is crucial in several respects. It literally shows the sequence of occurrences, which assists the coder in categorizing the behavior accurately by providing additional clues. The number identifies each single interval (e.g., the 11th interval in the fifth segment of coding). This identification is essential for testing interobserver reliability: Two coders can identify the specific intervals for discussion.

Time-on-Fitness Instrument (TOFI)

Segment (1 min)	Management	Wait	Rest/relaxation	Strength/stretch	Segment notes (activities, events . . .)
23	1 2	3 4 5 6 7 8 9		10 11 12	1-2—Getting heavy hands 3-9—Wait for the next exercise
24				1 2 3 4 5 6 7 8 9 10 11 12	
(25)		12	11	1 2 3 4 5 6 7 8 9 10	12—Getting up from the mat

Figure 21.1 Completed Time-on-Fitness Instrument (TOFI) recording sheet.

After an entire class observation, the observer makes appropriate entries under "General Field Notes" about any special or important features of teacher behavior or the setting that affected how the student spent his or her time. Then, at leisure, the observer totals the number of behaviors in each column and calculates the percentages. These percentages represent time spent in each category.

The coder's primary responsibility is to categorize student behavior using the objective characteristics of behavior as defined. Occasionally, the coder may have to make a professional judgment about the level of difficulty of the exercise based on the capability of the target student. For example, the same exercise, walking, can be coded as "cardiovascular" for some students and as "warm-up" for others. Occasionally, the coder may have to judge the intent of the behavior. The same exercise can be used for cool-down as well as for warm-up. Such judgment may depend on the clues from the instructor or the student and the conditions under which the class is conducted.

Five ground rules for coding TOFI data are as follows:

1. The coder analyzes the student behavior, making decisions in the following order:
   - Whether the behavior belongs to fitness or nonfitness time (i.e., whether the behavior is fitness related).
   - Whether the behavior involves physical movement. The coding sheet has shaded columns for those categories involving no physical movement and blank columns for all categories that do involve physical movement.
   - What specific category best represents the behavior observed.

   The behavior observed during an interval must be coded as one of the nine categories on the coding sheet. The system is inclusive.

2. Nonfitness time involves decisions about the categories management, wait, and other. The class time is defined by the schedule published in the YMCA program catalog. If the activity is advertised as an 8:00 p.m. to 9:00 p.m. class, the coding starts at 8:00 p.m. and ends at 9:00 p.m.
   - If the instructor is late while the student is waiting, code "wait."
   - If the instructor is ready to begin, but no student has yet arrived, then code "other."
   - If the target student leaves during the middle of coding, code "other" for the rest of that 1-minute coding segment. Then select and code another student.
   - If the instructor ends the class early, continue coding the behavior of the target student until he or she goes out of gym. At that point, code "other."
   - Coding stops at the end of the scheduled class time, even if the class is still in progress.
   - Wait is used only in obvious situations in which the instructor or the context provides definite clues. *Examples:* The instructor says, "Let's wait!" Or the tape player stops in the middle of dancing, so the students have to wait for music to start again.

- Management is often coded when the student changes body position. *Examples:* Changing position from left to right, getting up from the mat, and getting into the push-up position. This is not rest/relaxation because, as defined, rest/relaxation involves no physical movement.
- Situational specifics for any of these three categories may be recorded as segment notes or general field notes.

3. If two or more types of behavior occur during an interval, code the type of behavior that consumes the greater portion of the interval. *Example:* If the student warms up for 2 seconds and rests for 3 seconds, code "rest."

4. If two types of behavior occur *simultaneously* during an interval, code the type of behavior that better represents the behavior observed according to the category definitions. Do not code both behaviors. This system is mutually exclusive. However, the subscript, dash (—), is used to indicate that a coded category was accompanied by a knowledge behavior such as receiving instruction, measuring pulse, or watching a demonstration. If the student receives instruction from the teacher while using Heavy Hands during the first and the second intervals (see Segment 24 of Figure 21.2) the two intervals are coded with subscripts (i.e., 1—, 2—).

Time-on-Fitness Instrument (TOFI)

Segment (1 min)	Management	Wait	Rest/relaxation	Strength/stretch	Segment notes (activities, events . . .)
24				1- 2- 3 4 5 6 7 8 9 10 11 12	How-to: "Keep your back straight and arms out this way"

Figure 21.2 Completed Time-on-Fitness Instrument (TOFI) recording sheet with subscripts.

5. When in doubt, code the behavior, circling the interval number to indicate doubt, and move on. Right after that coding segment, go back to review it in the following order of priority:

- By looking at the intervals that occurred before and after the behavior in question. *Example:* Walking should be coded as "warm-up" if it occurs before jogging and as "cool-down" if it occurs after jogging.
- By figuring out what part of class this particular interval belongs to: beginning, middle, or end. *Example:* The beginning exercises

are seldom coded as "strength" or "cardiovascular" due to insufficient intensity.
- By regarding the behavior, in the absence of obvious indicators, as a continuation of the previous interval.
- After considering the previous suggestions, if still in doubt, leave it alone. The first impression is always better than second-guessing.

For practical reasons, each target student is coded for three alternating segments (the coder rests for 1 minute between each 1-minute coding segment). Thus the number of target students is determined by the length of the class (e.g., 10 target students for a 60-minute class and 5 students for a 30-minute class).

The first target student for observation is randomly selected 5 minutes before the beginning of a class. First, the coder counts the number of students that are present, thus assigning a number to each student, from left to right facing the front. Then, the coder selects one number among those assigned by using a table of random numbers. For example, if Number 7 is chosen out of 15 students, then Student 7 becomes the first target student. If Number 16 is chosen when only 14 students are present, then the number is skipped. Random sampling continues until a number—in this case, 14 or smaller—is chosen.

The second target student is selected at the end of the last coding segment for the first student. The student who is closest to the first target student is selected. If this includes more than one student, the student who is closest clockwise to the first student is selected. This procedure continues in selecting the sequence of target students until the end of a class. If a student who has already been observed is selected again, then the choice is the next closest student. In this way, the same student may not be observed twice in a class. Using this approach, the coder can observe a relatively large number of different students in each class. If fewer than 10 students in a 60-minute class or 5 students in a 30-minute class are available, then the same student is observed twice.

SUMMARIZING AND INTERPRETING THE DATA

To gather data about how students allocate their time among the nine student behavior categories, the TOFI uses 5-second interval recording (12 codes per minute) during alternating 1-minute segments of the class (Figure 21.3). The 1-minute observations that cover 30 minutes of a 60-minute class produce 360 coded intervals. At the end of each class,

Time-on-Fitness Instrument (TOFI)

Date: _____   YMCA: _____

No. of students: _____   Instructor: _____

Class time: from _____ to _____   Session no./total sessions: _____ / _____

Segment (1 min)	Nonfitness time			Passive fitness time		Transitional fitness time		Active fitness time		Segment notes (activities, events . . .)
	Management	Wait	Other	Rest/relaxation	Knowledge	Warm-up	Cool-down	Strength/stretch	Cardiovascular	
Total										

General field notes (instructors, students, setting, etc.)

Figure 21.3   Time-on-Fitness Instrument (TOFI) recording sheet.

the observer totals the number of intervals in each column and calculates the percentages. For example, if one column's total is 36, then this is 10% of a 60-minute class. These column percentages represent time spent in each category in that particular class.

REFERENCE

Golding, L.A., Myers, C.R., & Sinning, W.E. (Eds.) (1982). *The Y's way to physical fitness* (rev. ed.). Chicago: National Board of YMCA.

Chapter 22

Direct Instruction
Behavior Analysis (DIBA)

Dorothy B. Zakrajsek
Deborah Tannehill

Direct instruction is a model of teaching that is conceptually and operationally based on a combination of behaviors that were synthesized from process/product research (Rosenshine & Furst, 1971). Fielding, Kaneenui, and Gersten (1983) refer to direct instruction as a tightly structured approach to teaching in which the learner is shown explicitly how to perform skills, has ample practice time to master skills, receives frequent feedback on learning progress, and experiences success at each learning phase. Rosenshine (1979) says that direct instruction includes clear learning goals, sufficient time for instruction and practice, monitored student performance, low-level cognitive questions, immediate and specific feedback, extensive content coverage, and learning goals and materials appropriate for the student's ability. Proponents of direct instruction claim that learning achievement is increased through active teacher participation and on-task student behavior.

Direct Instruction Behavior Analysis (DIBA) features those behaviors identified by direct instruction researchers (Good & Grouws, 1977, Rosenshine, 1976, 1979; Rosenshine & Furst, 1971) and interpreted for physical education by Graham and Heimerer (1981). DIBA was designed to collect data on teacher and student behaviors that can be used in analyzing teaching performance with the direct instruction teaching model.

CATEGORY DESCRIPTIONS

DIBA comprises 15 categories: 8 categories plus 3 subscripts to further define teacher behavior and 4 categories to describe student behavior.

Teacher Behavior

Teaching Informing (I)

Teacher tells, explains, demonstrates, reviews, or summarizes.

Teacher Observing (O)

Teacher silently observes, watches, or monitors student performance.

Teacher Structuring (S)

Teacher stresses objectives and important points, directs performance, or signals transitions.

Teacher Questioning (Q)

Teacher asks questions that are intended to evoke a verbal or motor response.

Teacher Praise/Encouragement (P)

Teacher praises, commends, accepts, or encourages student performance or attempts.

Teacher Feedback (F)

Teacher gives feedback that is immediate, specific, task relevant (can include correct or incorrect responses).

Teacher Controlling (C)

Teacher uses disciplinary comments or actions to criticize or to justify authority.

None of the Above (N)

Teaching behaviors are not related to the instructional process (teaching and learning).

Enthusiasm (E)

A subscript E is used with the teacher behaviors if they are emitted in a way that interest and excitement are apparent through tone of voice, gestures, or facial expressions.

Lack Clarity (C)

A subscript C is used with teacher behaviors (informing, structuring, questioning, or feedback) to denote unclear interactions. Subscript C should be based on student reaction (e.g., puzzled looks, questions, and confusion) in following directions.

Modeling (M)

A subscript M is used with teaching behavior (informing, structuring, questioning, and feedback) to denote those times when the teacher is showing or demonstrating nonverbally how to perform or how not to perform a skill.

Student Behavior

Motor Engaged (M)

Student is actively engaged in an appropriate motor task/activity.

Cognitive Engaged (C)

Student listens to or reads about subject matter and gains information.

Response Preparing (R)

Student gets ready to respond to a learning task (R); gets equipment or relocates (R_T); waits for a turn (R_W).

Off-Task (O)

Student is not engaged in an appropriate motor or cognitive task. *Examples:* Student is getting a drink of water or taking a break.

RECORDING PROCEDURES

Three-second interval observe and record procedures are used. Acceptable levels of interobserver reliability can be established with Equation 3.1 (in chapter 3) after five or six hours of training. The following recording procedures govern the data collection.

1. Start recording when the teacher officially begins the class and stop when the teacher determines the close of class.

2. Record behaviors in 3-second intervals. Observe the teacher for 3 seconds and during the next 3 seconds record the behavior. Then observe the target student for 3 seconds and during the next 3 seconds record the behavior. The sequence is as follows:
   - Observe teacher 3 seconds
   - Record teacher behavior 3 seconds
   - Observe target student 3 seconds
   - Record student behavior 3 seconds

   Ten behaviors, 5 teacher and 5 student, are recorded per minute.
3. Select a target student at random. Record all student behaviors using only the target student.
4. If you use more than one target student, only observe one at a time.
5. Use a split-column format for recordings and enter them horizontally (see Figure 22.1).

Direct Instruction Behavior Analysis (DIBA)

Figure 22.1 Direct Instruction Behavior Analysis (DIBA) recording sheet.

Comments

Comments _____

Teacher behaviors		Student behaviors	
I Informing	F Feedback	M Motor engaged	
O Observing	C Controlling	C Cognitive engaged	
S Structuring	N None of above	R Response preparing	
Q Questioning	(E) Enthusiasm	R_T Getting equipment or relocating	
P Praise/encourage	(C) Clarity	R_W Waiting for a turn	
	(M) Modeling	O Off-task	

6. Record behavior changes if observed during the 3-second interval and adjust by slowing the subsequent recording pace.
7. Use subscripts depending on the information sought.

SUMMARIZING AND INTERPRETING THE DATA

Tally the number of behaviors for each teacher and student category. Figure the percentage of each category by dividing the category tallies by the number of total tallies (use the DIBA summary form, Figure 22.2).

Direct Instruction Behavior Analysis (DIBA)

Teacher behaviors	Number of tallies	Percent[a]
Informing (I)		
Observing (O)		
Structuring (S)		
Questioning (Q)		
Praise/encourage (P)		
Feedback (F)		
Controlling (C)		
None of the above (N)		
	Total _____	
Enthusiasm[b] (E)	Total _____	_____%
	$(I+S+Q+P+F)$	
Clarity[c] (C)	Total _____	_____%
	$(I+S+Q+F)$	
Modeling[d] (M)	Total _____	_____%
	$(I+S+Q+F)$	

Student behaviors	Number of tallies	Percent[a]
Motor engaged (M)		
Cognitive engaged (E)		
Response preparing (R)		
Getting equipment or relocating (R_T)		
Waiting for a turn (R_W)		
Off-task (O)		
	Total _____	

[a]Divide the number of tallies per behavior by the total number of tallies.

[b]Divide the number of enthusiasm tallies by the total number of tallies for informing, structuring, questioning, praise, and feedback.

[c]Divide the number of clarity tallies by the total number of tallies for informing, structuring, questioning, and feedback.

[d]Divide the number of modeling tallies by the total number of tallies for informing, structuring, questioning, and feedback.

Figure 22.2 Direct Instruction Behavior Analysis (DIBA) summary form.

The percentages of teaching behaviors can be analyzed according to the direct instruction teaching model. The subscripts allow for a closer examination of those behaviors that are more elusive in the overall generalization of limited teacher behaviors. The student behavior percentages allow for an analysis of on- and off-task behavior and how much time the students are engaged in learning. Information for DIBA can be used to compare instructional effectiveness as defined by direct instruction.

REFERENCES

Fielding, G., Kaneenui, E., & Gersten, R. (1983). A comparison of an inquiry and a direct instruction approach to teaching legal concepts and applications to secondary school students. *Journal of Educational Research*, **76**(5), 288-292.

Good, T., & Grouws, D. (1977). Teaching effects: A process-product study in fourth grade mathematics classrooms. *Journal of Teacher Education*, **28**(3), 49-54.

Graham, G., & Heimerer, E. (1981). Research on teacher effectiveness: A summary with implications for teaching. *Quest*, **33**(1), 14-25.

Rosenshine, B. (1976). Recent research on teaching behaviors and student achievement. *Journal of Teacher Education*, **27**(1), 61-64.

Rosenshine, B. (1979). Content, time and direct instruction. In P.L. Peterson & H.J. Walberg (Eds.), *Research on Teaching: Concepts, findings, and implications* (pp. 57-74). Berkeley, CA: McCutchan.

Rosenshine, B., & Furst, N. (1971). Research in teacher performance criteria. In B.O. Smith (Ed.), *Research in teacher education* (pp. 94-103). Englewood Cliffs, NJ: Prentice-Hall.

Chapter 23

Observational Recording Record of Physical Educator's Teaching Behavior (ORRPETB)

Michael J. Stewart

The Observational Recording Record of Physical Educator's Teaching Behavior (ORRPETB) is a multidimensional instrument that can be used in a lab or field setting. It has the capabilities of recording instructional climate, interaction, teacher behavior, or any combination thereof. It addresses teacher performance directly by assessing teacher behavior and indirectly by assessing the performance of students. The instrument consists of 27 teacher behavior categories, 4 student behavior categories referred to as *climates*, and 5 teacher-student behavior categories referred to as *interactions*.

The instrument has been tested for interobserver reliability in a lab as well as a field setting. The method used to compute interobserver reliability was interval-by-interval (see Equation 3.1). An agreement is any interval in which two independent observers record the presence of the same climate, behavior, or interaction. A disagreement is any interval in which two independent observers record a different climate, behavior, or interaction. The percent of agreement for observer reliability was calculated for the categories of climate, behavior, and interaction, as well as for an overall figure. The agreement for climate was 93%; behavior, 83%; interaction, 91%; and combined total, 82%.

CATEGORY DESCRIPTIONS

Climates

Climates are indirect assessments of teacher performance determined by what the students of the class are doing.

Instructional Time (I)

The period of time in the class when, theoretically, the opportunity for the student to learn is present. Students can receive information either verbally or nonverbally. During this time, 51% or more of the students are not engaged in physical activity. *Examples:* Students are listening to a lecture, watching the teacher or another student model a skill, watching a film, listening to a tape recorder, participating in a class discussion, or answering teacher questions.

Management Time (M)

The period of time in the class when, theoretically, the opportunity to learn is not present. During this time, 51% or more of the students are involved in activities that are only indirectly related to the class learning activity. There is no instruction, demonstration, or practice. *Examples:* The students are changing activities, numbering off for an activity, listening for roll call, getting out or putting away equipment, or moving to another environment for an activity.

Activity Time (A)

The period of time in a class when 51% or more of the students are involved in actual physical movement in a manner that is consistent with the specific goals of the particular environment. *Examples:* They are performing exercises, drills, participating in a group or individual sport, providing assistance for a partner or group, waiting in line for a turn, or taking an exam.

Waiting Time (W)

The period of time in a class when 51% or more of the students are prohibited from being categorized in other classroom climates. In other words, they are not in the elements of instructional, management, or activity time. *Examples:* They are waiting for class to begin; waiting for instruction to resume when it has been interrupted by another teacher, student messenger, parent, principal, or public address system; responding to a fire drill; or waiting for the instructor, student, or both to repair equipment.

Interaction

Interaction occurs when the teacher initiates verbal or nonverbal communication toward a student or group of students, or responds either verbally or nonverbally to student behavior. Interaction is divided into five categories. When recording interactions, the observer should ask two questions: What is the size of the group (individual, group, class)? Which sex is the interaction directed toward (male, female, or both)?

Individual (I)

The teacher is talking or responding nonverbally to one student.

Group (G)

The teacher is talking or responding nonverbally to more than one student but not the entire class.

Class (C)

The teacher is talking or responding to the entire class.

Male (M)

The teacher is talking to all individuals in the class who are male.

Female (F)

The teacher is talking to all individuals in the class who are female.

Teacher Behavior

This category accounts for teacher reactions to student behavior.

Lecturing or Orienting (LO)

The teacher gives facts or opinions about content or procedures and expresses his or her own ideas or the ideas of someone else. The teacher may be lecturing or orienting one or many students, who may or may not be engaged in activity during this time.

Asking Questions (AQ)

A teacher asks a student or group questions about content or procedures with the intent that an individual or group of individuals will answer. Students may or may not be engaged in activity during this time. Questions such as "How many times can you bounce your ball?" and "Can you make a shape with your legs?" are also included in this category.

Answering Questions (AQ)

A teacher answers students' questions about content or procedures.

Listening (L)

The teacher responds by listening to the student's question or response.

Monitoring (MO)

A teacher observes the class without reacting verbally to the behaviors of the students; the teacher is not being addressed by a student or group of students. He or she could be standing in one place or walking about the class area, but maintaining eye contact with the class is necessary. Observing a film with the class is included in this category.

Nonfunctional (NF)

The teacher displays behaviors not related to the ongoing activities of the class. The students may or may not be involved in activity during this time. *Examples:* The teacher is grading papers, writing a hall pass, talking to another teacher, talking to a student not in the class, or putting up equipment for the next activity or class.

Managing (MG)

The teacher expresses behaviors that are related to the class, but clearly not contributing to its educational outcomes. The students may or may not be involved in activity during this time. *Examples:* The teacher is repairing equipment or apparatus that has broken during the course of the class, sweeping water off a court that is to be used during the class, moving a mat to another area, or retrieving balls or other objects that have been used in a drill or activity.

Skill Feedback

Any information, either verbal or nonverbal, that the teacher makes available to the student to improve the next response. Feedback is positive, negative, or corrective in nature, and the first two are either general or specific.

Positive Skill Feedback—General (FG+). General praise, either verbal or nonverbal, that occurs during or immediately following a skill attempt. It is very important that these comments are intended for skill attempts and not social behaviors. *Examples:* "Yes! Good! Great! All right! Okay! At-a-girl!" "At-a-boy! Way to go! Right-on! Terrific! Good job!" "That's right! Good for you!" A wink. Thumbs up. A nod. A friendly slap on the back. A smile.

Positive Skill Feedback—Specific (FS+).   Specific, verbal praise that occurs during or following a skill attempt. *Examples:* "Yes, you kept your toes straight!" "Good, you followed through that time with a relaxed motion!" "Way to go, you kept your eye on the ball that time!" "Great, you came out of the pike at the right moment!" "At-a-girl, your back-swing was much smoother!"

Negative Skill Feedback—General (FG–).   General scolding, either verbal or nonverbal, that occurs during or immediately following a skill attempt. *Examples:* "Bad" "You can do better!" "Not good enough!" "How many times do I have to tell you?" A frown. Shaking the head.

Negative Skill Feedback—Specific (FS–).   Specific, verbal scolding that occurs during or following a skill attempt. "Terrible. Your arms weren't straight until you made contact!" "Bad; you swung down at the ball!" "You can do better; your legs were bent during the entire movement!" "I can't believe it; your legs were 2 ft apart when you entered the water!"

Corrective Skill Feedback (CF).   Corrective verbal information given during or following a skill attempt. Often corrective feedback can become negative skill feedback, and the tone or volume of the voice will be the indicator. Remember that this feedback corrects a skill performance rather than scolding it. *Examples:* "Keep your arms straight." "Stay on your toes." "A little bit more follow-through." "Keep your chin close to your chest."

Corrective Skill Feedback + Positive (CF+) or Negative (CF–) Skill Feedback.   Corrective information given during or following a skill attempt plus a positive or negative statement or gesture. *Examples:* "Fantastic! Now keep your arms straight next time." "Bad; keep your chin close to your chest next time." A wink. "A little more follow-through and you'll have it."

Modeling

A skill or activity used to show a student or students the correct or incorrect way to perform a skill or behavior. Verbal instruction may or may not accompany modeling, but the behavior should be recorded as modeling and not lecturing or orienting.

Teacher Modeling—Positive (TM+).   The teacher demonstrates the correct way to perform a skill or behavior. *Examples:* Demonstrating a correct forward roll, or demonstrating the correct method of lining up at the door and standing in the correct place.

Teacher Modeling—Negative (TM–).   The teacher demonstrates the incorrect way to perform a skill or behavior. *Examples*: Demonstrating the incorrect way to bump a volleyball, or the incorrect way to walk to the door and line up (running to the door and sliding on the floor).

Student Modeling—Positive (SM+).   The teacher uses a student or students to demonstrate the correct way to perform a skill or behavior. *Examples:* Demonstrating the correct way to perform a jump shot in basketball, or pointing out one or more students who are being quiet and attentive during the lecture.

Student Modeling—Negative (SM–).   The teacher uses a student or students to demonstrate the incorrect way to perform a skill or behavior. *Examples*: Demonstrating the incorrect way to throw a shot put in a track meet warm-up, or pointing out a student who pushes and shoves while getting hoops from the equipment bin.

Social Behavior

The teacher reacts verbally or nonverbally to the social behavior of a student or students.

Praise—General (PG).   Positive or supportive general statements or gestures made by the teacher during or following a behavioral episode. *Examples:* "Good!" "Perfect!" "Tremendous!" "Okay!" Thumbs up. A pat on the back.

Praise—Specific (PS).   Positive or supportive specific statements or gestures made by the teacher during or following a behavioral episode not related to skill attempts. *Examples:* "Good; everyone is quiet and listening." "Perfect Gladys; you stopped talking on the signal." "Tremendous, class; you lined up without pushing today." "Great, Joshua; you are holding your ball and waiting for directions."

Nagging (N).   A teacher verbally or nonverbally scolds a student or students at a low intensity for an undesirable social behavior. *Examples:* "I told you to get in line." "You're making too much noise." "Sh . . . Didn't I say to stop talking?" "I said move quietly." Shaking the head.

Getting Nasty (N–).   A teacher verbally or nonverbally scolds a student or students at a high intensity for an undesirable behavior. *Examples:* Yelling or screaming. Using obscene language. Making sarcastic remarks. Physically pushing, moving, or hitting a student or students.

Hustling (H)

A teacher uses verbal statements or gestures to activate or intensify previously directed behavior. The tone of voice and the enthusiasm level are extremely important in this category. These are motivating statements and gestures, and caution should be taken not to mistake them for negative skill feedback-general or specific. *Examples:* "Run, run, run!" "Harder!" "Faster, faster!" Clapping hands quickly. Jumping up and down.

Appropriate Punishment (P)

Specific penalties imposed by the teacher on those students who break the class rules by exhibiting disruptive or deviant behaviors. The fact that many of the penalties may not seem appropriate is irrelevant; a philosophical judgment should not be made as to their appropriateness. *Examples:* Administering time out from reinforcement. Sending a student or students to the principal's office. Having a student or students apologize to another student or the teacher.

Physical Contact (PC)

The teacher physically touches a student during a skill attempt or explanation of a skill. If verbal statements accompany the physical contact, then it should be recorded as such. *Examples:* Spotting a student or manually guiding a student through a skill.

Teacher Officiating (TO)

The teacher acts as an official during a game or activity, and his or her behavior cannot be classified in the preceding categories.

Teacher Participation (TP)

The teacher participates in a game or activity and is not involved in the teaching process.

RECORDING PROCEDURES

Figure 23.1 is an example of an ORRPETB recording sheet. At the top of the record there are spaces for basic information. These should be completed before actual recording takes place. Below the basic information is the coding record itself. The intervals are numbered on the coding record, and every 10th interval is shaded to denote a rest period for the observer. The coding record consists of 80 intervals; because 8 of these are rest intervals, the coding record provides for 12 minutes of observation and recording. At the bottom of the coding record are categories and subcategories with their appropriate codes.

Observational Recording Record of Physical Educator's Teaching Behavior (ORRPETB)

Recorder —————————————— Teacher ——————————————

School ——————————— Page ——————————— Grade ———————————

Environment ——————— Activity ——————————— Date ———————————

Time started ————Time finished ————— Reliability check Yes ———— No ————

```
      1  2  3  4  5  6  7  8  9 10 11 12 13 14 15 16 17 18 19 20
   C
   B
   I

     21 22 23 24 25 26 27 28 29 30 31 32 33 34 35 36 37 38 39 40
   C
   B
   I

     41 42 43 44 45 46 47 48 49 50 51 52 53 54 55 56 57 58 59 60
   C
   B
   I

     61 62 63 64 65 66 67 68 69 70 71 72 73 74 75 76 77 78 79 80
   C
   B
   I
```

Climate (C)		Behavior (B)			
Management	M	Lecturing or orienting	LO	Praise specific	PS
Instruction	I	Asking questions	AQ	Nagging	N
Activity	A	Answering questions	WQ	Getting nasty	N–
Waiting	W	Listening	L	Punishment	P
		Monitoring	MO	Positive skill feedback	
		Nonfunctional	NF	-general	FG+
		Managing	MG	Positive skill feedback	
Interaction (I)		Physical contact	PC	-specific	FS+
Individual	I	Hustling	H	Negative skill feedback	
Group	G	Teacher modeling,		-general	FG–
Class	C	positive	TM+	Negative skill feedback	
		Teacher modeling,		-specific	FS–
Male	M	negative	TM–	Corrective skill	
Female	F	Student modeling,		feedback	CF
		positive	SM+	Corrective skill	
		Student modeling,		feedback + positive	CF+
		negative	SM–	Corrective skill	
		Praise general	PG	feedback + negative	CF–
				Teacher officiating	TO
				Teacher participation	TP

Figure 23.1 Observation Recording Record of Physical Educator's Teaching Behavior (ORRPETB) recording sheet.

The ORRPETB recording procedure is interval recording, a method of recording the occurrence or nonoccurrence of a behavior within a specific time interval. Because teaching physical education involves a high frequency of behavioral episodes, a 5-second interval should be used to maintain a high correspondence between the actual and the recorded frequencies of occurrence. At the same time, a 5-second interval allows sufficient time for the observer to recognize and record behavior reliably.

When recording climates, behaviors, and interactions, the observer should consider and record those that occur for the longest time during the 5-second interval as the principal behavior. Exceptions to this rule are in the behavioral categories of physical contact, hustling, praising, nagging, getting nasty, punishment, or feedback. These are recorded as the principal behavior if they occur for any period of time. The reason for this exception is that these behaviors occur for short periods (sometimes only a second). Not acknowledging these very important teaching behaviors would give an inaccurate reflection of the teacher's behavior.

A cassette tape recorder and programmed tape is used as a timing device to indicate observation and recording intervals. Every 5 seconds the tape signals the observer to either observe or record. In addition, the tape indicates which interval the observer should be recording. This method permits the observer to maintain constant eye contact with the subject during the interval. Upon hearing the signal "observe," the observer watches the teacher and students for 5 seconds. At the end of the 5-second observe interval, the tape should signal "record." In addition to the record signal, a number ranging consecutively from 1 to 80 should be included on the tape so the observer knows which interval to mark. The observer is then given 5 seconds to refer to the behavior indicators at the bottom of the coding sheet and record the Climate, Behavior, and Interaction. Following the 5-second recording interval, the observer receives another observe signal.

SUMMARIZING AND INTERPRETING THE DATA

After the observational period is completed, the information on the coding records is transferred to a summary sheet to give the teacher a better idea of his or her teaching performance. Figure 23.2 is a summary sheet to use with this instrument. The teacher or recorder begins by counting the intervals of each category of the instrument and recording the number of category intervals in the appropriate area on the summary sheet. When all intervals are accounted for, a percent of occurrence is calculated for each category of the instrument by entering the total number of recording intervals during the observational period. The total number of category intervals and the total number of intervals during the observational period should be equal. Furthermore, after the percent of occurrence has been calculated for each category, those percentages should total 100. If a teacher or supervisor would like to combine selected behaviors into such general categories as positive behaviors or negative behaviors, this can be done simply by identifying those behaviors considered positive and those considered negative and adding the subcategories together. This would give a much more general picture of the teaching performance, but sometimes this might be desired.

**Observational Recording Record of Physical Educator's
Teaching Behavior (ORRPETB)**

Name ————————————————— Date ——————————————————

Category	Code	Number of category intervals	Total number of intervals for observation period	Percentage of occurrence
Climate Management	M			
Instruction	I			
Activity	A			
Waiting	W			
Subtotal				
Interaction Individual	I			
Group	G			
Class	C			
Male	M			
Female	F			
Subtotal				
Behavior Lecturing or orienting	LO			
Asking questions	AQ			
Answering questions	WQ			
Listening	L			
Monitoring	MO			
Nonfunctional	NF			
Managing	MG			
Physical contact	PC			
Hustling	H			

(Cont.)

Figure 23.2   Observation Recording Record of Physical Educator's Teaching Behavior (ORRPETB) summary sheet.

Teacher modeling, positive	TM+			
Teacher modeling, negative	TM–			
Student modeling, positive	SM+			
Student modeling, negative	SM–			
Praise general	PG			
Praise specific	PS			
Nagging	N			
Getting nasty	N–			
Punishment	P			
Positive skill feedback-general	FG+			
Positive skill feedback-specific	FS+			
Negative skill feedback-general	FG–			
Negative skill feedback-specific	FS–			
Corrective skill feedback	CF			
Corrective skill feedback + positive	CF+			
Corrective skill feedback + negative	CF–			
Teacher officiating	TO			
Teacher participation	TP			
Subtotal				
Grand total				100%

Figure 23.2 (Continued)

ACKNOWLEDGMENT

The instrument described in this chapter was developed as part of the author's dissertation. Appreciation is extended to Daryl Siedentop for his many suggestions and helpful guidance in every phase of the development of the instrument.

Chapter 24

Observation Instrument for Content Development in Physical Education (OSCD-PE)

Judith E. Rink

The purpose of the Observation Instrument for Content Development in Physical Education (OSCD-PE) is to describe the process of content development in physical education activity classes (Rink, 1979). All teaching behavior is categorized. Although behaviors that make no contribution or only an indirect contribution to lesson content are recorded, the most description is provided on behaviors that directly contribute to lesson content. These behaviors are coded into three major facets simultaneously: communication function, content function, and source.

To understand how these behaviors function in a lesson, all movement tasks are underlined and the beginning and end of time allotted for activity are indexed in the observational record. This provides a record of what takes place during activity and during transitions between activities.

OSCD-PE is a difficult instrument to learn to use in its entirety. It takes approximately 40 hours to learn how to record in a continuous fashion for research purposes. A training manual is available for those who wish to learn to use it independently. In the development of the instrument, reliability varied from .70 to .90, depending on the context and difficulty of the lesson. Most research in which OSCD-PE has been used has reported reliabilities above a .80 using simple percentage of agreement on the categories of the instrument.

The advantage of OSCD-PE is that it provides a script of a lesson that can be directly compared with other lessons. Almost all behaviors and instructional events that are part of most other descriptive analytic tools in the physical education literature can be obtained using OSCD-PE, in addition to the content dimension that is not part of other tools. Of particular value is the information provided on refining behaviors of the teacher and determining how managerial behaviors function in a lesson.

OSCD-PE does not provide information on the accuracy, appropriateness, or quality of a teacher's behavior. Because only student verbal behavior that involves an interaction with the teacher is recorded, there is no way to determine the effect of teaching behavior on student responses. Therefore, the observer can report only that a behavior was exhibited but cannot provide information on the quality of that behavior. In situations where teachers seem to do everything right, but do not base what they do on what students do, this is a problem.

CATEGORY DESCRIPTIONS

Communication Function

This function focuses on the type of communication used for a given behavior.

Soliciting

Any spoken or unspoken nonappraisal behavior that evokes or is intended to evoke a behavior from another person in the instructional situation. Soliciting behaviors in physical education generally involves giving commands to do something or asking questions that require a response.

Responding

Any spoken or unspoken behavior that is a clear response to an event in the instructional situation. Responding behaviors in the physical education setting are generally answers to verbal questions.

Initiating

Any spoken or unspoken behavior that presents information to others that is not directly elicited by an antecedent behavior or event. Initiating behaviors in physical education settings are lecture-type behaviors—those that provide information without expecting an immediate response. Directions on how or why to do something usually fall into this category.

Appraisal

Any spoken or unspoken behavior that directly and explicitly communicates a judgment about the person, group, or product of behavior. Appraisal behavior makes a judgment about past performance and is not a corrective statement that solicits future behavior. Appraisals must be explicit.

Content Function

The content function concerns the role the behavior plays in the development of lesson content.

Informing

Any spoken or unspoken behavior that is intended to communicate substantive information to the learner and does not have a refining, extending, or applying function. Informing behaviors do not develop content; they merely introduce content information to the learner.

Refining

Any spoken or unspoken behavior that is qualitatively related to improving substantive motor performance. Refining behaviors can be solicitations (corrective feedback), appraisals (specific evaluations of performance), initiations (lecture on how to improve performance), or responses (answers to a question on how to perform better).

Extending

Any spoken or unspoken behavior that is quantitatively related to either reducing or expanding the content of substantive material. Extending behaviors usually make things more or less difficult, or are related to variety of response.

Applying

Any spoken or unspoken substantive behavior that introduces or sustains a focus on the use of motor activity that is related to the use of that movement rather than the movement performance itself. Application content in physical education is usually competitive in either a self-testing or a game situation.

Conduct

Any spoken or unspoken behavior that structures, directs, or reinforces the explicit or implicit behavior code of a given situation. Conduct behaviors are disciplinary behaviors.

Organization

Any spoken or unspoken behavior that structures, directs, or reinforces the arrangement of people, time, or equipment to create conditions for substantive learning. Organizational behaviors are management behaviors without the conduct category.

Source/Recipient of Behavior

The source of behavior is coded differently depending on whether the teacher or a student is the source of the behavior. If the former, the category is coded to reflect to whom the teacher is directing the behavior. If the latter, the category is coded to reflect the nature of that source (a single student, class, or small group).

Class

Whole class.

Individual

One or two students.

Small Group

Over three students but not more than half the class.

Individual/Public

An individual but in a manner that the whole class can hear.

Other Categories

These other categories are not content related and do not fit the afore-mentioned areas.

Indirect/Overt (51)

Behavior that creates or maintains the conditions for learning without being directly related to the lesson content. *Examples:* Injured students, off-topic discussions, and attendance.

Indirect/Covert (52)

Observing behavior.

Nonfunctioning (60)

Behavior that makes neither a covert nor an overt contribution to the lesson.

Movement Task (—)

Any solicitation requesting students to engage in substantive movement content (can be informing, refining, extending, or applying).

RECORDING PROCEDURES

1. Behavior is recorded every time it changes categories. If the same behavior is sustained for over 5 seconds, it is coded again for the following 5-second interval.
2. A two-digit number is used for recording. The first number represents the communication function of the behavior and is coded for soliciting, responding, initiating, or appraising, as is appropriate. The second number represents the content function of the behavior and is coded 1-6 for informing, refining, extending, applying, conduct, or organization, as is appropriate. If the behavior is not content related, the symbols for nonfunctioning (60), indirect/overt (51), or indirect/covert (52) are used.
   A sample recording form is provided in Figure 24.1. It is divided into columns representing the facet of the Source/Recipient of behavior.
3. The teacher is assumed to be the source of the behavior unless an "S" is used to indicate student or an "O" is used to indicate another element in the instructional situation.
4. The behavior is assumed to be positive unless it is circled to indicate a negative behavior.
5. The movement task is underlined when it is phrased as a directive in the lesson. If it is not phrased as a directive, it is underlined as an initiation behavior at some point in the explanation of the task.
6. A slash to the left of the column indicates when activity begins. A slash to the right of the column indicates when allotted activity ends.
7. Behavior directed to only one student consecutively is bracketed to indicate how much time the teacher is spending with one individual.
8. Demonstrations are indicated with the subcode "D."

Observation Instrument for Content Development in Physical Education (OSCD-PE)

Page no. _____

I. D.   Jr. High Coed Tennis _____   Date _____   Coder _____

Description of content forehand/backhand tennis -- individual skill

Arrangement of equipment 1 court; balls and rackets for every student

C	I	G	I/C
36			
36			
16			
			36
			36
			36
36			
31			
31			
			36
			36
15			
31			
31			
31			
36			
36			
		S16	
		26	
/16			
	31		

C	I	G	I/C
	31		
			40
			41
			12
			12
12			
			(42)
			12
			12
			12
			42
			12
			12
16			
16			
31			
32			
(32D)			
32			
(42)			

C	I	G	I/C
32			
(42)			
12			
		S22	
42			
42			
32			
/16			
		12	
			41
		12	
		11	
		12	
		20	
		42	
16			
		12	
36			
		12	

(T) Teacher	(1) Soliciting	(1) Informing	(C) Class	(51) Indirect–overt
(S) Student	(2) Responding	(2) Refining	(I) Individual	(52) Indirect–covert
(O) Other	(3) Initiating	(3) Extending	(G) Group	(60) Noncontributing
	(4) Appraising	(4) Applying	(I/C) Individual/	
		(5) Conduct	Public	
		(6) Organization		

Figure 24.1 Completed Observation Instrument for Content Development in Physical Education (OSCD-PE) recording sheet.

SUMMARIZING AND INTERPRETING THE DATA

Data are summarized by each of the major facets of the instrument as well as individual behaviors. These data are best reported in terms of rate per minute of a lesson for comparison purposes. Figure 24.2 offers another form for data analysis.

Observation Instrument for Content Development in Physical Education (OSCD-PE)

Teacher _____   Lesson no. _____

Specific behavior   Total

```
10 ___ ___    20 ___ ___    30 ___ ___    40 ___ ___        ___ ___
11 ___ ___    21 ___ ___    31 ___ ___    41 ___ ___        ___ ___
12 ___ ___    22 ___ ___    32 ___ ___    42 ___ ___        ___ ___
13 ___ ___    23 ___ ___    33 ___ ___    43 ___ ___        ___ ___
14 ___ ___    24 ___ ___    34 ___ ___    44 ___ ___        ___ ___
15 ___ ___    25 ___ ___    35 ___ ___    45 ___ ___        ___ ___
16 ___ ___    26 ___ ___    36 ___ ___    46 ___ ___        ___ ___
```

Totals

```
___ ___    ___ ___    ___ ___    ___ ___        ___ ___

                       51 ___    52 ___
```

Lesson phases

_____ Beginning before activity (number of intervals).

_____ Total number of behaviors recorded.

_____ Percentage of activity time (number in activity divided by total).

_____ Average transition time (time between tasks divided by number of transitions).

_____ Average activity time (total activity time divided by number of different tasks worked on).

_____ S/T Student/Teacher verbal interactions (total number of different).
_____ T/S

_____ Average feedback episodes (total number of separate feedback incidents divided by total feedback behavior during activity).

_____ Demonstration during activity time.

_____ Demonstration not during activity time.

Figure 24.2 Observation Instrument for Content Development in Physical Education (OSCD-PE) data analysis sheet.

The following are other useful constructs:

- Time spent before activity starts, in inactivity, and transitions between activities.
- Types of tasks, listed in order of occurrence, to provide a gross picture of content development.
- Average time spent with one individual in a feedback context.
- Use of demonstration (where and to what extent it occurs).

The first interpretation an observer should make is the extent to which management or content behavior is exhibited. This reveals the teacher's managerial skills. If management is a problem, it is possible to sort out what the teacher is doing or not doing by the specific types of behavior he or she exhibits and where they occur in the lesson. With poor management, generally few expectations are communicated (35, 36) or reinforced (46, 45), and desist behaviors are used a great deal (circled 15 and 16). Management that occurs right after a task is delivered generally indicates poor task communication. Management that occurs toward the end of activity generally indicates poor task pacing.

The way in which content is developed is the unique feature of the OSCD-PE. Task progressions with no refining or extending tasks usually indicate a complete lack of concern for progression in complexity and no emphasis on quality of performance. Strategies for refining can be sorted into individual feedback, class refining, and amount of time spent with individuals. In addition, attempts to modify tasks for individuals can be obtained by tasks underlined in the "Individual" or "Group" column of the recording sheet.

Lessons that have a variety focus are discriminated by extensions coded with a "V" and explored in terms of the examples of and solicitations for variety given. Lessons that have an application focus can be sorted into those that have a qualitative focus (refining) and those in which the teacher plays primarily a referee or cheerleader role.

REFERENCE

Rink, J. (1979). *Development of an observation system for content development in physical education.* Unpublished doctoral dissertation, The Ohio State University, Columbus.

Chapter 25

Qualitative Measures of Teaching Performance Scale (QMTPS)

Judith E. Rink
Peter H. Werner

The purpose of the Qualitative Measures of Teaching Performance Scale (QMTPS) is to describe qualitative aspects of teacher process characteristics in an effort to determine why some teachers are more effective than others in effecting student learning. The QMTPS is divided into four major constructs: type of task, task presentation, student response appropriate to task focus, and specific congruent feedback. An interobserver agreement of 90% has been achieved for this observation instrument.

The QMTPS has the following limitations:

- The QMTPS is related to but is not a direct measure of effective teaching.
- The QMTPS was originally designed to assist researchers in gaining more qualitative insight as to how more effective teachers differed from less effective teachers in a study concerning the jumping and landing abilities of children. Although thought to be generic in nature, the use of the QMTPS has not been used in other teaching studies.
- Effective teaching goes beyond the constructs of academic learning time, number of practice trials, content development, and management skills of the teacher. The QMTPS identifies several additional constructs (task presentation, student response, and congruent feedback) that seem to be critical to teacher effectiveness. As a result, the QMTPS can only be considered as one of a battery of instruments that, when used properly, can yield a more complete picture of the link between instruction and learning.

CATEGORY DESCRIPTIONS

Type of Task

The type of task concerns the nature of the movement activity that the teacher poses to the students for them to execute. There are five types of tasks.

Informing

A task that names, defines, or describes a skill or movement concept with no focus other than just to do it. It is usually the first task in a sequence of tasks.

Refining

A task that qualitatively seeks to improve motor performance. Most often this type of task focuses on improving the mechanics of the skill or tactical/strategic aspects of play.

Extending

A task that quantitatively changes the original task content by manipulating the level of difficulty of conditions under which the task is performed or that seeks a variety of responses.

Repeat

A simple repetition of the previous task.

Applying

A task that focuses student performance outside the movement itself. It is usually competitive or self-testing in nature.

Task Presentation

Task presentation concerns the delivery of information by the teacher to the students. There are five categories.

Clarity

Teacher's verbal explanation/directions communicate a clear idea of what to do and how to do it. This judgment is confirmed on the basis of student movement responses to the presentation and is relative to the situation.

Yes. Students proceeded to work in a focused way on what the teacher asked them to do.

No. Students exhibited confusion, questions, off-task behavior, or lack of intent to deal with the specifics of the task.

Demonstrate

Modeling desired performance executed by teacher, student(s), and/or visual aids.

Yes. Full model of the desired movement.

Partial. Incomplete model of task performance exhibiting only a portion of the desired movement.

No. No attempt to model the movement task.

Appropriate Number of Cues

The degree to which the teacher presents sufficient information about the movement task without overloading the learner.

Appropriate. Three or fewer new learning cues related to the performance of the movement task.

Inappropriate. Either more than three or no new learning cues related to the performance of the movement.

None Given. No attempt at providing learning cues was made.

Accuracy of Cues

The degree to which the information presented was technically correct and reflected accurate mechanical principles.

Accurate. All information presented was correct.

Inaccurate. One or more incidences of incorrect information.

None Given. No cues given.

Qualitative Cues Provided

Verbal information provided to the learner on the process or mechanics of movement.

Yes. Teacher's explanation or direction included at least one aspect of the process of performance.

No. Teacher's explanation or direction included no information on the process of performance.

Student Responses Appropriate to Task Focus

This category measures the degree to which student responses reflect an intent to perform the task as stated by the teacher.

All

No more than two students viewed on the video screen exhibited inappropriate responses.

Partial

Three or more students exhibited inappropriate behavior on the video screen.

None

No students exhibited appropriate behavior.

Teacher Specific Congruent Feedback

The final category looks at the degree to which teacher feedback during an activity is congruent with (matched to) the focus of the task.

Yes

More than two incidences were evident in which teacher feedback was congruent with the task.

Partial

One or two incidences of congruent feedback were evident.

No

No congruent feedback was given.

RECORDING PROCEDURES

A videotape of a given lesson is used to record QMTPS data. This is for the purpose of assessing the categories of type of task, task presentation, congruent feedback, and student responses. A task is a unit of work given verbally and/or visually by the teacher that focuses students on the intended skill or aspect of that skill to be executed once activity is initiated. The observer stops the videotape after each task is delivered by a teacher to identify the task and code the section of the instrument on task presentation. He or she stops it again after an activity to code student responses and teacher feedback.

SUMMARIZING AND INTERPRETING THE DATA

Data are recorded in number of occurrences and converted to percentages of the teacher task-student response unit of analysis for each category in each construct (Figure 25.1). There are five categories in the presentation of task area, one for student response appropriate to focus, and one specific congruent feedback area. Each of these seven areas is totaled and converted to percentage. Responses in the most desirable category (scores of 1) are summed and averaged for a total QMTPS score. For example, in Figure 25.1 the teacher gave a total of 12 tasks. After the initial informing task, four refining tasks focused on quality, six tasks focused on extending the skill in difficulty or variety, and one repeat task was given by the teacher.

In the area of task presentation, the teacher was clear in instruction about tasks 6 out of 12 times, or 50% of the time. The teacher gave a full demonstration once, a partial demonstration once, and no demonstration 10 times during task delivery. An appropriate number of cues was given during 2 of the 12 tasks. These cues were accurate 5 out of 12 times, and in 4 out of 12 instances they were qualitative. For the category, student responses appropriate to the task focus, all students responded appropriately 33% of the time; 50% of the time students responded inappropriately. Specific congruent feedback was given by the teacher in 1 of the 12 tasks. The scores in the most desirable categories were 50%, .08%, 16%, 42%, 33%, 33%, and .08%; the mean of these scores, 27, is the total QMTPS score.

Recording the type of tasks a teacher gives creates a picture of the intent to focus on quality movement, to increase or decrease the difficulty or introduce variety through task progressions, or to engage students in self-testing or gaining activities. Although no one best pattern emerges, over a period of time a balance of type of tasks should occur.

Task presentation dimensions reveal the teacher's ability to select accurate qualitative learning cues and to communicate them to the learner. The construct of task presentation is a measure of the teacher's attempt to give the learner an accurate motor plan. Student responses should technically be of higher quality if the teacher has been able to communicate clearly (Werner & Rink, 1986). Task presentation, however, is also an indirect measure of task appropriateness. These categories describe the task-oriented and movement-quality foci of the lesson. Tasks that have no

Qualitative Measures of Teaching Performance Scale (QMTPS)

Teacher _____ Coder _____

Focus of lesson _____

Lesson number _____

Task Number	Type of task	Clarity	Demonstration	Number of cues	Accuracy of cues	Qualitative cues	Student response appropriate to focus	Specific congruent feedback
1	I	2	3	2	1	1	3	3
2	R	2	3	2	1	2	3	3
3	E	2	3	2	1	1	2	3
4	E	1	3	1	1	2	1	2
5	E	1	3	1	3	2	2	3
6	R	1	2	2	1	1	1	2
7	E	1	1	2	2	1	1	3
8	R	1	3	2	3	2	1	1
9	E	1	3	2	3	2	3	3
10	Re	2	3	2	3	2	3	3
11	R	2	3	2	3	2	3	3
12	E	2	3	2	3	2	3	3
13								
14								
15								
Totals		1–6 2–6	1–1 2–1 3–10	1–2 2–10	1–5 2–1 3–6	1–4 2–8	1–4 2–2 3–6	1–1 2–2 3–9
Percent for each category		1–50 2–50	1–08 2–08 3–84	1–16 2–84	1–42 2–08 3–50	1–33 2–67	1–33 2–16 3–50	1–08 2–16 3–75
Percent most desirable		50	08	16	42	33	33	08

Type of task
I–Informing
R–Refine (quality)
E–Extend (variety)
Re–Repeat (repeat same task)
A–Apply self-testing

Clarity
1–Yes
2–No

Demonstration
1–Full
2–Partial
3–None

Number of cues
1–Appropriate
2–Inappropriate
3–None given

Accuracy of cues
1–Accurate
2–Inaccurate
3–None given

Qualitative cues
1–Yes
2–No

Student responses
1–All
2–Partial
3–None

Specific congruent feedback
1–Yes
2–Partial
3–No

Total QMTPS 27

Figure 25.1 Qualitative Measures of Teaching Performance Scale (QMTPS) recording sheet.

qualitative focus and do not lead to improved performance or focused practice are filtered out.

The next construct describes student responses appropriate to the task focus (Rink & Werner, 1985). This category focuses on the degree to which student responses reflect an intent to perform the task as stated by the teacher. Appropriate responses are considered those in which the students show an intent to use the information on skill performance given by the teacher. Student responses fall into the category of providing for practice. The ideal comparison is to evaluate the relationship between the response of the student and the learning goal. This instrument looks at the relationship of the student response and the intent of the teacher. When students formulate motor plans and emit appropriate responses, student learning should occur.

The last construct of the instrument is that of teacher specific congruent feedback. This category addresses the degree to which teacher feedback during activity matches or is congruent with the task focus. The congruency component, in terms of giving students consistent messages on the focus of the task and the results of their efforts, is very important to developing accountability for the task. Congruent feedback gives students a progress report of their efforts as related to the task and/or what they can do to improve their performance.

Total QMTPS scores reflect the quality of the teacher's work with students and generally suggest his or her effectiveness in terms of product measures. In one study (Werner & Rink, 1984), the teacher who produced the most consistent student achievement had the highest QMTPS total score. Although data can only be supportive rather than predictive because of the low sample size used in the study, it is interesting to note that, as scores on the QMTPS total score went up, so did effectiveness.

The purpose of the QMTPS is to look at the relationships among task presentation, student responses, and teacher feedback identified in the model for skill acquisition earlier. The characteristics of task presentation focus on clarity and specificity of presentation. If the task is appropriate and well presented there should be a direct relationship to quality student responses. In addition, if teacher feedback is congruent with the task presentation and appropriate to the responses of students, it should serve to further improve the quality of student responses.

REFERENCES

Rink, J., & Werner, P. (1985, August). *Student responses as a measure of teacher effectiveness*. Paper delivered at the International Conference on Research in Physical Education and Sport, Garden City, New York.

Werner, P., & Rink, J. (1984, July). *Effects of intervention in the teaching process on jumping and landing abilities of second grade children*. Paper presented at the Olympic Scientific Congress, Eugene, Oregon.

Werner, P., & Rink, J. (1986). *Identifying effective instructional skills for teaching jumping and landing*. Unpublished paper, University of South Carolina, Columbia.

Chapter 26

West Virginia University Teaching Evaluation System and Feedback Taxonomy

Andrew H. Hawkins
Robert L. Wiegand

The West Virginia University Teaching Evaluation System was developed to provide a rich, empirical source of information that could inform evaluative judgments made by physical education professionals regarding their subject matter lessons and programs. The generic system is useful across a wide variety of subject matter activities. Further, it is useful regardless of the type of lesson, its length, class size, or the kind of programmatic context in which the lesson resides.

The system was designed to include a comprehensive, mutually exclusive set of categories for both teacher behavior and the behavior of students in the teacher's class. The teacher response class categories were functionally defined through content analysis of qualitative field notes taken while observing a variety of preservice and in-service teachers engaged in the instruction of several subject matter activities. Student response classes are identical to the learner involvement level categories of the Academic Learning Time-Physical Education (ALT-PE II) system (Siedentop, Tousignant, & Parker, 1982).

The system is designed for use with an electronic recording regimen. However, there is no reason why a more traditional interval recording regimen could not be used with the system's category definitions. For the purposes of this chapter, only the electronic regimen is explained. This preferred recording methodology is capable of providing real-time information for each category for duration and frequency and their derivatives: mean, minimum, and maximum lengths of occurrences; percentage of total time; and rate (frequencies per unit of time). The electronic recording regimen thus provides a rich data display with a great capacity to inform evaluative decisions. Approximately 8 hours of instruction and practice generally produces desired accuracy, reliability, and agreement levels (.85) for undergraduate, graduate, and in-service-level data collectors.

Accuracy is assessed through observation comparisons with several short segments (4 minutes) of criterion videotapes. Reliability is assessed through comparisons of an accurate observation to another observation conducted on the same data sample a week or more later. Interobserver agreement is assessed by comparisons of two simultaneous independent observations of the same behavior sample. Assessments of all three dimensions of data quality are encouraged to enhance believability.

Because the system is designed to profile behaviors observed during student-contact class time, information relevant to daily planning is only indirectly related to data emerging from this system. Specific data profiles may indicate certain problems in the daily planning process, but the precise nature of the problems is not self-evident and the profile requires the trained and experienced interpretation of a teacher educator or other similarly informed professional.

The generic nature of the system requires that all data emerging from a lesson be interpreted in light of certain contextual factors like activity, placement in unit, class size, total time, and so forth. This is particularly true with the student categories, as ALT is only definable in light of a lesson's subject matter goals. Thus no ideal data profile exists that generalizes across the myriad of instructional settings used in physical education.

Finally, as in all category systems, categories are somewhat arbitrary delineations between certain response classes. In other words, the total behavioral sample is subdivided into functionally defined groups of behaviors that are thought to have some relationship to teaching effectiveness according to the informed opinion of experienced teacher educators. It remains to be seen whether all the response classes as defined herein are profitable in understanding essential relations in the teaching-learning environment; some categories should perhaps be further subdivided to reveal significant relationships, whereas others may have to be combined for the same result. The categories included in this revision represent the current thinking of the authors based on the best available evidence, but balanced against the need to minimize the total number of categories because system simplicity enhances data quality.

CATEGORY DESCRIPTIONS

Teacher Behavior

General Observation (1)

Teacher watches student groups or individuals engaged in any category of student behavior. The teacher must not be engaged in any other category of teacher behavior for the observer to code this category. General observation includes passive supervision, and there is no relationship of the observation to an instructional focus.

Encouragement (2)

Teacher makes a verbal statement whose purpose is to enhance the students' perception of their ability to accomplish a subsequent task. The teacher is not telling the students what to do (an instructional prompt), but is clearly trying to build confidence. *Example:* "You can do it." "If you did the last task you can surely do this."

Positive Feedback (3)

Teacher makes a positive verbal statement or gesture following an appropriate student behavior (skill or organization) that is clearly designed to increase or maintain such responses in the future. The statement or gesture must follow soon enough after the behavior for the student to clearly associate it with the behavior.

Corrective Feedback (4)

Teacher makes a negative or critical verbal statement or gesture following an inappropriate student behavior (skill or organization) that is clearly designed to decrease such responses in the future. The statement or gesture must follow soon enough after the behavior for the student to clearly associate it with the behavior.

Management (5)

Teacher is engaged in carrying out a non-subject-matter task (e.g., setting up equipment, taking roll, collecting papers, etc.). Teacher may be directing students verbally in a management task.

Instruction (6)

Teacher is verbally describing to the students how to do a skill, or is using a verbal prompt to direct students in attempting a skill or activity. The activity must be a subject matter task for the observer to record Instruction.

Modeling (7)

Teacher demonstrates to students how to do a subject matter task, or participates with students in a subject matter task or activity.

Physical Guidance (8)

Teacher physically guides students through a subject matter task or activity. *Examples:* A physical guidance prompt or spotting, as long as there is physical contact.

Nontask Verbal (9)

Teacher talks to students about non-subject-matter and nonmanagerial subjects. *Examples:* Commenting on student's clothing or talking about what one student did over the weekend.

Off-Task (10)

Teacher does not pay attention to what are clearly his or her responsibilities regarding the class at hand. *Example:* A teacher makes notes on what to do during football practice while he or she is teaching a physical education class.

Specific Observation (11)

Teacher watches one student engaged in a subject matter task for the purpose of providing feedback related to performance. Teacher position must be proximal to student position so that observation is clearly focused on a specific student who is performing. Specific observation could be scored when teacher is watching pairs or small groups when the instructional focus is clearly on a group task. *Example*: Observation of five players executing a fast break during an instructional session on the fast break.

Student Behavior

Motor Engaged (ME) (13)

The student is engaged in a subject matter motor activity.

Motor Appropriate (MA) (14)

The student is engaged in a subject matter motor activity in such a way as to produce a high degree of success.

Motor Inappropriate (MI) (Manually Calculated)

The student is engaged in a subject-matter-oriented motor activity, but the activity-task is either too difficult for the individual's capabilities or so easy that practicing it could not contribute to lesson goals.

Motor Supporting (MS) (15)

The student is engaged in a subject matter motor activity whose purpose is to assist others in learning or performing the activity. *Examples:* Spotting in gymnastics, feeding balls to a hitter in a tennis lesson, throwing a volleyball to a partner who is practicing set-up passing, or clapping a rhythm for a group of students practicing a movement pattern.

Cognitive (C) (16)

The student is appropriately involved in a cognitive task. *Examples:* Listening to a teacher describe a game, listening to verbal instructions about how to organize, watching a demonstration, participating in a discussion, or watching a film.

On-Task (ON) (17)

The student is appropriately engaged in carrying out an assigned non-subject-matter task (management, transition, or warm-up). *Examples:* Moving into squads, helping to place equipment, counting off, doing warm-up exercises, and moving from the gym to a playing field.

Off Task (18)

The student is either not engaged in an activity he or she should be engaged in or engaged in an activity other than the one he or she should be engaged in—behavior disruptions, misbehavior, and general off-task behavior. *Examples:* Talking when a teacher is explaining a skill, misusing equipment, fooling around, fighting, and disrupting a drill through inappropriate behavior.

Interim (19)

The student is engaged in a noninstructional aspect of an ongoing activity. *Examples:* Retrieving balls, fixing equipment, retrieving arrows, or changing sides of a court in a tennis match.

Waiting (W) (20)

Student has completed a task and is awaiting the next instructions or opportunity to respond. *Examples:* Waiting in line for a turn, having arrived at an assigned space and waiting for the next teacher direction, standing on a sideline waiting to get into a game, or having organized into the appropriate formation and waiting for an activity to begin.

RECORDING PROCEDURES

The electronic regimen was designed to be used with the hand-held Datamyte 801 (part of the 800 series), which is a hard-wired micro-processor, so designated because the programming for frequency and duration recording of behavioral events is engineered into the hardware. Thus the machine is user-friendly, requiring no programming expertise or training. The data are accessed through a Liquid Crystal Display (LCD) immediately following data collection. Complete data profiles must be transcribed by hand onto data summary sheets (Figure 26.1).

There are electronic alternatives to the Datamyte hardware. Several companies market a portable event recorder that is similar in capacity to the Datamyte 1000 series. Some are capable of being programmed to collect frequency and duration data, but programs designed for the West Virginia University system have yet to be developed. A program does exist for an interval recording system (McKenzie & Carlson, 1984), however, and slight modifications of that program may be useful for an interval record-ing regimen for the West Virginia University system. The approximate cost of the TRS 80 Model 100 is $500.

The West Virginia University Teaching Evaluation System is designed to be used in the touch mode of the Datamyte 801. In this mode once an event key is depressed and released the event timer is activated and continues to accumulate time until another event key is depressed. At that moment the timing of the first event ceases and the second begins. There are 20 numeric event keys on the Datamyte 801. The teacher response classes correspond to Keys 1-11 as indicated in the category definitions. The eight student response classes correspond to Keys 13-20.

The Datamyte 801 also allows the user to program 10 predetermined sequences of up to four consecutive response classes. In the West Virginia University system nine teacher response class sequences and one student response class sequence are selected. Sequences 1 through 9 include the following: 6-11-3, 6-11-4, 7-11-3, 7-11-4, 8-11-3, 6-3, 7-3, 8-3, and 11-3. These teacher response class sequences are optional and others of interest may be substituted by the user. Sequence 10 is the student response class sequence 13-14. This sequence is not optional, for reasons that will be-come apparent as the recording procedures are described.

To record responses using this system the observer identifies either the teacher's or the student's response class immediately after the behavior begins and presses and releases the corresponding key. When the sub-ject changes to a new response class, the observer presses and releases the key corresponding to the new response class. This process continues throughout the observation period.

There are only three response classes that are exceptions to this process: motor engaged (ME), motor appropriate (MA), and motor inappropriate

West Virginia University Teaching Evaluation System

Teacher __J.C.__ Observer __Hawkins__ Date __11/19__

Observation # __2__ Activity __Stunts & Tumbling__ Placement in unit __#4__

Station or (whole) (circle)

Number of students __22__

Student teaching:
School __Wiles Hill__
Directing teacher __Klemick__

Goals: Teacher ↑ Feedback to 3/min
       Students ↓ On-task to <30%

Sequence data		
Sequence	Frequency	Rate
1. 6-11-3	3	.26
2. 6-11-4		
3. 7-11-3		
4. 7-11-4		
5. 8-11-3	2	.17
6. 6-3	4	.35
7. 7-3	1	.09
8. 8-3	3	.26
9. 11-3	4	.35

Teacher

Category	Dur.	Freq.	Mean	%	Min.	Max.	Rate
1 General observation	1.06	17	.06	9	.01	.21	1.47
2 Encouragement	.00	0	.00	0	.00	.00	.00
3 Positive feedback	.76	23	.03	7	.01	.08	1.99
4 Corrective feedback	.10	2	.05	1	.03	.07	.17
5 Management	4.84	42	.12	42	.01	.68	3.63
6 Instruction	2.09	28	.07	18	.01	.46	2.42
7 Modeling	.60	3	.20	5	.09	.35	.26
8 Physical guidance	.53	11	.05	5	.01	.20	.95
9 Nontask verbal	.12	3	.04	1	.03	.06	.26
10 Off-task	.00	0	.00	0	.00	.00	.00
11 Specific observation	1.48	33	.04	13	.01	.13	2.85
Teacher totals	11.58						

Student

Category	Dur.	Freq.	Mean	%	Min.	Max.	Rate
13 Motor engaged	3.72	41	.09	34			3.75
Sequence 10	2.79	26	.11	26	.04	.28	2.38
Motor appropriate (13-14)							
Motor inappropriate	.93	15	.06	9			1.37
15 Motor supporting	.00	0	.00	0	.00	.00	.00
16 Cognitive	.00	0	.00	0	.00	.00	.00
17 On-task	3.89	15	.26	36	.03	.62	1.37
18 Off-task	.21	2	.11	2	.05	.16	.18
19 Interim	1.84	35	.05	17	.01	.14	3.20
20 Waiting	1.25	6	.21	11	.06	.30	.55
Student totals	10.91						
CAL: Motor engaged	GP13-14	13	D-F	D-Total			Fr-Total
Motor inappropriate	GP13-14-S10	13-S10	D-F	D-Total			Fr-Total

Figure 26.1 Completed West Virginia University Teaching Evaluation System data summary sheet.

(MI). The type of motor engagement may not be readily identifiable until after the event has been completed. Therefore, when a student begins a motor activity, the observer immediately presses and releases Key 13. If the student's motor activity is deemed appropriate at the completion of the event, the observer presses Key 14 and then immediately presses and releases the key corresponding to the next student response class.

The Datamyte, as previously mentioned, is programmed by the user to recognize the 13-14 sequence as Sequence 10. Therefore, pressing 13 followed by 14 codes a particular motor event as appropriate. MI frequencies and durations are derived by subtracting MA (Sequence 10) from ME (13).

Observations are alternated between the teacher and the students. The target students are randomly selected prior to the start of class, and a randomly ordered sequence is prescribed. Observation begins with the teacher and lasts approximately 2 minutes. The observer then spends approximately 15 seconds finding the first target student. This student is observed for approximately 2 minutes, another 15-second interval allows the observer to refocus on the teacher, and the second 2-minute teacher observation period begins. This process continues until the class ends, or until such time as the observer decides to cease observation. (The Datamytes have a "clear/off" key that allows observations to be interrupted without losing any data. This key is pressed to allow for the 15-second transition periods.)

If it is unrealistic for the observer to conduct the observation during the entire class, then specified class portions may be sampled. Two strategies are suggested. First, portions of the initial, middle, and final thirds of the class time may be recorded to represent all phases of the class. Second, the observer may be able to determine from the teacher that certain portions of the class will differ qualitatively from other portions based on different organizational patterns, and so forth. In this case observers may wish to purposefully sample each of these distinctive portions so the data represent all of them, or, better yet, to conduct separate observations on each portion.

As previously mentioned, observations alternate between the teacher and a randomly selected student. Each subject is observed for approximately 2 minutes with 15 seconds allowed for transitions to a new subject. It is important to note, however, that observations should not begin at an arbitrary temporal location. Rather, the first time a subject changes to a new response class after the observer begins watching becomes the starting point for each observation. This time is noted on a watch with a second hand. This observation period is terminated at the first behavior change following the 2-minute time period, at which time the "clear/off" key is pressed rather than a new response class key. The purpose of this procedure is to prevent pseudodurations in the initial and culminating events, with the accompanying data distortions.

SUMMARIZING AND
INTERPRETING THE DATA

The observer's task upon completing the observation is to transcribe the data compilations from the Datamyte's LCD to a data summary sheet. Most relevant data are available from the LCD; however, some important data require calculations using frequency and duration data available from the Datamyte, easily accomplished with a pocket calculator. The steps in the summarization process are as follows:

1. Generate total observation time for all teacher response classes. Press "Group 1, 2, 3, 4, 5, 6, 7, 8, 9, 10, 11, Duration" and record at "Teacher Totals" under the Duration column.
2. Generate total observation time for all student response classes. Press "Group 13, 14, 15, 16, 17, 18, 19, 20, Duration" and record at "Student Totals" under the Duration column.
3. Generate the total duration for each response class. Press "Duration, 1" and then record at appropriate location in the Duration column; press "2" and record, press "3" and record, and continue in this manner for each of the following response classes: 4, 5, 6, 7, 8, 9, 10, 11, 15, 16, 17, 18, 19, 20. (*Note.* Do not generate durations for 13 or 14 during this step.)
4. Generate the total frequency for each response class. Press "Frequency, 1", and then record at the appropriate location in the Frequency column; press "2" and record, press "3" and record, and continue in this manner for each of the following response classes: 4, 5, 6, 7, 8, 9, 10, 11, 13, 15, 16, 17, 18, 19, 20. (*Note.* Do not generate frequency for 14 during this step.)
5. Generate the means for each response class. Press "Mean, 1" and then record at the appropriate location in the Mean column; press "2" and record, press "3" and record, and continue in this manner for each of the following response classes: 4, 5, 6, 7, 8, 9. 10, 11, 15, 16, 17, 18, 19, 20. (*Note.* Do not generate means for 13 and 14 during this step.)
6. Generate the minimum durations for each response class. Press "Min/Max, 1" and then record at the appropriate location in the Min column; press "2" and record, press "3" and record, and continue in this manner for each of the following response classes: 4, 5, 6, 7, 8, 9, 10, 11, 15, 16, 17, 18, 19, 20. (*Note.* Do not generate minimums for 13 or 14.)
7. Generate the maximum durations for each response class. Press "Shift, Min/Max, 1" and then record at the appropriate location in the Max column, press "2" and record, press "3" and record, and continue in this manner for each of the following response

classes: 4, 5, 6, 7, 8, 9, 10, 11, 15, 16, 17, 18, 19, 20. (*Note*. Do not generate maximums for 13 or 14.)

8. Generate frequencies for the preprogrammed instructional sequences. Press "Seq. 1, Freq." and record in the Sequence Data section in the Frequency column; press "Seq. 2, Freq." and record, Press "Seq. 3, Freq." and record, and continue through Sequence 9. (*Note*. It is necessary to press "Seq." before the event key and follow with "Freq." for each datum. Failure to do so will result in reprogramming another sequence while losing data for the desired sequences.)

9. Generate duration for ME. Press "Group, 13, 14, Dur." and record in the appropriate location in the Duration column.

10. Generate duration, frequency, mean, minimum duration, and maximum duration for MA. Press "Seq. 10, Dur." and record in the proper location in the Duration column; then press "Freq." and record in the proper location in the Frequency column. Press "Mean" and record in the proper location in the Mean column. Press "Min/Max" and "Shift, Min/Max" and record in the proper location in the Minimum and Maximum columns. (*Note*. It is not necessary to press "Seq. 10" again after the first time to generate the frequency, mean, minimum, and maximum data.)

11. Generate duration for MI. Subtract MA duration from ME duration and record in the proper location in the Duration column.

12. Generate frequency for MI. Subtract MA frequency from ME frequency and record in the proper location in the Frequency column.

13. Generate mean durations for ME. Divide the ME duration by the ME frequency and record in the proper location in the Mean column.

14. Generate mean duration for MI. Divide the MI duration by the MI frequency and record in the proper location in the Mean column.

15. Generate the percent for each student response class. Divide the duration for each student response class by the Student Totals-Duration and record in the percent (%) column.

16. Generate the rates for each student response class. Divide the frequencies for each student response class by the Student Totals-Duration and record in the Rate column.

17. Generate the percent for each teacher response class. Divide the duration for each teacher response class by the Teacher Totals-Duration and record in the % column.

18. Generate the rates for each teacher response class. Divide the frequencies for each teacher response class by the Teacher Totals-Duration and record in the Rate column.

19. Generate the rates for each programmed sequence. Divide the fre-

quency of each sequence by the Teacher Totals-Duration and record in the Rate column in the Sequence Data section.

The interpretation process designed for the West Virginia University Teaching Evaluation System involves five essential steps:

1. Student teacher's self-analysis
   - Data prediction: Estimate important student and teacher data from your lesson (see Figure 26.2).
   - Intuition: Intuitively react to the lesson regarding strong points, weak points, what would be changed next time, and so forth.

Name __J.C.__   Placement in unit: 1 ② 3

1. Estimate the percentage of time you spent in each of the following behavior categories during the class you just taught. Your total of all categories must equal __90__ .

   A. Making general observations of the class operation .... _10_
   B. Managing the operations of the class .... _20_
   C. Providing verbal instruction .... _20_
   D. Modeling for a student .... _0_
   E. Physically guiding a student through a motion .... _20_
   F. Making specific observations of students for the purpose of providing instruction .... _20_

   Total .... _90_

2. Estimate the rate per minute at which you engaged in the following behaviors:

   A. Encouraged students .... _.50_
   B. Reinforced students .... _1.00_
   C. Provided corrective feedback .... _.50_

3. Estimate the percentage of time your students engaged in the following behaviors during the class you just taught. The total must equal __100__ .

   A. Engaged in motor appropriate activity .... _60_
   B. Engaged in motor inappropriate activity (e.g., too easy, too difficult) .... _10_
   C. Supported other students' motor appropriate activity .... _10_
   D. Engaged in cognitive behavior .... _5_
   E. Engaged in management behaviors preparing to practice or perform .... _2_
   F. Engaged in behaviors irrelevent to the class .... _0_
   G. Rested between activity .... _6_
   H. Waited their turn to perform .... _7_

   Total .... _100_

Figure 26.2 Completed student teacher self-analysis form.

2. Student teacher's description of positive aspects of lesson

- Data: Highlight the important aspects of the data that reflect positive aspects of the lesson, describing why it is important to continue in that manner.
- Intuition: Describe the portions of the lesson that you thought were intuitively good, without regard to the data. Call attention to aspects of teaching that often do not appear in the data.
- Data plus intuition: Describe the aspects of the lesson that you intuitively thought were positive and relate those feelings to data that tend to corroborate them.

3. Student teacher's needs for improvement

- Data: Describe portions of the data that need to be improved. Consider only the most important aspects of the data even though there may be problems with minor variables as well. Don't give the students in the class too many things to think about for their next lesson.
- Meaning: Describe why it is important to change the negative aspects of the data by describing just what the data reveal about the lesson and what an improvement in the data would reveal about future lessons.

4. Guidance for student teacher for future lessons

- Suggestions of strategies for improvement: Strategies designed to improve the data in subsequent lessons have been developed and appear as the Taxonomy of Feedback Strategies (Tables 26.1 and 26.2). The strategies are organized according to lesson deficiencies as indicated by specific data patterns. For example, the student response class pattern of Low MA-high waiting is associated with four strategies that have been seen to improve the lesson deficiency. The observer selects one of the strategies that will most likely result in improvement in the data pattern and suggests that the student teacher implement it. Generally, one student response class pattern and one teacher response class pattern are the focus for strategy selection. Data observers are not limited to the strategies contained herein, only to their own thoughtful experience as teachers or teacher educators. However, the taxonomy does provide a useful frame of reference for guiding student teachers in solving lesson problems.

5. Student teacher's goals

- Student: Select the most important student behavior category that needs improvement and establish a reasonable data-based goal for the next observation, based on the strategy suggestions made earlier.

- Student teacher: Select the most important teacher behavior category that needs improvement and establish a reasonable data-based goal for the next observation, based on the strategy suggestions made earlier.

Table 26.1 Taxonomy of Feedback Strategies: Student Response Class Strategies

Student response class patterns	Strategy/feedback
Low motor appropriate, high waiting	*Equipment utilization* Use additional equipment or improve utilization of current equipment. *Group size* Reduce group size. *Supplemental activities* Incorporate activities not requiring much additional space or equipment (e.g., fitness). *Competition* Design and implement competitive drills.
Low motor appropriate, high interim	*Equipment control* Develop settings in which equipment is less likely to get away (e.g., use hitting cage in golf lessons). *Motivation* Design and implement an extrinsic motivation system when students display high interim levels as a means to avoid the prescribed activity (e.g., allow students to participate in an activity of their choice after they complete a set number of objectives).
Low motor appropriate, high off-task	*Equipment utilization/group size* Use additional equipment or reduce group size to reduce waiting time, which often provides opportunities for off-task behavior. *Supplemental activities* Use activities that may not need more equipment to reduce waiting, thus decreasing opportunities for off-task behavior.

(Cont.)

Table 26.1   (Continued)

Student response class patterns	Strategy/feedback
	Supervision pattern Revise supervision and instruction pattern. Target students who need help and/or attention prompts and then provide the necessary instruction and feedback. *Motivation* Employ an extrinsic motivation system. *Instructional system* Revise instructional sequence by including more rigorous and challenging tasks.
Low motor appropriate, high on-task	*System communications* Teach the system early and thoroughly so students have a clear understanding of what to do, where, and when before the class moves into activity. *Motivation* Employ an extrinsic motivation system.
Low motor appropriate, high cognitive	*Instructional episodes* Not always undesirable. Certain activities require detailed demonstrations or instructions. If the teacher's instructional episodes were few but occupied much class time, it suggests students had little time to engage in the activity. Teacher needs to establish activities in which the students can begin working and then offer as many short, individual episodes as necessary. *Instructional materials* Use other visually or task-oriented cognitive activities such as stations in which students read materials, watch film loops, make paper-pencil responses, and so forth. Such a station is designed to enhance the student's cognitive understanding of the activity while involving him or her more actively in the subject matter.

Student response class patterns	Strategy/feedback
Low motor appropriate, high motor supporting	*Motor supporting* Motor supporting activities are often essential in the teaching/learning process of motor skills. Generally, they are not detrimental and can be beneficial when the motor supporting student can offer pertinent feedback to the performer. Also, many motor skills need to be practiced in a controlled setting to allow the performer to concentrate on the proper mechanics. *Alternate practice aids* Revise the management plans to avoid the need for motor supporting (e.g., practice soccer kicking techniques using a wall for rebounding and "feeding").
Low motor appropriate, high motor inappropriate	*Instructional system* Revise the objectives or their sequence in light of student abilities. The objectives should challenge all students, yet allow them to succeed. *Instructional intensity* Task may seem inappropriate due to the students' not understanding how to perform it. Teacher should offer supplementary and more intense instruction (e.g., modeling and physical guidance). *Extrinsic motivation* Design and employ an extrinsic motivation system when planning and instruction errors are not the cause of high levels of motor inappropriate activity.

Table 26.2   Taxonomy of Feedback Strategies: Teacher Response Class Strategies

Teacher response class patterns	Strategy/feedback
Low specific observation, high general observation	*Supervision* Data will reveal how active or passive the teacher's supervision was during the class. A high percentage in general observation indicates inactivity. Teacher should use general observation to target individuals who need help and then proceed directly to them to offer help.
Low instructional rate, high management time	*Management system* Teacher should devise an instructional system that allows the students to manage themselves. Teacher is then free to provide an appropriate rate of instruction (e.g., make a tape that cues students when to move to the next phase in the lesson).
Low instructional rate, high instructional time	*Instructional rate* Much time in instruction but with few episodes indicates the teacher spent too much time in whole class instruction, which reduces the time students can be motor-appropriately engaged. Teacher should allow students to become appropriately engaged and then provide instruction in short, individual episodes as needed. *Instructional intensity* Usually verbal prompts are sufficient to elicit the desired student activity, but sometimes more intense instruction is required. A student's inability to perform may be due to not understanding the task. Teacher can give further instruction by modeling or physical guidance. If a constant model is needed (dance), teachers should employ another expert to model so they can provide the necessary instruction.
Low feedback rate, high instructional time	*Feedback* After every instruction and observation sequence, teacher should offer feedback to the student(s) about performance. Feedback is essential because a student needs to know if the performance was correct or where improvements are needed.

REFERENCES

McKenzie, T., & Carlson, R. (1984). Computer technology of exercise and sport pedagogy: Recording, storing, and analyzing interval data. *Journal of Teaching in Physical Education*, 3(3), 17-27.

Siedentop, D., Tousignant, M., & Parker, M. (1982). *Academic learning time-physical education*. Unpublished manual, School of Health, Physical Education and Recreation, The Ohio State University, Columbus.

RELATED REFERENCES

Cool, R., Hawkins, A., & Wiegand, R. (1987, April). *Evaluation master teacher performance: A five year longitudinal study*. Paper presented at national convention of the American Alliance for Health, Physical Education, Recreation and Dance, Las Vegas.

Landin, D., Hawkins, A., & Wiegand, R. (1986). Validating the collective wisdom of teacher educators. *Journal of Teaching in Physical Education*, 5(4), 252-271.

Chapter 27

Instrument for the Analysis of the Pedagogical Functions of Physical Education Teachers (PEDFUNC)

Bruce L. Morgenegg

The Instrument for the Analysis of Pedagogical Functions of Physical Education Teachers (PEDFUNC) is designed to investigate how physical education teachers use language to move events along toward some learning or performance end. Four categories describe the use of language and each has a pedagogical function: structuring, soliciting, responding, and reacting. Through structuring, participants set the context for subsequent behavior; it is a preview of future events. Soliciting calls for an expected response from the receiver of the solicitation. Responding is the reciprocation of soliciting. Reacting serves to rate, evaluate, or modify the aforementioned pedagogical functions.

This taxonomy for analyzing language has stimulated numerous investigations concerning the frequency and ordering of teacher behaviors in a number of subjects and a variety of settings. Because these pedagogical functions have been extensively tested, it is assumed their validity has been established. The Bellack system was originally used in the classroom (Bellack, Kliebrad, Hyman, & Smith, 1966). The present instrument was modified for use in physical education, and the necessary modifications were monitored by Dr. Bellack. The reliability of the entire instrument has also been tested. Both intraobserver and interobserver reliability coefficients have averaged above 80%.

To date the instrument has been used only for research purposes. In its present form the various categories and the attending coding conventions can only be used with videotape. A digital clock imprint on the videotape is also necessary. These limitations preclude using it in a live setting. The functions of language are the primary analytic concern; the content of language is given only superficial attention.

CATEGORY DESCRIPTIONS

Function Dimension (FNC)

The function dimension is represented by four categories: structuring, soliciting, responding, and reacting. These pedagogical moves constitute the basic unit of discourse and describe the ways verbal and nonverbal communication is used by classroom participants. Structuring and soliciting are initiatory because they serve to get events under way. Responding and reacting are reflexive because their occurrence is dependent upon other moves.

Structuring

Moves that serve to identify and describe future activities that will occupy the efforts of the participants:

> Structuring moves serve the pedagogical function of setting the context for subsequent behavior in the gymnasium by (a) launching halting-excluding interaction in terms of the dimensions of time, agent, activity, topic and cognitive process, regulations, reasons, and instructional aids. (Bellack et al., 1966, p. 16)

Examples: "The next thing we do, we are going to do without making any noise." "All right, on the balance beam, as on any piece of equipment, you need a spotter, and it is the spotter's responsibility to know what the person is going to do and when he or she is to do it."

Soliciting

Moves that "elicit (a) an active verbal response on the part of the persons addressed to attend to something; or (b) a physical response" (Bellack et al., 1966, p. 19). With the solicitation, the agent expects and is trying to initiate a subsequent response by the person addressed. Solicitations may take all grammatical forms: declarative, interrogative, or imperative; however, the interrogative is the most common. Direct solicitations are commands or imperatives, whereas questions constitute indirect solicitations. *Examples:* "How many of you are thinking about moving to the middle of the biggest open space? Raise your hand." "Come over here and sit down."

Responding

Moves that fulfill the expectation of the soliciting moves. Therefore, responding bears a reciprocal relationship to soliciting (i.e., it occurs only in relation to it). In the classroom, speech is the most common response; in physical education, movement is a more common response form. *Example:* "Come over here and sit down." (Pupils sit down in the place designated by the teacher.)

Although pupils are the principal respondents, from time to time the teacher will respond to a pupil solicitation. *Example:* Pupil asks, "What's the score?" (soliciting). Teacher says, "Five to four" (responding).

Reacting

Moves that serve to modify (by clarifying, synthesizing, expanding) or rate (positively or negatively) what was said or done in preceding moves. A preceding structuring, soliciting, or responding move provides the opportunity for a reaction, but does not necessarily elicit one. Reacting moves differ from responding moves; whereas a responding move is always directly elicited by a solicitation, preceding moves serve only as the occasion for the reactions. *Examples:* "That was very good." "No, wrong way, Dottie."

Postscript

Every teacher solicitation is coded according to the verbal or nonverbal nature of the expected response. Every teacher reaction is coded according to the verbal or nonverbal nature of the move that occasioned it.

Meaning Dimension (MNG)

The meaning dimension focuses on the content of a given communication. Classroom participants discuss two topics: One concerns the subject matter of the class and the other concerns assignments, materials, and class procedures. These two topics are classified as substantive and nonsubstantive.

Substantive

Communications that directly contribute to, or call for a demonstration of, one's knowledge of the subject matter or are directly related to the subject matter. For purposes of this study, the subject matter is the sports, games, exercises, and other related activities common to physical education. Information is subject matter oriented whenever it relates to the movement of the body or its parts, regulatory conditions (such as rules of the activity), people or objects in space, or the goal of the activity. *Examples:* "When the whistle blows, we are going to balance ourselves, using five parts of our body." "Jump to a front support and swing your leg around."

Nonsubstantive

Nonsubstantive utterances carry information about social, managerial, or procedural tasks. This information may support the subject matter, but does not directly contribute to one's knowledge or performance of it. *Examples:* ''Alright, get your shoes on and line up at the door.'' ''That's my grade book and you don't belong in there.''

Mode Dimension (MDE)

The mode dimension is represented by verbal and nonverbal categories that identify the manner of communication used in carrying out a pedagogical move.

Verbal

Behavior that is characterized by the use of language to communicate the function and meaning of a given move. Language may be written, but in physical education it is characterized mostly by the use of speech.

Nonverbal

Behavior that is characterized by the use of motions to communicate the function and meaning of a given move. Of particular concern are those motions that facilitate the teaching or learning process and have pedagogical significance. *Example:* The teacher demonstrates a handstand or blows a whistle to start the activity. (Personal motions of the teacher are not considered as part of nonverbal behavior.)

Direction Dimension (DIR)

The categories of the direction dimension are used to identify the three sizes of pupil groups the teacher addresses during a given pedagogical move.

Individual

Communications with one pupil only.

Group

Communications directed toward more than one pupil, but not the whole class.

Whole Class

Communications directed toward the whole class.

RECORDING PROCEDURES

Certain conventions are necessary to facilitate application of the categories to the videotapes. These conventions are as follows:

General Coding Instructions

The observer makes inferences from contextual cues about the intent of the teacher and codes behaviors accordingly (Bellack et al., 1966, p. 255). Grammatical form may give a clue, but is not decisive in coding. For example, a solicitation may be declarative, interrogative, or imperative. A response may be in the form of a question—frequently indicating the tentativeness on the part of the speaker. *Example:* "What should you be doing when your opponent gets ready to shoot the basket?" (Solicitation). "Put your hands up?" (Response).

An utterance may contain different pedagogical moves. A sentence cannot contain more than one pedagogical move. If two pedagogical moves appear in one sentence, the function is coded by the dominant message—structuring, soliciting, responding, or reacting.

The videotape recorder is stopped whenever necessary to make an entry. Replaying the tape may be necessary to verify a particular entry on the recording sheet. Because parts of a tape are occasionally inaudible, some behaviors cannot be entirely encoded. For this reason, a "Not Codable" designation is sometimes used. This code is also used if a given behavior cannot be classified by an existing category.

The general manner of coding is by a number that represents the appropriate category for that dimension. The coding numbers by dimension and category are shown in Figure 27.1.

Teacher behaviors are encoded by all of the above categories, whereas student behaviors are identified by source (SRC), function (FNC), target (TRG), moves in an interaction unit (MVS), and teaching cycles (CYE) only.

Pedagogical Moves

The basic coding unit is the *pedagogical move*. Changes in the source of the move (teacher or pupil), its function (structuring, soliciting, responding,

Pedagogical Functions of Physical Education Teachers (PEDFUNC)

Source (SRC)
1-Teacher
2-Student
0-Not codable

Function (FNC)
1-Structuring
2-Soliciting (direct)
3-Soliciting (indirect)
4-Responding
5-Reacting (neutral)
6-Reacting (positive)
7-Reacting (negative)
0-Not codable

Postscript (PST)
1-Verbal
2-Nonverbal
3-Verbal/nonverbal
0-Not codable

Meaning (MNG)
1-Substantive
2-Nonsubstantive
3-Substantive/nonsubstantive
0-Not codable

Mode (MDE)
1-Verbal
2-Nonverbal
3-Verbal/nonverbal
0-Not codable

Direction (DIR)
1-Individual
2-Group (more than one pupil but less than the whole class)
3-Whole class
0-Not codable

Target of Interaction Unit (TRG)
1-Individual
2-Group
3-Whole class
0-Not codable

Number of Moves During Interaction Unit (MVS)
1-8
9 or more

Quarter of Class Period (QRT)
1-First
2-Second
3-Third
4-Fourth

Tape Number (ID)
1-85

Figure 27.1   Coding numbers by category and dimensions for Pedagogical Functions of Physical Education Teachers (PEDFUNC).

or reacting), or its direction signal the beginning of a new move. Coding begins with the first manifestly educable statement relevant to conducting the class and its activities for the day.

Pupil interaction with the teacher is the only type of pupil behavior recorded; interaction with other pupils is not recorded. Interaction is the verbal or nonverbal communication of substantive or nonsubstantive meaning that has pedagogical significance to one or both of the target participants (i.e., teacher or pupil).

The coder records the beginning and ending times of the teacher's pedagogical moves. The time is entered in minutes and seconds, which are taken from the imprinted clock on the videotape. Onset and offset times must reflect at least a 1-second duration. An entry of 4:01-4:02 would be correct, whereas an entry of 4:01-4:01 would be incorrect. A pause in the teacher discourse or codable activity of more than 5 seconds signals the end of the previous move. The next codable activity begins with the next move of the teacher or pupil. The 5-second interval is not part of the move time. A move is the time between its onset and offset, less pauses lasting from 2 to 5 seconds. For example, a solicitation may last from 1:05 to 1:12; however, this may include a 4-second pause. Thus the time would be entered as 1:05-1:08 and counted as a 3-second, not a 7-second, solicitation.

Teacher participation (playing a game as one of the pupils) or observation is not considered pedagogically interactive. Therefore, instances in which a teacher is participating with the pupils are not coded even though there might be an occasional verbal interchange between teacher and pupils.

It may be difficult at times to distinguish between reacting and structuring because, in reacting to a pupil response, the teacher may refer to subsequent pupil behaviors (structuring) that should take place. If the discourse refers to future events, the function is coded as structuring. If the discourse refers to a past response, it is coded as reacting.

In coding structuring moves, keep in mind that they are not used to elicit a direct response. They only set the context for subsequent behaviors or activities. These moves differ from soliciting in that direction is implicit rather than explicit. Structuring moves, in other words, imply what action is to be taken, whereas soliciting moves explicitly outline what action is to be taken.

Discourse referring to elapsed or remaining time (as in basketball or hockey) is coded as structuring unless, of course, this information is called for by soliciting, in which case giving the elapsed or remaining time would be a response.

The solicitation may call for an immediate or future response. No specific deadline need be mentioned. Most solicitations call for an immediate response. The key guideline for identifying a solicitation is whether the move calls for an expected response or whether the solicitation is being used to initiate an immediate response. A whistle used to stop an activity is a solicitation. If a whistle is blown after a goal, it is coded as a reaction. The whistle didn't stop the activity; the act of making a goal did.

If there is a question about how to classify a teacher move (particularly in the case of soliciting or reacting), the coder must ask the question, Is the teacher trying to initiate a new response? If the coder decides that the teacher is trying to initiate a new response, the teacher's move is coded as soliciting. If the teacher is commenting on a pupil's prior response and not, in the judgment of the coder, trying to initiate a new response, the teacher's move is coded as reacting. The issue in question is whether the dominant function of language is to initiate a response or comment on a prior move.

Frequently, an exercise period precedes the events for the day. If the teacher solicits a response by cuing (giving an onset or offset signal), soliciting is entered. If the teacher counts cadence (establishes a rhythm), the entire cadence process is not considered a solicitation. For example, if a teacher counts "1, 2, 3, 1, 2, 3," only the solicitation that begins and ends the exercise is entered. If the teacher says "Down, up, down, up," individual solicitations are entered, because these represent individual cues. The difference between cuing and cadence is that the former is considered soliciting, whereas the latter is for maintenance of the rhythm of the exercise.

If a pupil solicitation gives rise to a teacher response and the pupil move is not verifiable, the pupil move is coded by inference from other contextual cues. If a teacher says, "yes," it is inferred that there was a prior pupil solicitation. Therefore, a pupil solicitation followed by a teacher response is entered on the coding sheet in that order.

Each solicitation is coded by the type of response the teacher expects, verbal or nonverbal. The code is entered in the appropriate Postscript column. If a response results from a prior move, the prior move is coded as soliciting. After a teacher solicitation, a 5-second period is allowed during which the observer monitors pupil response. If, after 5 seconds, the pupils with which the teacher communicated have an estimated majority response (51% of the group), a pupil response is entered on the coding sheet. If a pupil response cannot be verified by seeing its execution or by context, a response is not entered. If a response begins during a solicitation, it is entered after the teacher completes the solicitation. The duration is measured from when the teacher begins; it does not end with the pupil response.

Most reacting moves are not difficult to distinguish, except perhaps when reacting gives way to structuring, or in the case of distinguishing a reaction from a solicitation. Each reaction is coded by the type of move that occasioned the reaction, whether it is verbal or nonverbal. The number code is entered under the postscript heading. A reaction does not necessarily rate or evaluate. Reactions can also serve to clarify, synthesize, expand what has been said or done previously, or comment on a preceding move, but they do not call for a response. Reacting moves also serve to express feelings, opinions, and personal comments about other moves, but, again, they do not call for a direct response by the pupil or teacher. Summaries are coded as reactions.

Teachers react to physical moves made by pupils that were not the immediate result of a teacher solicitation. For example, a teacher might comment positively on a movement or action by a pupil that has only a distant connection with solicitation. Preceding moves that were not seen are not entered even though they might be inferred.

Meaning Dimension

Each pedagogical move is coded according to its meaning (i.e., whether it is substantive or nonsubstantive). Pedagogical moves are substantive when they contain information that relates to the subject matter: past, present, or future movement of the body or its parts; information about regulating environmental conditions; and temporal or spatial elements that are relevant to the accomplishment of an activity goal. The pedagogical move may also contain information about cognitive processes related to goal accomplishment.

Discourse that defines a particular location in the gym would be coded as nonsubstantive, whereas information about body or team position would be coded as substantive. Thus, "Go to that end of the gym" is nonsubstantive discourse, and "You're in their zone!" is substantive discourse. Nonsubstantive pedagogical moves contain information about such verbal and nonverbal events as making assignments, moving equipment, calling roll, planning activities, commenting on pupil physiognomy or standards of behavior, or maintaining the social system of the gymnasium. An utterance may carry both substantive and nonsubstantive information. If so, "3" is coded under meaning.

Mode Dimension

Each pedagogical move is coded according to the medium of communication used. In coding a pedagogical move as having a verbal mode, the observer is indicating that the teacher used speech exclusively to structure, solicit, respond, or react. A nonverbal code indicates the teacher used a pedagogically relevant nonverbal cue to carry out a particular pedagogical move. A "3" is coded if the verbal and nonverbal modes were used simultaneously during any part of the pedagogical move.

Direction Dimension

If a teacher is communicating with an individual and then directs the discourse to a different individual, two separate incidents are coded even though in both incidents the teacher was communicating with an individual. The same conventions are to be used for communications with groups. In addition, class size may vary. If, for example, the teacher sends part of the class outside the gym, the group with which he or she is working constitutes the class. The teacher may divide the class into groups and work on a nonrotating basis with one of the groups. In this case, the group constitutes the new class.

Target of Interaction Unit

Every time the direction of the discourse changes to a new individual or group, a notation is made under the target dimension. This convention is also in effect when the class is addressed anew, the discourse having previously been directed toward a group or individual.

Interaction Unit

To study the extent (in numbers of moves) and composition of the teacher-pupil interchange, an interaction unit (Neujahr, 1970) was employed. An interaction unit is a series of interchanges between the teacher and discrete groupings of pupils. Every time the target of a continuous series of interactions changes, a new interaction unit begins. The interaction unit is identified by the number of pedagogical moves used between teacher and pupil. If, for example, a teacher interacts with a series of different individuals, the observer codes one interactive unit for each interaction with a different pupil or group of pupils.

Teaching Cycles

Cycles are predetermined patterns of pedagogical moves. A cycle begins with an initiatory move (structuring or soliciting) and continues until the next structuring move or unstructured solicitation. Cycle combinations and their assigned numbers are as shown in Figure 27.2. When a cycle is completed, the appropriate cycle number is entered on the coding sheet according to its initiator (teacher or pupil). To speed coding, do not enter cycles until the tape is completely coded.

Using the Recording Sheet

Each line of the recording (Figure 27.3) represents behavior of either the teacher or a pupil. Figure 27.4 shows how the coding sheet might look after coding four pedagogical moves. Move 1 lasted 31 seconds; it was a structuring move (FNC-1) executed by the teacher (SRC-1). The meaning of the move was substantive (MNG-1), communicated by the verbal mode (MDE-1), and directed toward the class (DIR-3). With Move 1, the

```
 1. STR
 2. STR  SOL
 3. STR  REA
 4. STR  REA  REA...
 5. STR  REA  RES
 6. STR  SOL  RES   RES...
 7. STR  SOL  REA
 8. STR  SOL  REA   REA...
 9. STR  SOL  RES   REA
10. STR  SOL  RES   REA   REA...
11. STR  SOL  RES   REA   RES...
12. STR  SOL  RES   REA   RES...  REA
13. SOL
14. SOL  RES
15. SOL  RES  RES...
16. SOL  REA
17. SOL  REA  REA...
18. SOL  RES  REA
19. SOL  RES  REA   REA...
20. SOL  RES  REA   RES...
21. SOL  RES  REA   RES...  REA...
```

Legend

STR-Structuring   RES-Responding
SOL-Soliciting   REA-Reacting
...-One or more additional moves of the kind
designated. For example, RES... means
one or more additional responses to the
same solicitation.

Figure 27.2 Teaching cycle combinations and numbers. *Note*. Reprinted by permission of the publisher from Bellack, Arno et al., *The Language of the Classroom*. (New York: Teachers College Press, © 1966 by Teachers College, Columbia University. All rights reserved.), page 195.

teacher initiates an interactive unit targeted toward the class (TRG-3). The interaction unit contained one move (MBS-1), which is classified as Cycle Number 1–structuring (CYC-1). Move 2 was initiated by a pupil (SRC-1) and was an indirect solicitation (FNC-3). It initiated an interaction unit consisting of two moves (MVS-2). The second move of the interaction unit is Move 3 by the teacher. Move 3 was a 1-second teacher (SRC-1) response (FNC-4) that contained substantive information (MNG-1), was communicated by speech (MDE-1), and was directed toward one pupil (DIR-1). Move 3 brings to a close a pupil-initiated cycle consisting of a solicitation by the pupil and a response by the teacher (CYE-14). The cycle number would be recorded on the line for Move 2. The last three numbers on the fourth move are identification numbers. The first of these is the quarter of the class period and the last two digits are the tape number.

After a tape has been completely coded, tally the interaction units by counting the number of moves between TRG entries. Enter number of units on the same line as the TRG number of that interaction unit. After tallying interaction units, assign cycle numbers to the appropriate move combinations within each unit.

**Instrument for the Analysis of Pedagogical Functions of
Physical Education Teachers (PEDFUNC)**

TMB	TME	SRC	FNC	PST	MNG	MDE	DIR	TRG	MVS	CYE	CYE	QRT	ID	ID

TMB-beginning time   MNG-meaning   CYE-cycle number
TME- ending time   MDE-mode   QRT-quarter
SRC-source   DIR-direction   ID-tape number
FNC-function   TRG-target
PST-postscript   MVS-moves in interaction unit

Figure 27.3   Instrument for the Analysis of Pedagogical Functions of Physical Education Teachers (PEDFUNC) recording sheet.

SUMMARIZING AND INTERPRETING THE DATA

Bellack et al. (1966) suggested that language used between teachers and pupils serves four functions: to structure, to solicit, to respond, and to

Move number	TMB	TME	SRC	FNC	PST	MNG	MDE	DIR	TRG	MVS	CYE	QRT	ID
1	06:07	06:38	1	1	0	1	1	3	3	1	1		
2	00:00	00:00	2	3	0	0	0	0	1	2	14		
3	06:41	06:42	1	4	0	1	1	1	0	0	0		
4	06:43	07:08	1	1	0	1	1	3	3	1	1	2	58

TMB-beginning time	MNG-meaning	CYE-cycle number
TME- ending time	MDE-mode	QRT-quarter
SRC-source	DIR-direction	ID-tape number
FNC-function	TRG-target	
PST-postscript	MVS-moves in interaction unit	

Figure 27.4 Instrument for the Analysis of Pedagogical Functions of Physical Education Teachers (PEDFUNC) recording procedures.

react. Furthermore, they point out that teachers and pupils use language according to a set of implied rules that are consistent with their respective roles as players in a communication game (Bellack et al., 1966; Wittgenstein, 1958). This is not a game in the usual sense of the word—a power struggle in which secret strategies are carried out by the players to take advantage of one another's weaknesses and emerge victorious. This is a game only in the sense that there are agreed-upon, implicit rules that the participants (teachers and pupils) follow. The only ostensible win is some degree of pupil learning.

The regularity of behavior patterns for both teacher and pupil seems to warrant the conclusion that this communication game is in effect in the gymnasium and that it can be characterized by a general set of rules. Although these generalized rules paint a certain descriptive portrait of teacher-pupil interactions in the gymnasium, they do not deny that each class is different in the way the communication game is played. Indeed, there is great diversity in the distribution of each pedagogical move, its content, direction, and so on. However, if these results are at all indicative of the population as a whole, then these rules seem to govern the ebb and flow of communications while defining the respective roles of teacher and pupils, at least in a descriptive sense. The major rules describing the teacher's role are as follows:

- The teacher plays a very active role by carrying out over half of the pedagogical moves for teachers and pupils combined, with soliciting and reacting being the most frequently used. (This is not to imply that the pupils are not active; they are very busy responding to the teacher's solicitations and interacting with other pupils.)
- The duration of the teacher's pedagogical moves is relatively short. Soliciting, responding, and reacting moves last between 2 and 3 seconds, whereas structuring moves average 12 seconds in length.

- In using soliciting moves, teachers tend to expect a nonverbal response more than they expect a verbal response, and they use the direct form five times more frequently than the indirect form.
- Elementary teachers react twice as often as secondary teachers, and elementary teachers react to nonverbal activities of the pupil more than they react to verbal activities.
- Concerning the sequential nature of teaching, nearly all cycles and interaction units are initiated by the teacher. Both cycles and interaction units are short; they usually last for two moves or less.
- Although substantive meaning dominates the content of the moves, the verbal mode is used more frequently than the nonverbal mode. Single pupils are the primary focus of attention during a solicitation, whereas a structuring move is mostly directed to the whole class.

Because the camera focuses on the teacher, not on the student, a limited amount of pupil data is available. Nevertheless, the roles for pupils seem to be governed by the following rules:

- The pupils' most active pedagogical role is responding to teacher solicitations.
- Elementary pupils engage in structuring slightly more than secondary pupils do.
- Pupil solicitation is usually indirect.
- Pupil-initiated cycles and interaction units are few in number and are usually composed of not more than two moves.
- When pupils react, it is in a neutral, rather than a positive or negative, form.
- Pupil responses are, for the most part, nonverbal.

REFERENCES

Bellack, A.A., Kliebrad, H.A., Hyman, D.T., & Smith, F.L., Jr. (1966). *Language of the classroom*. New York: Teachers College Press.

Neujahr, J. (1970). *An analysis of the teacher-pupil interaction when instruction is individualized*. Unpublished doctoral dissertation, Teachers College, Columbia University, New York.

Wittgenstein, L. (1958). *Philosophical investigations*. Oxford: Basil Blackwell.

Chapter 28

Physical Education Teachers' Professional Functions

William G. Anderson

The Physical Education Teachers' Professional Functions system was conceived as part of the Videotape Data Bank Project carried out over a period of several years at Columbia University. The system is designed to describe the behavior of physical education teachers during normal class periods. It is a multidimensional system, which means that each segment of teacher behavior is coded several times, once per dimension. Six dimensions are included: function, function subscript, mode, direction, substance, and duration. Each of these dimensions is divided into several categories; the category that best describes what the teacher is doing is selected as the code for that segment of teacher behavior. For example, if a teacher tells a student "Bend your wrist when you shoot the foul shot," it is coded as follows: preparatory instructing (function), does (function subscript), talks (mode), one student (direction), basketball skill (substance), and 3 seconds (duration).

To better understand subsequent sections of this report, the reader is advised to review the summary list of dimensions and categories that comprise the system (Table 28.1). The substance dimension is not included in this report because of its length and its idiosyncratic relationship to the subject matter being taught. Interactive behavior is expanded from its usual content to include behavior that involves conveying nonverbal messages, observing movement behavior, and participating in movement activities.

The ultimate purpose of this system is to describe behavior of physical education teachers and communicate it to others in the profession. Categories classify teacher behavior using terminology and concepts that are familiar to and have common meanings among professionals. The system was designed as a research instrument to be used to describe videotaped teacher behavior. It provides an account of what the teacher does from the moment he or she enters the gymnasium until the moment he or she leaves.

This system uses the function dimension as the key descriptive dimension. The extensive number of function categories is designed to enhance

Table 28.1   Summary List of Dimensions and Categories for Physical Education Teachers' Professional Functions

---

Function

Interactive

Preparing for motor activities
 1. Organizing
 2. Preparatory instructing
 3. Providing equipment or readying environment

Guiding the performance of motor activities
 4. Concurrent instructing
 5. Officiating
 6. Spotting
 7. Leading exercises
 8. Intervening instruction
 9. Observing the performance of motor activities
10. Participating in motor activities
11. Other interacting related to motor activities

Other interactive behaviors
12. Administering
13. Establishing and enforcing codes of behavior
14. Other interacting

Noninteractive intervals

15. Dealing with equipment
16. Other noninteractive intervals

Indiscernible intervals

17. Insufficient audio/video
18. Absent from gymnasium

Subscripts

1. Does
2. Shares
3. Delegates

Direction

1. One student
2. Group/whole class of students
3. Combination of one student and whole class
4. Other persons
5. Other combinations of one student, whole class, and other persons

Mode

1. Talks
2. Listens
3. Observes (silently)
4. Demonstrates
5. Uses student demonstrator
6. Uses aids
7. Uses signaling devices
8. Writes or provides written material
9. Manually assists
10. Participates
11. Performs physical task

---

the specificity of description within this dimension. Furthermore, changes in function categories define the basic unit of behavior used for analysis. (A unit of behavior begins when a teacher starts to carry out a particular function and ends when he or she starts to carry out another function.) Thus other dimensions are coded in relation to the function dimension (the coder first determines the function of the teacher's behavior and then determines the subscript, mode, direction, substance, and duration of the behavior exhibited during the function). Finally, the categories enable the coder to classify behavior according to the professional function accomplished or attempted and to avoid, wherever possible, the use of covert teacher intentions or effects on students as a basis for classification.

Categories in the other dimensions add substantially to the descriptive power of the system by accounting for the extent to which the teacher carries out the function or shares it (function subscript), the manner of communication used (mode), the persons toward whom the teacher's behavior is directed (direction), and the subject matter of the interaction (substance). The categories across all dimensions provide a relatively comprehensive picture of teacher behavior, although they represent only one of many possible ways of conceptualizing what teachers do.

The reliability of the system was determined on two occasions. Two judges independently coded 5-minute segments from five randomly selected videotapes. A second-by-second analysis of interobserver agreement was calculated. Acceptable levels of agreement were achieved in all major dimensions: function, 86.7%; mode, 87.6%; direction, 91.6%; and substance, 99.6%. The level of agreement for the function subscripts was considerably lower: 72.3%. Subsequently, a master code for these five segments was developed through negotiation between the two judges. A third judge coded the same segments and achieved the following levels of agreement with the master code: function, 92%; mode, 95%; direction, 81%; substance, 99%; and subscripts, 79%.

In a fundamental sense, the description produced is limited to the dimensions, categories, definitions, and ground rules that comprise the system. However, the following limitations are also noted.

First, all interactive intervals and silent observation periods of less than 5 seconds are not accounted for. Instead, they are coded as part of the preceding interactive unit. This produces a distortion in the descriptive record reducing the time allotted to noninteractive intervals and silent observation periods and increasing the time allotted to other categories.

Second, the system describes interactive behavior and ignores concurrent noninteractive behavior. For example, when the teacher instructs a student and at the same time walks across the gym, the instruction is coded but the walking is not. As a consequence, the descriptive record does not account for much of what the teacher does in relation to the environment or to his or her own person.

Third, although common professional terminology was used to name categories, those terms had to be precisely defined to be useful in the system. This could lead to misreading the descriptive record if the reader relies upon his or her own conception of the meaning of the terminology.

And finally, the accuracy with which behavior is coded is limited by the evidence available to the observer. Tapes don't always provide a clear record of teacher actions and student talk. On such occasions this may lead to erroneous coding.

To understand the category descriptions that follow, it is important to know the following key definitions. *Motor activities* are goal-directed movement activities normally considered part of the subject matter of physical education such as games of low organization, games of high organization, sports, exercises, exploratory movements, and fundamental movements. *To be performed* refers to activities engaged in during the videotaped class periods or a subsequent class period. *Determining* is interacting for the purpose of making a decision (in relation to the listed function). *Providing information* involves making information (e.g., facts, concepts, ideas, relationships) available to students by any one or a combination of such processes as fact stating, explaining, interpreting, justifying, defining, soliciting, responding, and reacting. *Equipment* refers to all physical objects normally considered to be physical education equipment or used in the class as equipment. *Interactive behaviors* are characterized by conveying or receiving messages to/from others by talking/listening, writing, demonstrating, signaling, or assisting; participating with others in performing a task; or observing the behavior of others (using one or more of the communication modes in the mode dimension). *Noninteractive be-*

haviors are characterized by not communicating, observing, or participating with others.

CATEGORY DESCRIPTIONS

The dimension definitions and categories of the Professional Functions system are provided. Ground rules for coding behaviors are also described.

Interactive Function Dimension

This dimension identifies the purpose of the teacher's interactive behavior (behavior that uses one of the interactive functions in the mode dimension).

Organizing

Providing information about the students' future location, position, grouping, role (a description that carries with it a set of distinguishing duties such as goalie, team captain, etc.), and ordering of performance (indicates when students are to perform in relation to other students, i.e., "John goes first") in relation to the motor activities to be performed. *Examples:* "O.K., Paul, these are your partners for today." "Line up in squads" (for exercises).

Organizing includes gathering people together to provide instructions about motor activities, providing feedback to students about organizing, and providing or getting information related to organizing. When the teacher tells the students what to do and at the same time assigns each student to a role or location, code as preparatory instructing.

Preparatory Instructing

Providing information that identifies the activity to be performed, or the behaviors (motor and/or cognitive) to be exhibited in performing the activity, and the rules governing the activity or rationales for participating in the activity. *Examples:* "Today we are going to do exercises with a jump rope." "Try it (bouncing ball) with your elbow." "Keep your head up when you dribble."

Preparatory instructing applies in those cases where knowledge of information directly affects the way the activity was performed. This includes verbal interchanges between student and teacher that are designed to prepare students for activity. When the teacher gives feedback to the student about student-provided preparatory information, it is coded as preparatory instructing. This category also includes information provided by a teacher or student demonstrator.

Providing Equipment or Readying the Environment

Interacting for the purpose of providing equipment or readying the environment for the motor activities. This applies only when the teacher interacts with others in providing equipment or readying the environment. *Examples:* "OK, everyone come over here and get a racket" (teacher watches students get rackets). Teacher silently hands jump ropes to students.

Concurrent Instructions

Providing information that identifies behaviors to be exhibited, rules to be followed, or the nature or quality of outcomes or behaviors being exhibited in performing the motor activity (but not information normally provided by an official). *Examples:* Student is crouching, ready to shoot the basketball; teacher says, "Shoot it easy." Students perform stages of a skill as the teacher gives cues, "Bring it back, start forward, follow through."

Concurrent instructions include all concurrent teacher comments that provide information intended to influence student performances, including feedback given to the student during or immediately after his or her performance. These may be cuing exercises (when words are a legitimate cue for what to do), but do not include merely counting cadence for exercises or using other word cues to keep students in time.

Officiating

Performing the recognized and established duties of an official in a game or sport. This includes performing the duties of an official (e.g., regulating starting and stopping of the activities, enforcing rules, keeping time, and keeping score) in a game or sport or activity for which there are no established duties of officials. *Examples:* Teacher blows whistle for rule violation. "Hacking foul, two shots." "The score of the game was 7 to 5."

This category includes officiating moves in all recognized professional games. Officiating does not include giving directions about what to do or setting down the rules; these are coded as instructing.

Spotting

Interacting with students to protect them against injury by taking a position and, when necessary, moving to protect a performer. *Examples:*

Student begins approach to vault; teacher is in spotting position. "Johnny, go and spot for Janey" (teacher delegates).

Spotting has priority over silent observation of motor activities. When a teacher is spotting and concurrently providing verbal information, code according to purpose of verbal information. Finally, spotting begins when teacher is in position to spot and student begins performance.

Leading Exercises

Interacting with students as they exercise by giving go and stop signals, counting cadence, or performing the exercise (so it can be followed simultaneously), for the purpose of regulating the students' performance. Instances when the teacher uses cues primarily to affect cadence and not to inform students of what comes next are coded as leading exercises. *Examples:* "Ready, begin, 1, . . . 2, 3, and stop." "All right, begin" (teacher does exercise and students follow).

Intervening Instruction

Providing information contingent on student performance that identifies behaviors to be exhibited; rules to be followed; concepts to be used; or the nature, quality, or outcomes of behaviors exhibited in performing the motor activity (but not information normally provided by an official). *Examples:* Teacher stops the basketball game and says, "You should have passed the ball to Johnny; he was free." At the end of the game the teacher reviews the students' performance.

Intervening instruction includes only those comments contingent upon student performance or events related to the performance that are intended to influence future performance (including feedback). Extended comments that occur immediately after student performance are considered intervening instruction, as are all remarks that essentially review past activities, even though they could be interpreted as preparation for upcoming activities. Finally, intervening instruction entails instances of delayed feedback, in which some other actions intervene between performance of the activity and feedback about the activity.

Observing the Performance of Motor Activities

Silently attending to, not actively guiding, students who are performing motor activities. Only silent periods of 5 seconds or more are recorded, and only observation of motor activities are included. Organizing or preparatory instructing is not included.

Participating in Motor Activities

Performing in a motor activity (not leading or demonstrating). Only periods of 5 seconds or more, during which the teacher is not performing other functions, are coded as participating. This does not include leading exercises. *Examples:* Teacher participates in a game of tag or plays in a volleyball game.

Other Interacting Related to Motor Activities

All other interactions directly related to motor activities that do not fall into previous categories. *Examples:* Discussions that would not influence performance, such as history of the activity, current events related to the activity, and spectator behavior. General encouragement such as "Go, go, go!" Phasing out the motor activity by handing in equipment.

Administering

Interacting with students about school, departmental, or class policies related to such things as dress schedules, attendance, excuses from gym, and so forth. *Examples:* Taking attendance. "Next week we will meet 45 minutes earlier."

Establishing and Enforcing Codes of Behavior

Interacting with students for the purpose of influencing their social-personal conduct, including disciplining, informing, commending, and determining. This category identifies behavior related to established (or implied) codes that delineate generically appropriate behavior and not behavior that is appropriate only for a specific activity or situation. It includes information about administrative codes. *Examples:* "Don't bounce the ball when I'm talking." "Put your shirt on."

Other Interacting

All other interactive behaviors that do not fall into previous categories, including those in which the purpose is unclear. Other interacting includes organizing for administrative tasks (e.g., attendance taking), interacting about personal matters, and discussing subject matter not related to the motor activities. Other interacting also designates silent observation of students not connected with carrying out one of the listed functions lasting more than 5 seconds. *Example:* "How is your brother feeling?"

Noninteractive Intervals: Dealing with Equipment

Getting out, placing, adjusting, or retrieving equipment. This category is characterized by periods of 5 seconds or more during which no interactive function is being carried out.

Noninteractive Intervals: Other Noninteractive Behaviors

All other noninteractive behaviors such as examining the roll book, tying shoes, waiting (not connected with carrying out listed function), changing location, and recording information on student performance. This includes noninteractive behaviors that are unclear.

Indiscernible Intervals: Insufficient Audio/Video

Unable to determine whether the teacher's behavior is interactive or noninteractive because the audiotape or videotape is unclear.

Indiscernible Intervals: Absent From Gymnasium

Teacher leaves the gymnasium.
   There are 10 general ground rules for coding the function dimension:

1. To identify the primary function of a teacher's interactive behavior, use the function category that best describes the purpose of the behavior at that moment. A function continues until a new interactive function category that best describes the purpose of the behavior or a noninteractive or indiscernible interval occurs.
2. Talking: When the teacher is talking, use the function category that best describes the purpose of the messages he or she is conveying. However, when the teacher is soliciting information from students, use the function category that best describes the purpose served by the information being solicited. When the teacher is telling the students to carry out one of the listed functions, use the function category that best describes the function the students are carrying out. (Use function subscript *shares* or *delegates* when this occurs.) The categories *observing* and *participating* are not used in these instances; they apply only when the teacher is observing or participating. Noninteractive categories are not applicable in these instances either.
3. Listening: When the teacher is listening to a student during an interchange, use the function category that best describes the purpose of the entire interchange. The interchange may consist of either student talking and teacher responding, or teacher talking and student responding.
4. Performing: When the teacher is performing a physical task, use the function category that best describes the purpose of the task.
5. Observes (Silently): Periods of silent observation lasting less than 5 seconds are considered to be pauses. When the teacher silently observes students performing motor activities for a period of 5 seconds or more, use the category *observing the performance of motor*

activities. When the teacher silently observes the students carrying out a task other than performing motor activities that he or she had asked them to carry out, use the function that best describes the purpose of the teacher's request. When the teacher silently observes students but without meeting any of the preceding criteria, code as *other interacting*.

6. Priority of Concurrent Functions: In some instances the teacher's behavior simultaneously accomplishes more than one interactive function. Use the following rules to help you decide which function to assign. When the teacher accomplishes one function by talking and another by doing or observing, use the talking function. When he or she accomplishes one function by listening and another by doing or observing, use the listening function. When he or she accomplishes one function by doing and another by observing, use the doing function. In other words, the order of priority is *talks, listens, performs, does, observes*.

7. Uncertainties: When the behavior is clearly interactive, but the specific function is not clear, choose the best interactive category. When the behavior is clearly not interactive, choose the best noninteractive category. Use *indiscernible* only when you cannot determine whether the teacher is interactive or noninteractive. When a teacher's interactive behavior is interrupted or stopped before the function of the behavior becomes apparent, code it either *other interacting related to motor activities* or *other interacting*. When evidence points equally toward classifying an event in a category of other and in a more descriptive category, code it in the more descriptive category.

8. Audiovisual Aids: When the teacher uses an audiovisual aid such as a record or film to convey continuous messages to the students, code the onset of the use according to the function being carried out by the aid. Thereafter, disregard the function being carried out by the aid and code the function of the teacher's behavior. When the teacher attends exclusively to the messages coming from the aid and does not otherwise interact, code as *other noninteractive behavior*.

9. Idiosyncratic expressions of habitually used words that merely fill space and are not intended to convey a message are not coded independently. Consider them part of the ongoing unit.

10. Nonverbal gestures are not considered for coding functions.

Function Subscript Dimension

This dimension indicates the extent to which the teacher carries out the function by himself or herself or shares it with others. For each interactive functional unit use one of the following subscripts.

Does

The teacher's behavior carries out the function.

Shares

The teacher and student share in carrying out the function.

Delegates

The teacher delegates carrying out the function to the students.

The function subscript dimension has four general ground rules for coding:

1. When the primary function is carried out by providing information
   - and the information is supplied entirely by the teacher, use *does*.
   - and part of the information is supplied by the teacher and part by the student, use *shares*.
   - and the teacher directly solicits the information from the student(s), use *shares*.
   - and students directly solicit the information from teacher, use *shares*.
   - and the teacher merely assigns the student a role that will involve providing the information, use *delegates*.

   Examples: "In doing the forward roll, tuck your chin to your chest" (preparatory instructing, does). "Keep your chin on your chest, and what else?" Student responds, "Hands on mat, shoulder-width apart" (*preparatory instructing, shares*).
2. When the primary function is carried out by performing a physical task (this is normally the case in providing equipment and spotting),
   - and the teacher performs the task, use *does*.
   - and the student(s) and teacher perform the task, use *shares*.
   - and the teacher merely tells/asks the student to perform the task (but does not perform it himself or herself), use *delegates*.

   Examples: Teacher spots for a student who is vaulting (*spotting, does*). Teacher gets equipment out of closet; students come up to take equipment (*providing equipment, shares*). Teacher tells students to get equipment; students go get it (*providing equipment, delegates*).
3. When the primary function is carried out by both providing information and performing a physical task (this often happens in demonstrating, officiating, other interacting, and administering), use the following guidelines:
   - When the teacher does it all, use *does*.
   - When the student does part or all of the performing or providing information (and the teacher does the rest), use *shares*.

- When the teacher merely assigns someone to perform the function (and does not perform the task or provide any of the information himself or herself), use *delegates*.

Examples: Teacher demonstrates head stand and provides concurrent commentary (*demonstrates, does*). Teacher has student demonstrate skill while teacher provides concurrent commentary (*demonstrates, shares*). Teacher has squad leaders take attendance in their squads, then report to him or her (*administering, shares*). Teacher asks student to demonstrate skill, then merely watches demonstration (*demonstrates, delegates*).

4. When the function is *observes* or *participates*, the only subscript used is *does*.

Direction Dimension

This dimension identifies the persons toward whom the teacher's interactive behavior is directed.

One Student

Teacher's behavior is directed toward one student (or one student at a time), whether or not that behavior is perceived by others.

Group/Whole Class of Students

Teacher's behavior is directed toward more than one student or to the entire class (may include one group at a time).

One and Group/Whole Class

Teacher's behavior is directed simultaneously at one student and the whole class.

Other Persons

Teacher's behavior is directed at persons other than students in class.

Other Combination

Teacher's behavior is directed at all of the preceding groups.
The direction dimension has two ground rules:

1. *Student* refers to any person officially enrolled in the class.

2. When teacher's function is coded as *observe*, code direction as follows:
   - When teacher is clearly attending to only a single student's performance, code direction as *one student*.
   - When teacher is attending to two or more students performing at same time, code direction as *one and group/whole class*.

Mode Dimension

The mode dimension identifies the way(s) in which the teacher interacts with others, that is, the way(s) in which he or she conveys messages to others, receives messages from others, or acts upon them.

Talks

Conveys verbal messages.

Listens

Attends to verbal messages from others.

Observes

Silently attends to the behavior of other people.

Demonstrates

Performs motor activity that conveys messages.

Uses Student Demonstrator

Has student demonstrate motor activity.

Uses Aids

Uses audiovisual or visual aids to convey messages.

Uses Signaling Devices

Uses mechanical devices (e.g., whistle, drum, hand claps, etc.) to convey messages.

Writes or Provides Written Materials

Conveys written messages.

Manually Assists

Touches other person in a way that affects person's movement.

Participates

Performs motor activity as a participant.

Performs Physical Task

Performs physical task other than those previously listed (e.g., handing out equipment).

This dimension uses three ground rules for coding:

1. Code all modes that occur during a unit. *Exception.* Code *observes* only when it is the exclusive mode used in a unit. Because *observes* occurs continuously in all interactive units, it is assumed to be one of the modes used in each unit and therefore need not be coded repeatedly.
2. Code *listens* only when there is evidence that the teacher is listening to or has received the student's message, such as when the teacher asks a question and then silently attends to the student's verbal response or when the student makes a request to which the teacher responds.
3. *Demonstrates* and *participates* are used only when the teacher performs a motor activity or part of a motor activity, such as showing students the correct position for hands in performing a stunt.

RECORDING PROCEDURES

The following recording procedures are designed for use with videotape recordings of teacher behavior.

1. As you view the tape, ask yourself, "What function is the teacher performing?"
2. When the function is discernible, stop tape. (Use "Stop" on the machine.)
3. Record the function.
4. Rewind the tape.
5. Replay the tape; search for the moment at which the function begins.
6. Stop the tape. (Use "Still" on the machine.)
7. Record the time, which must be imprinted on the tape beforehand.
8. Record other dimensions.

9. Play the tape; search for additions to mode, direction, and function subscript dimensions. If additions are required, stop the tape and make additions. Search for new function.
10. Repeat Steps 1-9.

If the teacher engages in silent observation for what you think is a period of 5 seconds or more, go through Steps 2-9, coding the function as observed. If, when the subsequent function is coded and timed, it turns out that the observation period was less than 5 seconds, cross out the entire observation code.

The unit of analysis used in this system is a segment of teacher behavior devoted to the accomplishment of a single primary interactive function. The primary function is the function category that best describes the purpose of a teacher's behavior at a point in time. A new functional unit begins when a new primary interactive function is detectable. All pauses between words, sentences, and movements are considered part of a single unit, provided the words or actions that surround the pause are devoted to accomplishing the same function. (A pause is a period of less than 5 seconds during which no detectable interactive function is being carried out.) Pauses occurring between words or actions that accomplish different functions are coded as part of the preceding function. Periods of 5 seconds or more during which no interactive function is being carried out are coded as *noninteractive* intervals or *indiscernible* intervals. Therefore, the functional unit ends at the point at which (a) another unit begins, (b) a 5-second noninteractive interval begins, or (c) a 5-second indiscernible interval begins. Contiguous pauses of different kinds that add up to more than 5 seconds are coded as a unit according to the predominant type of behavior displayed during the period (*silent observing, noninteractive,* or *indiscernible*).

SUMMARIZING AND INTERPRETING THE DATA

With appropriate computerization, the data obtained from this system can be summarized and displayed in a number of ways. Table 28.2, which is taken from Barrette's (1977) observation study of 40 physical education classes, is one way of presenting the information. Barrette (1977) and Anderson and Barrette (1978) provide other illustrations for displaying data. Basically, the system yields information about how teachers spend their class time in terms of the purpose of their actions and how, with whom, and about what they communicate. The information that emerges has several possible interpretations, including those of most interest to the teacher whose behavior has been recorded. Some questions that can be answered by applying this system to a sample of tapes are posed by Barrette (1977):

- How is teacher behavior distributed within the function dimension with regard to the frequency and duration of behavior for all classes? For secondary classes? (Total duration and total frequency; mean duration and mean frequency per class; percent duration and percent frequency; mean duration per occurrence of function.)
- What is the frequency of occurrence and duration of substance categories with respect to coded teacher behavior in the function dimension for all classes? For elementary classes and secondary classes? (Proportional occurrence of substance categories for all classes; mean duration of substance per class.)
- How do teachers carry out functions with respect to the function subscript, mode, and direction dimensions of their behavior? What is the frequency of exclusive use of categories in these dimensions when coded with the function dimension?
- What is the range, variability, and percentile norm distribution for function dimension behaviors for all classes?
- To what extent do functions teachers engage in change with respect to successive time segments within the class period? For example, when do teachers spend more of their observation time—in the second quarter or third quarter of the class?

The Physical Education Teachers' Professional Functions system is designed for descriptive research on teaching. As part of the Videotape Data Bank Project, it was used by Barrette (1977) to describe teacher behavior in 20 elementary and 20 secondary classes. A more extensive summary of results is reported in *What's Going on in Gym: Descriptive Studies of Physical Education Classes*, Anderson and Barrette (1978).

A simplified version of the system was used by Goldsmith (1979) as part of a training procedure to help preservice teachers increase awareness and control of their instructional behaviors. The system has been translated into French by researchers at the University of Quebec and is currently being used to analyze teacher behavior in Quebec province. A simplified version of the system appears in Anderson (1980). This version can be used in live settings and caters more to in-service and preservice training.

REFERENCES

Anderson, W.G. (1980). *Analysis of teaching physical education*. St. Louis: C.V. Mosby.

Table 28.2 Duration and Frequency of Occurrence for 18 Function Dimension Categories

Function category	Total class time (sec)	Total frequency	Percent of class time	Percent frequency	Mean duration/ occurrence (sec)	Mean duration/ class (sec)	Mean frequency class
Organizing	5,639	4,222	7.1	5.2	13.2	141.0	10.6
Preparatory instructing	11,307	764	14.2	9.5	14.8	282.7	19.1
Providing equipment	1,664	317	2.1	3.9	5.3	41.6	7.9
Concurrent instructing	13,615	1,433	17.1	17.8	9.5	340.4	35.8
Officiating	5,950	1,131	7.5	14.1	5.3	148.8	28.3
Spotting	553	103	.7	1.3	5.4	13.8	2.6
Leading exercise	919	54	1.2	.7	17.0	23.0	1.4
Intervening instructing	4,458	472	5.6	5.9	9.4	111.5	11.8
Observing	16,827	1,360	21.1	16.9	12.4	420.7	34.0
Participating	846	68	1.1	.8	12.4	21.2	1.7
Other interacting related to motor activity	5,085	648	6.4	8.1	7.9	127.1	16.2
Administering	3,578	204	4.5	2.5	17.5	89.5	5.1
Establishing and enforcing codes of behavior	1,602	260	2.0	3.2	6.2	40.0	6.5
Other interacting	3,030	365	3.8	4.5	8.3	75.8	9.1
Dealing with equipment	439	66	.6	.8	6.7	11.0	1.7
Other noninteractive intervals	3,247	320	4.1	4.0	10.1	81.2	8.0
Insufficient audio/video	558	45	.7	.6	12.4	14.0	1.1
Absent from gymnasium	359	16	.5	.2	22.4	9.0	.4

Note. From *A Descriptive Analysis of Teacher Behavior in Physical Education Classes* (pp. 69-70) by G.T. Barrette, 1977. Unpublished doctoral dissertation, Teachers College, Columbia University, New York.

Anderson, W.G., & Barrette, G.T. (Eds.) (1978). *What's going on in gym: Descriptive studies of physical education classes.* (Monograph 1, Motor Skills: Theory Into Practice). Newton, CT: Motor Skills: Theory Into Practice.

Barrette, G.T. (1977). *A descriptive analysis of teacher behavior in physical education classes.* Unpublished doctoral dissertation, Teachers College, Columbia University, New York.

Goldsmith, R.C. (1979). *A procedure to help preservice teachers in physical education enhance their control, awareness, and satisfaction.* Unpublished doctoral dissertation, Teachers College, Columbia University, New York.

RELATED REFERENCE

Kim, D. (1983). *A comparison of teaching behaviors between Korean and Idaho secondary physical education teachers.* Unpublished doctoral dissertation, University of Idaho, Moscow.

PART IV

COACH/ATHLETE CLIMATE ANALYSIS

The process of systematically observing and coding teaching behaviors has steadily gained favor in the athletic arena, where coaching behaviors are now routinely subjected to analysis. Tharp and Gallimore (1976) were among the first to report observational data on coaching behavior after coding several practice sessions of UCLA basketball coach, John Wooden. Since then, systems have been designed specifically for observing athletic roles or recording behaviors in either competitive sports or physical education.

Quarterman's Physical Education Teacher/Coach Observation System is based on the latter. He presents 12 teacher/coach categories that are really six pairs of verbal/nonverbal behaviors directed toward either students' skill attempts or students' class behaviors. The categories are formulated on the principles of operant reinforcement theory and provide insight relative to positive or negative feedback during athletic practice or skill rehearsal in physical education class.

The Coaching Behavior Recording Form, described by Langsdorf, is essentially the same category system developed by Tharp and Gallimore (1976). However, Langsdorf has increased its operational use by providing more descriptive category terms, introducing practice segment study, and expanding the means for summarizing and interpreting the data. Twelve categories are designated, permitting a study of the nature and the amount of coaching actions during practice or segments of practice.

Rushall developed two observation schedules that attend to teacher/coach (TOS/COS) and pupil/athlete (POS/AOS) behaviors. The categories in each pair are identical, but the environment—whether educational or athletic—determines the nature of the analysis. The TOS/COS is comprised of seven groups of behaviors that include such generalized activities as feedback, correcting, instructing, environment management, questioning, observing, and doing nothing. The POS/AOS outlines nine groups of participant behavior that note performance, effort, interaction, questioning, directing, responding, attending, destructive, no activity, and injury.

The Lombardo Coaching Behavior Analysis System (LOCOBAS) records and describes the interaction between the coach and athletes, officials, coaches, and others within the context of sport. Specifically, LOCOBAS focuses on the interaction between the coach and other significant participants in the athletic contest and on the quality of the interaction. A five-category instrument, LOCOBAS provides descriptive data about the target audiences of interaction during competitive athletic events.

Sinclair's Feedback Analysis Profile (FAP) measures several characteristics of verbal feedback given by coaches during practice sessions. The focus of FAP is on the instructional style of the coach specific to athletes' motor skill development. Each feedback episode is coded to reflect the presence or absence of the particular characteristic under observation. The system can also be used in physical education.

The Arizona State University Observation Instrument (ASUOI), developed by Lacy and Darst, provides a method of collecting data on coaching behavior in practice sessions. Either event or interval recording techniques can be used with this system. By altering the definitions of the behavioral categories slightly, the authors have developed a system that can also be used effectively in physical education. Though it is a relatively simple instrument to use, it yields valuable information to provide insight into the improvement of coaching and teaching behavior.

Tannehill and Burton modified Stewart's ORRPETB (chapter 22) to assess coaching behaviors of youth basketball coaches. The Coaching Observational Recording System (CBORS) is a multidimensional observation instrument that employs a time-sampling method of recording. The instrument can be used with all sports in practice or game situations. Information is coded according to four coaching climates, four types of interaction, and six categories of coaching behaviors. A summary of the information provides the coach with a profile of the organizational climate, the direction of interaction, and numerous coaching behaviors.

McKenzie and Giebink designed The Hierarchical Observation Method for Analyzing Sportsmanship (THOMAS) to assess player sportsmanlike and unsportsmanlike behavior in competitive game play. The system may be extended to include practice sessions in physical education classes. Sportsmanship behaviors are recorded under physical, verbal, and nonverbal responses. This hierarchical arrangement determines the order of entry if two behaviors occur simultaneously. The authors offer several suggestions for expanding and integrating their uses of the instrument.

REFERENCE

Tharp, R.G., & Gallimore, R. (1976, January). What a coach can teach a teacher. *Psychology Today*, pp. 75-78.

Chapter 29

Physical Education Teacher/Coach Observational System

Jerome Quarterman

The Physical Education Teacher/Coach Observational System was designed specifically for describing and analyzing behaviors of the physical education teacher and athletic coach. It focuses on verbal as well as nonverbal behaviors, with categories developed in terms of reinforcement theory. These data can help a physical education teacher or coach discern which behaviors are appropriate to specific learning environments (e.g., gymnasium, swimming pool, or athletic field) and which are inappropriate. The behavior categories in this system are defined in terms of *operant reinforcement theory*, which states that the immediate consequences of behavior shape future behavior. According to this theory, the frequency of a desirable behavior can be increased through positive or negative reinforcement, and the frequency of an undesirable behavior can be reduced through punishment or reinforcement of other desirable behaviors that are incompatible with the undesirable behavior. Because behavior is a function of its consequences, teachers and coaches should know how to deliberately and selectively dispense reinforcing consequences. For instance, teachers who praise students for practicing appropriate skills in a basketball class are more likely to observe such behaviors thereafter.

The sole component for determining the reliability of the instrument was interobserver agreement, or the percentage of agreement between two or more persons for each of the individual behavior categories during a single observation session. All individual categories yielded an 80% or higher interobserver agreement. Individuals can be trained to use the instrument with a minimum of 80% reliability with a few hours of practice.

CATEGORY DESCRIPTIONS

Six similar verbal and nonverbal teacher/coach behaviors are observed under two major categories, students attempting a skill during practice, and students' general social behavior. Only these positive, negative, and corrective behaviors are tallied.

Students' Skill Attempts

Positive Verbal Behavior

Verbal comments indicating praise or support that imply positive feelings about the student's skill attempt in class. *Examples:* ''Very good!'' ''At-a-boy!'' ''Great job!'' ''Way to go!'' ''That's the way to do it!'' ''Right-on!''

Positive Nonverbal Behavior

A body contact, hand gesture, or facial expression indicating positive feelings about the student's skill attempt in class. *Examples:* Patting a student on the shoulders, hugging a student, mussing the hair of a student, clapping, making an ''OK'' signal, winking, laughing and raising the eyebrows, shaking the head, and so forth.

Corrective Verbal Behavior

A verbal comment indicating that the student's skill attempt was not satisfactory. *Examples:* ''Not exactly; keep your head back!'' ''Keep your eyes on the ball!'' ''Keep those arms straight!'' ''Arch your back!'' ''Follow through on the swing!''

Corrective Nonverbal Behavior

A body contact, hand gesture, or facial expression indicating that the student's skill attempt was not satisfactory. *Examples:* Holding or turning a student's head in the correct position; getting a student's arm, body, legs, or feet into correct position; pushing hands in the air; or dribbling in the air.

Negative Verbal Behavior

A verbal comment that implies negative feelings about the student's skill attempt in class. *Examples:* ''That's not good enough.'' ''That's terrible.'' ''You're just loafing.'' ''Awful.'' ''Uh-uh.''

Negative Nonverbal Behavior

A body contact, hand gesture, or facial expression indicating negative feelings about the student's skill attempt in class. *Examples:* Pushing, pulling, hitting, or holding a student (physical restraint); clapping for attention; signaling thumbs down; frowning; scowling; or looking angry.

Students' Class Behaviors

Positive Verbal Behavior

Verbal comments by the teacher that praise or imply positive feelings about the student's class behavior. *Examples:* "Fine job today." "Keep up the good work." "You're the best." "A super job."

Positive Nonverbal Behavior

A body contact, hand gesture, or facial expression indicating positive feelings about the student's class behavior. *Examples:* Patting on the shoulders, hugging a student, mussing a student's hair, clapping, making an "OK" signal, laughing, raising the eyebrows, or shaking the head.

Negative Verbal Behavior

A verbal comment that implies negative feelings about the student's undesirable class behavior. *Examples:* "No, no!" "Cut it out!" "Stay in line!" "Just look at this class!" "Be quiet!"

Negative Nonverbal Behavior

A body contact, hand gesture, or facial expression indicating negative feelings about the student's class behavior. *Examples:* Clapping for attention, signaling thumbs down, placing a finger over the lips for quiet, or folding the arms and staring at an individual or group of students.

Verbal Punishment

Verbal comments imposing penalties on students who break the class rules or demonstrate disruptive or deviant behaviors. *Examples:* "Get out of the class!" "Stand in the corner for the rest of the class period!" "Run 20 laps around the gym!" "Do 15 push-ups!"

Nonverbal Punishment

Refers to a body contact, hand gesture, or facial expression indicating penalties on students who break the class rules or demonstrate disruptive or deviant behavior. *Examples:* Holding a student to keep him or her from fighting, physically moving a student from one place to another when he or she is unruly, giving a hand signal, or nodding the head or rolling the eyes for a student to sit in the corner or to leave the gym area.

RECORDING PROCEDURES

Teaching behaviors are recorded by event recording (Hall, 1971). Predefined, observable behavior is recorded as it is witnessed by the observer. For example, when the observer notes the teacher making such positive verbal comments as "Very good," or "Great job, Bobby," he or she marks a tally under this category, thus producing a numerical output that is converted to rate per minute. Event recording is done continuously or during separate time intervals throughout a teaching session. According to Siedentop (1976), a valid measure of teacher behavior can be obtained by doing event recording for a short period and repeating it throughout a teaching session. For example, a valid measure of teacher behavior was obtained from five 3-minute and one 5-minute recording sessions separated by five 2-minute rest sessions (Figure 29.1). Two-thirds, or 20 minutes, of the total teaching session was recorded. During the 2 minutes when no observation was being recorded, the observer made relevant comments under "Specific Interval Notes."

Physical Education Teacher/Coach Observation System

Teacher _Jones_   Grade _5th_   Activity _Volleyball_
Time _10:00-10:30_   Date _11/25_

Time intervals	Students' Skill Attempts						Students' Class Behaviors					
	Positive		Corrective		Negative		Positive		Negative		Punishment	
	VBL	NVBL	VBL	NVBL	VBL	NVBL	VBL	NVBL	VBL	NVBL	VBL	NVBL
10:00-10:03								ЖЖI * 6	IIII 4	III 3	I 1	
10:05-10:08					ЖЖ 5	II 2	II 2	II 2	IIII 4			
10:10-10:13	II 2	I 1	ЖЖ 5	ЖЖI 6	ЖЖII 7	III 3						
10:15-10:18	II 2	II 2	ЖЖ 5	ЖЖIII 8	ЖЖI 6	ЖЖ 5						
10:20-10:23	II 2	II 2	II 2	IIII 4	ЖЖII 7	ЖЖ 5	III 3	ЖЖ 5	I 1	II 2		
10:25-10:30	IIII 4	ЖЖ 5					II 2	I 1	ЖЖ 4	IIII 4	III 3	II 2
Total for 20 minutes	10	10	12	18	25	15	7	8	15	10	6	3
Rate per minute	.5	.5	.6	.9	1.25	.75	.35	.4	.75	.5	.3	.15

Specific interval notes:

* The students entered the gym in a very disorderly manner (yelling out, running, etc.)

Figure 29.1   Completed Physical Education Teacher/Coach Observation System recording sheet.

SUMMARIZING AND INTERPRETING THE DATA

An event recording format (Figure 29.1) was used in the intervals described in the previous section to obtain a sampling of 20 minutes of teacher behaviors taken from the 30-minute teaching session. The data were then converted to rate per minute by dividing the total events recorded by 20.

The totals and the rate per minute of the individual cells can answer questions about the kinds of behaviors used by the teacher (e.g., the ratio of positive to negative behaviors used by the teacher while the students were attempting skills; see Figure 29.1). The teacher expressed 10 positive verbal behaviors, 10 positive nonverbal behaviors, 25 negative verbal behaviors, and 15 negative nonverbal behaviors. The negative behaviors outweighed the positive behaviors by a 2-to-1 ratio.

The rate per minute of positive and negative behaviors can be determined by dividing the total by 20. There were 20 positive behaviors (1 per minute) and 40 negative behaviors (2 per minute).

With this information, the teacher can make decisions about changing or modifying his or her verbal and nonverbal behaviors. In the example above, the teacher probably needs to increase his or her positive behaviors and decrease his or her negative behaviors to be more effective in the class.

REFERENCES

Hall, R.V. (1971). *The measurement of behavior*. Lawrence, KS: H and H Enterprises.

Siedentop, D. (1976). *Developing teaching skills in physical education*. Boston: Houghton Mifflin.

RELATED REFERENCES

Quarterman, J. (1978). *A descriptive analysis of teaching physical education in the elementary schools*. Unpublished manuscript, The Ohio State University, Columbus.

Quarterman, J. (1980). An observational system for observing the verbal and nonverbal behaviors emitted by physical educators and coaches. *The Physical Educator, 37*, 15-20.

☐ *Chapter 30*

Coaching Behavior Recording Form

Edward V. Langsdorf

The Coaching Behavior Recording Form was used initially to collect data for a specific research project. It remains essentially a data collecting instrument for determining the nature and amount of specific coaching behavior that occurs during a given practice session or within particular segments of a practice session. Although basically a research tool, it has potential for practical application by coaches and teachers as a self-evaluation and peer-evaluation device.

The form features descriptive terms that identify commonly observed coaching behavior (first described by Tharp & Gallimore, 1976; more recently confirmed by Langsdorf, 1979). Space is provided on the form for recording discrete instances of observed coaching behavior as they occur throughout the course of a practice session. There is also a provision for dividing a practice session into segments (e.g., early practice as opposed to late practice, warm-up as opposed to team scheme, or individual practice as opposed to group practice) to determine variations in the amounts or kinds of coaching behaviors that may occur at different times during the same practice session.

With well-defined behavior categories and rigorous event recording procedures, the Coaching Behavior Recording Form is assumed to have content validity. Reliability for this form is determined at the time of data collection by periodically comparing the tallies of two independent observers throughout the course of data collection. In a recent study using this instrument (Langsdorf, 1979), the form was found to exceed the required reliability standard of .85.

When using a form such as this, the observer must consider the possibility of observer error. Well-defined behavior categories and practice in using the form will help eliminate this source of error, as will periodic reliability checks throughout the course of data collection. It is strongly recommended that pilot studies or trial runs, using potential subjects and reliability checks, precede any serious attempt to observe and record coaching behavior.

Event recording for extended periods of time (2 to 3 hr) or over many consecutive days can become a tedious, monotonous task. When this occurs, observer accuracy falls off. A possible solution for this problem might be videotape or audiotape recording to allow for more thorough analysis of verbal and nonverbal behavior.

Finally, the instrument cannot qualify behavior. No attempt is made to determine how good or how poor an instructional behavior is in terms of effectiveness. The form is capable of providing only quantitative information.

CATEGORY DESCRIPTIONS

The Coaching Behavior Recording Form (Figure 30.1) contains 10 categories of commonly recognized coaching behaviors, provisions for other categories of behavior that may be unique to an individual coach, and a provision for uncodable behaviors.

Instruction

Verbal statements about what to do or how to do it; statements on the fundamentals of blocking, tackling, or strategy. *Examples:* "Keep your head up on the block." "Left guard, on 48 power, you pull and turn up the hole."

Hustle

Verbal statements to activate or intensify previously instructed behavior (a verbal cue, usually shouted by the coach). *Examples:* "Drive, Drive, Drive!" "Hit, Hit, Hit!"

Praise

Verbal compliments or encouragements. *Examples:* "Way to go, gang." "Nice tackle." "Good job."

Nonverbal Reward

Nonverbal compliments or encouragements. *Examples:* A pat on the back, a smile.

Scold

Verbal statements of displeasure. *Examples:* "What a stupid play that was." "That was the worst excuse for a block."

Nonverbal Punishment

Scowls, gestures of despair, and temporary removal of a player from scrimmage; includes any hands-on action. *Examples:* Pulling or pushing a player or rapping a player's helmet.

Scold/Reinstruction

A combination category in which a single verbal behavior refers to a specific act, contains a clear scold, and reasserts a previously instructed behavior. *Examples:* "How many times do I have to tell you, John, that you cut to the right off your left foot?"

Modeling-Positive

A demonstration of how to perform. *Example:* Actually getting down in a football stance and showing a player or players how to execute a particular block.

Modeling-Negative

A demonstration of how not to perform. *Example:* Showing a player how he incorrectly executed a block by re-creating the incorrect blocking form.

First Name Use

Using a player's first name when speaking to him or her. *Examples:* "Nice catch, Mary." "Bruce, that was a terrible block."

Other

Any behavior not falling into one of the preceding categories. *Example:* A coach uses questioning as a teaching behavior.

Uncodable

Behaviors not clearly heard or seen.

The coaching behavior categories described above have been used successfully in basketball and football coaching and seem suitable for most team sports. To determine the number of specific behaviors that might occur during the entire course of a particular practice session, one would probably not use practice segments. However, for someone interested in comparing the amounts or kinds of behavior occurring at different times in a practice session, the form accommodates data collection by practice segments (see Figure 30.1). For example, high school and college football

Coaching Behavior Recording Form

Date_____ Practice session _____ Observer's name _____

Behavior category	Seg. ___ Time ___	Seg. ___ Time ___	Seg. ___ Time ___	Seg. ___ Time ___	Seg. ___ Time ___	Seg. ___ Time ___	Seg. ___ Time ___
Instruction							
Hustle							
First name use							
Praise							
Nonverbal reward							
Scold							
Nonverbal punishment							
Scold/ reinstruction							
Modeling– positive							
Modeling– negative							
Other							
Other							
Other							
Uncodable							

Figure 30.1 Coaching Behavior Recording Form.

practices (and many other team sports) are often divided along these or similar segments:

- Warm-up: Usually the first part of the practice session, organized so that the entire team is together. It includes such activities as loosening up, doing calisthenics, stretching, and performing a circuit of footwork drills.
- Individual: Breakdown of the team by positions to work on fundamental skills specific to that position (e.g., receivers with the receiving coach to work on a specific pattern or patterns).
- Group: Breakdown of the team by combination of positions to work on coordinating specific fundamental skills (e.g., receivers, running-

backs, quarterbacks, and a center all working on pass plays at the same time).

- Scrimmage: Gamelike practice that consists of an offensive team and a defensive team working against one another.

By providing space for seven distinct segments, the form allows flexibility when observing a coach who may include more or fewer than the four suggested segments for football. As an example, Langsdorf (1979) added two segments, one on one and conditioning, which appeared in the daily football practice scheme quite regularly. In the same study, it was also observed that not every practice session contained the same number of segments. Some were occasionally omitted, depending on what the coach wanted to accomplish during that particular practice session.

RECORDING PROCEDURES

Using the form is quite simple; however, it is recommended that anyone intending to use it practice observing and recording with the form prior to data collection. Event recording is the recording method used, whereby each discrete occurrence of the defined behavior is recorded as it is observed by making a tally adjacent to the defined behavior category and under the appropriate segment heading. This procedure yields the total number of times a particular behavior occurs during a practice session or within a particular practice segment. Figure 30.2 is an example of a completed coding form.

SUMMARIZING AND INTERPRETING THE DATA

Once collection has been completed, the data are put into some usable form. There are at least three methods of data analysis. First of all, one could simply examine the raw data and compare the number of behaviors that occur in the various categories. However, more meaningful comparisons are possible by determining percentages of behavior and adding the time element to produce a behavior rate (all three of these forms of data summarization are found in Table 30.1). Comparison by percentage seems considerably less cumbersome than comparing raw data figures to examine differences between behavior categories for an individual coach. A behavior rate figure provides a more complete picture of how much actual behavior took place during a particular period of time. Furthermore, percentage and rate figures allow for comparison between two or

Date __4/4__   Practice session __13__   Observer's name __Ed Langsdorf__

Behavior category	Seg. _warm_ Time 17:00	Seg. _1 on 1_ Time 4:00	Seg. _Ind._ Time 34:00	Seg. _Group_ Time 46:00	Seg. _Scrim_ Time 34:30	Seg. _Cond._ Time 5:30	Seg. ___ Time ___
Instruction	I	HHT II	HHT HHT IIII	HHT HHT HHT HHT HHT HHT IIII	HHT HHT HHT II	II	
Hustle	IIII		II	HHT HHT III		I	
First name use		II	II	HHT HHT HHT HHT HHT HHT II	HHT III		
Praise		II	I	HHT II	III	I	
Nonverbal reward							
Scold				HHT HHT HHT	HHT HHT		
Nonverbal punishment					HHT		
Scold/ reinstruction		III	II	HHT HHT HHT HHT II	HHT HHT HHT		
Modeling– positive		II	IIII	HHT II	III		
Modeling– negative		II	I	II	II		
Other							
Other							
Other							
Uncodable							

Figure 30.2 Completed Coaching Behavior Recording Form.

more coaches (or teachers) much more readily than do behavior totals as obtained from raw data. It should be noted that percentage figures and rate figures reveal similar but different information.

Totaling the number of tallies adjacent to each behavior category in Figure 30.2 reveals that instruction behavior occurred 75 times during this practice session, hustle behavior occurred 20 times, and praise behavior occurred 15 times. The number of times each behavior occurred during each segment (if it occurred at all) can also be determined from Figure 30.2.

In addition to recording each instance of behavior, the observer can use a stopwatch to record the length of each segment and the total length of practice. By timing segment lengths and total practice time, the ob-

Table 30.1 Example of Data Comparison Using Total Behaviors, Percentage of Behavior, and Behavior Rate

Category	Total	Percent	Behaviors per min
Instruction	1,780	35.94	.73
Hustle	723	14.60	.30
Scold/reinstruction	603	12.17	.25
Praise	542	10.94	.22
Scold	527	10.64	.22
Modeling-positive	289	5.83	.12
Nonverbal punishment	120	2.42	.05
First name use	110	2.22	.05
Modeling-negative	66	1.33	.03
Nonverbal reward	30	0.61	.01
Other	45	0.91	.02
Uncodable	59	1.19	.02
Total	4,894	98.80	2.02

server can determine rate of behavior (expressed in behavior per minute) for a practice session or for individual segments within a session. In Figure 30.2 warm-up lasted 17 minutes; one on one, 4 minutes; individual, 34 minutes; and so forth. The total time for the session was 141 minutes.

Table 30.2 presents percentages and rates of behavior for two subjects. A comparison of these percentages shows that Subject 2 had a higher percentage of behavior falling into the instruction category than did Subject 1. Similar comparisons can be made between these two subjects for each behavior category. Further examination of Table 30.2 shows that even though Subject 2 had a greater percentage of instruction than did Subject 1, his rate of behavior for that category was slightly less. In effect, Subject 1 displayed more instruction behavior per unit time than did Subject 2. It is therefore evident that comparisons of coaching behavior involving two or more coaches are enhanced by using both percentage and rate figures.

The comparisons discussed here used percentages and rates determined from total behaviors observed over several hours of practice time spanning a number of practice sessions. Other data summary possibilities exist, including week-by-week analysis and practice segment analysis.

Table 30.2   Example of Percentage and Rate Comparisons for Two Subjects

	Subject 1		Subject 2	
Category	Percent	Behaviors per min	Percent	Behaviors per min
Instruction	35.94	.73	50.30	.65
Hustle	14.60	.30	12.70	.16
Scold/reinstruction	12.17	.25	8.00	.10
Praise	10.94	.22	6.90	.09
Scold	10.64	.22	6.60	.09
Modeling-positive	5.83	.12	2.80	.04
Nonverbal punishment	2.42	.05	0.00	.00
First name use	2.22	.05	1.65	.02
Model-negative	1.33	.03	1.60	.02
Nonverbal reward	0.61	.01	1.20	.02
Other	0.91	.09	2.40	.03
Uncodable	1.19	.02	6.60	.09

REFERENCES

Langsdorf, E.V. (1979). *A systematic observation of football coaching behavior in a major university environment.* Unpublished doctoral dissertation, Arizona State University, Tempe.

Tharp, R.G., & Gallimore, R. (1976, January). What a coach can teach a teacher. *Psychology Today*, pp. 75-78.

□ *Chapter 31*

Teacher/Coach and Pupil/Athlete Observation Schedules

Brent S. Rushall

The Teacher/Coach and Pupil/Athlete Observation Schedules are designed for use in sporting and physical education environments. The former is used for observing teacher or coach behaviors. In an educational setting the schedule is called the Teacher Observation Schedule (TOS), and in a sporting environment it is called the Coach Observation Schedule (COS). Similarly, the latter is used for observing pupil or athletic behaviors. In educational settings participants are observed using the Pupil Observation Schedule (POS), and in sports athletes are observed using the Athlete Observation Schedule (AOS).

The COS/TOS classifies seven groups of behaviors: feedback and rewarding; correction and prohibiting; questioning; directing, explaining, and informing; monitoring and attending; managing; and no activity. These categories, based on the work of Breyer and Calchera (1971), provide an assessment of the behaviors exhibited by a coach. The schedule focuses on the way consequences for participant behaviors are provided, the type of directions or setting events demonstrated, the form of non-interactional behaviors occurring, and the occurrence of activities not related to control functions. From these emphases an estimate of the teacher's/coach's potential effectiveness can be formed.

The AOS/POS categorizes nine groups of behaviors: task performance and participation, participant interaction, questioning, directing, response to teacher/coach, attending, destructive activity, no activity, and injury. The analysis provides an assessment of an individual's participation. The schedule focuses on task application, personal interactions, attention, and activities that are not related to the prime environmental purpose. Information is developed that evaluates the participant's behaviors, which in turn can be used as the feedback for the teacher/coach or the participant. It could also serve as an index of the effectiveness of the teacher/coach for controlling a participant's behavior.

The validity of the schedules was established in two ways. First, the categories were validated by empirical observation of instances of the behaviors they defined. Second, an evolutionary process was followed by extensively using the schedules with a number of observers and environments. Definitions were refined so that categories were mutually exclusive. The criterion for acceptance of the scale was 100 hours of use without the occurrence of a dual-classification behavior. The exhaustion of all possible behaviors in each schedule is due primarily to the no activity category, which is a catchall classification for behaviors that are not related to the aims and content of coaching or teaching. Interobserver reliability was established using the percentage of agreement explained in chapter 3.

CATEGORY DESCRIPTIONS

Coach/Teacher

Feedback

The coach provides information to tell the participant the performance was satisfactory and should be repeated in the same manner, or the performance was satisfactory but can be improved by incorporating additional features included in the feedback communication. Feedback can concern both skill and general behaviors and must stipulate what to do on the next occurrence of the behavior. *Examples:* "That was a good arm extension. Try to keep it that way." "Your body position is almost perfect. Drop your head a little lower and it will be perfect."

Rewarding

The coach openly demonstrates pleasure with the behavior of a participant or group, conveying a positive feeling about or acceptance of the behavior. It can be verbal or nonverbal. Rewarding is differentiated from feedback in that it is purely directed at some past performance, and informational content does not indicate what to do on the next occurrence of the behavior. *Examples:* "That is the finest technique I've seen you do." Excited clapping.

Correcting

The coach provides information to tell the participant his or her performance was not satisfactory and how it must be altered to continue. The content should include the performance characteristics that must be introduced for at least a satisfactory performance. This contrasts with feedback in that correcting implies that the performer still has to achieve an adequate performance. Correcting can concern both skill and general behaviors and must stipulate what to do on the next occurrence of the behavior. *Examples:* "Your racket head was too low. Raise it up to a position higher than your wrist when you play the next backhand." "Your time was poor. Next time try to keep an even pace throughout the whole race rather than saving your effort until the end."

Prohibiting

The coach disciplines or openly displays displeasure with an individual or group, conveying a negative feeling about or unacceptability of the behavior to which it is related. It can be verbal or nonverbal. Prohibiting is differentiated from correcting in that it is purely directed at some past performance and the informational content does not indicate what to do on the next occurrence of the behavior. *Examples:* "That was a poor shot." Thumbs-down sign.

Questioning

The teacher asks a question related to the subject matter.

Directing

The teacher directs an individual or group to do something directly related to the subject matter. The content does not refer to any previous behavior. *Examples:* "Throw the ball again." "Change to a slower rhythm."

Explaining

The teacher explains, elaborates, or summarizes previous material or paraphrases a statement that was not understood. The content must be related to the subject matter. This behavior is very noticeable when new information is being presented. *Examples:* "There are three rules that you must remember. They are . . ." "This is the way to stand in the ready position. The feet should . . ."

Informing

The teacher answers an individual's question, which must be related to the subject matter.

Monitoring

The teacher surveys the activity environment without focusing on a particular individual.

Attending

The coach listens or pays attention to what an individual or group is doing or saying. The coach obviously focuses upon some activity or behavior.

Managing

The coach engages in behaviors that lead up but are not directly related to a learning situation or subject matter. *Examples:* Establishing order, getting a piece of equipment, or checking attendance.

No Activity

The teacher is not involved in verbal or nonverbal activity relevant to the team or subject matter. As a rule, no interaction between the teacher and participants is evidenced. To record this behavior it must be the only category demonstrated in the observation time period. *Examples:* Looking out a window, not being present in the environment, talking to a visitor, or answering the telephone.

Athlete/Pupil

Task Performance

The individual performs a physical activity that is related to the sport or subject matter. Two levels of analysis are considered to assess how the individual is applying himself or herself.

Task Effort.   The level of effort applied to performing a defined physical activity that provides an estimate of how hard the individual is working.

- *Maximum (EM):* The observer considers the level of effort to be maximum or very high. Facial expressions, bodily cues, or sounds that accompany high levels of effort must be evident to record this classification.
- *Adequate (EA):* The observer considers the level of effort to be adequate.
- *Inadequate (EI):* The observer considers the level of effort to be below

an acceptable level. Facial expressions, bodily cues, and utterances indicating the performer is loafing must be evident to record this category.

Task Participation. The topography or form of the behavior. An assessment is made as to whether the performer is executing the required behavior. This category requires the observer to make two decisions about the physical activity of the individual—how hard and how well he or she is working need to be determined. Consequently, for an occurrence of this category two check marks should be entered on the daily recording sheet.

- *Adequate (PA):* The observer considers that the performer is doing the activity in the appropriate form.
- *Inadequate (PI):* The observer considers that the performer is not doing the activity in the appropriate form.

Participant Interaction

The participant interacts verbally with another participant. This does not include questioning or directing behaviors.

Positive. The individual interacts with another participant by providing encouragement, positive sanction, feedback, explanation, or pleasant connection. Neutral interactions are also recorded in this category.

Negative. The individual interacts with another participant by providing unpleasant associations or discipline. Displeasure or animosity is conveyed in the tone and content of the confrontation. This behavior is only verbal. Obvious physical intervention should be recorded as destructive activity.

Questioning

The participant asks a question concerning the subject matter or organization.

Athlete/Pupil (AP). The participant asks another athlete/pupil a question.

Coach/Teacher (CT). The participant asks the coach/teacher a question.

Directing

The participant directs another individual to do something related directly to the subject matter. *Examples:* ''Be ready for your turn.'' ''Move to the end of the line.''

Response to the Teacher/Coach

The participant gives opinions or information as a response to teacher/coach-initiated questions.

Attending

The participant pays attention to what another individual, group, or the coach/teacher is saying or doing about some activity or behavior that is related to the subject matter.

Destructive Activity

The participant physically performs an act that interferes with the functioning of another individual or group.

No Activity

The individual does something that is not related to the subject matter or the attainment of the training session goals. This must be a physical act because all verbal behaviors are accounted for in other categories. This must be the only behavior category exhibited in the observation time period for it to be recorded. *Examples:* Tying a shoe, waiting for a turn, and looking out a window.

Injury

The participant is injured and does not take part in activity.

RECORDING PROCEDURES

The easiest and most popular method of observing is time sampling. The ongoing behavior is classified at the end of a predetermined period of time. For this set of tools, a 10-second interval is recommended. Shorter periods fatigue the observer, and longer periods require more time to attain stable or representative data. Time periods can be read from a stopwatch or wristwatch. Preferably, tape recordings giving the periodic instruction ''observe'' should be used, although the consistency of time interval needs to be calibrated periodically. With time sampling, only the behavior that is displayed at the end of the time interval is classified.

Time-sampled event recording has also proven to be successful (MacEachern, 1972; Rushall & MacEachern, 1977; Rushall & Smith, 1979; Smith, 1972). All behaviors that occur during a time period are classified. If the observation period is not too long, observer reliability is not noticeably affected. A period of 5 seconds is the easiest to handle. The greater the time period, the larger the number and frequency of observed categories; therefore, observation periods of over 10 seconds are not recommended.

In time-sampled event recording, a tape recording is used to signal observation and recording periods. Such a recording signals the onset of a 5-second observation period with the command "observe" and terminates it with the command "record."

It is suggested that observations be done in 5-minute blocks as indicated on the daily recording sheets for the schedules (see Figures 31.1 and 31.2). Behavior occurrences are indicated by check marks on the daily

Teacher/Coach Observation Schedule

Teacher/coach name _____ Activity_____

Session number _____ Conditions _____ Date _____

Behavior category		Time interval						
		0-5	5-10	10-15	15-20	20-25	25-30	Total
Feedback	F							
Reward	R							
Correcting	C							
Prohibiting	P							
Questioning								
Directing	D							
Explaining	E							
Informing	I							
Monitoring	M							
Attending	A							
Managing								
No activity								

Comments

Figure 31.1 Teacher/Coach Observation Schedule recording sheet.

recording sheets for each schedule. These are totaled for each 5-minute block of the total observation session. A more sophisticated recording method involves recording each occurrence as a consecutive number, which allows one to interpret the sequence of behaviors. Behavior patterns are more readily observed when their response sequences are available.

Pupil/Athlete Observation Schedule

Pupil/athlete name _____ Activity_____

Session number _____ Conditions _____ Date _____

Behavior category		Time interval						
		0-5	5-10	10-15	15-20	20-25	25-30	Total
Task effort, maximum	EM							
Task effort, adequate	EA							
Task effort, inadequate	EI							
Task participation, adequate	PA							
Task participation, inadequate	PI							
Participant interaction, positive	P							
Participant interaction, negative	N							
Questioning, athlete/pupil	AP							
Questioning, coach/teacher	CT							
Directing								
Response to teacher/coach								
Attending								
Destructive activity								
No activity								
Injury								

Comments

Figure 31.2   Pupil/Athlete Observation Schedule recording sheet.

SUMMARIZING AND INTERPRETING THE DATA

The traditional frequencies and percentage of behavior occurrence are readily discerned from the daily recording sheets. Thus it is possible to identify how much time was consumed by a particular behavior category and to compare the proportions between categories. When behavior occurrences are sequenced, it is possible to use time-series analyses or cluster analyses to determine patterns of responding. Such analyses extend the observations to discussions of styles of behavior and comparisons of consistencies and inconsistencies within individuals and between individuals. Further interpretations depend on the inventiveness of the researcher.

REFERENCES

Breyer, N.L., & Calchera, D.J. (1971). A behavioral observation schedule for pupils and teachers. *Psychology in the Schools, 8*, 330-337.

MacEachern, J.A. (1972). *Effects of systematic behavioral feedback on teaching behaviors of student teachers.* Unpublished master's thesis, Dalhousie University, Canada.

Rushall, B.S., & MacEachern, J.A. (1977). The effects of systematic behavioral feedback on teaching behaviors of student physical education teachers. *Canadian Journal of Applied Sport Sciences, 2*, 161-169.

Rushall, B.S., & Smith, K.S. (1979). The modification of the quality and quantity of behavior categories in a swimming coach. *Journal of Sport Psychology, 1*, 138-50.

Smith, K.C. (1972). *The modification of a competitive swim coach's behavior.* Unpublished master's thesis, Dalhousie University, Canada.

RELATED REFERENCES

Danielson, R.R. (1974). *Leadership in coachings: Description and evaluation.* Unpublished doctoral dissertation, University of Alberta, Canada.

Richards, A.A. (1975). *A study of the relationship between teaching behaviors and performer behaviors in the physical education setting.* Unpublished master's thesis, Dalhousie University, Halifax, Nova Scotia.

Rushall, B.S. (1977). Two observation schedules for sporting and physical education environments. *Canadian Journal of Applied Sport Sciences, 2*, 15-21.

Rushall, B.S. (1980, April). *Coaching styles for various sports.* Paper presented at the annual convention of the American Alliance for Health, Physical Education, Recreation and Dance, Detroit.

Chapter 32

The Lombardo Coaching Behavior Analysis System (LOCOBAS)

Bennett J. Lombardo

The purpose of the Lombardo Coaching Behavior Analysis System (LOCOBAS) is to describe and record the interaction between the coach and athletes, officials, assistant coaches, and others within the context of sport. Specifically, LOCOBAS focuses on two variables: (a) the interaction between the coach and other significant participants and nonparticipants in the athletic contest and (b) the quality of the interaction.

LOCOBAS is a five-category observation instrument that provides descriptive data related to the quantity and quality of the interaction of the coach as well as the target of such behavior. LOCOBAS was designed for use during athletic competition; it is not as useful or responsive when employed in practice sessions.

LOCOBAS, an interval system, provides information about the sequence of the interaction between the coach and the other participants in the athletic contest. Patterns of behavior are easily determined via an analysis of pairs of behaviors.

Interobserver reliability was reported at .946 ($p < .01$) using Kendall's coefficient of concordance with the correction applied for tied rankings. Interobserver reliability, employing the percent agreement method, was determined to be .81.

LOCOBAS does not have the capability of describing the specific content of the player-coach interaction, nor can it provide data about the appropriateness of the behavior observed. As with other descriptive instruments, LOCOBAS provides bits of information about the rightness of such interaction. Also, LOCOBAS, as it describes the quality (as defined by the system) of the coach's interaction, does not distinguish among the various, specific types of positive, neutral, and negative coaching behaviors.

CATEGORY DESCRIPTIONS

Positive

A positive evaluation.

Verbal (1). Coach praises, accepts, commends, laughs, encourages, urges on, or provides positive feedback or reinforcement.

Nonverbal (11). Coach claps, pats on head, shakes hand, embraces happily, dances about, or nods affirmatively.

Neutral

Absence of positive or negative evaluation.

Verbal (2). Coach gives directions, orders, makes superficial remarks, gives information, lectures, or gives commands.

Nonverbal (12). Coach points, directs, gives signals, waves arms to move players, or demonstrates.

Negative

A negative evaluation.

Verbal (3). Coach criticizes, scolds, is sarcastic, expresses anger, swears, curses, screams, hisses, jeers, threatens, or provides negative feedback.

Nonverbal (13). Coach hits, strikes, kicks, spits, throws objects, shakes head, grimaces, frowns, flails arms, scowls, or shakes the body of an athlete.

On-Task Behavior (700)

No apparent interaction but coach is obviously involved in the action of the game; the activities of the players, fans, and officials; and so forth. Use this category when the coach is not interacting with another individual, yet is still absorbed in the game. *Example:* The coach is seated and is intently focused on game play, but not interacting with anyone verbally or nonverbally.

Off-Task Behavior (800)

No apparent interaction and the behavior of the coach is off-task. The coach is involved in tasks unrelated to the action of the game, the competition, and its participants. Employ this category when the coach is obviously absorbed or distracted by activities not central to the athletic event. *Example:* Coach is looking up into the stands.

RECORDING PROCEDURES

The observer uses the following symbols to prefix the data recorded (i.e., the individual tallies). This indicates the individual nature of the behavior and the specific individual(s) with whom the coach interacts.

- One individual (I)
- Players, coach's team (1)
- Assistants, coach's team (2)
- Game officials (3)
- Others (fans, opposition coaches, players, etc.) (4)

The recorder/observer observes and records all interaction that involves the coach under observation. Therefore, it is imperative that the observer stay alert and follow the coach throughout the course of the coding session. Prior to the start of the athletic event, the observer assumes a position such that the verbal and nonverbal behavior of the coach under observation can be noted. The position of the observer is critical because the observer can only record what he or she can observe and hear. Poor positioning will result in the loss of data. The observer records the interaction on the tally sheet at 5-second intervals and/or on every change of behavior, indicating both the nature of the interaction (i.e., positive, neutral, or negative) and to whom it was directed. The observer continues in this way for the entire length of the contest (Figure 32.1).

Whenever the coach interacts with athletes, the observer must decide whether the coach is directing his or her behavior to either a group (i.e., more than one athlete) or one individual. The letter "I" is used to indicate interaction directed to one individual and is placed beside the relevant code. For example, if the coach calls out, "Great play, Mary," the observer records "I1" (Individual, positive, verbal). If the coach orders, "John, move back," the observer records "I2" (Individual, neutral, verbal).

Each time the coach's behavior is coded the observer records a numerical symbol consisting of two or three digits. The initial digit represents the group or person(s) with whom the coach interacts. If the interaction is verbal, then the observer codes 1, 2, or 3. For example, 33 represents a negative verbal interaction between a coach and an official (e.g., "Ref, that was a lousy call!"), whereas an interaction coded "I" indicates a positive verbal interaction between the coach and athlete(s) (e.g., "Beautiful catch!").

Lombardo Coaching Behavior Analysis System (LOCOBAS)

Identification _____ Page _____

01_____	21_____	41_____	61_____	81_____
02_____	22_____	42_____	62_____	82_____
03_____	23_____	43_____	63_____	83_____
04_____	24_____	44_____	64_____	84_____
05_____	25_____	45_____	65_____	85_____
06_____	26_____	46_____	66_____	86_____
07_____	27_____	47_____	67_____	87_____
08_____	28_____	48_____	68_____	88_____
09_____	29_____	49_____	69_____	89_____
10_____	30_____	50_____	70_____	90_____
11_____	31_____	51_____	71_____	91_____
12_____	32_____	52_____	72_____	92_____
13_____	33_____	53_____	73_____	93_____
14_____	34_____	54_____	74_____	94_____
15_____	35_____	55_____	75_____	95_____
16_____	36_____	56_____	76_____	96_____
17_____	37_____	57_____	77_____	97_____
18_____	38_____	58_____	78_____	98_____
19_____	39_____	59_____	79_____	99_____
20_____	40_____	60_____	80_____	100_____

Figure 32.1 Lombardo Coaching Behavior Analysis System (LOCOBAS) recording sheet.

If the interaction is nonverbal only, the coder uses the teen equivalent of the LOCOBAS category (i.e., 11, 12, 13), prescripted with the lead digit code indicating the person or group with whom the coach interacts. For example, a positive nonverbal interaction between the coach and officials is coded "311" (a thumbs-up signal to referee). If the coach stands with arms out and shrugs her shoulders, nonverbally trying to learn the referee's decision, then code "312" (neutral). If the coach waves his hand at the official in disgust, code "313" (negative). Whenever the coach is talking and demonstrating or gesturing at the same time, the observer simply codes the verbal symbol (i.e., two-digit number) and encircles it.

The final chore for the observer is to complete the variable data sheet, which provides descriptive information about the game setting. The observer should do this as soon as the data are made available to him or her. This may occur prior to, during, or after the observation period (Figure 32.2).

Lombardo Coaching Behavior Analysis System (LOCOBAS)

Time _____ Date _____ Day _____

Observer # _____ Observation # _____ N = ____ n = ____ N - n = ____

Coach	Team/athletes	Crowd
Age: ____ -25	**Sport:** ____ baseball	**Size:** ____ sparse
____ 26-34	____ softball	____ average
____ 35-44	____ basketball	____ large
____ 45+	____ soccer	**Involve-** ____ active
Race: ____ white	____ football	**ment:** ____ average
____ black	____ volleyball	____ passive
____ mixed		____ out of
____ other	**Organiza-** ____ Little League	control
Dress: ____ formal	**tion:** ____ youth sports	**Objectivity:** ____ good
____ informal	____ JHS	____ poor
Sex: ____ male	____ SHS	____ mixed
____ female	____ collegiate	**Home** ____ ahead in
Activity ____ active	**Race:** ____ white	**team** score
level: ____ average	____ black	**status:** through-
____ passive	____ mixed	out game
	____ other	
	Sex: ____ male	____ trailing
	____ female	most of
	____ coed	game
	Record: ____ winning	____ see-saw
	____ average	
	____ losing	
	Team _____	
	name: _____	

Comments:

Figure 32.2 Lombardo Coaching Behavior Analysis System (LOCOBAS) variable data sheet.

SUMMARIZING AND INTERPRETING THE DATA

The data are summarized by first tallying the frequencies for each of the individual categories of LOCOBAS (i.e., positive verbal, positive nonverbal, etc.). In this way, the total number of tallies for each specific category are obtained (e.g., frequency total for neutral, verbal interactions). After having determined the frequencies for each of the individual categories, the coder can easily obtain the total number of

Lombardo Coaching Behavior Analysis System (LOCOBAS)

N = Total behaviors   N = 673
n = Total noninteractive behaviors   n = 388
N - n = Total interactive behaviors   N - (Sum NonIA) = $673 - 388 = 285$

Observer # __1__ Observation # __35__ Date __3/27__ Day __Monday__ AM (PM)

LOCOBAS category	Frequency	Behaviors (%)	Interactive behaviors (%)
11 Player-positive, verbal	11	1.63	3.86
12 Player-neutral, verbal	101	15.01	35.44
13 Player-negative, verbal	6	0.89	2.11
111 Player-positive, nonverbal	11	1.63	3.86
112 Player-neutral, nonverbal	61	9.06	21.40
113 Player-negative, nonverbal	14	2.08	4.91
21 Coach-positive, verbal	6	0.89	2.11
22 Coach-neutral, verbal	18	2.67	6.32
23 Coach-negative, verbal	1	0.15	0.35
211 Coach-positive, nonverbal	13	1.93	4.56
212 Coach-neutral, nonverbal	17	2.53	5.96
213 Coach-negative, nonverbal	2	0.30	0.70
31 Officials-positive, verbal	—	—	—
32 Officials-neutral, verbal	6	0.89	2.11
33 Officials-negative, verbal	5	0.74	1.75
311 Officials-positive, nonverbal	—	—	—
312 Officials-neutral, nonverbal	6	0.89	2.11
313 Officials-negative, nonverbal	7	1.04	2.46
41 Others-positive, verbal	—	—	—
42 Others-neutral, verbal	—	—	—
43 Others-negative, verbal	—	—	—
411 Others-positive, nonverbal	—	—	—
412 Others-neutral, nonverbal	—	—	—
413 Others-negative, nonverbal	—	—	—
Individual behaviors	58	8.62	20.35
700 On-task behaviors	386	57.36	—
800 Off-task behaviors	2	0.30	—
Total noninteractive behaviors	388		

Figure 32.3 Completed Lombardo Coaching Behavior Analysis System (LOCOBAS) data summary sheet.

interactions for the observation period by summing all LOCOBAS categories. Next, each individual LOCOBAS category is divided by the total number of tallies recorded to obtain the percentage of occurrence for each interactive category (Figure 32.3).

Another set of parameters is obtained by examining only the interaction. This data set is obtained by subtracting the total of noninteractive coaching behaviors (on-task and off-task behaviors) from the total number of behaviors recorded in the observation period. The researcher compares each interactive category with the total number of interactive behaviors in the observation under consideration (the researcher may wish to analyze the interaction only, rather than the interaction and the noninteractive coaching behaviors).

Specifically, the data reveal percentage figures indicating the coach's

- verbal interaction, total;
- nonverbal interaction, total;
- positive, neutral, and negative interaction, verbal;
- positive, neutral, and negative interaction, nonverbal;
- interaction with individual athletes on his or her team;
- interaction with officials, fans, and others at the athletic event;
- interaction with his or her assistants;
- total noninteractive, on-task behavior;
- total noninteractive, off-task behavior; and
- total interaction versus noninteractive behavior.

The entire data set provides the researcher with a description of the climate of the athletic setting. Although the instrument is easy to use, the data indicate the level of encouragement, support, and process-oriented behavior manifested by the athletic leader. When analyzed in conjunction with the information gleaned from the variable data sheet, the data provide a clear, albeit limited, profile of the coach's behavior within the context of the competitive sporting event.

Chapter 33

Feedback Analysis Profile (FAP)

Gary D. Sinclair

The Feedback Analysis Profile (FAP) was developed as an awareness tool for the purpose of focusing the attention of beginning coaches on selected elements operating in any feedback or learning situation. Consequently, the completed profile creates a sensitivity toward this aspect of their instructional style and highlights any excessive tendencies that coaches may have developed while interacting with athletes.

Because effectiveness and efficiency of practice time are functions of the feedback process, coaches must be aware of the communication variables they are using during practice and, more importantly, why and how they are being used. It has become increasingly obvious to informed observers that Drucker (1969) was quite right when he stated, "There is a significant difference between efficiency—doing things right—and effectiveness—doing the right thing" (p. 19).

FAP provides a perceptual framework and cognitive organizer that focuses attention on what is occurring in the instructional setting. The data summaries cannot be considered to fully describe the instructional act, but they present a representative sampling and an overview of general tendencies or a behavioral style. As the success of any coaching effort is determined by the appropriateness of the communication relative to the situation and objectives sought, interpretation of the profile is essentially descriptive in nature.

CATEGORY DESCRIPTIONS

The FAP behavior categories (Figure 33.1) reflect what research says about the characteristics of effective communication and thus serve to bridge the gap between learning theory, instructional design, and successful teaching practice (Brophy & Good, 1978; Darst, Mancini, & Zakrajsek, 1983; Fishman & Tobey, 1978; Magill, 1985; Medley, 1979; Morgenegg, 1978; Siedentop, 1983). Coaches must concern themselves with whom they are directing their remarks, in what social setting (publicly or privately) these remarks are being made, and whether the remarks are positive or negative in character. They should be aware of the focus of their comments, that is, whether they are addressing the action or the behavior of the athlete and, if skill is the focus, whether they are centering on a correct or incorrect aspect of the performance. The specificity or generality of any comment is also a concern relative to its need to be on-task. The timing and the nature of the intent (e.g., evaluative, prescriptive) of any feedback influence the learning process. Ideally, the complete interaction procedure should be informative to the athlete.

Feedback Analysis Profile (FAP)

Name_____ Sport/activity_____ Game/practice level ____Sex___Age____

Direction		Focus			Character		On–task		Specific		Timing			Intent				Totals	
		Skill		Beh	+	–	Yes	No	Yes	No	Con	Ter	Del	Evl	Des	Pre	Aff		
		√	X																
Individual	Private																		
	Public																		
Group	Private																		
	Public																		
Team/ class																			
Totals																			

√ - Correct
X - Incorrect
Beh - Behavior
+ - Positive
– - Negative
Con - Concurrently

Ter - Terminal
Del - Delayed
Evl - Evaluative
Des - Descriptive
Pre - Prescriptive
Aff - Affective

Figure 33.1 Feedback Analysis Profile (FAP) recording sheet.

Direction

Is the feedback directed to an *individual*, an instructional *group* of individuals (squad, forwards, backs, etc.), or the whole *team*? When direction is established, it is noteworthy to determine whether the interaction occurred *privately* or *publicly* (i.e., could it be heard by all those in the vicinity?).

Focus

Is the feedback directed to the actual performance of the *skill* or to the athlete's *behavior*? If the feedback is directed to the skills, is a *correct* (✓) or *incorrect* (X) segment of the action referred to?

Character

Even though the feedback interaction is corrective in intent, does its nature reflect a *positive* or *negative* attitude toward the athlete?

On-Task

Did the feedback refer to the aspect of the action that was cued prior to its initiation (*yes* or *no*)? *Example:* If the coach comments on the leg and hip action of "sitting into the ball" during a golf swing after he or she told the athlete to concentrate on the left arm in the downswing, then the feedback is not on-task.

Specific

Did the feedback offer usable information specifically related to the task (*yes*), or was it a general uninformative comment (*no*), even though it was on-task?

Timing

The temporal location affects the use of the time between trials. Was the feedback delivered *concurrently* during the action or *terminally* (i.e., immediately upon conclusion of the action), or was it *delayed* for a period of time after the action was completed?

Intent

What was the intent of the feedback?

Evaluative.   Feedback that provides an assessment or value judgment of the success of the action in terms of the goal set. *Examples:* "That's better." "Not so good." "Good—a '7' on the rating scale."

Descriptive.   Feedback that informs the athlete of what was done with no accompanying value judgment—the problem-solving approach.

Prescriptive.   Feedback that identifies the changes in performance that are necessary for improved results.

Affective.   Feedback that has the sole purpose of motivating the athlete to encourage persistence at the task or to reinforce a correct action.

RECORDING PROCEDURES

As a coach responds to an athlete's performance, the observer codes each feedback episode to reflect the presence or absence of the characteristics defined. For example, the following feedback episode, "Hey, Johnny! That swing needs improvement. Adjust your racket face angle," is described as "individual, public, error focused (x), positively delivered (+), on-task but general, terminal, evaluative, and prescriptive," and would be recorded/coded as a "1" in the category in the "Individual, Public" row.

SUMMARIZING AND INTERPRETING THE DATA

The summary of the feedback monitoring period presented in Figure 33.2 reveals that eight feedback episodes in total were recorded.

- Direction: Of these eight, seven (or 88%) were directed to an individual, and in 72% of the episodes they were delivered publicly. Only one of the eight (12%) was group oriented, and it, too, was a public announcement. Thus 75% (six of eight) of the individual feedback comments were shared with the entire team/class.
- Focus: Six of the eight (75%) comments were skill-execution oriented and 100% were error centered. The remaining two feedback statements referred to a behavior element.
- Character: Seven of the eight (88%) episodes were negative.
- On-Task: Six (75%) of the feedback statements were not on-task.
- Specific: Five (63%) comments were general or uninformative.
- Timing: Seven (88%) were delivered after the task was completed.
- Intent: Seven (88%) of the feedback statements were evaluative, with only one (12%) offering any prescriptive information.

The example describes a time period in which the vast majority of feedback episodes (88%) were delivered to the athletes publicly. The main focus was upon skill or proficiency of performance (75%), with all comments being error oriented. Only 33% of the comments were on-task and

Feedback Analysis Profile (FAP)

Name_____ Sport/activity _Track_ Game/practice level _Univ._ Sex _F_ Age _18-21_

Direction		Focus			Character		On–task		Specific		Timing			Intent				Totals		
		Skill		Beh	+	–	Yes	No	Yes	No	Con	Ter	Del	Evl	Des	Pre	Aff			
		√	X																	
Individual	Private	7	8		7	8	7	8	7	8		78		78					2	7	
	Public	1 2 3 4	6		1 2 3 4 6		1 2 3 4 6	6	1 2 3 4	4 6	3	1 2 3 4 6		1 2 3 4 6					5 73%	88%	8
Group	Private																		0	1	
	Public	5			5		5		5			5					5		1	12%	
	Team/class																				
Totals		0 6 6 75%	2	1	7 88%	2	6 75%	3	5 63%	1	7 88%	0	7 87%	0	1 12%	0				
		8		8		8		8		8			8								

√ - Correct
X - Incorrect
Beh - Behavior
+ - Positive
– - Negative
Con - Concurrently

Ter - Terminal
Del - Delayed
Evl - Evaluative
Des - Descriptive
Pre - Prescriptive
Aff - Affective

Figure 33.2 Completed Feedback Analysis Profile (FAP) summary sheet for eight episodes.

63% were general in nature. Eighty-eight percent of the time the intent was evaluative only (i.e., of little informative value), and all comments were negative in tone. Such an interactive experience does not produce the rapid progression in learning that coaches should be striving for.

The performance reveals some potential danger points if this profile actually becomes the style of a developing coach/teacher. This person not only has a tendency to share his or her thoughts with everyone in the vicinity, but also focuses upon errors and communicates in a predominantly negative manner. To complicate matters further, the majority of the feedback comments were off-task, general, and evaluative in nature. Unfortunately, an informative and encouraging atmosphere is not being created here.

Further, it would not be surprising if the athletes' morale and productivity in the practice environment or the workplace decreased. To be aware of such a profile would help beginning as well as experienced coaches alter their styles for the benefit of the athletes and/or the team. Effective instruction is dependent upon meaningful communication. Consequently, coaches should regularly monitor and assess their information feedback skills for excessive tendencies and/or trends. This process enables coaches to make a sound analysis of where they are in relation to where they want to be in their coaching styles. Coaches are thus able to make effective decisions relating to needed modifications in certain aspects of a performance. Consequently, it is suggested that a multiple baseline summary graph (MBSG) of selected elements of the FAP be constructed to vividly portray dominant communication tendencies (Figure 33.3). Then, definite plans can be made to restructure the feedback situation to produce conditions that foster effective learning and positive attitudes.

As an example, selected elements from the FAP (Figure 33.2) are arbitrarily chosen as the focus for modification over a series of six coaching sessions. The coach being monitored decides that it is necessary to decrease the focus on errors and increase the number of reactions to correct aspects of performance. The negative character of feedback comments must be decreased and the prescriptive (information content) element must be introduced. In addition, this prescriptive focus should be phrased such that the comments are on-task and specific to the task.

Coaches must be aware of what they are or are not doing in the instructional setting. They should have a thorough understanding of the conditions of feedback inherent to their sport to train, evaluate, and control the quality of the athlete's performance. Consequently, a systematic observation instrument like FAP creates an awareness of the coaches' instructional styles. As such, an instrument such as FAP highlights any excessive tendencies that coaches may have developed in their interaction with athletes. Interpretation of a feedback profile is based upon a knowledge of the purpose and goals of the situation being monitored and recorded. The coach's behavior should reflect the components regarded as necessary to the learning process (e.g., specific, on-task, informative, etc.) while being sensitive to the needs of each situation. It is not intended that a stereotyped feedback behavior style be developed, but rather, within the framework of an informative interaction, feedback behavior be delivered specific to the needs of the situation.

Beginning coaches should concentrate on making specific, on-task, prescriptive comments in a positive tone and reinforcing correct actions,

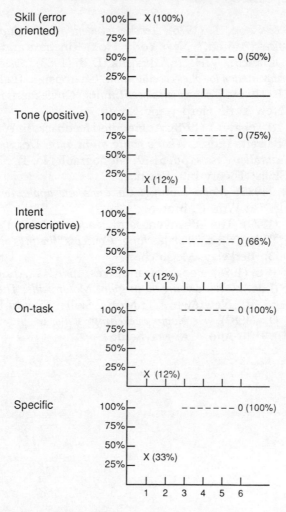

Figure 33.3   Feedback Analysis Profile (FAP) multiple baseline summary graph of selected feedback categories.

as well as correcting errors. Realistic improvement goals or targets should be set for future sessions. Completing the MBSG daily will facilitate this process. As each successive coaching session is monitored and recorded, beginning coaches should get better at interpreting the probable impact of their coaching efforts.

FAP has been used with the Canadian Ski Coaches Federation and British Columbia Judo and Synchronized Swimming teams.

REFERENCES

Brophy, J., & Good, T. (1978). *Teacher-student relationships: Causes and consequences* (2nd ed.). New York: Holt, Rinehart and Winston.

Darst, P.W., Mancini, V.H., & Zakrajsek, D.B. (1983). *Systematic observation instrumentation for physical education*. Champaign, IL: Leisure Press.

Drucker, P.F. (1969). *The age of discontinuity: Guidelines to our changing society*. New York: Harper and Row.

Fishman, S., & Tobey, C. (1978). Augmented feedback. In W.G. Anderson & G.T. Barrette (Eds.), *What's going on in gym: Descriptive studies of physical education classes* (pp. 51-62, Monograph No. 1), Newtown, CT: Motor Skills: Theory Into Practice.

Magill, R.A. (1985). *Motor learning: Concepts and applications* (2nd ed.). Dubuque, IA: Wm. C. Brown.

Medley, D. (1979). The effectiveness of teachers. In P. Peterson & H. Walberg (Eds.), *Research on teaching: Concepts, findings and implications* (pp. 26-43). Berkeley: McCutchan.

Morgenegg, B.L. (1978). Pedagogical moves. In W.G. Anderson & G.T. Barrette (Eds.), *What's going on in gym. Motor skills: Theory into practice* (pp. 63-74). Newtown, CT: Motor Skills: Theory Into Practice.

Siedentop, D. (1983). *Developing teaching skills in physical education* (2nd ed.). Palo Alto, CA: Mayfield.

Chapter 34

The Arizona State University Observation Instrument (ASUOI)

Alan C. Lacy
Paul W. Darst

The Arizona State University Observation Instrument (ASUOI) was originally designed for collecting information on the behaviors of coaches in practice settings, but it can also be used for observing teachers in the physical education environment. The rationale for the ASUOI has its origins in a number of studies completed from 1976 to 1983. The evolution of this instrument began with an investigation of the behaviors of John Wooden, basketball coach at UCLA, for 15 sessions during the 1974-75 season. Tharp and Gallimore (1976) devised a 10-category system to observe Wooden. Among the most interesting findings was that 50.3% of his behaviors fell into the instruction category, and an additional 8% were in the category of scold/reinstruction. Langsdorf (1979) developed a modified version of the Tharp and Gallimore instrument to objectively observe the behaviors of Frank Kush, then head football coach at Arizona State University, during 18 spring football workouts. Results of the study showed that 36% of all behaviors were in the instruction category, and an additional 12% were in the scold/reinstruction category.

Dodds and Rife (1981) completed a descriptive-analytic study on a highly successful women's field hockey coach using an instrument based on the work of Tharp and Gallimore. The instruction and criticism/cue categories accounted for 51% of the total observed behaviors. Lacy and Darst (1985) used an 11-category instrument based on the Langsdorf instrument to research the behaviors of a group of 10 winning high school head football coaches and reported 42.5% of the group's behaviors were in the instruction category. Model (1983) completed a similar study on 6 losing high school football coaches and found that 54.8% of the behaviors exhibited were in the instruction category.

Though various researchers have had slight variations in the behavior categories observed, it becomes clear that behaviors of an instructional nature represent a dominant percentage of observed behaviors. Because informative statements concerning the skills and strategies of the particular sport are crucial to effective teaching in the athletic environment, the ASUOI has expanded and modified several behavior categories to create a more sensitive tool capable of collecting more specific data on coaching behaviors.

This instrument is characteristic of the criteria identified to satisfy requirements of both face and content validity. Because the ASUOI categories are specifically defined and obviously related to coaching behaviors, face validity is apparent. Because a rational basis exists for the selection of the behavior categories and these behaviors are representative of coaching behavior as supported by previous research, the instrument also possesses content validity. Interobserver reliability was established using both event and interval recording procedures. The percentage of agreement exceeded the 85% criterion level in all behavior categories as well as in the total number of behaviors observed.

CATEGORY DESCRIPTIONS

The ASUOI represents a refined observational tool based on the instruments and findings of the previously discussed research. The instruction category has been subdivided to provide more insight into this critical aspect of teaching/coaching behavior. These subcategories are preinstruction, concurrent instruction, postinstruction, questioning, and physical assistance. In total, there are 14 behavior categories, 7 of which are directly related to the instructional process. The ASUOI also includes a bi-level coding format in the behavior categories of praise, scold, and hustle. These categories are divided into high-intensity or regular/high-intensity behaviors. Because nonverbal praise and nonverbal scold are difficult to observe and code accurately in live recording situations, the nonverbal and verbal categories of these two behaviors have been combined. If video playback is available, then the categories may be separated.

Use of First Name (1)

Using the first name or nickname when speaking directly to a player. *Examples:* "Nice pass, Bill!" "Tank, that was poor form on that tackle."

Preinstruction (2)

Initial information given to player(s) preceding the desired action to be executed. It explains how to execute a skill, play, strategy, and so forth associated with the sport.

Concurrent Instruction (3)

Cues or reminders given during the actual execution of the skill or play.

Postinstruction (4)

Correction, reexplanation, or instructional feedback given after the execution of the skill or play.

Questioning (5)

Any question to player(s) concerning strategies, techniques, assignments, and so forth associated with the sport. *Examples:* ''Who do you block on 44 dive?'' ''What is the proper grip on the backhand?''

Physical Assistance (6)

Physically moving the player's body to the proper position or through the correct range of motion of a skill. *Examples:* Guiding the player's arm through the movement of a forehand in racquetball or aligning a golfer's stance for a correct swing.

Positive Modeling (7)

A demonstration of correct performance of a skill or playing technique.

Negative Modeling (8)

A demonstration of incorrect performance of a skill or playing technique.

Hustle (9)

Verbal statements intended to intensify the efforts of the player(s). *Examples:* ''Run it out, run it out.'' ''Push yourself, push yourself.''

Praise (10)

Verbal or nonverbal compliments, statements, or signs of acceptance. *Examples:* ''Good effort on defense.'' Smiles. Thumbs-up sign. Pat on the back.

Scold (11)

Verbal or nonverbal behaviors of displeasure. *Examples:* ''That was a terrible effort.'' Scowling. Kicking the ground. Throwing a clipboard.

Management (12)

Verbal statements related to organizational details of practice sessions not referring to strategies or fundamentals of the sport. *Examples:* "Make five lines facing me on the sideline." "Put the basketballs in the ball bag."

Uncodable (13)

Any behavior that cannot be seen or heard or does not fit into the above categories. *Examples:* Checking injuries, joking with players, being absent from practice setting, or talking with bystanders.

Silence (14)

(Used only with interval recording.) Periods of time when the subject is not talking. *Examples:* Players are warming up or running sprints, player is talking, or coach is monitoring activities.

RECORDING PROCEDURES

Event recording is one method of collecting data on coaching behaviors with the ASUOI. Event recording involves placing a tally mark on the coding form (Figure 34.1) each time one of the predefined behavior categories is observed. This procedure results in a cumulative record of discrete events occurring during the observation period.

If the observed behavior is one of the three bi-level categories (hustle, praise, scold), then a circle should be made around the tally mark if the behavior is considered to be of high intensity. If the observer is not concerned with discriminating between high- and regular/low-intensity behaviors, this option is eliminated.

Observations are made for the entire practice session or for predetermined times in the workout with rest periods between data collections (e.g., 10 minutes coding, 2 minutes rest, 10 minutes coding, 2 minutes rest). A stopwatch is used to record the observation time to the nearest 30 seconds on the observation tally sheet so that rate per minute (RPM) can be calculated. RPM is calculated by dividing the number of behaviors by the minutes observed. If 30 Hustles were coded during 60 minutes of observation, then the RPM for the hustle category would be .50. The RPM for each behavior category, as well as the RPM for total behaviors during the entire observation period, should be calculated.

Interval recording is another method that is used with the ASUOI. When using this procedure, the observer must characterize each 5-second time interval with one of the predefined behavior categories. The behavior

Arizona State University Observation Instrument (ASUOI)

Date __11-15__ Coach __Darst__ Sport __Basketball__ Observer __Lacy__

Categories	Time _____	Time _____	Total	RPM	Percentage
Use of first name	╫╫ ╫╫ ╫╫ ⦀⦀	╫╫ ╫╫ ╫╫ ⦀	30	1.5	15.5
Preinstruction	╫╫	⦀⦀	7	.35	3.6
Concurrent instruction	⦀⦀⦀	⦀	4	.2	2.1
Postinstruction	╫╫ ╫╫ ╫╫ ╫╫ ╫╫ ╫╫ ╫╫ ⦀⦀	╫╫ ╫╫ ╫╫ ╫╫ ╫╫ ╫╫ ╫╫ ╫╫	81	4.05	41.2
Questioning	⦀⦀⦀⦀	⦀⦀	6	.3	3.1
Physical assistance	⦀⦀		2	.1	1.0
Positive modeling	⦀⦀⦀	⦀⦀⦀⦀	7	.35	3.6
Negative modeling	⦀⦀	⦀	3	.15	1.5
Hustle	╫╫ ╫╫	╫╫ ⦀⦀⦀	18	.9	9.3
Praise	⦀⦀⦀⦀	╫╫ ⦀	10	.5	5.2
Scold	⦀⦀⦀	⦀⦀⦀⦀	7	.35	3.6
Management	╫╫ ╫╫ ╫╫ ╫╫ ╫╫ ⦀⦀	╫╫ ╫╫ ╫╫ ⦀⦀⦀⦀	46	2.3	23.7
Uncodable	⦀⦀	⦀	3	.15	1.5
Total	102	92	194	9.7	

Comments __Preseason Practice - 20 minutes total observation__

Figure 34.1 Completed Arizona State University Observation Instrument (ASUOI) event recording sheet.

category that dominates a particular interval is coded on the interval observation sheet (Figure 34.2). The silence category is added for use in the interval recording procedures.

Using the numbers assigned to the behavior categories, the observer codes the appropriate number on the coding sheet for each interval. Behaviors are coded in a vertical direction on the coding sheet for each 5-second interval. The numbers representing hustle, praise, and scold can be circled to indicate a high-intensity level, if desired. The use of first

Arizona State University Observation Instrument (ASUOI)

12	14	14	7	4	13	4	14	10	1/12	4	3	14	5	14	5	14	14		
12	14	14	12	4	13	10	14	1/10	11	4	14	14	14	14	14	14	14		
12	14	14	12	6	12	14	14	14	9	6	14	14	14	14	4	11	14		
13	14	14	11	4	12	14	14	14	2	4	1/3	14	4	13	4	4			
12	14	1/3	1/3	7	12	1/10	14	14	2	5	4	14	4	14	10	4			
12	3	5	4	14	12	9	14	14	14	14	4	12	14	14	4	4			
1/5	4	14	6	14	2	9	14	14	14	14	5	12	14	14	14	14			
2	4	14	4	14	2	6	14	Rest	14	5	14	12	1/9	14	14	14			
2	14	4	4	14	2	7	14	1/10	14	14	14	12	14	1/2	14	10			
2	14	4	14	14	14	7	14	14	14	10	9	14	14	2	14	4			
7	14	4	14	14	14	3	1/3	14	14	14	4	1/4	14	14	14	4			
2	1/10	9	14	14	14	4	14	12	14	14	7	4	1/6	3	14	14			
7	9	7	14	14	1/11	4	14	12	1/4	14	14	8	4	14	1/10	14			
1/5	10	8	14	14	4	14	14	12	1/4	14	14	7	4	4	14	14			

Coach _Claxton_   Date _4-15_   Observer _Lacy_

School _Grand Canyon H.S._   Sport _Tennis (varsity boys)_

Comments _Record (10 min.) - Rest (2 min.) - Record (10 min.)_
Mid-Season - Day after match.

Behavior codes

1. Use of first name
2. Preinstruction
3. Concurrent instruction
4. Postinstruction
5. Questioning

6. Physical assistance
7. Positive modeling
8. Negative modeling
9. Hustle
10. Praise

11. Scold
12. Management
13. Uncodable
14. Silence

Figure 34.2 Completed Arizona State University Observation Instrument (ASUOI) interval recording sheet.

name category (coded as 1) should be coded in the same space as the independent behavior it accompanies. For example, praise used in conjunction with use of first name would be coded as 1/10. For accurate coding, the observer should memorize the numbers for each behavior category.

There are several factors to consider in choosing either event or interval recording procedures. Event recording is simpler to learn and use and generally enables the observer to record for longer periods of time. However, for an accurate analysis, both RPM and percentage of behaviors must be calculated and considered. There is also no information provided concerning the length of a particular behavioral episode. For instance, it may take the coach 60 seconds to organize a drill, but it would be coded with one tally mark in the management category on the observation sheet.

In contrast, when using interval recording, the observer can analyze the length of a particular behavior. If the coach takes 60 seconds to organize a drill, this management behavior would be coded in 12 consecutive 5-second intervals. Periods of silence can be coded as well. This information is not available with event recording procedures. Accurate interval recording requires more practice and more concentration on the part of the observer. Observations are usually made for shorter periods of time interspersed with rest periods. If care is taken to observe representative portions of the workout, the data collected are an accurate appraisal of coaching behaviors. The percentage of intervals is calculated, and, because the intervals that are observed represent time, it is not necessary to calculate RPM.

SUMMARIZING AND INTERPRETING THE DATA

Whether event or interval recording is used, the data derived from the ASUOI provides quantitative information concerning behaviors exhibited during the observation period. It is important to realize that no qualitative judgment is made concerning the coded behaviors. A high rate of instructional behaviors does not guarantee that the instructions given were of value.

When using event recording, the observer should also calculate the percentage of occurrence for each behavior category. Langsdorf (1979) pointed out that use of first name is not independent in that it must be used in combination with another behavior. By including the instances of first name occurrence in the calculation of percentages of independent behavior, the coder decreases the percentages of all other behaviors and distorts their values. Thus, to calculate percentages, the total of each behavior category should be divided by the total number of independent behaviors, *excluding* the use of first name category.

If 25 praises were coded out of a total of 200 independent behaviors, then 12.5% of all behaviors were in the praise category. By dividing the number of use of first name occurrences by the total number of independent behaviors, the percentage that use of first name accompanied an independent behavior can be calculated. If 50 use of first name behaviors were coded with 200 total independent behaviors, then 25% of all independent behaviors were accompanied by the use of first name.

Indications of both frequency and duration of behaviors are available with interval recording. The number of intervals for each behavior indicates frequency, and the number of intervals consecutively recorded for a particular category indicates the duration of that behavior. Major sequences of behaviors can be determined by using a matrix system following the guidelines of the Flanders' Interaction Analysis System (Flanders, 1970).

The percentage of intervals should be calculated for each independent behavior category. The first step in this process is to count the number of intervals in which each behavior has been coded on the interval recording coding sheet and transfer this information to the appropriate space on the interval recording worksheet (Figure 34.3). Next, divide the number of intervals coded for each independent behavior by the total number of intervals observed. This number represents the percentage of intervals that each independent behavior category was observed. Although this is not an exact measure, it gives a general appraisal of the time devoted to each behavior category. Percentage of intervals accompanied by use of first name can also be calculated.

Because research of coaching behaviors is relatively new, there are a number of possibilities for future study. Most completed research using the behavior categories in the ASUOI has concentrated on winning coaches of team sports. Claxton (1985) has used the ASUOI to study high school tennis coaches, but this is only the starting point to understand-

Arizona State University Observation Instrument (ASUOI)

Categories	Number of intervals	Percentage of intervals
1. Use of first name	18	7.5
2. Preinstruction	11	4.6
3. Concurrent instruction	8	3.3
4. Postinstruction	34	14.2
5. Questioning	8	3.3
6. Physical assistance	4	1.7
7. Positive modeling	8	3.3
8. Negative modeling	2	0.8
9. Hustle	8	3.3
10. Praise	12	5.0
11. Scold	8	3.3
12. Management	19	7.9
13. Uncodable	4	1.7
14. Silence	114	47.5
Total	240	100

Figure 34.3 Completed Arizona State University Observation Instrument (ASUOI) recording worksheet.

ing coaching behavior in the many individual sports. Studies involving different sports with different age groups, particularly younger ages, would add to the data base of coaching behaviors. Behavioral studies on less successful coaches could also be beneficial. Research on the behaviors of male and female subjects coaching the same sport might provide interesting insights. With more females participating in sports, it would be appropriate to compare the behaviors of coaches as they worked with male and female athletes. Descriptive-analytic as well as intervention research is a possibility with the ASUOI.

The practitioner can also use the ASUOI to provide information for self-evaluation of coaching behaviors. The coach can determine if behavioral tendencies remain consistent during various phases of the season (e.g., preseason, regular season, play-offs), after winning and losing games, during different parts of the practice session, or from season to season. Two areas of particular interest should be the praise-to-scold ratio and the amounts of time spent in managerial activities.

Though the ASUOI has been associated with the study of behaviors in the coaching environment, it also can be used effectively for studying teaching in physical education classes. The use of systematic observation instrumentation such as the ASUOI is crucial for continuing to enhance the knowledge base concerning effective teaching-learning strategies in competitive sports and physical education.

REFERENCES

Claxton, D.B. (1985). *A behavioral analysis of more and less successful high school tennis coaches*. Unpublished doctoral dissertation, Arizona State University, Tempe.

Dodds, P., & Rife, F. (1981). *A descriptive-analytic study of the practice field behavior of a winning female coach*. Unpublished manuscript, University of Massachusetts, Amherst.

Flanders, N.A. (1970). *Analyzing teaching behavior*. Reading, MA: Addison-Wesley.

Lacy, A.C., & Darst, P.W. (1985). Systematic observation of behaviors of winning high school head football coaches. *Journal of Teaching in Physical Education*, 4(4), 256-270.

Langsdorf, E.V. (1979). *A systematic observation of football coaching behavior in a major university environment*. Unpublished doctoral dissertation, Arizona State University, Tempe.

Model, R.L. (1983). *Coaching behaviors of non-winning high school football coaches in Arizona*. Unpublished doctoral dissertation, Arizona State University, Tempe.

Tharp, R.G., & Gallimore, R. (1976, January). What a coach can teach a teacher. *Psychology Today*, pp. 75-78.

Chapter 35

Coaching Behaviors Observational Recording System (CBORS)

Deborah Tannehill
Damon Burton

The Coaching Behaviors Observational Recording System (CBORS) is a multidimensional behavioral observation instrument suitable for use in lab or field settings. CBORS was modified from Stewart's (1980) Observational Recording Record of Physical Educators' Teaching Behavior (ORRPETB, chapter 23) specifically to assess coaching behaviors of youth basketball coaches. The multidimensional nature of CBORS is designed to identify the (a) coaching climate, (b) type of interaction, and (c) specific coaching behaviors typically used by coaches in practice and game situations. The four coaching climates, four types of interactions, and six categories of coaching behaviors comprising this instrument are clearly defined and differentiated. With systematic training, observers can be taught to collect reliable and valid data that provide a behavioral profile of coaches. Although CBORS was originally developed to assess coaching behaviors of youth basketball coaches, it should be equally valid for assessing coaching behaviors in all sports.

The development of CBORS was prompted by the need to find a behavioral observation instrument that could be used to evaluate the effectiveness of the American Coaching Effectiveness Program (ACEP) Level 1 coaches' education program in enhancing key coaching behaviors of youth basketball coaches. An evaluation of existing behavioral instruments concluded that Stewart's ORRPETB came closest to meeting the needs of this type of investigation, although extensive modifications were necessary to meet all the requirements of this study. Specifically, the ORRPETB was modified by (a) eliminating interactional categories for males and females while adding a category for no interaction and (b) modifying the coaching behavior category extensively. ORRPETB's 15 original categories of coaching behaviors were reduced to 6 by eliminating 4 categories, combining 6 others, and adding 1 additional category.

Moreover, subcategories for modeling, skill feedback, and social behavior were modified extensively.

A comprehensive 24- to 30-hour observer training program was developed to ensure high interobserver reliability through a multistage process that included (a) systematic study of a training manual; (b) group instruction of a CBORS training videotape that provided actual demonstrations of climate, interaction, and coaching behavior categories in a basketball setting; (c) written tests in which trainees were required to define CBORS categories and score behavioral examples; (d) the scoring of six videotapes of actual youth sport basketball practices and games; and (e) extensive practice in the use of CBORS in actual field settings.

Interobserver reliability was computed separately for climate, interaction, and coaching behaviors using Equation 3.1. CBORS proved to have high levels of reliability in all three behavioral categories, demonstrating interobserver reliability levels in excess of 90% for over 5,600 behaviors.

A potential source of error in using CBORS is the observer's expectations about what will be observed. Biases and expectations can cause observers to selectively attend to certain elements and to erroneously disregard other behaviors that are not consistent with their expectations.

CATEGORY DESCRIPTIONS

CBORS records 4 athlete behaviors (climates), 4 coach-athlete behaviors (interactions), and 19 coaching behaviors organized into 6 major categories. Such a multidimensional approach to behavioral observation not only allows the researcher to assess the specific number of times different coaching behaviors are used, but also provides information on (a) how practice time is allocated between instruction, practice, management, and waiting; and (b) whether coaching behaviors are addressed toward individuals, small groups, or the entire team (see Table 35.1).

Climates

Behavioral climates assess athlete behaviors by describing how athletes spend their time during practice and games.

Instructional Time (I)

The period of time during practice/competition when, theoretically, the opportunity to learn is present. Players can receive information either verbally or nonverbally. Also, during this time, 51% or more of the players are not engaged in physical activity. *Examples:* Players listen to a description of a new skill or strategy, watch the coach or another player model a skill, watch a film, participate in a team discussion, or answer a question.

Table 35.1   Coaching Behaviors Observational Recording System (CBORS)

Climate
I   Instructional time
M   Management time
P   Practice time
W   Waiting time

Interaction
I   Individual
G   Group
T   Team
N   No interaction

Coaching behaviors
1. Instructional behaviors
   L   Lecturing
   Q   Questioning
   MO   Monitoring

2. Modeling behaviors
   M+   Positive modeling
   M−   Negative modeling

3. Skill feedback behaviors
   SF+   Specific positive skill feedback
   GF+   General positive skill feedback
   SF−   Specific negative skill feedback
   GF−   General negative skill feedback
   CF+/CF−   Corrective skill feedback plus positive/negative feedback

4. Encouragement behaviors
   E   Encouragement
   H   Hustling

5. Social behaviors
   PR   Praise
   C   Criticism
   PU   Punishment

6. Noninstructional behaviors
   MG   Managing
   ND   Nondirected
   CA   Coach absent

Management Time (M)

The period of time during practice/competition when, theoretically, the opportunity to learn is not present. During this time, 51% or more of the players are involved in activities that are only indirectly related to the sport involved. Management time occurs when there is no instruction, demonstration, practice, or performance of skills. *Examples:* Players change drills or activities, participate in warm-up activities prior to formal practice, listen to travel plans or specifics on the upcoming game or practice, or put up or take down equipment.

Practice Time (P)

The period of time in practice/competition when 51% or more of the players are involved in actual physical movement in a manner that is consistent with specific practice/competition objectives. *Examples:* They may be engaged in performing drills, participating in a scrimmage/game, or actively involved in performance of strategy recognition or adjustment drills. Any basketball-specific drills used for the warm-up such as shooting lay-ups, offensive cutting and screening drills, defensive sliding drills, and dribbling drills are coded as practice time.

Waiting Time (W)

The period of time in practice/competition when 51% or more of the players are prohibited from being classified in other practice/competition climates. In other words, they are not involved in instruction, practice, or management behaviors. *Examples:* They are waiting for practice/competition to begin; waiting for practice/competition to resume after it has been interrupted by another coach, team manager, parent, referee, or player; or waiting for some type of equipment repair to be completed.

Interactions

Behavioral interaction refers to situations in which the coach initiates verbal or nonverbal communication with a player or group of players or responds verbally or nonverbally to a player's behavior.

Individual (I)

The coach talks or responds nonverbally to a single player. The coach must (a) communicate with the player one on one; (b) specifically pull the player aside during drills, a scrimmage, or a game; or (c) use the player's name. *Example:* ''Great shot, Mike!''

Group (G)

The coach talks or responds nonverbally to more than one player but less than half of the team.

Team (T)

The coach responds verbally or nonverbally to more than one-half of the team. Team interaction is assumed unless the coach is clearly talking to a single individual or a specific group.

No Interaction (N)

No interaction is occurring verbally or nonverbally. *Example:* The coach just monitors the athletes during a scrimmage or game.

Coaching Behaviors

CBORS divides coaching behaviors into six major categories. Each major coaching behavior category is further subdivided into appropriate subcategories.

Instructional Behaviors

Verbal and nonverbal coaching behaviors used to teach players how to perform new skills, strategies, or plays or to provide further instruction for the refinement of existing skills, strategies, or plays.

Lecturing (L). Coach provides verbal statements about what to do or how to do it, the strategy involved in a specific play, or general rules that must be observed during play. The coach may be lecturing or orienting one or more players who may or may not be engaged in activity during this time. If the coach simultaneously lectures and models correct or incorrect behavior, the behavior is modeling not lecturing.

Questioning (Q). Coach asks a player or group of players questions about a skill, procedure, or strategy with the intent of eliciting a verbal or non-verbal response. Players may or may not be engaged in activity during this time. In addition, a coach may listen to players' responses to his or her questions and listen to players' questions about execution of a skill, procedure, strategy, or tactic and respond with an appropriate answer. *Examples:* "Where is your position in setting up this play?" "Can anyone show me the play we have been working on?"

Monitoring (MO). Coach observes practice without reacting verbally or nonverbally to the behaviors of his or her players. That is, the coach is neither being addressed by a player or a group of players nor talking to them. The coach could be standing in one place or walking around the practice area, but maintaining eye contact with the players is necessary.

All action behaviors should be given higher coding priority than monitoring during observation periods. Thus, if a coach monitors for 4 seconds, and then says, "Great shot, Tom!" during the remaining second of the observation period, general positive skill feedback should be coded instead of monitoring. *Examples:* Coach ignores a very noticeable mistake on the part of a player or team or watches a film with the team.

Modeling Behaviors

A skill demonstration by player or coach designed to show the correct or incorrect way to perform a skill or play. If verbal instruction accompanies modeling, the behavior should be coded as modeling, not lecturing. Corrective skill feedback that is provided nonverbally via modeling without verbal instructions should be coded as positive or negative modeling.

Positive Modeling (M+).   The coach or player demonstrates the correct way to perform a skill or play. *Examples:* Coach or player demonstrates a lay-up shot, rebound block-out technique, or correct defensive position.

Negative Modeling (M−).   The coach or player demonstrates the incorrect way to perform a skill or play. *Examples:* He or she demonstrates incorrect follow-through on a jump shot, a poor cut on an offensive play, or a poorly executed pass.

There are situations when modeling may include multiple modeling behaviors in a sequence such as a correct demonstration, followed by what was done incorrectly, and finally a correct demonstration again. Regardless of how many behaviors are modeled in the sequence, each modeled behavior in the sequence should be recorded separately in order of occurrence (e.g., M+ −, M− +, M+ − +).

Skill Feedback Behaviors

Any information, either verbal or nonverbal, that the coach makes available to his or her players to improve the next behavioral response. Positive or negative gestures are considered skill feedback, whereas actual modeling of correct or incorrect behavior is considered modeling. It is very important that feedback behaviors be limited to skill attempts and not be used for social behaviors.

Specific Positive Skill Feedback (SF+).   Verbal praise that occurs during or following a specific skill attempt. *Examples:* "Yes, you followed through well on that shot!" "Good, that was a more aggressive move!"

General Positive Skill Feedback (GF+).   Verbal or nonverbal praise that occurs during or following a general skill attempt. *Examples:* "Yes! "Great!" "At-a-girl!" A wink. A nod. A friendly pat on the back.

Specific Negative Skill Feedback (SF−).   Verbal scolding that occurs during or following a specific skill attempt. *Examples:* "Come on, you shot without looking at the basket!" "Terrible! You took your eye off your man."

General Negative Skill Feedback (GF−).   Verbal or nonverbal scolding that occurs during or following a general skill attempt. *Examples:* "You can do better than that! We are supposed to be a team." A frown. Shaking the head. Throwing up the arms.

Corrective Skill Feedback Plus Positive/Negative Skill Feedback (CF+/CF−).   Corrective information given during or following a skill attempt that may be accompanied by a positive or negative statement or gesture. (Corrective verbal feedback that includes modeling is coded "CF+" or "CF−" and not "modeling.") *Examples:* "Fantastic! Now follow through more with your wrist next time." A wink. "A little more backspin and you'll have it."

Encouragement Behaviors

Statements coaches make to their players to encourage increased effort or performance. Encouragement behaviors may be general in nature or specifically designed to encourage hustle.

Encouragement (E).   Noncontingent use of verbal or nonverbal behaviors to motivate maintenance or improvement of skilled performance. Encouragement refers to efforts to motivate enhanced skilled performance rather than increased effort, and encouragement also relates to hopes for future performance not directly related to previous mistakes, skill attempts, and so forth. *Examples:* "Come on, team, let's get a basket!" "That's the way to go, gang, keep up the good work!"

Hustling (H).   Verbal statements or gestures to activate or intensify previously directed behavior. Tone of voice and enthusiasm level are extremely important in this category. These are motivating statements and gestures, and caution should be taken not to mistake them for one of the skill feedback categories. *Examples:* "Work harder! You can play good defense if you work at it." "Hustle! Dive for that loose ball."

Social Behaviors

The coach reacts verbally or nonverbally to the social behavior of a player or team.

Praise (PR).   Positive or supportive statements or gestures made by the coach during or following a social behavioral episode. *Examples:* "Good!

Everyone is ready to listen to directions for the next drill!'' "Great, Tom! You are here on time!'' (with a pat on the back).

Criticism (C). Coach verbally or nonverbally scolds a player or team in a high- or low-intensity manner for undesirable social behavior. *Examples:* "Leave the ball alone until I finish giving instructions.'' Physically pushing or grabbing a player and moving him or her back in line.

Punishment (PU). Specific penalties imposed on those players who break team or practice rules. *Examples:* Coach administers a time-out for horseplay during practice, has a player run laps or do push-ups, or waves the arms around in disgust as he or she verbally reprimands a player for misbehavior.

Noninstructional Behaviors

Behaviors that are unrelated to improvement of player or team performance.

Managing (MG). Practice-related coaching behaviors that don't contribute directly to achievement of practice/game objectives. The players may or may not be involved in activity during this time. *Examples:* The coach is sweeping the court, moving equipment to another area for the next drill, retrieving a ball from the stands, reminding players who they are guarding, announcing substitutions, or reassigning positions.

Nondirected (ND). The coach displays behaviors not related to ongoing practice activities. The players may or may not be involved in activity during this time. *Examples:* The coach is joking or talking with another coach or player about their school experiences, friends, family members, or daily activities; making arrangements for cars to take players to the next game; or talking or joking with a parent.

Coach Absent (CA). The coach is not present in the practice area but should be. *Examples:* The coach is late arriving at practice or gets called away from practice.

RECORDING PROCEDURES

CBORS uses a time-sampling method. Because continuous categorization of coaching behaviors becomes very difficult in highly interactive sports such as basketball, a time-sampling technique allows for more reliable and valid data. CBORS samples climates, interactions, and coaching behaviors for 5-second intervals and then provides 5 seconds to record data. Observers collect data for 3 minutes and then take a 3-minute rest.

Observers station themselves at a point from which they can observe the coach in an unobtrusive manner. Observations are recorded on a CBORS coding sheet (see Figure 35.1). Observers watch the coach during practice/game action and categorize the appropriate climate (C),

Coaching Behaviors Observational Recording System (CBORS)

Observer _____   Coach _____

Team _____   Date _____

Time started _____   Time finished _____

Climates (C)		Coaching behaviors (B)		Encouragement behaviors	
Instruction	I	Instructional behaviors		Encouragement	E
Management	M	Lecturing	L	Hustling	H
Practice	P	Questioning	Q	Skill feedback behaviors	
Waiting	W	Monitoring	MO	Specific positive skill feedback	SF+
		Modeling behaviors		General positive skill feedback	GF+
		Positive modeling	M+		
		Negative modeling	M–	Specific negative skill feedback	SF–
Interactions (I)		Positive/negative modeling	M+–		
Individual	I	Negative/positive modeling	M-+	General negative skill feedback	GF–
Group	G	Social behaviors		Corrective positive skill feedback	CF+
Team	T	Praise	PR		
No interaction	N	Punishment	PU	Corrective negative skill feedback	CF–
		Criticism	C	Noninstructional behaviors	
				Managing	MG
				Nondirected	ND
				Coach absent	CA

Figure 35.1 Coaching Behaviors Observational Recording System (CBORS) recording sheet.

Coaching Behaviors Observational Recording System (CBORS)

Category	Code	Number of occurrences	Total intervals	Percentage of occurrences
Climates				
Instruction	I			
Management	M			
Practice	P			
Waiting	W			
Interactions				
Individual	I			
Group	G			
Team	T			
No interaction	N			
Coaching behaviors				
Instructional behaviors				
Lecturing	L			
Questioning	Q			
Monitoring	MO			
Modeling behaviors				
Positive modeling	M+			
Negative modeling	M–			
Positive/negative modeling	M+ -			
Negative/positive modeling	M– +			
Social behaviors				
Praise	PR			
Punishment	PU			
Criticism	C			
Encouragement behaviors				
Encouragement	E			
Hustling	H			
Skill feedback behaviors				
Specific positive skill feedback	SF+			
General positive skill feedback	GF+			
Specific negative skill feedback	SF–			
General negative skill feedback	GF–			
Corrective positive skill feedback	CF+			
Corrective negative skill feedback	CF–			
Noninstructional behaviors				
Managing	MG			
Nondirected	ND			
Coach absent	CA			

Figure 35.2 Coaching Behaviors Observational Recording System (CBORS) summary sheet.

interaction (I), and predominant coaching behavior (B) for each 5-second period and then record these behaviors in the appropriate boxes during the next 5-second interval. The Numbers 1 through 6 represent 1 minute of recording. Ten seconds are used to observe and record a behavior for each category ($10 \times 6 = 60$ seconds). Observers may use a prerecorded audiocassette tape that directs them when to observe and when to record, thus ensuring that observation and recording intervals are uniform in length. After 3 minutes of coding, observers take a 3-minute rest, thus enhancing observer accuracy by limiting sampling to alternate 3-minute intervals throughout practices and games.

SUMMARIZING AND INTERPRETING THE DATA

CBORS provides a behavioral coaching profile of an individual coach by assessing three separate categories of information about his or her coaching behaviors in practice and game settings. Following an observation, the data are transferred to a summary sheet to provide the coach with an overall picture of his or her coaching behaviors (Figure 35.2). The number of occurrences for that particular behavior is divided by the total number of intervals for each section (climates, interactions, and coaching behaviors) to get the percent of occurrences.

CBORS can be used to compare the performance of a single coach with previously collected coaching behavior data or with normative data and/or to compare the coaching behaviors of groups of coaches. These observational data may also be analyzed with descriptive statistics and a variety of inferential statistical techniques.

Chapter 36

The Hierarchical Observation Method for Analyzing Sportsmanship (THOMAS)

Thomas L. McKenzie
M. Patricia Giebink

Teaching socially desirable values is a goal of general education, and it is frequently reported to be one of the four major objectives of physical education (Siedentop, 1980). Although many instruments are available to assist researchers directly in observing student and teacher behaviors as they relate to fitness, physical skill, and cognitive development, there are few designed specifically to analyze social skills.

The Hierarchical Observation Method for Analyzing Sportsmanship (THOMAS) is designed to assess one particular aspect of social skill development commonly referred to as *sportsmanship*. Sportsmanship is only one of the several possible complex social values that physical educators may be interested in observing; other values include cooperation, leadership, and followership. The focus of THOMAS is on physical, verbal, and nonverbal responses of students that are associated with the concept of sportsmanship. Although the observation procedures used with the instrument are applicable to the study of other social values, the definitions described here are for sportsmanship alone. THOMAS was originally designed specifically to study competitive game-play situations. However, because social interactions occur throughout a physical education class, observations can be extended to include an entire class period or practice session.

Observers, after being trained systematically, can use THOMAS with high reliability. In one study in which the instrument was used, Giebink and McKenzie (1985) used several methods for determining reliability and reported the following interobserver agreement scores: (a) interval by interval, 96.5 to 100%; (b) scored interval, 75 to 100%; (c) unscored interval, 98.5 to 100%; and (d) mean of scored and unscored interval, 87.8 to 100%.

THOMAS uses interval recording techniques. Although there are many advantages to interval recording (e.g., it simplifies the tasks of the observers and permits the simultaneous study of large numbers of diverse behaviors) and it is widely used, it has some inherent weaknesses (Hartmann, 1982). With interval recording the behaviors targeted for observation are sampled during short intervals (e.g., 5 seconds) and coded if they are present or absent during this time period. Data are reported as percentage of intervals, and only an estimation of the actual frequency and duration of events can be made. In addition, with interval data a sequential analysis of events cannot be readily conducted.

CATEGORY DESCRIPTIONS

THOMAS permits observers to classify student social interactions into two main categories, sportsmanlike behavior and unsportsmanlike behavior, and to further classify them into physical, verbal, and nonverbal response categories. A *physical* response involves physical contact; a *verbal* response involves oral communication; and a *nonverbal* response involves physical movement but no physical contact.

Sportsmanlike Behavior

Positive social interactions related to game play or class activities. Sportsmanlike behavior involves a student interacting pleasantly with another student or teacher by providing encouragement, support, assistance, feedback, or explanation.

Physical Sportsmanlike Behavior. Assisting an injured classmate, helping a fallen teammate or opponent to get up, spotting, retrieving an object for a classmate, gently hugging another player, and giving a "high five."

Verbal Sportsmanlike Behavior. Consoling the injured, offering thanks, offering to equalize competition, and praising others or approving their behavior.

Nonverbal Sportsmanlike Behavior. Giving a thumbs-up gesture and clapping for a teammate or opponent.

Unsportsmanlike Behavior

Negative social interactions related to game play or class activities. Unsportsmanlike behavior involves a student interacting with another student or teacher in such a manner that intimidation, provocation, animosity, or disapproval are conveyed in the tone and content of the interaction.

Physical Unsportsmanlike Behavior.   Game (or class) rule violations such as hitting, kicking, grabbing, shoving, pushing, and taking equipment away from other students.

Verbal Unsportsmanlike Behavior.   Name calling, using profanity, ridiculing, arguing, and throwing tantrums.

Nonverbal Unsportsmanlike Behavior.   Obscene gestures, stalking off the court, refusing to participate, faking an injury, and deliberately delaying a game.

RECORDING PROCEDURES

Interval recording techniques are used with THOMAS. Observers can either enter data directly into a portable microcomputer using the techniques described by McKenzie and Carlson (see chapter 4) or use standard interval recording techniques. With the latter method, a portable recorder accompanied by a programmed audiotape cassette directs observers through alternating 5-second observe/record intervals. Although procedures may vary with different research questions, a subject is typically observed for 1 minute (six observe intervals and six record intervals) before the focus is directed to a different subject. The tape, for example, instructs observers as follows: "Observe Subject 1. . . . record one. . . . observe Subject 1. . . . record two. . . . observe Subject 1. . . . record three." In compliance with the directions, observers focus on the first subject for 5 seconds to determine whether he or she emits sportsmanlike or unsportsmanlike behavior and then use the next 5 seconds to record the result of that observation in the appropriate space on the coding sheet, and so on.

When any behavior related to sportsmanship is observed during an interval, both the type (sportsmanlike or unsportsmanlike) and category (physical = P, verbal = V, and nonverbal = N) are coded (Figure 36.1). Unsportsmanlike behaviors are identified by encircling the code letter. If no behavior related to sportsmanship occurs during the interval, the observer draws a stroke through the recording space.

A hierarchical decision system is used to determine which single code is to be entered when more than one sportsmanship-related behavior occurs during the same interval. For type of interaction, sportsmanlike behaviors take precedence over unsportsmanlike ones, and for category, the order is physical, verbal, and nonverbal. For example, if a subject says, "I'm sorry you hurt your knee" while helping an opponent off the ground, the observer records a "P." If a subject yells at an opponent while simultaneously giving a "high five" to a teammate, the observer also records a "P." If a subject curses at a teammate while making an obscene gesture at him or her, the observer records a circled "V."

The Hierarchical Observation Method for Analyzing Sportsmanship (THOMAS)

Date _4-25_   Observer _Thom_   Activity_____

Type and valence   P = Physical
Circle if negative   V = Verbal
                     N = Nonverbal

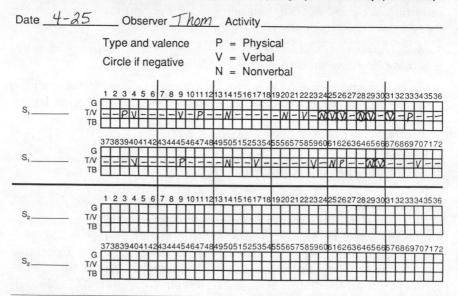

Figure 36.1 The Hierarchical Observation Method for Analyzing Sportsmanship (THOMAS) recording sheet (completed).

SUMMARIZING AND INTERPRETING THE DATA

Data are summarized by tabulating individual category codes and adding them together to determine sportsmanship valences. For example, Figure 36.2 shows that during 72 intervals of observing Subject 1, there were 5 Ps, 7 Vs, and 4 Ns (totaling 16 sportsmanlike intervals), and 5 circled Vs and 3 circled Ns (totaling 8 unsportsmanlike intervals) recorded. Percentages and ratios are also calculated. In this example, 25% of the intervals (i.e., observed intervals divided by total intervals and multiplied by 100) were sportsmanlike and 12.5% were unsportsmanlike; therefore, the sportsmanlike-to-unsportsmanlike ratio was 2:1.

THOMAS can be used for descriptive, correlational, and experimental studies, and thus data interpretation is highly dependent upon the research questions asked. For example, descriptive studies could examine sportsmanship behavior as it occurs in different sports (e.g., hockey, basketball) or sport settings (e.g., physical education class, intramurals), or as it is exhibited by different types of individuals (e.g., high skilled, low skilled). Correlational studies could compare sportsmanship ratings of individuals by teachers with observed scores for THOMAS, or deter-

**The Hierarchical Observation Method
for Analyzing Sportsmanship (THOMAS)**

Interval	Number	Percentage
Unscored	40	62.5
Scored	24	37.5
Sportsmanlike	(16)	(25)
Physical	5	7.8
Verbal	7	10.9
Nonverbal	4	6.25
Unsportsmanlike	(8)	(12.5)
Physical	0	0
Verbal	5	7.8
Nonverbal	3	4.7
Total	64	100

Sportsmanlike-to-unsportsmanlike ratio = 2:1 (2.00)

Figure 36.2 The Hierarchical Observation Method for Analyzing Sportsmanship (THOMAS) summary sheet with data for Subject 1.

mine the relationship between observed sportsmanlike behavior and the closeness of game scores. Experimental studies could examine the effectiveness of different interventions on rates of sportsmanlike and unsportsmanlike behaviors. Along this line, Giebink and McKenzie (1985) reported two studies in which the instrument was used to examine the effectiveness of three intervention strategies (instructions and praise, modeling, and a point system) on children's sportsmanship in a physical education class and in a recreation setting.

When using THOMAS, observers typically record information in addition to the data specifically related to sportsmanship. For example, game type and teacher behavior (particularly proximity) are probably related to students' sportsmanship behavior. The sample recording sheet (Figure 36.1) includes spaces for coding these two contextual variables, game type (G) and teacher behavior (TB). Researchers interested in such variables could assess sportsmanship behavior with THOMAS while simultaneously coding related events with their own interval systems or previously published ones, such as Stewart's Observational Recording Record of Physical Educator's Teaching Behavior (ORRPETB, chapter 23) for teacher behavior.

REFERENCES

Giebink, M.P., & McKenzie, T.L. (1985). Teaching sportsmanship in physical education and recreation: An analysis of interventions and generalization effects. *Journal of Teaching in Physical Education, 4,* 167-177.

Hartmann, D.P. (Ed.) (1982). *Using observers to study behavior.* San Francisco: Jossey-Bass.

Siedentop, D. (1980). *Physical education introductory analysis* (3rd ed.). Dubuque, IA: Wm. C. Brown.

PART V

ETHNOGRAPHY: QUALITATIVE ANALYSIS

During the last decade, educational researchers have adopted qualitative techniques for studying classroom phenomena. Physical education followed suit and in the early 1980s began to consider qualitative approaches as another means for explaining the instructional process. Today, sport pedagogists have, in general, accepted these data-generating techniques and are slowly incorporating them into their research tools. Because ethnographic or qualitative methods are quite new to physical education, we have included them in the following section. By making these descriptive technologies available, we hope that sport pedagogists can more readily make choices about using them independently or integrating them with quantitative methods.

Griffin and Templin provide a concise and descriptive overview of qualitative data collection methods that easily distinguishes them from conventional quantitative methods. They discuss what qualitative research is, the theoretical framework on which it is based, and how it can be used in physical education. Methodology is explained according to what the researcher does, how data are collected, and how data are analyzed. They conclude by identifying several caveats that should prepare the newcomer for this kind of research. A list of references of more detailed information about qualitative research is included, as well as published qualitative studies in physical education.

Goc Karp discusses the roles and functions of the researcher who chooses participant observation. She systematically outlines the process of how to conduct a study covering entry into the fields, observation, recording, data analysis, and presentation. This method is further clarified through an example illustrating the process, including an analysis of the data.

McBride offers three interview techniques followed by an application of one method, the Drive-Reduction Quotient (DRQ). The DRQ is a modification of an instrument that has its origin in social and psychological casework studies. It is a specific method of analysis that can be used to quantify data gathered from structured interviews. A sample interview and scoring instructions are included.

Chapter 37

An Overview
of Qualitative Research

Pat Griffin
Thomas J. Templin

The second period physical education class at Big City Middle School is playing soccer. The teacher has placed two piles of sweatshirts at each end of a large open field to serve as goals. There are no field markings. Four boys run up and down the field following the ball. Several other students stand silently in their assigned position until the ball comes near, then they move tentatively toward the ball to kick it away. Three girls stand talking in a tight circle near the far end of the field. They are startled when the ball rolls into their group, and two boys yell at them to get out of the way. They do and then regroup after the ball and the boys go to the other side of the field. Two boys, who have not touched the ball during the class, engage in a playful wrestling match near one goal. The teacher stands in the center of the field with a whistle in his mouth. He hasn't said anything since he divided students into teams at the beginning of class. He has blown the whistle twice to call fouls. The students play around him as if he were not there. A bell rings and all the students drop their pinneys where they are and start toward the school building. Belatedly, the teacher blows his whistle to end the game and begins to move around the field picking up pinneys.

After class, as we walk back to the building, the teacher says, "These kids are wild. If you can just run off some of their energy, they don't get into so much trouble in school. This group especially, not too many smarts (taps his temple), don't get into much game strategy." (He sees a boy and girl from the class standing near the door of the girls' locker room talking.) He yells, "Johnson, get your butt to the shower and stop bothering the ladies." He smiles at me. "You've got to be on them all the time." He looks up and sighs, "Well, two [classes] down, three to go."

This vignette is an example of a qualitative description of an episode in a physical education class. In qualitative research, detailed descriptions of a physical setting and what people say, do, think, and feel in that setting form the basis for developing an in-depth understanding of a particular situation, event, group of people, or individual. The goal is to portray accurately the experiences and perceptions of the participants.

Though qualitative research is used extensively in sociology and anthropology, its acceptance in education and physical education is comparatively recent. Qualitative research and its underlying theoretical paradigm provide an alternative to the more traditional quantitative mode of understanding life in physical education.

CHARACTERISTICS OF QUALITATIVE RESEARCH

Bogdan and Biklen (1982) identify five distinguishing characteristics of qualitative research that are useful in understanding this methodology.

1. *The natural setting is the direct source of data and the researcher is the key instrument*. Researchers go to the schools, playgrounds, school board meetings, gymnasiums, or playing fields to gather data. Because of their concern for context-specific knowledge, researchers believe it is essential to observe and talk to participants in their natural setting. Further, the researcher uses her or his own observations of and interactions with participants to gather data, rather than relying on paper-and-pencil tests or other predesigned instruments.

2. *Qualitative research is descriptive*. Rather than intervening in the setting in an attempt to manipulate or change behavior or perceptions, the qualitative researcher attempts to provide a detailed description of the setting as it is. Thus qualitative data consist of descriptions of the participants, the physical setting, and interactions that occur among participants. As much as possible, the participants' own words are used in these descriptions in the form of direct quotes from interviews and observed interactions. The researcher creates a rich narrative account of life in the setting under study rather than reducing these descriptions to numerical form.

3. *Qualitative researchers are concerned with process rather than simply with outcomes*. Qualitative researchers focus on answering questions that begin with "how" or "what is," rather than "how many," "how come," or "what causes." This emphasis on process comes from a belief that understanding how participants perceive themselves and their setting and how they make sense of their experience can provide valuable information.

4. *Qualitative researchers analyze their data inductively*. In a qualitative study, researchers do not begin with a hypothesis to prove or disprove or with a preconceived theoretical frame in which to categorize their observations. Instead, initial focusing questions (Patton,

1980) guide beginning observations. As data are collected, the researcher begins analysis so that data collection and analysis occur in a cyclical fashion, with each round of collection and observation informing subsequent rounds. In this way, theory is created from and grounded in the data. This grounded theory (Glaser & Strauss, 1976) is an essential component of qualitative research.

5. *Meaning is of essential concern to the qualitative approach*. Qualitative researchers want to understand how participants make sense of their experiences. The emphasis is on accurately describing participants' perspectives on events and people in their settings.

These characteristics of qualitative research reflect a particular theoretical frame of reference. A theoretical frame of reference can be defined as a set of assumptions that guide how each of us views the world. Though many researchers choose methods without explicit attention to their theoretical underpinnings, such an understanding can enrich the research process and discourage the random selection and misuse of method.

THE NATURALIST PERSPECTIVE IN QUALITATIVE RESEARCH

For most researchers the use of qualitative methods requires a major shift in frame of reference. Research methods classes typically focus on quantitative methods: proving or disproving hypotheses, the scientific method, development of instrumentation, statistical analysis, and identifying a quantifiable relationship among variables through manipulation and control. This research tradition grows out of a positivist paradigm that sharply contrasts with the naturalist paradigm undergirding the use of qualitative methods (Lincoln & Guba, 1985).

In the naturalist paradigm, realities are multiple, constructed by participants, and holistic. Thus it becomes impossible to identify a single reality true for all participants. Additionally, the relationship between the research and the participants in the naturalist paradigm is interactive. From the naturalist perspective it is not possible for the researcher to be separate from the setting and participants in the traditional sense of being objective or independent. A researcher working from the naturalist paradigm also believes that it is not possible to generalize research findings in the ways positivist researchers do. Rather, knowledge is context specific.

Further, the naturalist researcher doesn't believe it is possible to identify linear, one-way, cause-and-effect relationships on research with people and social interactions. Instead, all elements in a social setting are interactive and simultaneously affect each other. The naturalist researcher also believes that all research is value bound. To claim to be value free ignores how values influence the researcher at every stage of the process, from identifying a topic and methods to analyzing and discussing the data.

This brief description of the naturalist perspective is intended to provide readers with an introduction to the theoretical underpinnings of qualitative methods. This understanding can help readers make more informed choices by matching their own views of the world with the research methods they intend to use.

USEFULNESS OF QUALITATIVE RESEARCH IN PHYSICAL EDUCATION AND SPORT

Reading a qualitative research report is often more like reading a story as compared to reading a quantitative research report. The short episode described in the beginning of this chapter is typical of what might be included in an article to illustrate a particular theme identified during a research project. Because of the storylike quality, there is a human dimension to qualitative reports that is filtered out when social interactions are reduced to numbers. Readers get a feel for the situation and the people being described. The descriptions evoke emotional responses, and readers are invited to compare the described setting to their own schools, students, colleagues, and themselves. As a result, qualitative research reports or even excerpts from reports serve as provocative discussion materials in both undergraduate major classes and in-service teacher programs. For college teacher educators, who are often accused of being out of touch with the realities of teaching in the schools, involvement in a qualitative research project can provide an in-depth experience in the schools not possible while visiting student teachers or leading an in-service workshop for teachers.

Ultimately, the most valuable contribution qualitative research can make to physical education is to provide multiple and varied rich descriptions of what is going on in teacher education programs; school gym classes; and the minds of teachers, teacher educators, and students in these programs. This understanding can assist the evaluation and improvement of not only the specific programs studied, but also the readers who gain insights into their own professional work as a result of reading or discussing a qualitative study.

Now that we have briefly described what qualitative research is, the theoretical underpinnings on which it is based, and how it can be useful in physical education, we need to discuss what a qualitative researcher does. This description is intended to be an overview. There are several excellent texts, which are listed at the end of the chapter, for those who may want more in-depth study.

ASKING A QUESTION

The initial step in a qualitative study is to ask a question that is appropriate to qualitative methods. This means the question must ask for descriptions.

- How do girls and boys interact in a middle-school team sports class?
- How do teachers perceive their role as cooperating teachers when working with student interns?
- What contextual factors in the school affect physical education programming? How do they affect programming?
- What is the nature of the relationship between college teacher educators and public school teachers?
- What is it like to teach physical education in an urban, multiracial school?

These are all examples of the kind of questions appropriate to qualitative analysis. Each calls for a descriptive-analytic response. There are no hypotheses proposing relationships among variables to be proven or disproven.

QUALITATIVE DATA COLLECTION

Three modes of qualitative data collection are typically used: direct observation, interviews, and document collection.

Direct observation requires the researcher to go to the research setting and spend a significant amount of time there. As soon as possible after an observation, the researcher writes field notes, which are narrative descriptions of what was observed and what people did and said, and physical descriptions of places and people.

Observation can be overt or covert. In overt observation all participants know the researcher is present to observe and conduct research. During covert observation the researcher does not inform the participants of her or his research activities. Observers can also assume a participant or nonparticipant role. A nonparticipant observer avoids active participation in the research setting and restricts interactions to research-related discussions. A participant observer takes an active role in day-to-day life with other participants while simultaneously observing and gathering data.

Interviewing can also take several different forms. Some qualitative studies use interviews with participants as the sole form of data collection. These studies focus on understanding participants' perceptions— their thoughts and feelings about themselves and their setting. Other studies integrate interviews and observations, which enables the researcher to understand observed behaviors from the participants' perspective, what motivates participants' behavior, and what meaning observed behaviors have for the participants. In this way, the researcher avoids solely relying on her or his interpretations of observations.

Interviews can be formal or informal, but a common characteristic of qualitative interviews is that they tend to be open ended. Rather than preplanning a detailed protocol of questions to be asked of all participants, the researcher may use a less structured question guide. Questions focus on helping the researcher better understand the participant's perspective that emerges during the course of observations or prior interviews.

Document collection entails gathering written material that helps the researcher describe and make sense of the setting. Lesson plans, memos, diaries, school handbooks, curriculum guides, student course evaluations, graffiti, or school policy statements are all examples of documents used as sources of data in qualitative studies. Less frequently used qualitative data collection methods include taking photographs or video and audio recording.

Qualitative researchers use triangulation as one important way to cross-check their understanding of gathered data (Denzin, 1978; Templin, 1983). When triangulating data collection methods, the researcher uses two or more ways to gather data. Using direct observations and interviews together in one study is an example of triangulating data collection. The purpose of triangulation is to help the researcher accurately present findings from the participant's perspective and to minimize the effects of the researcher's biases in interpreting meaning from the data. Triangulation is also used to elicit multiple data sources by observing and interviewing different participants in the same setting. A third kind of triangulation involves the use of multiple observers or interviewers to collect data during one study.

QUALITATIVE DATA ANALYSIS

As stated earlier, one of the characteristics of qualitative research is that the data are analyzed inductively. Rather than fitting data into preconceived categories on an observation instrument or explaining data in terms of a theoretical framework identified at the outset of the study, the researcher organizes as the study evolves. Data collection and analysis occur simultaneously in a cyclical fashion. Data from observations, interviews, and document collection are organized into different categories that express themes of meaning. Subsequent data collection and analysis are used to confirm, disconfirm, or modify emerging themes. In a qualitative study it is possible that this on-going collection and analysis of data will lead to a shift away from the focusing questions chosen at the beginning of a study. Though this change in focus would be problematic in a quantitative study, qualitative researchers must be open to such a change if it more accurately captures the participants' perspective than the original focus questions did.

TRUSTWORTHINESS OF QUALITATIVE RESEARCH

Most of us are more familiar with the means by which the trustworthiness of quantitative research is determined. We have learned that internal validity, external validity, reliability, and objectivity are the accepted criteria for judging the quality of quantitative study. Because qualitative research and the naturalist paradigm on which it is based are different from quantitative research and its positivist underpinnings, different criteria are needed to determine trustworthiness.

Lincoln and Guba (1985) propose four criteria more consistent with the naturalist paradigm: credibility, transferability, dependability, and confirmability. These criteria are analogous, respectively, to their quantitative counterparts internal validity, external validity, reliability, and objectivity.

1. Credibility: Do the participants find the researcher's analysis and interpretation credible?
2. Transferability: Is there enough detailed description of the research setting for readers to make reasoned judgments about the transferability of results to their own settings?
3. Dependability: Is there an adequate description of the research process available to enable an independent auditor to retrace the decision-making process followed by the researcher during the study?
4. Confirmability: Can the findings of the study be tracked back through the analysis steps to the original data, and are interpretations and patterns reasonable?

Lincoln and Guba also suggest specific strategies for implementing each of these trustworthiness criteria. (For an example of how these criteria can be used in a study of the teacher education process in physical education, see Steen, 1985, 1986.)

CAUTIONS ABOUT CHOOSING QUALITATIVE METHODS

Qualitative research is an attractive choice for increasing our understanding of physical education programs, students, and teachers. The vivid descriptive narratives make the research come alive, the contextual integrity of different settings is respected, and, without preconceived hypotheses, the chance of imposing meaning on a setting is decreased. Additionally, the extended contact with teachers and students in programs under study can increase the researcher's sensitivity to the day-to-day experiences of participants in physical education.

There are, however, several cautions to be considered when choosing to use qualitative methods. Do not assume that because qualitative research does not use statistical analysis it is less complicated or requires less preparation than quantitative research. To complete a qualitative study effectively requires extensive planning and preparation to understand the methodology. Because the underlying theoretical framework and the data collection and analysis techniques are different from the more familiar quantitative styles, time must be taken to practice collecting and analyzing qualitative data and to read qualitative studies before attempting to implement one.

Doing qualitative research is time-consuming. Added together, the aspects of conducting a study added together require a major time commitment: observing and interviewing participants, traveling to and from the setting, writing up field notes, transcribing interviews, analyzing data, reanalyzing data, refocusing subsequent observations and interviews, meeting with coresearchers, and writing the final report.

Additionally, the volumes of data generated during observations and interviews can be intimidating. The organization of field notes, interview transcripts, and documents into coherent and meaningful clusters requires complex record keeping and the ability to boil down hundreds of pages of description into a manageable and trustworthy manuscript.

Because the researcher is the instrument, potential problems with reactivity, bias, and human relations are more apparent than when the same problems arise using quantitative methods. Qualitative researchers accept these characteristics of human interaction as a natural part of the research process. Rather than attempting to achieve objectivity, an impossibility in the naturalist paradigm, the qualitative researcher strives for neutrality. She or he must develop the ability to identify and monitor personal biases and feelings that, unrecognized, could subvert observation and interview skills as well as data analysis. This self-knowledge is essential to writing descriptive field notes rather than unintentionally interpretive accounts of participants' activities.

Qualitative research requires interaction with participants. Effective communication skills such as nonjudgmental listening and questioning facilitate developing the mutual respect and trust needed for participants to share their feelings and perceptions honestly.

At the other extreme there is the problem of identifying too closely with participants and losing the neutrality of the observer's perspective. A qualitative researcher spends a great deal of time with participants, learning about their lives and sharing experiences. It is not unusual to develop a sincere caring and empathy for participants. If this feeling causes the researcher to lose her or his neutrality and begins to affect data collection and analysis, resulting in distortions of findings, then the integrity of the study is lost. Anthropologists call this problem "going native."

A related caution concerns ethical dilemmas. Though ethical dilemmas in qualitative research are no more pressing than those in quantitative methods, they may seem more acute because of the intensity and sustained nature of the face-to-face contact between researcher and participants. Examples of potential ethical dilemmas encountered in the process of doing a qualitative study include the following: how to protect the participants' anonymity, whether or not to share field notes or the final report with participants, what to do if the researcher observes or is told about something illegal or immoral during an observation, and how to protect a participant's self-esteem without compromising the accuracy and integrity of the research when the two are in conflict. Balancing a concern for the equitable and respectful treatment of participants with the importance of accurately describing their lives can be difficult without easy solutions. These dilemmas and the large number of others than can arise must be addressed seriously and thoughtfully with a strong prejudice toward protecting the interests of the participants.

One final caution is noted; however, there is hope that in the near future qualitative researchers will no longer need to be concerned about it. The positivist paradigm and the quantitative research methods it reflects are the dominant research mode in the educational community. Most research methods classes are, in reality, quantitative research classes. Until recently, the review boards of most journals in education and physical education consisted of quantitative research experts who judged qualitative studies by quantitative standards. For assistant professors working for tenure, there is still the risk that quantitative researchers from the hard sciences will discount qualitative research without understanding the theoretical and methodological differences.

The situation, however, is changing. Qualitative research is on the cutting edge of educational research innovation and as such is rapidly achieving legitimacy. The number of qualitative studies appearing in the *Journal of Teaching in Physical Education* and the *Research Quarterly for Exercise and Sport* has increased dramatically over the past 5 years. Additionally, there were numerous sessions at the 1986 American Educational Research Association annual conference that focused on qualitative methods. This trend is encouraging for researchers interested in qualitative research.

TAKING THE NEXT STEP

A reference list is included for readers who are interested in more detailed information about qualitative research. Several useful texts on qualitative methods, as well as a number of published qualitative studies in physical education, are listed. In addition, the next two chapters describe in more depth some of the data collection methods briefly described in this overview.

Whether readers are interested in conducting qualitative research or want to be more knowledgeable readers of qualitative studies, our hope is that this overview has provided a helpful introduction. Perhaps there is one final word we need to say about qualitative research. After considering our cautions about complexity, time, ethical dilemmas, human relations concerns, and the fact that it is not for everyone, we find doing qualitative research fun, meaningful, and challenging. What more can a researcher ask?

REFERENCES

Bogdan, R., & Biklen, S. (1982). *Qualitative research for education: An introduction to theory and methods*. Boston: Allyn and Bacon.

Denzin, N. (1978). *The research act: A theoretical introduction to sociological methods*. New York: McGraw-Hill.

Glaser, B., & Strauss, A.L. (1967). *The discovery of grounded theory: Strategies for qualitative research*. Chicago: Aldine.

Lincoln, Y.S., & Guba, E.G. (1985). *Naturalistic inquiry*. Beverly Hills, CA: Sage.

Patton, M.Q. (1980). *Qualitative evaluation methods*. Beverly Hills: Sage.

Steen, T.B. (1985). *A case study of teacher socialization in physical education during training experiences: A qualitative analysis*. Unpublished doctoral dissertation, The Ohio State University, Columbus.

Steen, T. (1986, April). *Auditing qualitative research: A technique for establishing the dependability and confirmability of naturalistic inquiries*. Paper presented at the meeting of the American Alliance of Health, Physical Education, Recreation and Dance, Cincinnati, OH.

Templin, T. (1983). Triangulating ALT-PE: A research consideration. *Journal of Teaching in Physical Education*, **1**, 38-41.

RELATED REFERENCES

Bain, L. (1976). Description of the hidden curriculum in secondary physical education. *Research Quarterly*, **47**(2), 154-160.

Bain, L. (1985). A naturalistic study of students' responses to an exercise class. *Journal of Teaching in Physical Education*, **5**(1), 2-12.

Earls, N. (1981). Distinctive teachers' personal qualities, perceptions of teacher education and the realities of teaching. *Journal of Teaching in Physical Education*, **1**(1), 59-70.

Faucette, N., & Graham, G. (1986). The impact of principals on teachers during in-service education: A qualitative analysis. *Journal of Teaching in Physical Education*, **5**(2), 79-90.

Goetz, J.P., & LeCompte, M.D. (1984). *Ethnography and qualitative design in educational research*. Orlando, FL: Academic.

Griffin, P. (1983). Gymnastics is a girl's thing: Participation and interaction patterns in middle school gymnastics classes. In T. Templin & J. Olson (Eds.), *Teaching in physical education* (pp. 71-85). Champaign, IL: Human Kinetics.

Griffin, P. (1984). Girls' participation patterns in a middle school team sports unit. *Journal of Teaching in Physical Education*, **4**(1), 30-38.

Griffin, P. (1985). Boys' participation styles in a middle school physical education team sports unit. *Journal of Teaching in Physical Education*, **4**(2), 100-110.

Griffin, P. (1985). Teachers' perceptions of and reactions to sex equity problems in a middle school physical education program. *Research Quarterly for Exercise and Sport*, **56**(2), 103-110.

Griffin, P. (1985). Teaching in an urban multiracial physical education program: The power of context. *Quest*, **37**(2), 154-165.

Locke, L., Griffin, P., & Templin, T. (Eds.) (1986). Profiles of struggle. *Journal of Physical Education, Recreation and Dance*, **57**(4), 32-60.

Placek, J. (1984). A multi-case of teacher planning in physical education. *Journal of Teaching in Physical Education*, **4**(1), 39-49.

Placek, J. (1985). Teacher educators and students: The communication gap. In M. M. Carnes (Ed.), *Proceedings of the Fourth Curriculum Theory Conference* (pp.193-203). Athens, GA: The University of Georgia.

Templin, T. (1979). Occupational socialization and the physical education student teacher. *Research Quarterly*, **50**, 482-493.

Templin, T. & Griffin, P. (1985). Ethnography: A qualitative approach to examining life in physical education. In C.L. Vendien & J.E. Nixon (Eds.), *Physical education teacher education* (pp. 140-146). New York: Wiley and Sons.

Tousignant, M., & Siedentop, D. (1983). A qualitative analysis of task structures in required secondary physical education classes. *Journal of Teaching in Physical Education*, **3**(1), 47-57.

Chapter 38

Participant Observation

Grace Goc Karp

Participation observation is a method of collecting data that employs a variety of techniques well suited to the study of physical education. Templin and Griffin (1985) suggest that these qualitative approaches can "illuminate naturalistic real world behaviors sometimes missed in quantitative approaches to studying physical education" (p. 145). The techniques used in participant observation provide information that is used as baseline data, process data, values data, as well as answer research questions and provide theories (LeCompte & Goetz, 1982). The role of the observer, the stages of conducting a participant observation study, the techniques of data gathering, the analysis of data, and an example are presented and discussed in this chapter.

ROLE OF THE OBSERVER

There are many roles open to the observer in participant observation. These roles range from an observer who has minimum involvement in the activity to a complete participant who is totally involved in the activity. Selection of roles should be related to the type of information being sought, the degree of involvement permitted in the setting and with the people involved, and the personality of the investigator. The roles of the observer in Figure 38.1 have been compiled from the frameworks used by qualitative researchers (Gans, 1982; Junker, 1960; Patton, 1983; Spradley, 1980).

Degree of involvement			
High			Low
Complete participant	Participant as observer	Observer as participant	Complete observer

Figure 38.1 Participant observation continuum.

Complete Participant

In this role the investigator becomes completely involved in the situation, thereby maximizing direct contact with the actual situation in which events are occurring. After the event the participant becomes the researcher and documents what happened. This method often presents ethical and validity problems because the researcher's identity is usually hidden from the subjects under investigation.

The complete participant role has some advantages. Through total involvement certain hidden characteristics of the situation can be discovered, which without direct involvement could neither be experienced nor understood. The role also exposes the investigator to different subjective aspects of the situation. A major disadvantage of this role is that it is very difficult psychologically for the investigator to be a total participant and an observer at the same time. Total involvement in a situation may also lead to distortions or biases on the part of the observer. This role is probably most successful when the investigator is less familiar with the situation and therefore able to see the tacit rules of the situation more clearly.

Participant as Observer

In this role the investigator is a partial participant in the situation, enabling him or her to function more effectively as a researcher. The investigator seeks to maintain a balance between being an insider and being an outsider, between participation and observation. Because the observer's activities are not wholly concealed, it is important to clearly communicate to the subjects the purpose (general or specific) and consequences of the research that might result from the findings.

The advantages of this role are similar to those of the complete participant. The investigator is able to appraise the situation with less pressure, and some of the biasing influences that may be felt in the complete participant role are alleviated. The major disadvantage is that the subjects under investigation may change their behaviors, knowingly or unknowingly, because they know they are being observed.

This role is often used when situations are not suitable for the investigator to be a participant or when participant opportunities are limited or unavailable. The data collected from this observation are used to delineate categories of activities and to map movement in the physical environment.

Observer as Participant

The investigator in this role has limited participation in the situation and is free to observe to a greater extent. Again, because the observer's activities are not wholly concealed, the purpose and the consequences of the research should be conveyed at the outset.

An advantage of this role is that the investigator can observe more and, if necessary, participate or interact to increase the amount of information sought. A disadvantage is that limited involvement increases the chances of misinterpreting one's observations and data.

Steps must be taken to develop channels of communication. Informal and formal interviews and other informants help to increase and verify the information gleaned. The observer as participant role is often adopted when the investigator has very little opportunity to become involved or when the investigator feels more familiar with the situation being studied.

Complete Observer

This role is often referred to as the nonparticipant. A true nonparticipant observation would use hidden cameras or one-way mirrors, thereby avoiding interaction. However, in educational settings social interaction is unavoidable. Thus, even though the complete observer should avoid interaction with the subjects or the situation, some interaction will occur. The investigator often becomes the spectator and usually finds observation posts from which to observe and record.

This role is most successful in providing preliminary information for a study or when recording the actions of the subjects and not their feelings or attitudes. A disadvantage of this role is that misinterpretations can occur about the observations and data. The complete observer is often used when a particular situation does not allow for any participation or when the investigator wants to avoid involvement.

In summary, each role has its own range of participation, observation, and involvement. An investigator may in fact use one or more roles on this continuum to obtain relevant information. Similarly, each role has its different limitations and problems of reliability and validity (LeCompte & Goetz, 1982). The effective investigator needs to understand the limitations and problems associated with each role and to take steps to reduce their impacts.

A major concern regarding all observational data is the subjectivity of the observer concerning the covert and overt nature of the observations (Patton, 1983). This concern also raises ethical issues as described by Griffin and Templin in chapter 37. This issue demands a careful weighing of the purposes of the research; the situation; and the rights, interests, and sensitivities of the subjects concerned (Spradley, 1980).

STAGES IN CONDUCTING A PARTICIPANT OBSERVATION STUDY

There are three stages in conducting participant observation: entry, data gathering, and closure.

Entry

Entry involves informing the participants about the nature of the field-work, negotiating with the participants about how it is to be conducted, and making an entry into the setting.

Data Gathering

In the data gathering stage the investigator begins by identifying and being identified with the setting and the people or situation under study. This may create a variety of anxieties for the investigator (Gans, 1982). In some situations, key informants need to be identified, cultivated, and trained in their roles. As the investigator becomes comfortable in the setting, routines are generally established. Consideration must be given to the advantages and limitations of using these routines (e.g., standing and observing from the same place, observing the same people, and/or using the same questioning techniques).

Closure

During closure the investigator verifies the data, recognizing that some-times this cannot be accomplished until all the data have been completed and analyzed. However, formal and informal interviews at the end of the observation period are a means for verifying and connecting elements within the data as well as clarifying perceptions and gaining other insights.

TECHNIQUES OF DATA GATHERING

Several details must be considered before beginning data collection. The observer needs to formulate a working plan that identifies what to ob-serve and how to organize the data gathering process. Suggestions and guidelines follow.

Duration of the Observation

The length of time during which observations take place depends on accessibility to the situation and the nature of the questions being studied. A holistic perspective involves a longer time period than a more focused perspective. Observations range from daily 1- or 2-hr segments to those made across a total school year. It is important that the duration of the observation covers a full cycle of events that relate to the question under investigation. For example, a study regarding curriculum may involve observations prior to, during, and after the school year.

Focus of the Observations

The focus of the study can range from observation of all the components involved in a situation to one of the components. Once a study has begun, the focus may expand or narrow depending on what the observations reveal. The focus may also be determined by limited resources, time, and the complexity of the situation.

What to Observe and Record

Because it is impossible to observe everything, the investigator must organize what to observe and when to observe. This is done by asking descriptive questions that begin with "what," "where," "who," and "why." These questions translate into descriptive observations of the setting, people, activities, relationships, feelings, and so forth. The following guidelines (Patton, 1983; Spradley, 1980) are used in most studies, but need not be limited to the contents described here.

1. The setting, dates, and time: The description of the setting should be sufficiently detailed to permit the reader to visualize the setting. Dates and times should be clearly stated.
2. The human/social setting: This should describe the subjects and the ways in which people interact.
3. The activities and the behaviors of the participants: This section describes what happens in the setting in terms of *what* people do.
4. The investigator's relationship and perceptions: This describes the investigator's observational position, role, feelings, and perception (e.g., degree of influence on the subjects, insights, ideas, questions).
5. An event or sequence of events: Some events are described in a sequence of observations (i.e., through data collection of an introduction, action, interaction, highlight, review, and closure).
6. Informal interactions and unplanned activities: These descriptions provide crucial data and insights about the observed behaviors. Informal interviewing helps to verify perceptions gleaned from the data. Alternative perspectives are also gained by the researcher by participating in after- or before-school activities.
7. The language used: Recording the exact language used by the participants provides a better reflection of the subjects and their world. These words provide meanings that can be attached to certain aspects of the situation.

8. Nonverbal behaviors: This description includes individual and group body language, physical groupings, dress, gestures, and the like.
9. Events that do not occur: These observations should be carefully documented. They should only be described if the event was proposed or expected to occur, or if the investigator is experienced in this particular situation and would have expected the event to happen. Although these descriptions may be judgmental, they can also provide important comparative information.
10. Unobtrusive measures and documents: These descriptions incorporate record keeping and environmental observations such as dusty equipment, dates on documents, description of the notice board, lesson plans, handouts, records, and so on.

Recording

Observations are recorded in detail either during or immediately following the specific event. Recording is facilitated through a variety of means. Field notes and audiotaping are the primary tools used in participant observation, although videotapes, photographic materials, and computers make fieldwork more efficient and comprehensive. Field notes are recorded on paper or cards, or in a journal, or transcribed from videotapes and audiotapes. The method of writing field notes is individualistic, and each investigator employs techniques that are deemed most appropriate for his or her situation. Burgess (1982), Dobbert (1982), and Lofland (1974) offer a variety of commentaries and suggestions on the technique of writing field notes.

DATA ANALYSIS

Data analysis in participant observation takes place throughout the collection and the final summarization of the data. Time should be set aside following each period of observation and notation for reviewing notes and adding recollections and interpretations (Babbie, 1979).

Process

The process of observation and analysis is interwoven. The original questions and theories may or may not be answered. Analysis may lead to other questions and theories over the course of one's observations. Each new observation may lead to identifying a new variable or meaning that eventually provides a conceptual framework for further observations.

Similarly, a new variable or connection may lead to a reconsideration of the original framework, theme, or idea. This, in turn, may require the investigator to use more focused observations, questioning techniques, or observational role. Thus the investigator can continually modify the design of the study and test theory against data (Glaser & Strauss, 1967). Inherent dangers to this process are the investigator's bias and the possible subjectivity of the data actually collected. The investigator may observe only those things that support his or her theoretical conclusions, or probe the subject with biased questions and comments.

Data analysis is mainly inductive. Babbie (1979), Dobbert (1982), Glaser & Strauss (1967), and Spradley (1980) suggest the following questions and guidelines for the initial analysis of the data. These guidelines can also be used for focusing future observations.

1. Note similarities and dissimilarities of behaviors and events. What are the norms for these behaviors? Are they universal? Do they occur frequently, and what is the distribution?
2. Note differences and deviations from the norm. What are they, and why do they occur?
3. Create a taxonomy of behaviors and categories.
4. Formulate relationships and meanings, and represent these schematically. Check causal propositions.
5. Organize the data into themes.
6. Determine theoretical understandings and compare and test them through contrasting questions and selecting or focusing observations.
7. Delimit the theories and categories.

Glaser and Strauss (1967) propose three approaches to analyzing the data:

1. Code the data first and then analyze. This form of analysis converts qualitative data into crude quantitative form, often in order to test hypotheses.
2. Inspect the data for new properties of the theoretical categories. For this form of analysis, coding would be an unnecessary limitation if one wanted to generate new ideas and concepts.
3. Use both approaches in comparing and analyzing the data. This form of analysis generates theory more systematically than the other approaches.

Validation and Verification

As described earlier, steps must be taken to validate and verify both the process used by the investigator and the data collected from the study.

LeCompte and Goetz (1982) present a thorough overview of the problems encountered in this method of research. McCall and Simmons (1969) and Patton (1983) provide numerous ways of dealing with these problems. They suggest that a triangulation of research methods can be used to verify the data (e.g., surveys, documents, and interviews). Similarly, the perspectives of multiple observers could be recorded and used to validate the information. Also, the subjects involved in the study could be asked to verify the data analysis. Researchers should consider the methods they will employ to validate their study before the data collection begins.

PRESENTATION OF FINDINGS

Presenting the results of the participant study involves organizing the data and presenting the findings.

Organization of the Data

The following tasks are important in the organization of the data.

- List the variables, categories, and domains.
- List the categories analyzed and the extent of the analysis (e.g., complete, partial, incomplete).
- Collect the sketch maps, drawings, and schemes.
- List the themes, major and minor.
- Select examples for the preceding factors.
- Identify questions and themes that organize the data.
- Index the notes by recording page numbers appropriate to the presentation.
- Organize and label miscellaneous data.
- Organize the ideas for additional research possibilities and topics.

Presentation of the Findings

Formatting the presentation of the findings is usually determined by the research methodology. Typically, some categories developed in the analysis of the research are used to organize the presentation of themes. The original questions posed for the research can be used to organize the data. Similarly, a report format or case study can be used to present the findings. For further examples, refer to Dobbert (1982) and Burgess (1982), who each include a number of formats in their descriptions of participant observation methodology.

SUMMARY

Participant observation is used to provide descriptive data for answering descriptive and speculative questions. A variety of roles with varying degrees of involvement, participation, and observation are used. Each role has its advantages and limitations, which should be understood and prepared for prior to the study. The techniques for data gathering are clearly defined and must be followed diligently. This method uses analytic inductive strategies for analysis.

EXAMPLE USING COMPLETE OBSERVER ROLE

Setting: Junior high school. Teachers being observed have their office in the changing room.

Research Question: What are the planning behaviors of these teachers?

Duration of Study: Observation of every day in the 3-week unit.

Status: Teachers know the study is to observe their teaching behaviors.

Field Notes:

Date: Tues., Feb. 15

Day: 3

Grade: 6

7:50 a.m. Passed custodian in the corridor; it seems nobody is around. Walked into the changing room. Jane is sorting out pinneys, looks very busy. Had to squeeze past Tina to get to and from the corner where the pinneys are. Tina is working at the desk. Both say "Hi." I respond and say I have to write a few things down. Is it OK if I sit in the changing room? It'll help get me out of the way. Both smile and get on with their work. Sit in the changing room—still can see both teachers. Tina seems to be writing on a small piece of paper. She's copying from a notebook. Jane gets a cup of coffee and offers me one; I accept. Ask both teachers what time they come in—7:40 a.m. Tina's still writing but on a larger sheet of paper. She gets up and puts a notice on the board in the changing room—looks like team allocations? We talk about how boring it must be for me to watch. I say it's a pleasant change to get out of the university (laugh). Tina goes back to desk, puts the piece of paper on top of the roll sheet on her clipboard.

8:25 a.m. Bell rings. Students rush in to change. Both teachers interact and start to put equipment out into the gym. Tina tells them to look at the board for their station before they go into the gym.

8:35 a.m. Students in the gym, by the gym door answering roll call. I sit on the steps, corner of gym. Boys with the male teacher are ready to start a warm-up routine on the balcony. Girls, downstairs in the gym, are very well aware of the boys and only half-heartedly participate in the warm-up. Jane and Tina are numbering stations, putting balls at each station. A prechosen (?) student is taking the class through a warm-up routine. Tina looks at her clipboard and introduces the lesson on lay-up shooting. Talks about dribbling, take-off, release of the ball. Demonstrates, points out to watch where the ball is in relation to herself as she does it. Repeats the teaching points. Instructs them in a drill—they have to do it three times each side. Gets three students from each team to get pinneys from Jane, and tells them to go to their stations. As they go to their stations, Jane and Tina talk, Jane nods and goes to the stations at the other side of the gym, Tina helps at the other two stations. After the next drill, Tina blows the whistle and brings the students in with balls. Students go into the changing room while Jane collects the balls and pinneys. Tina is checking something on her roll sheet—roll? Tina goes into the office and writes something on the small card. Both teachers discuss the students' performance in the second drill; Tina: ''Didn't get the leap part very well, did they?'' Jane: ''No, they need to work on pushing off the opposite leg—maybe we should do a drill, like 1-2-3-up as a warm-up.'' Tina: ''Maybe'' (nods her head). Bell rings, the students start to leave; Jane and Tina start to get the equipment ready.

(Additions written after school.)

About 40 students, about 6 to a station.

First drill: Each student with the ball does lay-up from one side, then the other.

Second drill: Three students on each side, one ball, rest of balls in the bags. Tina told them to put balls in bag. Receiving side and shooting side in drill.

Analysis:

Time: Planning, approx. 30 min

Type: Lesson plan in the form of notes; notes seemed a list of teaching points, copied from unit plan?? Need to check what that notebook contains.

Also prepared notice for station allocation.

Tina added to the t. point list after the class?? Not to the unit plan??

Objective: To practice the activity? To see what parts of the skill they could do? Not sure, wonder what they'll do next lesson?

Relationships: Team teaching. Seems Tina instructs the students, therefore does the planning for that instruction. But Jane gives feedback; wonder if she plans for the feedback. Jane prepares and organizes the equipment—when does she think about that? Need to check amount of planning time on other days. Must get to school earlier! Need to see what the list says, t. points or activity? Why need notes after 13 years experience?

REFERENCES

Babbie, E.R. (1979). *The practice of social research*. Belmont, CA: Wadsworth.

Burgess, R.G. (Ed.). (1982). *Field research: A sourcebook and field manual*. London: Allen & Unwin.

Dobbert, M.L. (1982). *Ethnographic research*. New York: Praeger.

Gans, H. (1982). The participant observer as a human being: Observations on the personal aspects of fieldwork. In R.G. Burgess (Ed.), *Field research: A sourcebook and field manual* (pp. 56-61). London: Allen & Unwin.

Glaser, B.G., & Strauss, A.L. (1967). *The discovery of grounded theory: Strategies for qualitative research*. Chicago: Aldine.

Junker, B.H. (1960). *Field work: An introduction to the social sciences*. Chicago: University of Chicago Press.

LeCompte, M.D., & Goetz, J.P. (1982). Problems of reliability and validity in educational research. *Review of Educational Research*, **52**(1), 31-60.

Lofland, J. (1974). Styles of reporting qualitative field reports. *American Sociologist*, **9**(3), 101-111.

McCall, G.J., & Simmons, J.L. (1969). *Issues in participant observation*. Reading, MA: Addison Wesley.

Patton, M.Q. (1983). *Qualitative evaluation methods*. Beverly Hills: Sage.

Spradley, J. (1980). *Participant observation*. New York: Holt, Rinehart, & Winston.

Templin, T., & Griffin, P. (1985). Ethnography: A qualitative approach to examining life in physical education. In C.L. Vendien & J.E. Nixon (Eds.), *Physical education teacher education* (pp. 140-146). New York: Wiley and Sons.

RELATED REFERENCES

Becker, H.S. (1970). Problems of inference and proof in participant observation. In W.J. Filstead (Ed.), *Qualitative methodology* (pp. 189-201). Chicago: Markham.

Becker, H.S., & Geer, B. (1982). Participant observation: The analysis of qualitative field data. In R.G. Burgess (Ed.), *Field research: A sourcebook and field manual* (pp. 238-250). London: Allen & Unwin.

Fawcette, N. (1984). Implementing innovations: A qualitative analysis of the impact of an in-service program on the curricula and teaching behaviors of two elementary physical education teachers. *Dissertation Abstracts International*, **45**, 1683A.

Goc Karp, G. (1984). Theoretical and experiential planning models in secondary school physical education. *Dissertation Abstracts International*, **46**, 1866A.

LeCompte, M.D., & Goetz, J.P. (1984). Ethnographic data collection in evaluation research. In D.M. Fetterman (Ed.), *Ethnography in educational evaluation* (pp. 37-59). Beverly Hills: Sage.

Placek, J. (1982). An observational study of teacher planning in physical education. *Dissertation Abstracts International*, **44**, 4409A.

Schwartz, M.S., & Schwartz, C.G. (1955). Problems in participant observation. *American Journal of Sociology*, **60**(4), 343-353.

Sweeney, M.A. (1984). Teacher socialization: The pre-practicum experience with third-year human movement majors. *Dissertation Abstracts International*, **45**, 1069A.

Tousignant, M.G. (1982). Analysis of the task structures in secondary physical education classes. *Dissertation Abstracts International*, **43**, 1470A-1471A.

Wang, B.M. (1977). An ethnography of a physical education class: An experiment in integrated living. *Dissertation Abstracts International*, **38**, 1980A.

Chapter 39

Interview Techniques in Research

Ron McBride

The use of interviews as a data gathering technique is not new. Historically, interviews have played an important role in the fields of psychology and psychiatry where intensive research designs have typically been used. Behavioral researchers have used the interview to predict outcomes of national elections as well as to gauge reactions to foreign and/or economic policies of the government, measure employees' morale, and measure subjects' reactions to psychological experiments (Johnson, 1976). In pioneering the use of ethnographic methods as an alternate research model to traditional quantitative studies, anthropologists have long relied upon interviews in their field studies of preliterate societies (Biddle & Anderson, 1986).

The intent of interviewing, as stated by Patton (1982), is to find out "what is in and on someone else's mind . . . *not* put things in someone's mind" (p. 161). Interviews allow the researcher to gain knowledge about intrinsic factors that cannot be observed, including feelings, values, thoughts, and intentions. Interviewing, in sum, permits access to another person's perspective.

INTERVIEW CATEGORIES

There are three broad categories of interviews from which qualitative data are collected. Each approach has its strengths and drawbacks depending upon the purpose. The three categories are formal or structured interview, semistructured interview, and informal or unstructured interview.

Formal or Structured Interview

In a structured interview, the questions have already been decided upon prior to the interview session. The questions are carefully worded and are asked in the same order for all respondents (Maccoby & Maccoby, 1954). Data collected from this format are presumed to be systematic and objective and therefore more easily analyzed and interpreted. Because a standardized format is followed, potential interviewer effects from having different interviews for different respondents are reduced. Variation among interviewers is also minimized on those occasions where a number of different interviewers may be required. Further, it has been found that the uniformity of behavior on the part of the interviewer can be replicated by other investigators with relative ease (Phillips, 1971).

The weakness of the structured approach is that it does not permit the interviewer much flexibility or freedom to expand upon a respondent's answer or to pursue an issue that was not anticipated prior to writing the interview questions.

Semistructured Interview

In the semistructured interview, the interviewer has a specific number of major questions or issues to explore, but then is free to probe beyond the respondent's immediate answers. The questions or issues form a framework from which the interviewer develops additional questions to gain further information from the respondent—but always within the predetermined subject matter (Patton, 1980).

Informal or Unstructured Interview

The informal or unstructured interview is not confined by the guidelines of the two previous approaches and is often used as part of ongoing research ventures typified by participant observation studies. It relies solely on the interviewer's ability to create questions and probe issues as they arise in the course of the interview. No predetermined questions are prepared because the investigator has no knowledge of what may happen in a particular setting or how the respondent might react to a situation, interaction, and so forth. The interviewer, quite literally, must be able to adapt to what is happening in the immediate environment.

The strength of this format is that it allows the interviewer to be flexible and to develop each situation in whatever ways deemed appropriate. Greater attention can be paid to the individual differences of the respondents, and questions can be formulated and sequenced to obtain more in-depth information.

A major drawback to both the semistructured and the unstructured interview is that, although there is greater flexibility and individualization for the interviewer, there now exists the possibility that more data will be collected from one respondent than from another. Different questions may be asked of different participants, thus making data analysis difficult. The interviewer must be highly skilled in the interview process so that possible interviewer effects (e.g., personal characteristics, attention to detail, clerical ability, expectations concerning the subjects' responses, etc.) are kept to a minimum and that data gathered are meaningful to the outcome of the study. Additionally, the informal interview approach requires a greater time commitment, because several interviews with different participants may be required before a similar set of questions can be generated and posed to all.

USE OF INTERVIEWS

Despite some of the shortcomings outlined above, the interview process in recent years has, as has qualitative research in general, gained greater popularity in educational research. Investigators have realized that in the complex and sophisticated social milieu of the classroom, not all variables, interrelationships, and questions related to student cognition can be strictly quantifiable. The interview process is one such strategy used in this approach.

The use of interviews is also evident in some of the research currently being conducted in the physical education setting. Griffin (1984) used informal discussions and interviews with teachers to identify girls' participation patterns in a middle school sport unit. Placek (1984) used both informal and semistructured interviews to supplement information gathered from classroom observations and field notes to examine teacher planning habits with a group of four physical education teachers. Tinning and Siedentop (1985) also employed a number of formal interviews and many informal interviews in a study designed to identify the characteristics of tasks and accountability in student teaching. I myself, in the role of participant observer, spent 100 hours observing and interviewing a student teacher over an 11-week period.

The use of interviews in physical education research is, however, still very much in its infancy. Given the sophisticated skills required of an expert interviewer and the current trend of increased use of structured interview information to supplement other data (Korchin & Schuldberg, 1981), it may be prudent for the novice researcher to use a carefully conceived and systematic structured interview format that lends itself to data analysis.

One such approach that meets these criteria is a method formulated by Dollard and Mowrer (1947) to assess tension in written documents. The measure of tension is called the Discomfort Relief (or Drive Relief) Quotient (DRQ). The measure yields a relatively reliable, graphic picture of tension change over time. Originally designed for the social case record, the method is equally appropriate in an autobiography, psychoanalytic history, or any other kind of personal document (Dollard & Mowrer, 1947). This drive reduction unit is based on the premise that a successful case study should move from high to low tension levels. Therefore, counting the tension or discomfort words, clauses, or sentences appearing in several interview sessions, the researcher can quantify the element of drive reduction tension in a case record.

		+	−	N
1. How do you feel personally about your teaching, its effectiveness, your impact on the students, and so forth up to this point in your student teaching?				
Well, it depends on the day.	1		✓	
Sometimes I am pleased with it, but for the most part I really have to wonder if I'm really teaching.	2		✓	
Sometimes I really wonder if I am doing a good job or I am doing the things I'm supposed to, or if I'm just baby-sitting and just kind of going through the motions.	3		✓	
Some of the things I thought I'd taught in the beginning, like how to throw, and I watch them, and they throw the same way they did before, incorrectly and that kind of thing.	4		✓	
Judging from the kids' reactions, they still come out and want to know what game we are going to play.	5			✓
So they still look at it as play time or something like that.	6		✓	
They are not that interested in learning the skills and so I wonder if that is OK or if I hadn't done what I should have done all along.	7		✓	
I hadn't gotten them to the point I'd like to.	8		✓	
2. We've been focusing primarily on classroom organization, logistics of the classroom as an area of concern. How then, after our training sessions, do you feel about this concern now?				
Much better actually.	9	✓		
The things that I've done have helped quite a bit.	10	✓		
Just getting to think about it more, and, the things that I have done have forced me to organize right down to the last detail.	11	✓		
Which, before, I just kind of thought, well, you know, I don't know if it will come out well or just make a general framework and play most of it by ear.	12		✓	
Since I've done that, since I've started writing things out, it has helped quite a bit.	13	✓		
Things don't get nearly as messed up.	14	✓		
[What kind of "things" have helped you or assisted you?]				
All of them really.	15	✓		
The things like set, and all that kind of stuff we had last summer.	16	✓		

(Cont.)

Figure 39.1 Sample interviewing and scoring.

METHOD

By way of illustration, the sentence format of the DRQ is modeled. The first step is for the researcher to design a carefully worded structured interview relating to the variable or phenomenon under study. Each interview session (assuming that several will occur over time) is audiotaped and then transcribed. Each sentence is transcribed as a separate unit for analysis (see Figure 39.1). Trained independent scorers are required to

		+	–	N
But at the time I hadn't taught yet and it didn't make that much difference.	1		✓	
I just assumed that, well, it happens all the time; you do it all the time anyway and it's not something you really have to think about.	2			✓
And I'd pretty much forgotten about it until we went over it again and so it was a really good review.	3	✓		
I realized that it just doesn't happen, that you really have to plan ahead.	4	✓		
So all of it's been really good as far as drawing my attention to what I should be doing.	5	✓		
3. That leads me into the next question—have the sessions helped you at all in your teaching situation?				
Yeah, definitely.	6	✓		
As far as focusing my attention on really planning the lessons and having me do them beforehand.	7	✓		
Like I said, I had forgotten most of that stuff and of course you have to say something when you get out there.	8			✓
Last week in the seventh class I had a really good class.	9	✓		
As part of set, I wrote down all the things I wanted to say.	10	✓		
Before I just made a little note and never really looked at it.	11		✓	
This way, I wrote it out and said this, and this, and this.	12	✓		
And they were the most attentive that time than they ever had been.	13	✓		
Usually, when we came out there at the beginning they wanted to get going and it was hard to settle them down to tell them what we were going to do.	14		✓	
Probably it has just to do with me having more confidence going in, knowing exactly what I want to say and then it comes off better.	15	✓		
4. Do you feel the information gained from the training films in which we saw certain techniques modeled, as well as the notes and handouts, were useful and/or applicable to your teaching situation?				
Yes.	16	✓		
The handouts were especially helpful.	17	✓		

Figure 39.1 (Continued)

	+	–	N
The films were difficult because they were not PE and it's hard to apply to an actual teaching situation.			
1		✓	
But you at least get ideas or definitions of what it is supposed to be like.			
2	✓		

5. Could you give a capsule summary, then, of the effects the sessions have had on you in regard to the area of classroom organization?

Yeah. I suppose mainly that I can really do something about it.			
3	✓		
I think I always knew that things were getting out of hand because of me and not the kids. . . I knew it was me.			
4		✓	
It's shown me specific ways of how I can really do something about it.			
5	✓		
Before I kind of thought I should be able to do something about it, but I didn't really know what.			
6		✓	
Since doing these things and focusing my attention on different things . . . that's helped a lot.			
7	✓		
I think just the main thing has been getting my attention focused on what I can do.			
8	✓		

Totals: 24 14 3

$$DRQ = \frac{14}{14 + 24}$$

$$DRQ = .37$$

Figure 39.1   (Continued)

read the entire interview and analyze it sentence by sentence. This can generally be taught in only a couple of 1- to 2-hr training sessions. Figure 39.2 illustrates a list of sentence-scoring instructions used in a study of preservice teacher concerns (McBride, 1984).

SUMMARIZING AND INTERPRETING THE DATA

After the interviews have been scored, the number of positive, negative, and neutral sentences are tallied. The quotient is determined by the following equation:

$$DRQ = \frac{\text{Discomfort sentences}}{\text{Discomfort sentences plus relief sentences}}$$

Figure 39.1 also illustrates the scoring process (*Note.* The neutral sentences are not included in the final calculations.) Interobserver reliability can be assessed using Kendall's coefficient of concordance (Siegel, 1956). The coefficient (indicating the degree of association among the judges) can then be subjected to the appropriate test of significance.

Sentence Scoring Instructions

1. Attached are copies of transcripts from several interview sessions with a number of preservice teachers. The interviews are in no particular order or sequence, so do not approach them with any preconceptions as to how they should progress. Your task is to read each interview from beginning to end and score each sentence in terms of whether the information (a) concerns, (b) relieves, or (c) fails to affect you decisively one way or the other.

2. If you react with tension to a sentence (i.e., if it causes you concern or makes you feel annoyed, excited, or apprehensive) place a check mark in the minus (–) column.

3. If you react favorably to a sentence (i.e., if it gives you a sense of relief, relaxation, or satisfaction) place a check mark in the plus (+) column.

4. If you react neither favorably nor unfavorably, or if you find that your feelings are about evenly balanced, place a check mark in the neutral (N) column.

5. Take your time and read each interview carefully and try to score as naively and as spontaneously as you can.

6. Read both past and present references as if they were present. Thus "I was very concerned" is scored as minus and "I will be relieved" is scored as plus.

7. Each sentence on the transcript is numbered, so make sure that the total of all scores for each page corresponds to the number of sentences; no other calculations are required.

8. Please do not discuss the interviews with anyone else—they are confidential.

Figure 39.2   Sentence-scoring instructions for interview technique.

Investigators use the measure of tension data collected from their structured interviews to assess any changes over time. This approach is particularly well suited for studies dealing with teacher concerns, reactions to changes or innovations in their environment, and teacher anxieties, as well as addressing issues related to student cognition, concerns, and so forth. When the interview information is used in conjunction with other data, informed decisions regarding treatment programs or appropriate intervention strategies can be based upon objective data. The effectiveness of these decisions can be monitored through continued interviews and subsequent interview analysis.

REFERENCES

Biddle, B.J., & Anderson, D.S. (1986). Theory, methods, knowledge, and research on teaching. In M.C. Wittrock (Ed.), *Handbook of research on teaching* (3rd ed.) (pp. 230-252). New York: Macmillan.

Dollard, J., & Mowrer, R. (1947). A method of measuring tension in written documents. *Journal of Abnormal Psychology*, **42**, 3-32.

Griffin, P.S. (1984). Girls' participation patterns in a middle school team sports unit. *Journal of Teaching in Physical Education*, **4**, 30-38.

Johnson, R.F.Q. (1976). Pitfalls in research: The interview as an illustrative model. *Psychological Reports*, **38**, 3-17.

Korchin, S.J., & Schuldberg, D. (1981). The future of clinical assessment. *Journal of the American Academy of Child Psychiatry*, **17**, 1147-1158.

Maccoby, E.E., & Maccoby, N. (1954). The interview: A tool for social science. In G. Lindzey (Ed.), *Handbook of social psychology* (Vol. 1, pp. 449-487). Cambridge, MA: Addison-Wesley.

McBride, R. (1984). An intensive study of a systematic teacher training model in physical education. *Journal of Teaching in Physical Education*, **4**, 3-16.

Patton, M.Q. (1980). *Qualitative evaluation methods*. Beverly Hills: Sage.

Patton, M.Q. (1982). *Practical evaluation*. Beverly Hills: Sage.

Phillips, B.S. (1971). *Social research strategy and tactics*. New York: Collier-Macmillan.

Placek, J.C. (1984). A multi-case study of teacher planning in physical education. *Journal of Teaching in Physical Education*, **4**, 39-49.

Siegel, S. (1956). *Nonparametric statistics for the behavioral sciences*. New York: McGraw-Hill.

Tinning, R., & Siedentop, D. (1985). The characteristics and accountability in student teaching. *Journal of Teaching in Physical Education*, **4**, 286-299.

SUMMARY TABLE FOR SYSTEMS

Verbal and Nonverbal Interaction Analysis

System	Focus	Level of complexity	Recording technique	Verbal behaviors	Nonverbal behaviors
Interaction Analysis Systems (Flanders' Interaction Analysis System—FIAS)	Analyzes verbal interaction between teacher and students. Provides explanatory information for the following six instruments.	Low	Interval	Teacher Student	
Rankin Interaction Analysis System (RIAS)	Analyzes verbal and nonverbal interaction for preservice or student teachers.	Low	Interval	Teacher Student	Teacher Student
Behavior Analysis Tool (BAT)	Analyzes verbal and nonverbal interaction of teacher initiation, student response, and teacher reinforcement.	Medium	Interval	Teacher Student	Teacher Student
Cheffers' Adaptation of the Flanders' Interaction Analysis System (CAFIAS)	Analyzes verbal and nonverbal interaction between teacher and student.	Medium	Event Interval	Teacher Student	Teacher Student
CAFIAS Supervisory Feedback Instrument (CSFI)	Focuses on verbal and nonverbal interaction analysis between teacher and student with coding modifications to facilitate immediate feedback.	Medium	Event Interval	Teacher Student	Teacher Student
Self-Assessment Feedback Instrument (SAFI)	Analyzes verbal and nonverbal feedback interaction of the teacher and coach.	Low	Event	Teacher Coach	Teacher Coach

Instrument	Description		Data Collection Method		
The Dyadic Adaptations of the Cheffers' Adaptation of the Flanders' Interaction Analysis System (DAC)	Describes verbal and nonverbal dyadic interaction between teacher and a specific student.	Medium	Event Interval	Teacher Student	Teacher Student
Teacher/Student Climate Analysis					
Data Collection for Managerial Efficiency in Physical Education (DACOME-PE)	Focuses on the management component of physical education classes.	Low	Event Duration	Teacher	Student
Pattern Analysis	Describes how instructional time is allotted in the classroom.	Low	Interval	Teacher	Student
Flow of Teacher Organizational Patterns (FOTOP)	Analyzes time that the teacher spends in teaching and nonteaching activities.	Low	Interval	Teacher	Student
Student Teachers Observing Peers (STOP)	Focuses on paired student teachers providing instructional feedback for each other.	Medium	Event Duration Placheck	Teacher	Student
Systematic Observation of Student Opportunities to Respond (SOSOR)	Determines the effects of game modifications on student opportunities to participate.	Medium	Event		Student
Academic Learning Time-Physical Education (ALT-PE) (1982 Revision)	Focuses on motor activity, engaged levels of students, and class context.	Medium	Interval		Student
Teacher's Questionnaire on Students' Activities (TQSA) (Based on ALT-PE II)	Determines teachers' perceived awareness of their behaviors and student behaviors and actual occurrence.	Medium	Pre- and postclass questionnaire		Student

(Cont.)

Appendix (Cont.)

System	Focus	Level of complexity	Recording technique	Verbal behaviors	Nonverbal behaviors
Teacher Monitoring Analysis System (TMAS)	Codes teacher monitoring variables, location patterns, and grouping structures of students. Parallels ALT-PE in context and learner involvement variables.	High	Interval		Teacher Student
ALT-PE Microcomputer Data Collection System (MCDCS)	Focuses on four levels: pacing, content, learner moves, and level of subject matter difficulty. Computer program available.	High	Interval		Student
Time-On-Fitness Instrument: Time On-Task in Nonschool Settings (TOFI)	Focuses on how participant time is spent in adult fitness classes by targeting one person.	High	Interval		Student
Direct Instruction Behavior Analysis (DIBA)	Focuses on teaching behaviors from the direct instruction model of student behaviors.	Medium	Interval	Teacher	Student
Observational Recording Record of Physical Educator's Teaching Behavior (ORRPETB)	Codes climate, teaching behaviors, student behaviors, and teacher/student interactions.	High	Interval	Teacher Student	Teacher Student
Observation Instrument for Content Development in Physical Education (OSCD-PE)	Describes the process of content development in physical education classes	High	Interval	Teacher Student	Teacher Student

Instrument	Description				
Qualitative Measures of Teaching Performance Scale (QMTPS)	Codes relationships among task presentation, student responses, and teacher feedback with quality of student responses (video analysis only).	High	Event	Teacher	Student
West Virginia University Teaching Evaluation System and Feedback Taxonomy	Describes a comprehensive set of teacher and student behaviors. (Can be used with Datamyte 801). Student behaviors parallel ALT-PE.	High	Event, Interval	Teacher	Teacher, Student
Instrument for the Analysis of the Pedagogical Functions of Physical Education Teachers (PEDFUNC)	Codes language across four behavior changes: structuring, soliciting, responding, and reacting.	High	Event, Duration	Teacher	Teacher
Physical Education Teachers' Professional Functions	Describes several teacher roles, direction of teacher communication (grouping), and management behaviors (video analysis).	High	Event, Duration	Teacher	Teacher
Coach/Athlete Climate Analysis					
Physical Education Teacher/Coach Observational System	Describes positive, negative, and corrective reinforcement by the teacher/coach.	Low	Event	Teacher, Coach	Teacher, Coach
Coaching Behavior Recording Form	Analyzes coaching behaviors during practice.	Low	Event	Coach	Coach
Teacher/Coach and Pupil/Athlete Observation Schedules	Classifies several teacher/coach behaviors and student/athlete response behaviors.	Medium	Event, Time sampling	Teacher, Coach, Student, Athlete	Teacher, Coach, Student, Athlete

(Cont.)

Appendix (Cont.)

System	Focus	Level of complexity	Recording technique	Verbal behaviors	Nonverbal behaviors
Lombardo Coaching Behavior Analysis System (LOCOBAS)	Describes the interaction between coaches and athletes, assistant coaches, officials, and others during competition.	Medium	Interval	Coach	Coach
Feedback Analysis Profile (FAP)	Analyzes communication feedback of the coach during game/practice across several dimensions.	Medium	Event	Coach	
Arizona State University Observation Instrument (ASUOI)	Describes the coach's verbal and nonverbal behavior during practice.	Medium	Event Interval	Coach	Coach
Coaching Behaviors Observational Recording System (CBORS)	Analyzes several coach/athlete interactions and coaching behaviors using a multidimensional system.	High	Event Interval	Coach	Coach
The Hierarchical Observation Method for Analyzing Sportsmanship (THOMAS)	Assesses sportsmanlike and unsportsmanlike athlete behavior during competition.	Medium	Interval	Athlete	Athlete

Ethnography: Qualitative Analysis

Participant Observation	Collects descriptive data in answer to research and speculative questions. One component or a range of components may be observed over time.	Medium	Event Other	Teacher Coach Student Athlete	Teacher Coach Student Athlete
Interview Techniques in Research	Develops and analyzes structured, semistructured, and unstructured interviews.	Medium	Other	Teacher Coach Student Athlete	Teacher Coach Student Athlete